MW01148355

Joining the Clubs

Sports and Entertainment

Steven A. Riess, *Series Editor*

Other titles in Sports and Entertainment

Joining
the
CLUBS

The Business of the
National Hockey League
to 1945

J. Andrew Ross

SYRACUSE UNIVERSITY PRESS

J. Andrew Ross is a historian of sport and business. He holds a PhD from Western University and is a post-doctoral fellow at the University of Guelph. He can be reached through http://www.jandrewross.ca.

Contents

Illustrations

Photographs

Following page 186

Figures

Map

Tables

Acknowledgments

Writing history is a collective enterprise, and so there are many people I need to thank. Ben Forster got me interested in business history and encouraged me to start the project at the University of Western Ontario (now Western University), where I benefited from the support of faculty and my fellow students. Greg Marchildon, Keith Fleming, and Don Morrow gave valuable comments on the manuscript, and at the University of Guelph, Kris Inwood helped me carve out the time to revise.

Like businesses, academic research runs on money, and I was able to travel extensively to conduct research thanks to financial support from Western, the Social Sciences and Humanities Research Council of Canada, the Ontario Graduate Scholarships Program, and a Canada-US Fulbright Award. In New York, I was welcomed at International House and by the Economics Department of the Stern School of Business at New York University. I would like to thank the staff of these institutions and also the many librarians and archivists who helped with sources. A special appreciation goes to Miragh Bitove and Craig Campbell of the Hockey Hall of Fame and Museum Resource Centre and to Ken Leger, who donated NHL meeting minutes to the hall.

I am grateful to those individuals who helped with access to private papers, documents, and unpublished manuscripts: Lori Ball of Molson Coors (Molson fonds) and Pat Duggan and Howard Shubert (Thomas Duggan Collection). John Wong generously provided gate receipts and attendance figures from his own research, Hoagy Carmichael shared images of Lord Stanley, Len Kotylo copied his collection of legal documents, Stephen Hardy sent me several prepublished papers, Paul Kitchen allowed me a peek at his manuscript (now published) on the Ottawa

Senators, and Stan Fischler let me peruse his scrapbooks one memorable afternoon when the Devils were playing. A general thanks also goes to the members of the Society for International Hockey Research, whose player database, member insights, and Listserv I benefited from regularly. At the University of Guelph Library, Jenny Marvin helped design the map and Heather Martin advised on copyright issues.

The National Hockey League and club documents were particularly hard to come by, but the late John Halligan directed me to various obscure but enlightening documents and arranged permission to use the Rangers microfilm that turned out to be stored deep in the bowels of the Garden. Other requests to NHL clubs were generally met with courtesy, but as it turned out almost nothing had been retained from the pre-1945 era.

Finally, I would like to thank those who gave permission to use previously published material and images: University of Toronto Press, *Business and Economic History On-Line*, *Sport History Review*, and the Bank of Canada. The staff at Syracuse University Press was a pleasure to work with, and I want to thank series editor Steve Riess and the other readers for their encouragement and fine criticism.

Last but not least, I want to thank my family, who supported my decision to leave the present-day investment business and pursue the past business of hockey. In particular, I am grateful to Margaret, who joined me near the beginning of my journey and recruited two rookies, Luke and Hart, to play for our club. This book is dedicated to them.

Abbreviations

AAFC	Amateur Athletic Federation of Canada
AAU	Amateur Athletic Union (United States)
AAUC	Amateur Athletic Union of Canada
AHA	American Hockey Association (1926–27, AHL '30–32, then AHA again '32–42)
AHAC	Amateur Hockey Association of Canada
AHA of US	Amateur Hockey Association of the United States (1937–) (now USA Hockey)
AHL	American Hockey League (renamed AHA, 1930–32; formerly IAHL and Can-Am League, 1940–)
AL	American League (baseball)
AO	Archives of Ontario
BAA	Boston Athletic Association
BCA	Bank of Canada Archives
BIHA	British Ice Hockey Association
BPL	Boston Public Library Special Collections
CAAU	Canadian Amateur Athletic Union
CAC	Canadian Arena Company
CAHA	Canadian Amateur Hockey Association (1914–94) (now Hockey Canada)
CAHL	Canadian Amateur Hockey League (1899–1905)
Can-Am	Canadian American Hockey League (1926–36)
Can-Pro	Canadian Professional Hockey League (1926–29)
CBC	Canadian Broadcasting Corporation
CDT	*Chicago Tribune/Daily Tribune*
CHA	Canadian Hockey Association (1909–10)

CHA	Central Hockey Association (1925–26) (became AHA)
CHA	Canadian Hockey Association (Livingstone League)
CRBC	Canadian Radio Broadcasting Commission
CSM	*Christian Science Monitor*
EAHL	Eastern Amateur Hockey League (1933–53)
ECAHA/ECHA	Eastern Canada (Amateur) Hockey Association (1905–9)
EHL	Eastern Hockey League (1954–73)
FAHL	Federal Amateur Hockey League
FECB	Foreign Exchange Control Board (Canada)
G&M	*Globe and Mail* (Toronto)
HH	*Hamilton Herald*
HHFM	Hockey Hall of Fame and Museum
HHOF	Hockey Hall of Fame (later HHFM)
IAHL	International-American Hockey League (1936–40)
IBC	International Boxing Council
IHHOF	International Hockey Hall of Fame
IHL	International Hockey League: (1904–7); (formerly the Can-Pro, 1929–36)
IIHA	International Ice Hockey Association
IIHF	International Ice Hockey Federation (a.k.a. LIHG)
IIHL	International Ice Hockey League (a.k.a. LIHG)
IOA	Imperial Oil Archives
LAC	Library and Archives Canada
LIHG	Ligue Internationale de Hockey sur Glace (a.k.a. IIHL/IIHF)
LP	*La Presse* (Montreal)
MAAA	Montreal Amateur Athletic Association
MDS	*Montreal Daily Star/Montreal Star*
MG	*Gazette* (Montreal)
MLG	Maple Leaf Gardens
MSG	Madison Square Garden
MUA	McGill University Archives
NFL	National Football League
NHA	National Hockey Association (1909–17)

NHL	National Hockey League (1917–)
NL	National League (baseball)
NSS	National Selective Service (Canada)
NYDM	*New York Daily Mirror*
NYHT	*New York Herald Tribune*
NYRC	New York Rangers Collection
NYT	*New York Times*
OAAC	Ottawa Amateur Athletic Club
OC	*Ottawa (Evening) Citizen*
OHA	Ontario Hockey Association (1890–)
OPHL	Ontario Professional Hockey League (1908–11)
PCHA	Pacific Coast Hockey Association (1911–24)
PCHL	Pacific Coast Hockey League (1928–31, '36–41, '44–52)
PJ	*Le Petit Journal* (Montreal)
QUA	Queen's University Archives
TDS	*Toronto Daily Star/Toronto Star*
TG	*Globe* (Toronto)
USAHA	United States Amateur Hockey Association (1920–25)
WCHA/WCHL	Western Canada Hockey League/Association (1921–24)
WFP	*Winnipeg (ON) Free Press*
WHL	Western Hockey League (1924–26)
WPHL	Western Pennsylvania Hockey League

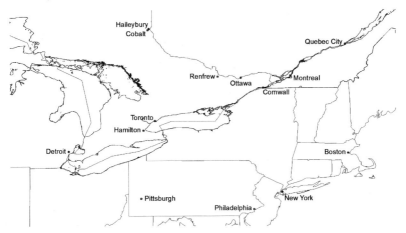

1. Cities important to the emergence and development of the National Hockey League and its predecessors. (Jennifer Marvin)

Joining the Clubs

Introduction

"A Rather Unique Sort of Organization"

The National Hockey League . . . is a rather unique sort of organization. It has no parallel that I know of anywhere, and even as a lawyer, I
would find it difficult to define what it really is other than the fact that it is
a name, the National Hockey League." Clarence Campbell delivered these
words in a speech to the Empire Club of Canada in March 1963. Since he
had been president of the forty-six-year-old National Hockey League for
seventeen years, the audience of Toronto businessmen might have found
it odd that Campbell would find his own organization "difficult to define"
other than by its name. And even the name was confusing: the league
spanned two countries, so which "nation" was actually being referred to?[1]

Campbell explained that while the league's business was mostly
straightforward—to sell hockey as entertainment—there were some special characteristics to consider. First, it was "a competitive league in sport"
but also "a partnership in business"; in other words, the product was competition between teams, but the clubs had to work together in a league—a
special business form used only in the sports industry. (Campbell noted
that the business had "no parallel" and was "frequently misunderstood,"
which seemed to be supported by the fact that it appeared to be outside
the regulation of any state, and he admitted that "it is not even registered
any place.") Second, the men who ran the NHL were not just businessmen but, according to Campbell, also "fundamentally sound sportsmen,"
implying that their role in hockey was at least partly cultural and not just
commercial. Third, he noted that "the nature of the business itself . . . is a
very compact group," an allusion to the small size (only six clubs) but great

power the NHL exerted as the only hockey major league. This power was also apparent in the fourth characteristic, which transcended commerce: Campbell spoke of "the extraordinary amount of influence which we exercise with respect to [the Canadian national sport] . . . not necessarily from our own choice, but from the nature of things."[2]

It was a fascinating description in which Campbell was essentially arguing that the league was unusual, but that it had apparently come about naturally and not through any conscious decisions of its makers. This idea seems paradoxical. If that were the case, then why did more businesses not naturally take up the same form? Or was there something peculiar about sports businesses?

Certainly, the economic form the NHL took was an anomaly in North American business. It was a cartel, a term Campbell understandably did not use, given its implications. A cartel is a group of producers who coordinate the supply, distribution, and price of a product, in this case major league hockey. The NHL could also be seen as a monopolist, because it was the only supplier of the top tier of professional hockey, and an example of an even rarer bird, the monopsony, because it was the only buyer of elite hockey-playing talent. That Campbell did not point out these features was not surprising, because they were supposed to be illegal, especially in the United States. The years before Campbell's speech had seen several court cases and congressional investigations into the legitimacy of the league forms used by major league sports like hockey.

Campbell was trying to convey the message that the NHL was more than just an economic structure. The nomenclature supported him by downplaying the business aspects. The NHL as well as baseball's National League (NL) and American League (AL), the National Basketball Association, and the National Football League (NFL) were called leagues or associations, not cartels; their members were clubs, not corporations; they were run by presidents and boards, but also commissioners, councils, and governors; their workers were players, not laborers; and their primary activities were games or sports. Campbell's Toronto audience likely did not question these terms and probably understood, consciously or not, that major league sports did not conform to the definition of a conventional business.

The idea of a dual or hybrid identity for major league sports is not surprising, given the historical context that existed between the identification of sport itself as an economic or as a cultural activity. The mass commercialization of sport had come during the second phase of the Industrial Revolution especially the period of rapid change from the mid-nineteenth century to before the First World War that provided the technology and the consumers to allow commercial sport to thrive. Having formerly been mostly outside or marginal to the market, sports and games were now brought inside to be priced and distributed. Game forms were commercialized, participants professionalized, and new industries formed to exploit the new leisure time of the working and emerging middle classes. Sport's very definition changed with these processes. While it had previously described generally upper-class pastimes, amusements, and recreations (like game hunting, horse racing, and gambling), it came to include the competitive games of the middle and working classes (like baseball, pedestrianism, or cycling), who were elaborating their own play culture and imbuing it with both economic and social importance. By the twentieth century, the transformation of play into work and the integration of sport into North American industrial society were in full swing, albeit unevenly across sports and spaces. Sports like baseball in the American urban Northeast led the way in professionalization, but others had different trajectories into the new century and their blossoming into fully commercial sports (or failure to do so) depended on the commercial opportunities of markets, the availability of infrastructure, and the willingness of entrepreneurs to promote them.[3]

Through the twentieth century, the sports industry matured, but the duality of economic and cultural natures was still evident. At its end, one observer noted that Major League Baseball was slightly smaller than the American envelope industry and three times smaller than the cardboard box industry, but as another astutely pointed out, "There is no cardboard box page in the daily paper." American sports like baseball retained a cultural mass that far outweighed their economic importance.[4]

It was perhaps owing to this queer identity that sports businesses were late gaining the attention of scholars, and the story of their development was primarily told through popular literature, which focused on on-field exploits. Only late did others take up the challenge to enlighten under-standing of the sport commercialization process, by studying the internal dynamics of the sports businesses that were often the most dominant insti-tutions of sport. Harold Seymour and David Voigt led the way in treating baseball as a historical business enterprise, and the era of free agency in the 1970s inaugurated a continuing interest in the economic dynamics of sport by Gerald Scully, Roger Noll, Rodney Fort, Andrew Zimbalist, and others. However, there are still relatively few detailed monograph treat-ments of specific commercial organizations or entrepreneurs, even though they were often the most prominent structures and agents of change in the modern sports era. The lack of attention has dimmed awareness and appreciation of the special characteristics that distinguish sports indus-tries from other mainstream commercial enterprises. Indeed, as Stephen Hardy argues, the historical analysis of the sport industry, its entrepre-neurs, and its markets is not limited to sports and business history, but can offer special insights into broader North American consumer culture and society. And as the Western industrial economy moves from manufactur-ing to service-sector domination, the study of culturally potent services like sport becomes even more compelling.[5]

While much of the early groundbreaking work in business history was concerned with large-scale, national mass manufacturers, in recent decades scholars have offered alternate models of industrial development that focus on small-batch and regional production. Sports industries have been rarely addressed, but would heed a recent call to consider the place of the national culture in which firms operate, along with their legal and political environments. Kenneth Lipartito emphasizes that business his-torians must consider the cultural influences on decision making and how entrepreneurs themselves *create* culture. Approaches that ignore these factors, he contends, reduce business behavior to the simple pur-suit of profit, growth, and stability and create "an untenable abstraction of human action."[6]

To understand a sports industry, the consideration of business in its social context is crucial. Teams and leagues responded to demographic change, new technology, and fan demand by pursuing particular strat-egies for attaining competitive balance, managing failure (losing), and creating the civic and national markets that went beyond a mere market relationship and contributed to their customers' identity formation. They modified the traditional adversarial divisions between firms through the cartel form, which encouraged a large degree of cooperation among firms. What was intriguing was that in addition to being illegal, cartels were usually unstable owing to incentives to cheat (producers sell outside the cartel system). Yet major league sports succeeded in becoming relatively stable formations and achieving implicit legitimacy by the state.[7]

So the business history of sport is also a story about culture. The local and regional variants of the North American social environment influenced the sports business, and this environment was crucial not just to business behavior, but to the evolution, form, and structure of the business. Culture influenced structure, and this structure was itself a form of cultural expression.[8]

The study of the NHL offers many opportunities to explore these expressions. Bruce Kidd was the first to produce an original history of the league and devoted a chapter in *The Struggle for Canadian Sport* (1996) to arguing that the league's commercializers usurped the place of community sport in the interwar years. The first book-length scholarly treatment of the league's history was John Chi-Kit Wong's *Lords of the Rinks* (2005), which provided a much-needed narrative of the history of elite commercial hockey from the 1890s to the 1930s, paying special attention to the internal workings of the NHL through its archival materials. His work shows the importance of contingency and how the NHL men made decisions to produce and create a certain brand of hockey. Yet there are still rich veins to tap on the business structure of the NHL, particularly the evolution of the league's form, its labor relations, expansion and contraction, the adaptation of the game to new markets, the importance of the media, and the league's relationship with the state.[9]

As Campbell impressed upon his audience, the NHL had grown to have a profound and general social and cultural influence, particularly in Canada. As such, we may need to think of the league as more than a business form, but also as an institution. Avner Greif defines an institution as "a system of rules, beliefs, norms and organizations that together generate a regularity of (social) behaviour." The hockey system was formed by many components—players, leagues, clubs, spectators, arenas, entrepreneurs, the media, as well as state, military, educational, and religious organizations—but the National Hockey League had an increasingly dominant role. This point is what Clarence Campbell was getting at when he spoke of the "extraordinary amount of influence" that it exercised. This book is about how those individuals who ran the NHL came to have such influence. It examines why and how the NHL eventually became the preferred mode for joining the elite professional hockey clubs and highlights the tensions that Campbell still identified decades later: between sportsmen and businessmen, partners and competitors, amateurs and professionals, national and business interests, and the cultural and commercial identities of an institution. In short, it examines "the nature of things" that made the NHL such a "unique sort of organization."[10]

By telling the history of the league's formation and early years, from the initiation of hockey in Montreal in 1875 to the end of the Second World War in 1945, I hope to convey for readers a deeper understanding of the process by which the NHL carved out its special place. The main sources for this story are league, club, and personal correspondence; financial documents; newspaper reports; government documents; and legal proceedings. Particular attention is paid to the internal relationships among the league's member clubs, executives, and players and its external relationships to other professional leagues, amateur hockey organizations, the media, customers, and the state. These sources help add to, and modify, prevailing interpretations of the league's history that are often incomplete or offer jaundiced interpretations of the league's behavior, especially about the roles and motivations of the entrepreneurs and organizers who directed it.

This book is primarily the story of the game off the ice, a play-by-play of the activity behind the scenes that determined the creation and definition of the hockey component of the sport-entertainment industry. It is about entrepreneurship, marketing, and labor relations, but above all organizational behavior. The emphasis of this book is weighted to the production, and not the consumption, of NHL hockey, and for this stress there is no apology, for the central focus is on, as Stephen Hardy recommends, "the central issues as the sports organizations defined them." The main issues were how the NHL cartel was organized to maintain long-term stability, the way in which it dealt with its labor force, and how it adapted its product and structure to the demands of local, regional, and international markets. It also pays close attention to the contingencies of a period characterized by war and peace, by economic stability and recession, and by momentous technological and social change of the modern age. Though often subtle, the history of NHL hockey production was also marked by social changes in class, gender, national identity, and ethnicity in the era, as well as an underlying tension over the perceived effects of modernity. Furthermore, the league's transnational aspect distinguishes its experience from the history of the other American major leagues, by speaking to our understanding of the interdependent relationship between the Canadian and American economies and cultures in an era of continental integration and globalization.[11]

In structure this book is chronological and begins before the league's formation in 1917, with a first chapter that surveys the social, economic, and cultural environment that fostered elite hockey from the last quarter of the nineteenth century to the First World War, the period in which the Montreal game gained prominence in Canada and the United States. Chapter 2 discusses the impetus to form the NHL, its competition with rivals, and its struggle to survive and grow. The campaign to transplant the league into the United States is the subject of chapter 3, which describes how the game was differentiated from amateur competitors and integrated with existing American sports networks. Chapter 4 is an analysis of the importance of arena building to continued league expansion and the subordination of potential competitors into minor leagues, with the NHL as the major league. The early years of the Great Depression are covered by chapter 5, which shows how the league tried to find the right relationship between clubs, rinks, and markets, against a background of economic retrenchment. Chapter 6 looks at the latter half of the 1930s, when the league began to contract and clubs had to revise relationships with their arena landlords. The league was also able to convince the amateur organizations to agree to help it develop a reliable player-supply system. Finally, chapter 7 explains the ambivalent role of the league in the Second World War as it adapted to the exigencies of wartime society on the home fronts of two nations and tried to reconcile its business mission with the national fight.

1

Industrializing a Game

1875–1916

On Wednesday, March 3, 1875, Montreal's *Gazette* reported that some members of the Victoria Skating Rink would gather that evening to play a "game of Hockey," an activity "much in vogue on the ice in New England and other parts of the United States." It was similar to another sport developed in Montreal, lacrosse, and the Scottish country game of shinty, an old stick and ball game, and apparently some of the players were already "reputed to be exceedingly expert." Unlike lacrosse and shinty, however, the hockey players would be using "a flat circular piece of wood" that was less likely to leave the ice surface and make its way into the crowd of spectators, who stood unprotected at rinkside.[1]

At the rink that night, two nine-man teams excited "much merriment as they wheeled and dodged each other," creating an "interesting and well-contested affair" for the spectators, who "adjourned well satisfied with the evening's entertainment." The players were members of the Montreal Football Club, another sport new to Montreal in this decade, and were captained by Charles Torrance, a scion of one of the wealthiest families in the city, and James Creighton, an engineer and part-time journalist. The city's other major evening daily, the *Montreal Evening Star*, carried a near-identical report, suggesting the details were provided by the same source, either by the rink management or by the players themselves, most probably Creighton. Elsewhere in the *Star* appeared another version of the event that suggests the game was not congenial to all the spectators. A Victoria Rink member wrote in to complain that the rink had been "monopolized by a select party in a game of shinny" without notice, the players had arrived late, and when some members went onto the ice before the end of the game, the hockey players attempted to drive them off and "one of their number in a most violent manner assaulted some juveniles with his shinny stick."[2]

We can trace an unbroken line from this Montreal game to the modern sport of ice hockey as practiced by the National Hockey League, the dominant commercial version. But as the *Gazette* report makes clear, while this diversion may have been new to rink subscribers, it was not original to Montreal. Cognates of the game preceded and coexisted with it elsewhere in Canada, as well as the United States and Europe, where proponents of bandy, hurling, shinty, lacrosse, and cricket took their games to the ice. For the most part, these events remained informal and sporadic, lacking in consistent rules and equipment and hindered by the lack of ice on which to play. In order to develop, outdoor ice sports needed a consistently cold climate and an institutional body to carry the sport to the next season after the ice melted. In Montreal two months of temperatures below freezing solved the climate problem, and its club-based sporting culture solved the other.[3]

Institutionalization is the process by which informal folk games become organized sports, and the nineteenth century saw it applied to all manner of games. In team sports, the codification of rules, the beginning of regular league play, and the payment of players have all been touted as the signal watersheds for the emergence of "modern" institutional sport. It is important not to see the process of institutionalization as leading necessarily to one particular form and to recognize that sport evolution was historically and socially contingent; in other words, there was no specific "modern" form that these historical developments were moving inexorably toward, but decisions were being made that produced varieties for different purposes, some more organized than others and some more persistent than others, depending on the social, cultural, and economic conditions. In the late nineteenth century, the conditions were favorable to the transformation of games into the organized sports of the industrial age.[4]

Up to the formation of the National Hockey League in 1917, the central facets of hockey institutionalization were the adoption and spread of Montreal Rules, the development of a competitive structure based on

league play, and the commercialization of relationships (especially of players) to the point that it can be seen to have created a new industry. The
main story is of the choices made by the men (and a certain kind of men)
who, under constraints of the social and commercial context, determined
the future directions of the sport. Bringing a cultural activity like hockey
into the modern industrial age was not an easy, natural, or inevitable process, but one that was contested right from the beginning, even more so
away from the ice than on it. The episode at the Victoria Skating Rink
already more than hinted at the arguments to follow. On the surface, it
was a novelty presented by like-minded sportsmen out for an evening lark,
but there were already tensions over the attempt to exclude spectators, the
definition of the rink as commercial enterprise or public space (or both),
the acceptability of violence, and the role of the media. Left unmentioned
were the dimensions of gender (women were passive observers), of technology (rink, ice, lighting, skates, and organization), as well as of class
and the urban environment (the rink was a members-only club for a city
minority with inversely proportional social and economic power). Before
the NHL could arrive, the game of hockey would require negotiation of
social, cultural, geographic, ideological, and economic boundaries to
allow for the industrializing of the game.[5]

Sporting Association

The Victoria Skating Rink was erected in 1862 north of Dorchester, between Drummond and Stanley Streets in St. Antoine's Ward, the heart
of the English-speaking (Anglophone) community of Montreal. Built as
a venue for the enjoyment of winter balls, masquerades, and skating in a
relatively comfortable indoor atmosphere, like many sports facilities the
Victoria was owned and run by its own members, many of whom also
belonged to other sporting clubs in a city that was becoming renowned for
its amateur sport culture.[6]

From the 1840s, affluent and socially ambitious Anglophone bourgeois Montrealers, primarily those individuals whom Gillian Poulter has
called the "professional and commercial middle classes," began in earnest
to organize sporting organizations. Clubs such as the Montreal Snow Shoe
Club, Montreal Lacrosse Club, and Montreal Football Club were at the

forefront of North American sport innovation and provided a model for other Canadian urban sportsmen and sportswomen as they thrived into the 1870s and 1880s. The drive to associate through club membership was not unique to Montreal, but was characteristic of bourgeois society in the United States and Canada. Over the course of the nineteenth century, the social changes wrought by the emergence of urban-industrial society and exacerbated by the dislocation of transatlantic migration strained traditional bonds of community, church, and kinship and introduced new separations based on class, skills, and occupation. In response, people sought to restore continuity and predictability and chose new rule-based voluntary organizations like sports clubs as the medium. As Ben Rader argues, the primary purpose of sports clubs was not sporting competition per se, but to define a new "subcommunity" to include (and exclude) based on ethnicity or social status. This separation was especially important in an era of rapid population growth, social mobility, and geographic expansion, which Robert Wiebe argues shifted society from one based on personal knowledge networks to one organized by formal networks with standardized symbols and signals. Wielding these symbols in a disciplined way through sport and nonsport social activities, sports clubs served to reinforce the community of the members, socialize its youth, and distinguish members from outsiders.[7]

In Montreal, Canada's largest (100,723 people in 1861) and most industrialized city, the associational impetus surged. Unlike the city's elite Anglo upper class, who engaged in traditional British sports such as curling, yachting, and cricket, the middle classes created sports clubs for various reasons, including the reproduction of a whole set of middle-class values, among them discipline, stamina, moral virtue, order, fair and "scientific" play, masculinity and manliness, urban boosterism, moral reform, and muscular Christianity. In addition, sport helped Anglophone Montrealers define a new Canadian national tradition distinct from the legacy inherited from the British. Some British borrowings, like football, were not yet standardized and could be modified, while other favorite activities borrowed from aboriginal culture, like snowshoeing, tobogganing, and lacrosse, could be "elevated" into modern, organized, and "Canadian" sports through imposition of rules and regulations. Winter sports had an important part to play in this national project, as they were also about the subjugation of nature, rationalizing the harsh climate and using them to create a unique "myth of the North" that differentiated English Canadian identity from the British, French Canadian, aboriginal, and American. These were Canadian specifics that contributed to a greater national purpose well beyond the construction of local subcommunities, a process that was particularly important to a country that had only confederated in 1867.[8]

Lacrosse was the classic product of this Montreal environment, a sport that was derived from an Iroquois activity, organized by Montreal sportsmen, and then consciously promoted as a national sport of Canada with standardized rules and a national association. Lacrosse's popularity bloomed almost overnight in 1867, when it eclipsed imports such as cricket and baseball owing to its class appeal, moral character, Canadian origin, and exciting play. Lacrosse also served as a model for new sport innovations that took place in the 1870s. Indeed, the organizer of the 1875 Victoria Rink hockey game, James Creighton, had experimented with lacrosse on ice at the Victoria Rink the year before, and the sport was to have a lasting influence on hockey's rules of play and organization.[9]

Unlike lacrosse and other popular Montreal sports, hockey's origins were neither strongly identified with an aboriginal game nor a direct British import ancestor. Rather, it appears to have emerged in different forms and at different times in places as dispersed as New England, Britain, Nova Scotia, and elsewhere. This development has led to a long debate about "the" origin of ice hockey, but it is clear that hockey is an example of convergent evolution, a concept from biology that describes how unrelated species develop similar features when evolving in similar environments. The availability of ice, skates, projectiles, and game making in different locales led to the formation of several hockey-like games. The existence of American and British antecedents was directly acknowledged in the *Gazette*, and we also know that Creighton was a former resident of Halifax, Nova Scotia, where similar games on the ice had been played and reported in newspapers since at least the 1860s and where the sticks used at the Victoria Rink game originated. But the Montreal species had the most favorable environment for growth and diffusion.[10]

For the next two seasons, play was sporadic, but in 1877 McGill University students organized the first hockey-specific club and exhibition fixtures began to be played with other local athletic clubs, including the St. James Club and the Metropolitan Club, where Creighton was also a member. Rules published in the *Gazette* in 1877 showed that Montreal hockey was modeling itself mainly on field hockey, with influences from lacrosse and association football.[11]

Into the early 1880s, however, games were one-off exhibitions by teams from McGill, the Victoria Rink (1882), the Crystal Palace rink (1884), and the Montreal Hockey Club (1884). And in comparison to lacrosse and baseball, which were played in neighborhoods all over the city, hockey was restricted to the St. Antoine's Ward and remained concentrated among English Montrealers. This limitation was mainly because any consistent participation in hockey depended on access to rinks. While still dependent on the weather outside to freeze the ice, covered rinks protected the surface from sun and precipitation and allowed an extension of the skating season from as little as six weeks to sometimes more than three months. By the mid-1880s, the popularity of hockey began to improve rink balance sheets, even though access to the rinks to play hockey was still restricted to a class of patrons who could afford it.[12]

The social character of the sport was confirmed by its appearance at the famous Montreal Carnivals of the 1880s. Ironically, the diffusion of the indoor sport was owed to outdoor performances at the Carnival, which brought together tourists and Montrealers who could afford the time for winter recreation. Members of the local sports clubs organized the events, which featured the now-traditional sports of snowshoeing, curling, and skating. In 1883 there was a hockey tournament on the St. Lawrence River with the Victorias, McGill, and a team from Quebec, playing seven-man hockey (instead of nine), a change that persisted. The annual Carnival allowed the tournament to become a regular championship event and heightened the profile of the sport in the city, and local clubs grew in number from four clubs in 1877 to eighteen in 1887. Just as important was the large number of visitors from outside Montreal who brought back the Montreal novelty to their own communities.[13]

The Carnival had been the inspiration of a member of the Montreal Amateur Athletic Association, a club known as the "Winged Wheel" from the design of its crest. The MAAA was formed in 1881 by joining together the Montreal Bicycle Club, Montreal Lacrosse Club, and Montreal Snow Shoe Club, with the object "to encourage athletic sports, to promote physical and mental culture among and to provide rational amusements and recreation for its members." While the MAAA was not an ethnically exclusive organization—there were significant numbers of Francophones and Jews—the membership was socioeconomically restrictive, and being composed in the majority of middle-class professional and commercial men of British Protestant origin, it reflected their cherished values of "muscular exertion, temperance, imperialism, and sporting excellence." In 1885 the Montreal Hockey Club joined the MAAA as a "connected" club, a status that maintained its autonomy but subscribed it to MAAA amateur ideology and organizational leadership and restricted its membership to MAAA members.[14]

The "amateur ideal" was a core component of the Canadian sporting tradition, a phenomenon derived from a British ideal that itself had roots in both an evangelical Christian morality that frowned upon sport and also a middle-class desire for class differentiation. Historian Adrian Harvey shows that "professional" and "amateur" did not come to be mutually exclusive concepts in Britain until after 1830, when sport became seen as "improper" and the upper and middle classes were demanding more separation in recreation, to exclude the lower. Thus, "professional" acquired a derogatory social class dimension to replace its original skill-related definition and was now related to money. "Amateur" thereby came to be defined as its opposite; whereas before the 1830s "amateur" was simply equated with "gentleman," now too it was defined by whether players were paid. By the late nineteenth century, increases in sporting activity resulting in wider class interactions contributed to greater desire to define boundaries between social positions. This ideology found fertile soil in Montreal, where the club culture of the Anglo-Protestant middle classes was keen to keep itself distinct from other socioeconomic, ethnic, linguistic, and religious groups. Soon after its foundation, the MAAA became one of the most powerful and prominent sport organizations in the country, and it supported a "simon-pure" definition of the amateur, as any person "who has never competed for a money prize, or staked bet, or with or against any professional for any prize, or who has never taught, pursued, or assisted in the practice of athletic exercise as a means of obtaining a livelihood." The Winged Wheel was also a prime mover in the creation of a national governing body for amateur sport, the Amateur Athletic Association of Canada in 1884, but in the ensuing two decades the social values and commercial principles of the association cohered less and less under the amateur rubric with the pressures brought by commercialization of sport and of hockey in particular as it spread beyond Montreal.[15]

Propagating the Montreal Rules

Though designed to include and appeal to a certain class of player and spectator, like other Montreal sports hockey also pretended to national importance. In the 1880s the "Montreal game" would spread out to new territory but also back to those individuals familiar with the informal games that were analogous to it. In this process, the Montreal game would be transformed and modified.

Following the lead of lacrosse, which formed a league system the year before, in the fall of 1886 the major elite clubs put their games on a regular footing with the introduction of the first organized league structure. In December five clubs—Montreal HC (Hockey Club), Victorias, Crystals, McGill, and Ottawa Generals—formed the Amateur Hockey Association of Canada (AHAC) at Victoria Rink. The rules used the previous winter at a season-long tournament with many of the same teams formed the basis for the AHAC code. The game was to be played by seven players a side, with two thirty-minute halves (plus overtime if needed), and rules specified the size of goals (six feet by four feet), pucks (three inches by one inch), and stick blades (no wider than three inches), as well as a range of fouls for which players could be sent off ("charging from behind, tripping, collaring, kicking or shinning"). The new AHAC code confirmed hockey as an onside game, where no attacking player could precede the projectile, a style of game shared with football and field hockey. This rule put a premium on individual stickhandling and rushing, and in its essentials the game remained relatively unchanged for the next quarter century.[16]

The other code established was the league form itself, which on the surface provided another layer of meaning for the games—competing for the championship—but underneath also solved some basic economic problems by reducing the transaction costs of organizing games. The challenge for early competitors was managing the costs of searching out other teams, arranging games, agreeing on rules, and then making sure opponents showed up to play. Commercial commitments such as renting arenas and selling tickets required secure and efficient arrangements beforehand, and the league form facilitated this management by bringing together clubs in a contractual relationship that provided the apparatus of coordination and discipline. Over time, the elite commercial hockey leagues would constantly adopt, adapt, and refine these mechanisms according to the demands of changing economic, cultural, and institutional environments.[17]

Just as lacrosse had been fashioned in Montreal and gained quick popularity across Canada from the 1860s, hockey was being structured for national diffusion. How else to explain the pretense of naming a league the Amateur Hockey Association *of Canada* when it had only one member outside Montreal? The AHAC hoped to accommodate clubs from beyond the island of Montreal through the use of the challenge format, where each game became a championship match. This format made interurban travel more attractive, because if the visiting team won, the games returned to its home rink until it was defeated. And its next game could not occur until other clubs had a chance to play the new champion. Yet therein lay the disadvantage: few games were actually played, and some teams might play more than others. In the first AHAC season, the Victorias played seven games but McGill only one, so the next year the league tried out the alternative system: a series format that scheduled six games for each team and awarded the championship to the club with the best record. This system seemed to work well, but inclusivity trumped balance in 1889 when the league returned to the challenge format to encourage teams from Ottawa, Quebec, or Toronto to join. By 1892 the desire to attract clubs from outside Montreal had succeeded too well: Ottawa defeated Montreal HC at the Crystal Palace rink, and for the rest of the season the Montreal teams had to travel to Ottawa, almost three hours by train, to play. It also made little sense when Montreal HC won the championship by defeating Ottawa in the last game of the season, Montreal's lone victory in a season when Ottawa had six! Moreover, Montreal fans had been deprived of league hockey, and, perhaps more important, the Montreal clubs (and rinks) were deprived of gate receipts, which were becoming a major incentive for organized league play. In 1893 the AHAC returned permanently to series play and accommodated Ottawa and Quebec by spacing out their trips to Montreal.[18]

Ottawa's success in the AHAC showed what quick hold the Montreal game had taken on the capital city's sporting elite. Two Ottawa men had seen the sport at the 1883 Carnival tournament and within two months organized a hockey club upriver in the nation's capital. As in Montreal, the club attracted young professional men, several of whom were actually experienced players, being recent McGill graduates recruited to work in the Dominion civil service. The club competed well against the Montreal clubs at the 1884 and 1885 Carnival tournaments and was one of the founding members of the AHAC. However, after the first AHAC season, the club foundered owing to poor leadership, difficulty finding cheap ice time, and the absence of local competition.[19]

After lying dormant for three years, the club was reinvigorated by the opening of the Rideau Rink and the leadership of both James Creighton, who had moved from Montreal, and Philip Dansken (P. D.) Ross, the publisher of the *Ottawa Journal*. Ross was a Montrealer who had played hockey and other sports at McGill and been a reporter for the *Toronto Mail* at the 1883 Carnival tournament. After assuming control of the *Journal* in 1887, he ingratiated himself into Ottawa high society and saw his interests in hockey and society converge at the Rideau Rink. The rink's patron was the new governor general, Frederick Arthur Stanley, 1st Baron Stanley of Preston, an Englishman who became an enthusiast after he first saw hockey at the 1889 Montreal Carnival and whose sons and daughter played regularly at Rideau Hall, the viceregal residence. Stanley may also have attended a game at the Rideau Rink that March when James Creighton and P. D. Ross captained two local club teams that included members of Parliament, staff members of the governor general, three of Stanley's sons, and other local notables. The core of these players, known as the Rideau Rebels, took the game across Ontario for matches in Lindsay, Toronto, and Kingston. Back at home, middle-class Ottawa enthusiasts created the Ottawa Amateur Athletic Club (OAAC) on the model of the MAAA and connected to it the new Ottawa Hockey Club, which in turn helped form a new city league and rejoin the city to the AHAC.[20]

Despite the move to the capital, in terms of economic power and population, the spread of hockey from Montreal to Ottawa was a move from metropolis to hinterland, but Ottawa's viceregal connection gave the sport a social and symbolic legitimacy among aspiring bourgeoisie across Canada. Ottawa also served as the bridge to Ontario, where hockey was beginning to catch on in university and urban sports clubs. One of Ontario's oldest cities, Kingston already had a tradition stretching back to the 1840s of informal shinny played by garrison troops on the St. Lawrence. The Montreal game was introduced by a McGill graduate in 1879, and an intercity league appeared from 1885 to 1887. In Toronto, Ontario's largest city (population 181,200 in 1891), sporting club culture flourished, and organized rule-based hockey had taken root in local curling clubs in the winter of 1888, inspired by news of the Montreal Carnival tournaments and the formation of the AHAC. By 1891 a Bankers' League became the first composed of employer-sponsored teams, and women's teams were also beginning play.[21]

When the Rideau Rebels went on a provincial tour in 1890, it spurred interest in forming an Ontario intercity league on the AHAC model. Later that year under Stanley's patronage, clubs from Ottawa, Kingston, Toronto, Bowmanville, and Lindsay formed the Hockey Association of Ontario. Ross helped draw up the rules, which were very similar to AHAC's except for a different variation on offside, an allowance for the goalie to use his hands, and additional prohibitions against profane or abusive language, cross-checking, and pushing. Again following the AHAC example, the association inaugurated junior (1893) and intermediate (1896) circuits to complement the top level, named senior. Although clubs went in and out of existence in the early 1890s, the Toronto district of the renamed

Ontario Hockey Association (OHA) remained vibrant and included clubs from southwestern Ontario. Soon the more than one dozen clubs from Ottawa to Stratford became an Ontario parallel to the Montreal-centric AHAC, with Ottawa the nexus where the two organizations met.[22]

The two regional leagues and the many intercity rivalries soon led to calls for a Canadian championship competition. At a dinner on 18 March 1892 honoring the Ottawa Hockey Club, the governor general's aide-de-camp announced that Stanley wanted to donate a challenge cup to be held by the championship hockey team in the Dominion. Ross and the local sheriff, John Sweetland, were appointed to act as trustees and asked to determine the rules. When the cup arrived from England the next year, it was engraved "Dominion Hockey Challenge Cup," but it was known by the title given in the *Ottawa Journal* article of 1 May 1893, "The Stanley Cup." Ross outlined the requirements for awarding the cup, beginning with Stanley's own five conditions—among them that the cup be "open to all, and thus, representative of the hockey championship as completely as possible, rather than of any one association"—and adding nine of his own. Most important, the trustees expected the OHA and AHAC to coordinate seasons so that their champions might challenge for "the Stanley Hockey Championship Cup" at the end. Stanley and Ross's attempt to use the cup to structure the elite hockey league relationship did not show early promise when Montreal HC initially refused to accept it, but within a decade the trustees' willingness to accept challenges for the Canadian championship from all across the country succeeded in bringing the game an increasingly national audience. The competition also led to revenue opportunities in the form of gambling and tickets that sped the arrival of a fully commercialized and professional version of the game.[23]

The cup's granting coincided with recovery from a general North American economic downturn in the mid-1890s. Organized hockey spread more rapidly; facilitated by university alumni networks, rail transportation, media publicity, and commercial opportunities, the Montreal game diffused to cities and towns far beyond the St. Lawrence and Ottawa Valleys—to western Canada, New England, and back to the Maritimes. In particular, the sport took solid root in Winnipeg, Manitoba, a city experiencing phenomenal growth as the main entrepôt of prairie development, and its clubs went on to win the Stanley Cup in 1896 and 1901, even before the first Ontario club did so (Ottawa in 1903). The ease and speed of the western diffusion were helped immensely by the availability of winter ice and general adoption of the Montreal Rules. In comparison, on the East Coast the older Halifax game persisted, with marked differences, including allowance of forward passing and a goal perpendicular to the modern setup that could be scored on from both sides. Owing to the interrelated factors of climate, lower skill level, lack of adherence to the Montreal game, and economic weakness, the Halifax game began to wane in the new century and did not spread.[24]

The diffusion of Montreal-style hockey into the United States ran into similar limitations as in the Maritimes, including climatic variability and competition from rival ice game variants. Ice games were not unknown to Americans: there are accounts of informal play in midcentury periodicals, and a version of hockey was played at St. Paul's School in New Hampshire as early as 1860. Harvard College students formed a Hockey Club in 1884 but by the end of the decade were playing a game called ice polo (also popular in the Maritimes). After some exhibition contests with Canadian teams, they were convinced they should "convert" back to hockey. In the mid-1890s the spread of artificial ice technology changed the spatial distribution of the game, and condenser technology allowed hockey to skip south to cities such as Baltimore, Philadelphia, and New York, thereby creating longer seasons in these cities than in more wintry climes like Boston or even Toronto. The new American enthusiasts invited the Montreal clubs to play exhibitions and compete, and in 1896 clubs joined together in leagues like Manhattan's Amateur Hockey League and Pittsburgh's Western Pennsylvania Hockey League (WPHL).[25]

In addition to the spreading of the sport through class channels and across geographic space, sport culture was also transmitted through the media of newspaper, magazine, and telegraphy. Since the 1860s, American and Canadian newspapers had created a "world of sport" for their readers, devoting regular inches to covering sports such as pedestrianism, billiards, football, baseball, lacrosse, horse racing, and rowing, as well as taking paid advertisements for events themselves. Special interest periodicals such as *Outing* in the United States and *Athletic Life* in Canada emerged in the 1890s to serve a specific market of sports-minded consumers, and telegraph companies made special arrangements to transmit real-time bulletins of games to audiences who could not attend in person. These technologies, along with rule books, helped disseminate play and knowledge of the sport beyond the urban centers of central Canada and the northeastern United States and sowed the seeds for propagation.[26]

The Commercial Game

While for some hockey was just a game to play, for others it was a commercial service to be exploited, but the borders between the two were becoming less distinct. Amateur clubs actually became the first sites of commercialization, particularly the ones in the larger urban centers that focused on the provision of facilities to spectator and participant. Despite being "clubs," sport organizations took on some of the commercial character and forms familiar to their members from their daytime occupations. Members paid fees to purchase a share both in the governance of the organization and in its product. As amateur clubs moved from intraclub to interclub play, and from intraurban to interurban play, expenses for travel and equipment grew and required extra financing, so clubs began to negotiate sharing of gate revenues and travel expenses. Indeed, the lubricant of the modern economic world, money, was soon common to all levels of sport to some degree. By the mid-1870s, lacrosse clubs' costs were being subsidized by their more affluent members. As historian Alan Metcalfe writes, money was "the focal point of industrial capitalism" and gave "sport one factor that tied everything together."[27]

Notwithstanding its amateur ideology, the MAAA was run as a business. Weekly meetings and strict and efficient management of money from membership fees and gate receipts were the foundation of its success. In 1886 the constitution was revised to remove the prohibition against charging admission for events. To encourage attendance and attract new members, matches and activities were advertised extensively in newspapers and on streetcar posters and fences at the association's grounds, and newspaper coverage of athletes and events added to the publicity and became increasingly essential to promotion.[28]

In the minutes and account books of the MAAA's connected hockey club, Montreal HC, we can see unfolding the new tensions and opportunities provided by a commercial approach. In 1896 the club hired a trainer, at first by game and then by season, and paid him a bonus if the team won the championship. Coaches arrived a few years later, usually veteran players from past campaigns. Another growing commercial engagement was evident with equipment and facility suppliers, as the sport's popularity caught the attention of sporting goods retailers and manufacturers. T. W. Boyd & Son, a local Montreal retail concern, asked the club to write a letter saying it used their brand of stick exclusively. In 1899 the American Spalding puck was made the official projectile of the Montreal elite league, and in 1902 the Spalding Company sponsored a whole hockey league in Montreal.[29]

Linkages with other businesses became more extensive as well. The infrastructure of transportation figured prominently, as trains and ferries brought teams and fans together, but most important for hockey was the physical infrastructure. Rinks were the key sites for turning indoor hockey's organized expression into a mass spectacle. Bringing the sport under covered space had several advantages, including gas (and, later, electrical) lighting, a measure of control over ice conditions, and the ability to charge for and restrict admission privileges. With the emergence of the AHAC, outdoor games now became the exception for elite matches. The growth of rinks as commercial enterprises changed the sport by separating further the participant from the spectator and by becoming less class restrictive by accepting any spectator who could pay. The club's relationship with the rinks also changed, from consumer of services to supplier. The Victoria Rink went from charging players for admission to their own games to giving the club free box seats and handing out season tickets, along with other concessions, in recognition of the attraction the clubs created for spectators.[30]

By 1897 the concessions were not enough to offset the limited capacity of the Victoria and other local rinks, and the elite hockey clubs began to discuss a new facility that could accommodate and seat larger crowds. The next year, the first Canadian indoor rink built for hockey opened at the corner of St. Catherine Street and Wood Avenue in Westmount, a wealthy English suburb of Montreal. Though still dependent on natural ice, the Westmount Arena was a clear improvement over the old rinks, with seating for six thousand, clear sight lines, and four-foot boards to protect spectators. As Howard Shubert notes, the arena was to provide the pattern for subsequent "arenas" built across North America and heralded the shift from a place of active participation in sport to a site of passive spectatorship. This shift was further reinforced by its ability to act as a multipurpose auditorium for the hosting of masquerades, band concerts, vaudeville, and conventions. Many of the arena's investors were of the same class that had always dominated Montreal sport. Among the notables were Andrew Gault, the "Cotton King of Canada"; James G. Ross, brother of P. D. Ross and partner in the family accounting firm; Louis Rubenstein, a champion figure skater; Russell Bowie, a star amateur hockey player; and Herbert Molson, of the famous brewing family. Many other scions of the Montreal business community and members of the Winged Wheel and Montreal HC participated, although initially there were only two French Canadian shareholders. The man in charge of the operation, as secretary-treasurer and manager of the Arena Company, was a former secretary and field captain of the Montreal Lacrosse Club, William A. Northey, who would become instrumental in organizing elite hockey in the city and maintaining the arena at its center.[31]

The clubs became comfortable with the commercial world of suppliers, servants, and facilities, but the commodification of the most important input of the game, labor, was still hotly contested. This friction was because new commercial opportunities conflicted with class and status priorities. Unlike ice time and skates, player labor could be had for free as long as hockey remained the preserve of the members of the leisured elite who could afford to play it in their (unwaged) spare time. Players chose to use the sport as a way to reinforce their class, socioeconomic status, and ethnicity, and not for income. This situation was generally the case until the mid-1890s, when, like sports before it, hockey became more broadly accessible to participants from other classes who had different priorities. This process seems to have been slower than for other sports like lacrosse, which did not require such specialized equipment and skill, namely, skates and skating, respectively. An example comes from the Irish Catholic Shamrocks club, where the lacrosse team was considered working-class but the hockey team retained the bourgeois character of the club's organizers. Even the French Canadians who began playing before the turn of the century were students at Montreal's elite classical colleges and thus children of the elite. Nonetheless, in the 1890s boys of different classes were playing shinny and hockey on the streets and rinks of Montreal. As men, they would form the player corps of the new century, albeit not without a considerable change in attitude to paid play.[32]

Even though professionals were not yet a threat, as early as 1886 hockey men were on the lookout for the disputes that had bedeviled lacrosse, and they made preemptively sure that the amateur code would rule in hockey as well. The AHAC constitution of 1886 took as its model the code of the National Amateur Lacrosse Association of Canada and, except for the sport's name, had near-identical objectives: "to improve, foster, and perpetuate the game of hockey in Canada; protect it from professionalism, and to promote the cultivation of kindly feeling among the members of the hockey clubs." The intent to protect hockey from professionalism is noteworthy because there is no evidence at this early date that professionalism was an actual problem. It may have been to preemptively protect hockey from those individuals who played professional lacrosse in the summer and might want to try their hands at hockey. In lacrosse the restriction to amateurs had been an attempt to exclude highly skilled aboriginals from playing on white teams, which skewed competition and affronted the ideology of social separation of classes and races. Aboriginal players were not considered an issue in hockey, and in fact the one aboriginal participant in the AHAC, Thomas Green, a member of the Six Nations Confederacy, was actually the first president of the league.[33]

The greater reason for resistance to professionalism was that it implied a different attitude toward sport, one that privileged winning over respectability and commercial lucre over social order. In lacrosse professional play was a scapegoat for a wider range of "problems"—gambling, poor refereeing, fistfights, fan rowdyism, and working-class participation—that had often preexisted or were unrelated to the issue of paying players. These issues began to emerge in hockey in the 1890s, and behaviors that had been considered acceptable among the elites, such as gambling (and pay-ment itself), were increasingly viewed with disdain.

Complicating matters was that distinguishing between amateurs and professionals was increasingly difficult. Frank Cosentino shows that up to the late 1870s and early 1880s, the main features of early Canadian ama-teurism, like its older British sibling, were class and skill level. The impor-tant class marker was being above manual labor or a "trade." In both countries the amateur definition then morphed into a definition based strictly on monetary payment. This shift was deceptively simple and cre-ated two problems. First, for years amateurs had been playing for prizes, including cash and medals, so the lines of acceptability had to be redrawn and agreed upon. Second, decrying the negative influence of money was a flagrant repudiation of the growing commercialization of the game in all its other aspects. Why should players be exempted from the market?[34]

The problem of professionalism was a symbolic contest of cultural meaning of the proper direction and purpose of hockey, a battle that would bedevil the sport well into the twentieth century. In the end, the elites of St. Antoine's Ward could not prevent the inexorable arrival of a new era of "mass sports," where the spectator was not playing for gentle-manly virtue, but paying for a spectacle and wanted to see a winning team, not necessarily a virtuous one. Some accepted the new paradigm and adapted their clubs and leagues to it, and some did not, but by the end of the first decade of the twentieth century hockey had a fully com-mercialized form from which a new industry would result with a new kind of entrepreneur to run it.[35]

In Leagues with Each Other

A few months before the Westmount Arena opened in 1898, the five-club AHAC senior series restructured under a new name, beginning a process of adaptation to the growing consumer demand for hockey and a concur-rent pressure to commercialize players. The elite clubs pursued a strategy of closing the league to outsiders in order to control production of elite hockey and stabilize the hockey labor market. Over the next ten years, they worked to find the right formula by experimenting with elite league form, function, and size and determining which mix of market scale, rink size, geographic dispersion, and ethnic and urban representation would produce the most successful hockey product.

The 1890s saw a proliferation of hockey clubs in Montreal and Ottawa, but also in small neighboring towns such as Cornwall, Ontario. As well, the game was attracting ethnic clubs—mainly Irish and French Canadian—who were successful at the junior and intermediate levels and looked for promotion to the AHAC's senior circuit. The existing league constitution provided for the promotion of a club to the senior series once it had won the intermediate series, and in 1898 the Ottawa Capitals, a rival of the Ottawa Hockey Club, asked to be admitted. At the annual meeting of the AHAC, the intermediate clubs made it clear they welcomed the chance to remove the dominant Capitals from their level and save on travel costs at the same time. But the Montreal senior clubs complained that if the Capitals were added as a sixth senior club, the series schedule would require midweek travel to Ottawa and an extended season. The other Ottawa club, Ottawa HC, worried that the Ottawa market could not support two senior clubs. Since both intermediate and senior divisions were allowed to vote, the Capitals had enough support to get promoted, but the senior clubs then resigned from the league to form a new organization, the Canadian Amateur Hockey League. Later it transpired that the senior breakaway had been planned all along to shake off the influence of the intermediate clubs, but the senior clubs did allow the intermediates to affiliate in a separately governed intermediate division of the CAHL, only with no more promotion mechanism.[36]

The breakup of the AHAC was an important moment that confirmed the elite club preference for a league that was closed to outsiders except by unanimous agreement among existing members. This development was not inevitable, but rather a choice between two well-known options in league organization. One was the National League in American baseball, which had closed membership from 1892, and the other was the English Football League, which adopted in the same year a divisional structure that allowed promotion and relegation of clubs from season to season. A closed league kept control over travel costs by allowing existing members to decide how many clubs were too many and how far was too far to travel. It was not too hard to imagine that if geographic extension made midweek travel necessary, then players might require money to take time off from their day jobs, and a full-time paid professional player corps might soon follow. The other advantage of the closed league was market control. Montreal had proved it could sustain several clubs, but in Ottawa the consensus was that one was enough. A closed league prevented clubs from eating into one another's customer bases and threatening the league as a whole, and this stability would also encourage infrastructural investment. (It is almost certainly not a coincidence that the Westmount Arena was built in the same year that the CAHL was formed.)[37]

The CAHL could still admit new members, but the requirement for unanimity was an obstacle. In 1899 McGill was declined because it had not won the intermediate championship. In 1901 the Crescents club of Quebec was refused on the grounds that "a six club league would prove an embarrassing and unwieldy proposition" (in other words, scheduling and travel would be too onerous). In 1902 Cornwall did not get the required unanimous approval, and the Aberdeens of Ottawa were simply not considered when they did not pay the application fee. Over time it seems the reasons got more specious and the debates in the boardroom more contentious, but the alternative of an open league seemed no better. In Ontario the OHA allowed all comers, but doing so led to instability and poor-quality hockey (an OHA team had yet to win the Stanley Cup). So for four years the CAHL refused to take in any new clubs and even restricted its clubs from playing exhibition matches during the season without league permission. In the fifth season, however, the CAHL clubs discovered the downside of creating a "close [sic] corporation" that did not accommodate expansion and growth: a rival league of jilted clubs could appear that, if it could obtain players, would threaten their monopoly.[38]

Moving players depended on changing the nature of their relationship to the club. In the nineteenth century there had been many common social bonds between hockey club members, but even before the turn of the century a gap was apparent between those members who were part of the club and the ones who actually played on the team. Club memberships exceeded the number who could participate in the games, and so a committee was usually appointed to choose the team that would be iced from week to week. As skill and age sorted them out, members specialized, with some playing in the games, others administering the club, and the rest providing social and financial support. This division of labor could lead to friction when success on the ice was not forthcoming. In October 1901 the resentment among Montreal HC players even spilled over into the newspapers. The *Montreal Daily Star* reported that players felt the committee's choices had compromised the club's chances to win the CAHL championship (they had finished fourth). Acting quickly, the club agreed to restore player input into picking the team and to allow players to elect their own coach and to hold regular committee-player meetings during the season to "ventilate and adjust" grievances. The new arrangements led to a championship season and the Stanley Cup, but it was not to last. As it turned out, roster control was not the only problem.[39]

The spirit of amateurism still prohibited monetary reward, but since the late 1890s the Montreal players—like others in the league—had been receiving more than just their names engraved on trophies. The Montreal HC club and its individual members supplied a wide range of goods for players, from the mundane, like fruit and reading materials, to lavish keepsakes, like gold watches and team photographs. After retaining the Stanley Cup in 1903, the players received diamond rings worth one hundred dollars each and one year's membership in the MAAA. The club also compensated individual medical expenses, equipment costs, and, for one player, overnight accommodation for match and practice nights. Recalling that the club was affiliated with the MAAA, the bastion of Montreal amateurism, one might speculate that other clubs would have done as much or more. The gifts and nonmonetary remunerations point to the growing pressure to pay players outright and also to the role that success in prestigious competitions such as the Stanley Cup was playing in creating that pressure to pay to win.[40]

Commercial, ideological, and geographic growth was pushing against the boundaries of the sport and demanding growth in the supply of expert players. Competition between clubs, between leagues, and between cities was creating a continuum of player-club relationships, from unpaid amateur to paid professional. Money encouraged mobility, but, in the beginning at least, amateur ideology ensured that compensation would be indirect. The earliest stories of players being directly paid for play came from Ontario and Pennsylvania, areas of high hockey interest with a scarcity of high-quality players. In 1896 a Pittsburgh club was writing to players in Montreal, offering off-ice jobs as well as travel and living expenses. In 1897 the OHA cracked down on rumored remuneration by passing a resolution that placed the burden on an accused player to prove he had *not* taken money. Later that season, when the manager of the Berlin (present-day Kitchener) club rewarded his players with ten-dollar gold coins as "souvenirs," the association expelled the whole team and declared them professional. The Berlin players were later reinstated, but it is interesting to note that three former Montreal Shamrocks played in the OHA that year, including Arthur Farrell, who returned to Montreal to play for the MAAA, and Charlie Liffiton, who followed a year later. It is unclear why these players left Montreal in the first place, but financial incentives can be assumed. At the turn of the century, the greater attraction for hockey mercenaries was the United States. Ottawa HC player Alf Smith went in 1901 to play for the Western Pennsylvania Hockey League, and the next year Ottawa lost three more players, including Bruce Stuart, the team's top scorer. Halfway through the 1903 season, the peripatetic Liffiton left Montreal again to play for the Pittsburgh Bankers of the semiprofessional WPHL. Other clubs in the CAHL and OHA were similarly raided, and it became evident that winning league championships and the Stanley Cup was no longer enough for the players.[41]

Defections to the United States bled the elite Montreal clubs, but in 1903 there was an amputation when almost the entire roster of Montreal HC defected and formed a new club, the Wanderer Hockey Club. The Wanderers' organizers, including James Strachan and William Jennings, ran the risk the league might simply isolate the club, but they had a plan. The continued intransigence of the CAHL's admission policy prompted the formation of a rival league composed of two clubs the CAHL had previously refused to admit (Cornwall and the Ottawa Capitals), along with a French Canadian club (Le National). The Wanderers joined this new league, which was christened the Federal Amateur Hockey League and led by the Capitals representative, William Foran, who by day was a high-ranking federal bureaucrat. The FAHL aimed to get access to senior hockey and the Stanley Cup competition, and the players expected to be rewarded as well. The new league's constitution was nearly identical to the code of the CAHL, except for two provisions: it provided for admission to the league with a majority vote, not unanimity—the major barrier to CAHL expansion—and it had a more relaxed policy about player compensation: the FAHL would allow payments to players.[42]

With all the players they needed, the FAHL clubs did not need to pry any more from CAHL clubs, and it also committed to arranging its games midweek so as not to compete directly with Saturday CAHL games. Yet the existence of two competing leagues radically changed the market of elite hockey by creating an alternative for dissatisfied players and league members. Club and player self-interest now trumped "kindly feeling" and gentlemanly respectability in relations between clubs. Within a month of the start of the 1903–4 season, this self-interest reared up. After Ottawa arrived more than an hour late for a game in Montreal, the other CAHL clubs tried to apply the required ten-dollar fine. Embittered, Ottawa resigned from the league in protest and began exploring a move to the FAHL. Considering the jump, the club confirmed with P. D. Ross that it could retain the Stanley Cup and defend it against challengers and then bring the prestigious trophy to the FAHL at the end of the season. With this promise in hand, Ottawa joined the Federal and brought the cup along, thereby changing the established practice of the cup staying in the league of the last champion until won by another. It also showed the power of the club and the weakness of the leagues in a two-league environment.[43]

The loss of Ottawa and the Stanley Cup was a blow to the prestige of the CAHL, and there were worrisome threats that the Shamrocks might also move and thus reduce the league to three clubs. Poor attendance in both leagues during the 1903–4 season suggested the Montreal market for senior hockey was oversaturated, but amalgamation talks in the fall failed to bring the parties together owing to residual bitterness over the mass defection of Montreal HC players to the Wanderers. After several club shifts, the leagues persisted through the 1904–5 season, unbalanced in the standings and at the gate (the FAHL Wanderers' games alone outdrew all the CAHL games combined). At this point, it was up to the only other power beside the clubs to step in to resolve the problem. In December 1905 the Westmount Arena warned there would not be enough ice to accommodate dates from both leagues and proposed (demanded?) a new alliance between the top clubs: Montreal HC, Victorias, Shamrocks, Quebec, Ottawa HC, and Wanderers. The pressure was heeded. On 11 December 1905, these six promptly abandoned their affiliations and formed the Eastern Canada Amateur Hockey Association (ECAHA). There had been talk of an eight-team league, but even a league of six was overly ambitious for some. As it was, there would be a game every three or four days from 3 January to 10 March—thirty in total. Those clubs who were left out screamed and hollered, but to no avail. The CAHL disbanded, and the FAHL became a shadow of its former self.[44]

The beginning of this new league was hardly harmonious. Forced together, the clubs experimented with neutral third-party administration in the form of the arena. As president they agreed on F. Howard Wilson, a director and major stockholder in the Montreal Arena Company, and William Northey, who ran the rink, was to be the paid secretary-treasurer. The ECAHA overcame some of the distrust and returned to using club representatives as league officers the next season, but in retaining Northey as a league administrator it began the long-term process of separating club and league management, which served the interest of moderating club conflict.[45]

While the Montreal clubs resolved their differences under an old model, a new league based on professional players was well under way in the United States. Unlike the Montreal elite leagues, or its Pittsburgh predecessor, the WPHL, the new International Hockey League placed the majority of its clubs in small towns, in this case the resource hinterland of Michigan's Upper Peninsula and New Ontario. The IHL was the brainchild of a Canadian dentist, Jack (Doc) Gibson, who was one of the players expelled in the Berlin OHA scandal. Gibson realized overt pay was essential to stock remote clubs in Houghton, Calumet, and Sault Ste. Marie (Canada and the United States), as well as Pittsburgh, as were salaries that were lucrative enough to tempt players from their urban day jobs for the short two- or three-month "bush" league hockey season, and also to convince them to permanently sacrifice their amateur status. The going wage was $15 to $40 a week, and it was enough to pull in many Canadian amateurs. Stars required more: the mercenary Charlie Liffiton briefly returned to play for the Wanderers for one game in 1905 before once again leaving to join Houghton of the IHL, where he was paid $1,350 and given a day job.[46]

For three seasons the IHL was a successful American adaptation of a Canadian sport model, transplanting players, officials, and rules to serve American audiences. Its use of outright professionalism caused some distress to Canadian elite hockey and in particular had an immediate deleterious effect on the OHA, from which most of the IHL players were lured. This defection made the Ontario league even more intransigent and conservative in its policies banning professionalism. In 1904 the OHA imposed residence regulations to control player movement, but the fact that many players were still resisting inducements from the IHL clubs suggests that the OHA was turning a blind eye to "shamateurism" among its own clubs, which often gave their players day jobs in the community, among other perquisites.[47]

The ECAHA resisted the effects of the IHL more successfully. It lost some players, and had to surreptitiously pay others more to keep them, but overall its ability to retain and rehire star players partly contributed to the demise of the IHL in 1907. The ECAHA clubs might have also taken note of the other challenges the IHL faced, such as sagging attendance, on-ice violence, poor refereeing, declining profitability, a general economic downturn, a general increase in costs, and, most important, the difference in size between cities in the circuit. In 1906–7 Pittsburgh outdrew Sault Ste. Marie (Michigan) and Calumet by more than four times each, and despite some sharing of gate receipts, this market imbalance had doomed the league. Another lesson was that the application of a salary limit had failed to contain the spending of the clubs and was ineffective when a rival league gave players leverage. Players had a new appreciation of their commercial value and a willingness to take action to achieve it (the Pittsburgh players had a successful strike in 1906), and they brought it back to the Canadian leagues.[48]

Another legacy of the IHL was the emergence of a national aspect. As a primarily American league, the IHL strengthened an association of the professional variety of the sport with the United States. Canadian newspapers were quite critical of the league and, no doubt fueled by resentment over the loss of local players, ascribed a package of undesirable elements—gambling, violence, and so on—to professionalism and to American influence. Though professionalism had been well on the way in Canada before the IHL, and the IHL was in many respects a binational business, the IHL introduced the idea that American commercialism was "tainting" the Canadian game, an idea that would persist.

The most obvious impact of the IHL was its amplification of the debate over professionalism in Canada. Over the course of the 1905–6 season, the issue was pressed in the newspapers, among the amateur governing bodies, and in the boardroom of the ECAHA. The overt salaries paid by the IHL and the loss of players brought the hypocrisy and cognitive dissonance of Canadian hockey amateurism to the fore, and hockey organizers and players adjusted their attitudes accordingly. There clearly was no going back to "simon-pure amateurism," as the skills required to play elite hockey were no longer available to the casual player. As one of the original amateurs, P. D. Ross, put it, "We expect the young athlete who has got into senior company to give up several hours a day to keep himself fit to give us the greatest possible amount of satisfaction and entertainment in physical sports." Ross's solution to the "heap of hypocrisy and lies" that athletics had become was to legalize semiprofessionals and allow them to compete side by side with amateurs, as long as their status was publicly announced. This idea addressed the social question, and Ross also had a solution for the economic one as well: he proposed salary limits to make sure that on-ice parity was maintained.[49]

The mixing of amateur and professional players had recently been proposed in lacrosse and was taken as a signal by hockey men that a softening of the hard line might be tolerated. Within the ECAHA, differences were evident between the clubs still backed by amateur athletic organizations, such as Montreal HC and Ottawa HC, and those stand-alone clubs like the Wanderers that felt less pressure to harmonize their commercial behavior with amateur ideology. The MAAA was becoming uncomfortable making exceptions for its hockey team and lobbied hard for a practical modification of amateur rules to allow amateurs and professionals to play together. In the spring of 1906, it declared all its teams were free to mix without threatening amateurs' status (the Montreal-based National

Amateur Lacrosse Union followed suit, dropping *Amateur* from its name for good measure). When the Canadian Amateur Athletic Union (CAAU), the national amateur sport governing body, retained the hard line that reflected the values of the members outside Montreal, particularly in Ontario, the MAAA set up a rival amateur body in 1907 called the Amateur Athletic Federation of Canada (AAFC), and an "Athletic War" broke out between proponents of a "pure" amateurism, like the Toronto-based Ontario Hockey Association, and those clubs (mainly from Montreal) that wanted either some realistic modification of amateur principles or acceptance of full professionalization of players.[50]

The ECAHA changed policy unilaterally at its annual meeting in November 1906, allowing open payment of players if their names were publicized. However, the lists that appeared were suspiciously dominated by amateurs, suggesting that clubs or players still did not want to admit reality. More important was the tendency for players to play one club off against another for higher salaries. James Strachan, the founder of the Wanderers, proposed that professionals be required to stay with a club for the whole season and the next, but this notion was not carried out. (Along with Ross's suggestion for a salary limit, it would become more attractive in years to come.) Getting cold feet, the Victorias tried to reverse course and return to the status quo ante of an all-amateur league, but it was too late. Professionalism had come to Canadian elite hockey, and clubs would have to either adapt to its exigencies or leave. In 1908 the clubs with the strongest ties to amateurism, Montreal HC and the Victorias, took the latter option. For the 1908–9 season, the ECAHA followed lacrosse precedent and dropped *Amateur* from its name, leaving no more arguments about whether to pay players.[51]

With the hockey issue resolved and the MAAA returned to amateurism, in 1909 the AAFC merged with the CAAU to form a new body, the Amateur Athletic Union of Canada (AAUC), which used a strictly graded amateur definition. Sports like hockey were now clearly divided between amateurs and professionals, who would no longer be allowed to play in the same leagues, not to mention together on the same teams. As a by-product of this division, the Stanley Cup now became the de facto exclusive domain of professional clubs. The trustees declared emphatically that "the Stanley Cup was not hung up for either amateur or professional hockey in particular, but for the best hockey." And the best hockey was on the professional side, a fact implicitly confirmed by a request by the AAUC for donation of a new cup, the Allan, to represent the amateur hockey champions of the Dominion. Though the professionals had won the Stanley Cup, it would be a long time before the "professional" brand lost its taint in the eyes of many hockey consumers.[52]

Business Principles

Full overt professionalism allowed the ECHA clubs (Ottawa, Wanderers, Shamrocks, Quebec) the freedom to structure their competitive space more fully on so-called business principles. Because the first principle of business is not necessarily a free market but one tilted in its favor, the league's priority was to tailor player movement and costs to its own needs.

The professional clubs were particularly troubled by players who signed contracts with two clubs in order to extract the best offer, and this situation was the result of several problems that needed resolution. The first was how to regularize the standing of the clubs as business entities, through incorporation or otherwise, so that contracts were legally binding. At least one player was concerned about the reliability of an unincorporated club as contractor, and there could be no resort to the law for either party if clubs had no agreed-upon legal standing. The second was how to get the clubs to agree not to steal each other's players, and here the trust of clubs in the league and its rules had to be established and reinforced. The third problem was how to stop players from jumping from club to club. Star players like Art Ross of the Wanderers were now demanding sixteen hundred dollars a season (the entire payroll of Montreal HC had been just over two thousand dollars the year before) and pitting one club against another. The movement of players had to be restrained so that economic order could be maintained.[53]

For the next decade, the main efforts of the league and its clubs were to develop effective solutions to these problems, and many of them turned on resolving a fourth problem: how to restrict competition for players from rival leagues. The Stanley Cup competition represented an opportunity for clubs from Ontario hinterland towns such as Haileybury, New Liskeard,

Cobalt, and Rat Portage to boost their profiles through sports competition. Backed by mining interests, these clubs would buy star players for a season and then challenge for the cup, with the gate revenues and wagers (sometimes tens of thousands of dollars' worth) making the whole venture worthwhile. The Montreal professional leagues had to come up with a model that could resist this centrifugal movement.

Before this competition could be addressed, there first had to be attention paid to the club governance structure within the ECHA. In the first decade of the twentieth century, running a hockey team became an expensive proposition, requiring capital and full-time attention. This development pressured the voluntary member-based community amateur clubs of the nineteenth century to reorganize into companies along fully commercial lines and restructure relationships according to commercial contract, not social comity. The local lawyers, pharmacists, and physicians who had governed the clubs often as part-time ventures and as a form of community service or class obligation were now being joined or replaced by new entrepreneurs who saw hockey more and more as an entertainment business, one requiring financial, not social, capital.

One of the most important new stages in this evolution was the idea that clubs could now be divorced both from their own members and from affiliated athletic clubs (like the MAAA and OAAC) and instead be *owned*. This change in character led to a dispute over the ownership of the Wanderers that wound up dissolving the ECHA itself.

The Wanderers club seems to have been the first club to have had formal ownership, and sometime before the fall of 1909 the club's principals transferred their stake to one among them, Fred Strachan (James's brother), who then sold shares to a group headed by P. J. Doran, the owner of the Jubilee Rink. This move was immediately challenged by one of the original owners, William Jennings, who claimed that Strachan did not have the right to sell the team. What concerned the other clubs was Doran's plan to move the Wanderers' games from the Westmount Arena to his own smaller-capacity rink, and in so doing reduce their gate receipts. With Ottawa's support, Jennings organized a new team to take the Wanderers' place and play at the arena. To further complicate league discussions in the fall of 1909, applications appeared from two other clubs eager to join the elite series: Le National, which had long been on the door-step of elite play and would appeal to the French Canadian audience in Montreal, and Renfrew, which was the champion of the FAHL. Renfrew was one of several clubs controlled by Ambrose O'Brien, the son of Ottawa Valley mining and lumber baron M. J. O'Brien, and he was keen to chal-lenge for the Stanley Cup. But only one club would be admitted. The four ECHA clubs needed a fifth to make the season ten games for each club on a home-and-home basis, and a league of six clubs was seen as creating too many games.[54]

To control the agenda, the Ottawa, Shamrocks, and Quebec clubs resigned from the ECHA and yet again reformed, this time as the Cana-dian Hockey Association (CHA). The action eliminated any existing rights to play in the elite series and was directed squarely at Doran's Wanderers. The threesome then held a meeting to consider applications from the Wan-derers, Le National, Renfrew, Cornwall, and Jennings's new All-Montreal team. After two hours of meetings, only Le National and All-Montreal made the cut. Incensed, the Wanderers' representative, Jimmy Gardner, reached out to Ambrose O'Brien, who had three clubs under his control and a big bankroll. O'Brien needed little convincing and agreed to form a separate circuit. Renfrew and his two other clubs in the northern Ontario mining towns of Cobalt and Haileybury would join with the ostracized Wanderers in a new league of their own, the National Hockey Association of Canada (NHA). Mirroring the CHA's addition of Le National, at Gard-ner's suggestion they also created another club, Les Canadiens, to appeal to the French Canadian audience of Montreal and provide a rival for the Wanderers.[55]

Having three established clubs, on the surface the CHA had the advantage, but the arena also had to be considered. It refused to freeze out the NHA, which had the top-draw Wanderers, and gave the upstart NHA access to the main Montreal hockey facility. The deep-pocketed O'Brien did the rest, luring star players such as Frederick (Cyclone) Taylor and the Patrick brothers, Lester and Frank, to play for Renfrew. Exaggerated reports of Taylor's salary exceeding five thousand dollars for a twelve-game season (O'Brien later recalled it was two thousand dollars) and the thousands O'Brien did pay to the rest of the team generated excitement in the press and changed the team's popular nickname to the "Millionaires." It did not take long for the CHA to submit. Only three weeks into the season, the reality of five professional hockey teams in Montreal competing for the same customers (making fifty games rather than twelve) had the CHA clubs asking for a merger. As the stronger party, the NHA dictated terms and accepted only the CHA's two strongest clubs, Ottawa and the Shamrocks. The two newcomers, Le National and All-Montreal, were frozen out.[56]

The new league was viable, but still needed realignment. The combination of big-city clubs and O'Brien's small-resource town clubs was unsustainable, just as it had been in the IHL. The economics of small arenas, small crowds, and high travel costs quickly culled two of the upper Ottawa Valley clubs. The association redistributed the Cobalt club to a new owner in Quebec City, Michael J. (Mike) Quinn, where the Anglophone club's challenge would be to sell the professional game in a strong amateur and increasingly Francophone market. The French Canadian Montreal club was given to a Montreal sports promoter, George Kendall, who went by the *nom de sport* of George Kennedy.[57]

Although he was of Scotch-Irish descent, George Kennedy was the guiding light behind the Club Athlétique Canadien, formed in 1908 with French Canadian partners to promote participation in wrestling, hockey, baseball, lacrosse, and other sports among Francophones. In the 1890s hockey's popularity had exploded beyond the west-end English elites to the east-end working classes, and Kennedy was eager to offer professional hockey to his customers, especially a French Canadian brand. Curiously, Kennedy's introduction to the league was not by application but through a lawsuit in which he claimed to own the right to the "Canadien" name in relation to sports. While the claim was probably unsound, Ambrose O'Brien was more than happy to sell the franchise to Kennedy, an owner more culturally in harmony with the intended French Canadian character of the club. As well, Kennedy's ambition and connections to the newspapers—especially the popular *La Presse*—promised to attract spectators, and he had several related interests in Montreal sport and entertainment: the Irish Canadians lacrosse team, a bowling alley, and a movie house. In November 1910 the NHA gave Kennedy the Haileybury franchise to move to Montreal, for which he paid seventy-five hundred dollars. To protect the desired ethnic homogeneity of the club, he was allowed to use only two non–French Canadian players, and in 1912 the other clubs agreed that the Canadiens would have the exclusive right to all French Canadian players.[58]

Renfrew was the last of the resource town clubs to persist, lasting until 1911, but then Ambrose O'Brien gave up hockey and allowed the franchise to be earmarked for Toronto expansion. The Cobalt and Haileybury moves completed the shift away from the hinterland and back to those major population centers of central Canada that were perceived to have the economic wherewithal to support a club—Montreal (467,000), Ottawa (87,000), Quebec City (78,000), and now Toronto (327,000).[59]

Back to one league, the clubs could return to refining the league's business mode. Continuing the process begun in the ECAHA, the NHA separated day-to-day league administration from club representatives by placing men with no direct affiliation with member clubs in executive positions, especially the paid post of secretary-treasurer. In a break from the amateur tradition, which had club representatives as president, vice president, secretary, and treasurer, the association initially had only two officers, a president and a secretary-treasurer, who could be the same person. The clubs retained decision-making power through the board of directors, which collectively supervised the affairs of the league and arbitrated disputes and appeals between clubs and with players. Its decisions were final, but the president did have an important mediating role, as did the secretary-treasurer as the day-to-day administrator. Recognized as a neutral arbiter who could put league interests ahead of club particularism, the president gradually became more autonomous in the areas of player suspension and officiating and began to exercise even wider influence.[60]

In the first season, however, it was Eddie McCafferty who did the most to shape the league's form. McCafferty was well known in Montreal sport as the secretary of the Montreal Royals of minor professional baseball's Eastern League, a club owned by Sam Lichtenhein, who also owned the Montreal Cotton & Wood Waste Company. Given the widespread anti-Semitism in Montreal, one might speculate that McCafferty may have been acting as proxy for the Jewish Lichtenhein, and his name was noted as the purchaser of the Wanderers in the fall of 1909. (Without a tenant for his rink, Doran likely saw little future in owning the club.) McCafferty incorporated the new club and sold shares to the public in order to broaden the ownership and increase its popularity, and it was no surprise when Lichtenhein took a large block of stock and became president of the corporation. McCafferty took a leading role in the formation of the NHA, acting as secretary at the formation meeting in December 1909, and he had definite ideas about the organization and future of the league. He ingratiated himself enough to leave the first meeting with a promise of a future Toronto franchise in the new league and the post of secretary-treasurer (although he was displaced from the latter to the board of directors by President T. Emmett Quinn, a former Shamrocks club officer, after the merger with the CHA).[61]

Along with Quinn and Dickie Boon, the Wanderers' manager, McCafferty devised a new governance and labor relations structure for the league to place it on a so-called business basis. The NHA revised the ECHA constitution in a deliberate departure from the past, and the new rules took up a whole page in the *Gazette*, detailing procedures for league administration, club responsibilities, and player relations. As well as a standard player contract, the league imposed restrictions on player remuneration and mobility. There would be a total salary limit of five thousand dollars for each club, a requirement to "waive" players past other clubs before they were moved out of the league, and a new "reservation clause" that allowed clubs to "draft" (list) up to ten players required for the next season and prevent them from joining other clubs. A business basis also meant regularizing communications with the media: future association meetings were to be private affairs, with the league president alone authorized to give out information about the proceedings. The constitution envisioned future expansion and international dominance of the sport, with the "of Canada" in the NHA name dropped in order "to permit of taking into affiliation hockey bodies that may be formed in the United States as well as in Canada, with a view to making it eventually the central organization in the game." The NHA would have continental and dominant ambitions. Where did these aspirations come from?[62]

Where the NHA's predecessors had borrowed the league governance form from lacrosse, these new business principles were borrowed directly from American baseball, perhaps owing to McCafferty's baseball background. The "Objects" section of the NHA constitution was nearly identical to the 1903 National Agreement that created the baseball duopoly between the National League and American League, as was the wording of the reservation clause. In scheduling the NHA also intended to use the baseball technique of the "road trip," whereby clubs completed a series of games in different cities before returning home. With geographically dispersed clubs, this idea made economic sense, and with professional players who were less reliant on day jobs, during the season, it was perhaps more feasible.[63]

The NHA went even further than its baseball cousins in adopting an institution that previous leagues had not: formal incorporation. In November 1911 the NHA clubs applied to form a federal corporation with fifty thousand dollars in share capital divided into five hundred shares of one hundred dollars each. The purpose of the corporation was "to encourage, develop and improve the National Canadian winter game of hockey and athletic sports and pastimes." The push may have come from Ottawa HC, known as the Senators, since the league's purpose was identical to that of the Ottawa Hockey Association, Ltd., which had been the second club after the Wanderers to incorporate (in 1911). The Canadiens followed in 1916, incorporating as The Canadian Hockey Club, Inc., and owned by Kennedy and six other owners. The motivation was in keeping with the growing size and commercial basis of the clubs. It also helped the signing of player contracts and, in Ottawa's case, set the table for the building of a new arena.[64]

The motives for incorporating the league itself are more subtle. The standard attractions of incorporation—limited liability for shareholders and the creation of a legal entity for business purposes—were probably not necessary, as the league itself made few contracts and did not create significant liability issues. There may have been a desire to give professional hockey a modern business form to distinguish it from the partnerships of the past and differentiate it from contemporary amateur organizations. It also created a formal barrier between leagues—in 1898 the CAHL had considered formally incorporating itself to create space between the senior and intermediate levels. But primarily, the motive was probably to address the instability that had characterized its forebears. Previously linked by class and fraternity, clubs were now bound by the responsibility of common ownership, and it was up to them to maintain the league as a viable commercial enterprise. League incorporation would be expected to address the interclub relationship by binding the clubs together as owners, thus hedging against the risk of defection and the creation of rival leagues, as well as providing stability for scheduling. The timing of the incorporation is also important in this regard, being undertaken before the anticipated move to Toronto (and perhaps further in the future). Incorporation may have given some peace of mind to the clubs of a league expanding in scale and scope.[65]

The strongest motivation for the reimagination of the hockey league form along business principles reflected the owners' desire to reduce the costs associated with their major expense, the players. Searching out talent, bargaining salaries, and then making sure players turned up to play (and did not jump to another club) were becoming more crucial to success. Exacerbating the problem was the creation of "star" players, highly skilled practitioners whose exploits drew customers to games irrespective of which uniform they wore. Through their own marketing and promotional efforts, clubs had helped give players like Fred Taylor their own brand equity and wished to retain control over it. But regulations could not just target the players, but had to include the clubs who bid for them, so control was implemented by restricting player freedom in tandem with imposing rules on the clubs for moving players.

The new labor policies created immediate resistance. Despite the benefits of the salary limit, it was not clear that all clubs were onside. The day the constitution was publicized, the *Gazette* reported that Ottawa would "ridicule" the idea of a salary cap and, if it were passed, "would observe it directly and ignore it indirectly, handing out what they pleased on the side of the players." Club disobedience, however, was minor compared to player reaction to the new rules. Within weeks of the announcement of the constitution, the papers reported on a rumored players' union. Wanderers player Art Ross, one of the beneficiaries of the rising trend in salaries, wrote an open letter to the *Montreal Herald* in order to "take up the cudgels on behalf of the players." Ross argued that, unlike baseball players, hockey players held other employment that was put at risk by possible injury and loss of time, "in addition to suffering a certain amount of distraction, which is almost bound to effect [sic] the prospects of advancement in business." (In essence, Ross was arguing that hockey players were semiprofessionals since they still held day jobs and had to be treated differently.) In spite of his high salary, Ross maintained that he "would gladly give back all I have made" to regain amateur standing and asserted that many other players felt the same way. But now that they were professional, and could not be reinstated as amateurs, the players simply wanted "what their skill is worth as revenue producers." Giving some indication of the magnitude of the proposed salary cap, according to Ross the Wanderers had been paying ten to fourteen thousand dollars in salaries and Ottawa ten to twenty-five thousand dollars over the past seasons, and both had "never been in the hole." The players were "not trying to bulldoze" the NHA, but simply wanted a fair deal.[66]

The day after Ross's letter appeared, the direction of the bulldozing became clear. After the Ottawa captain, Bruce Stuart, tried to organize a new players' league (with Art Ross backing the Montreal club), the clubs pushed back. At the NHA meeting the Montreal Arena announced a contract with the Wanderers and Canadiens that would prevent any "outlaw" player league from getting ice in Westmount. This announcement made the new league instantly unviable, so by mid-December the player revolt fizzled out. The league promptly promulgated the new standard player contract, giving clubs new latitude to "discipline, suspend, fine, or discharge" players, not only for incompetence on the ice, but also for behavior that was "intemperate, immoral, careless, indifferent . . . on or off the ice, as to endanger or prejudice the interest" of the club. League officers maintained that the new contract "would result in the operation of the National on a fair business-like basis, [and] that it will do away with contract jumping and make the professional league far more popular" (presumably by keeping the player rosters stable). Many players said they would refuse to sign, citing the reservation clause specifically as "worse than a life sentence," but lacking any alternative, most did. The money saved from salaries showed up that season on the clubs' bottom lines. Small-town Renfrew lost money, but Ottawa's profits were estimated at six to eight thousand dollars, the

Canadiens' at three to four thousand, the Wanderers' at two to three thousand, and Quebec's at nine hundred dollars.[67]

With these developments, the league addressed several transaction costs related to its business by fixing membership, formal scheduling, using a commercial organizational form, adopting league rules that constrained club behavior and player mobility, and delegating some enforcement power to its executive. But there were still problems. As it turned out, the salary cap was easier to legislate than to enforce, showing repeatedly that the greatest threat to league financial probity was not player freedom but club spending. And effective player control depended on the NHA being the only bidder for hockey talent (monopsony power), which could not last for long.

Entering the Bastion of Amateurism

After two seasons of reorganization, the NHA clubs were moving toward profitability and stability. Decisions to drop the rover position and commit to six-man hockey in 1911 helped open up the game and make it more exciting and also helped reduced the roster (and salary burden) to eight players from ten. The players' stamina was helped by a switch from half-hour halves to three twenty-minute periods, and such tinkering could be seen as part of a general economic trend toward efficiency and rationalization and greater speed. This thought was spelled out by a writer for the *Toronto Daily Star*, who reported that the roster reduction was being seen as "similar to the action of a big manufacturer in decreasing a working force. . . . One can easily see the day when the hockey player . . . will be traded and sold in the same manner that the largest baseball clubs across the border handle their men." The NHA's application of business principles to the sport was changing the motivations of athlete from "patriotic enthusiasm" to "a chase after the almighty dollar" and constituted nothing less than "the rebuilding of hockey as Canada's national winter pastime." The league's next play was to push south to Toronto, where the amateur mode still held sway.[68]

Toronto was Montreal's rival in size, in economic power, and also in its fanaticism for the winter game, and plans to bring professional hockey to the Queen City had been part of the ambition of the IHL and ECHA and had continued in the boardroom of the NHA. The successful export of professional hockey there could not be taken for granted, however. The experience of the Ontario Professional Hockey League (OPHL), which had struggled to operate in Toronto and southwestern Ontario from 1908 to 1911, showed that OHA amateur hockey was well established and would be hard to displace. There were many good teams with many local adherents and a strong critical tradition that saw professional hockey as having all the moral failings that could be associated with money and commerce, including dirty play, on-ice violence, a win-at-all-costs attitude, and match fixing. Led by the *Toronto Evening Telegram*, under its publisher and amateur hockey stalwart, John Ross Robertson, the Toronto press was eager to highlight these aspects and furthermore unwilling to acknowledge that the OPHL quality of play was superior to the OHA senior series. However, the immediate limitation to success in Toronto was infrastructure.[69]

The Mutual Street rink on which the OPHL Toronto Professionals played was physically small—at 168 feet by 78 feet, it was about 40 feet shorter and 12 feet narrower than the Montreal Arena—which meant the speed of the professionals could not be shown to any great advantage, and so it featured instead body contact and rough play. More important, the rink had capacity for only two thousand spectators, and the perception was that the extra costs of professional hockey could not be recouped even with capacity crowds, even when the rink owned the team. Alex Milne ran both the Toronto Professionals and the Mutual Street rink, but decided to withdraw the team for the 1910 season. He deemed it more profitable to accommodate eight amateur clubs, because "it pays us just as much to get a $100 amateur gate as it would to get a $500 pro gate. From the amateurs we get 65 per cent of the receipts, while we run the professionals ourselves, and the expenses are high." He also worried that a professional team had a heavy schedule that would eat into amateur ice time and would foster too much attention and seriously hurt interest in the amateur teams. A new rink was clearly needed, and there appeared to be no shortage of Toronto entrepreneurial energy eager to get involved in the ECHA or NHA franchise. In 1910 a group proposed building a tent over an outdoor rink that could seat four thousand, but the real solution was to create more ice and build a modern arena to surround it.[70]

Given the milder climate, a Toronto NHA franchise also had to be conditional on an arena with artificial ice, so that a season of sufficient length could be guaranteed, with sufficient seating capacity so that professional hockey could be profitable, and with sufficient rink size so that the speed of the professional game would not be hampered. Montreal capital stepped into the financial breach. In 1912 the Arena Gardens of Toronto opened on Mutual Street. It became known locally as the Mutual Street Arena after its location and its predecessor. Its modern steel construction, unobstructed views, and seventy-five hundred seats for hockey made it superior to both the old Mutual Street rink and even Montreal's Westmount Arena, and it was hoped it would open up the Queen City's full market potential for commercial hockey exploitation. The rink also showed that hockey was not the only business model being exported from Montreal. The Gardens was built by investors in the Montreal Arena along with local Toronto capitalists such as Sir Henry Pellatt and Lawrence (Lol) Solman. The Arena Gardens owners expected plenty of demand for ice from the local Toronto amateur clubs, but the main draw (and the Arena Gardens' commercial priority) would be the two new Toronto NHA franchises, Toronto HC (soon christened the Blueshirts) and the Tecumsehs. Unfortunately, construction delays meant the clubs would not take to the Gardens' ice until the 1912–13 season, but over the long term having two clubs was expected to justify the long road trips from Ottawa, Montreal, and Quebec City. After the demise of the OPHL, the NHA's two clubs would now be the only professional game in town. The challenge would now be to sell the professional NHA brand in the bastion of the amateur OHA.[71]

Duopoly

Artificial ice technology facilitated NHA expansion into southern Ontario, but it also made it feasible in even milder climates such as Canada's West Coast. In 1911 Frank and Lester Patrick, the former Renfrew hockey stars, announced the formation of the Pacific Coast Hockey Association (PCHA). Financed by their father and inspired by American artificial ice rinks like the St. Nicholas in New York City, the two brothers built rinks in Vancouver and Victoria and adopted a constitution that resembled the

NHA's. At first the Patricks de-emphasized their own role in the league executive (the first PCHA president was a former OHA executive, and Lester and Frank were listed only as directors), which suggested the initial goal was to bring in other owners and establish a cartel league, but the PCHA continued on as a league in which all clubs were owned by the league itself. This "syndicate" hockey model had significant advantages, especially for a new enterprise looking to control costs. It allowed the Patricks to acquire players for the whole league and assign them as needed to their three clubs (New Westminster, Vancouver, and Victoria), and, more important, common ownership also eliminated the fractiousness endemic to a cartel league like the NHA. (The downside was a constant insinuation that the outcome of league games was predetermined to maximize profits.) Being outsiders also meant the Patricks could ignore the NHA reservation clause and raid its clubs for players. Acquiring ready-made stars brought the ire of NHA club owners, who lost seventeen players, but the resulting high caliber of play brought the PCHA immediate high quality and legitimacy. William Foran, now a Stanley Cup trustee (replacing Sheriff Sweetland), accepted a PCHA challenge for the Stanley Cup after only the PCHA's inaugural season.[72]

The existence of an alternate employer for hockey talent rendered the NHA salary limit ineffective and forced clubs to outbid others to retain players. In the second PCHA season, 1912–13, the Canadiens' salary bill topped $8,000 and Ottawa's $10,000, leading to serious losses ($3,870.66 in Ottawa). That year the western league acquired the NHA's biggest star, Cyclone Taylor, after the NHA clubs fought over his services among themselves. Taylor's case showed how the semiprofessionalism of players complicated player control. He had been claimed by the Wanderers after Renfrew was dropped from the NHA in 1911, but he was unwilling to leave his job with the civil service in Ottawa to play in Montreal. Ottawa, his former club, held out for the right to use him for the 1911–12 season, as Lichtenhein threatened the Ottawa and other NHA owners. Taylor eventually solved the problem himself by getting himself transferred to the Immigration Branch office in Vancouver and playing for the PCHA in 1912–13.[73]

Other similar battles were waged over players, and Sam Lichtenhein's various maneuverings to control players were singled out and derided as "baseball diplomacy" in P. D. Ross's *Ottawa Journal*. An editorial criticized the Wanderers owner: he brings "baseball methods into hockey and reasons that a hockey player is as much the property of a club as the baseball player is of the club to which he belongs, forgetting that one man is doing nothing else but playing baseball, while the hockey player has other interests and only plays hockey for a couple of months." Echoing the comments of Art Ross in his letter during the aborted player revolt two years before, the *Journal* editor repurposed them to defend the community identity of players and their clubs. He reminded Lichtenhein that hockey players were paid less than ballplayers and needed to retain their other employment and also their community affiliations. The NHA owners would be wise to recognize that "there is some sentiment left in hockey, even if these magnates care to admit it or not," and that "we don't want to have the game reduced to the baseball standard, where not a single member of a team hails from the town for which he is playing."[74]

Professional hockey leagues were indeed well on their way to following baseball precedent, not only by dissociating player from locality, but also by agreeing to divide the national market among themselves. The two-season war between the associations was benefiting only the players and hurting the bottom lines of clubs in both leagues. Before the 1913 season, the rivals called a truce and entered into a four-year agreement that regulated the interleague competition for players by stipulating Canadian territorial rights (east of Port Arthur, Ontario [Thunder Bay], for the NHA, and west for the PCHA), recognizing each other's reservation clauses, and conducting an interleague draft. Any disputes between the leagues were to be resolved by what later came to be called the National Commission, another institution borrowed from baseball (though fated to be short-lived). Finally, the NHA and PCHA agreed to a championship series to alternate between West and East and assumed the Stanley Cup trustees would agree to this arrangement. After initial quibbles, the trustees placed the cup in the hands of the National Commission and from then on intended cup play to be restricted to champions of the NHA and

PCHA (and their successors and affiliates), with challenges from outside these leagues rarely accepted. When the PCHA admitted American clubs, the trustees were understood to have redesignated the trophy as symbolic of the "world championship," and not simply the Canadian.[75]

This agreement of national scope formed the basis for a two-league combine—a duopoly—that again restricted the freedom of the players. Following the baseball precedent, the NHA inserted a new version of the reservation clause directly into individual player contracts, calling it an "option clause," which gave the club the exclusive option to sign a player after the expiration of his contract. While the reservation clause had prevented other clubs within the league from signing away players from each other, the option clause was clearly intended to bind the player directly so that he could not leave the league entirely to play in another (that is, the PCHA). The new agreement had also made the NHA salary cap effective, but the imposition of a low six hundred dollars per man annual salary maximum once again drew player ire. Art Ross led the way, signing up Wanderers and Canadiens players to a new league that he said would pay them eight hundred dollars each. It did not pan out, but the NHA did agree to raise the limit to eight hundred dollars. The players suffered no repercussions, since decimating the clubs by suspending Ross and the other stars he had signed up would have had unfortunate consequences on the ice for the Montreal clubs.[76]

The interleague agreement did not prevent disputes from erupting in 1914–15 over the draft provision. The PCHA was allowed to pick one player from each of Ottawa, the Wanderers, and Quebec (for five hundred dollars each), but the NHA clubs refused to release two of the players. The Patricks held their ground, even after the National Commission arbitrator ruled in the NHA's favor in one case. Perceiving duplicity on the part of NHA president Emmett Quinn, the Patricks allowed themselves to be mollified by the offer of extra draft opportunities until after that spring's Stanley Cup series. But when there was no agreement forthcoming by the fall, the Patricks became exasperated and found an excuse to just steal five players from the Toronto Blueshirts. The NHA responded by treating all the PCHA players as free agents and raided the PCHA throughout the 1915–16 season. Frank Patrick allowed Portland, the PCHA champion, to play the Canadiens for the Stanley Cup, but said there would be no peace between the leagues as long as Emmett Quinn was NHA president.[77]

Resentment against Quinn had been building for some time within the league as well, arising again from his handling of the PCHA relationship. Lichtenhein even attempted to have himself installed as president at the 1915 annual meeting, and though Quinn was reconfirmed in office, he soon lost the confidence of George Kennedy as well. He resigned and was replaced by former Toronto Blueshirts owner Frank Robinson, but many of the presidential duties were given to the secretary-treasurer, Frank Calder, who had run the day-to-day operations of the association since 1914.[78]

Calder was the sports editor of the *Montreal Daily Mail*, but it was not unusual that he also took on an active managerial role in a sport he would have also reported on. Many journalists in the era—Elmer Ferguson, Michael J. (Mike) Rodden, T. P. (Tommy) Gorman, Charlie Querrie, and Lou Marsh, to name a few—supplemented their meager pay by serving as club and league public relations men, promoters, managers, and officials. Ironically, Calder had earned the job by showing a muckraker's independence in railing against perceived abuses in horse racing, wrestling, and hockey. As he recalled later, this reporting got the attention of the NHA owners: "When I became interested in [hockey] I was writing sport in a daily newspaper. Professional hockey was then in its infancy, just developing, the amateurs were being paid, they were in fact professionals. In my capacity as newspaper writer I raised considerable hell about these things that came to my attention. . . . Then having done that, there were certain other troubles developed which I kept pounding at continually and finally around 1914 they said 'You know so much about this god damn thing and how it should be done, you come and do it.[']" Calder was likely quoting Canadiens director George Kennedy, who supported his hiring despite the fact that he was also one of Calder's favorite targets. It was a brave choice, and a good one in the long run for the league. Events would show Calder to be an able administrator who combined a knack for mediating conflict with a keen survival instinct.[79]

There was conflict in spades. Besides the internal rifts in the league and outside trouble with the PCHA, the war in Europe had grown from a distraction in 1914 to an increasingly burdensome weight on Canadian society and economy. By the fall of 1915, demand for recruits was adversely affecting rosters and attendance was falling, leading to serious discussion about suspending play for the season. The clubs decided to continue and to cut player salaries instead.[80]

The league also had problems in individual markets. In Quebec the Bulldogs were failing to appeal to the French Canadian middle class in the city and had little success enticing local amateur players to make the jump to professional play or convincing the local press that the professional game was not corrupt and the games fixed. Ottawa ownership was reportedly looking to get out of hockey entirely, and Sam Lichtenhein complained continuously about losing money on the Wanderers.[81]

The greatest source of trouble was Toronto, where the clubs were constantly in flux and having a hard time distinguishing the NHL brand from high-quality amateur hockey. The various owners of the Toronto clubs had industrial, sport, and entertainment experience in professional lacrosse, baseball, and venue management, but they still struggled at the gate, changing names and owners with regularity as they tried to give Toronto spectators what they most seemed to want: a consistent and winning hockey team over the regular season. The amateurs played only short tournaments, where losing was not as evident, but at twenty-two games the NHA clubs' season was much longer than the amateur and a losing record could be fatal. In 1912–13 the Tecumsehs went bankrupt after a season of seven wins and thirteen losses and were sold to a Montrealer, Tom Wall, who renamed them the Ontarios. The next season saw the rival Blueshirts win the NHL championship and the Stanley Cup (Toronto's first), but the Ontarios lost even more games (sixteen) and were sold again.[82]

It was a bit of a coup when the NHA owners convinced a successful local amateur hockey organizer, Edward James (Eddie) Livingstone, to take over the Ontarios franchise in December 1914. Livingstone was the son of a prosperous Toronto printer and a partner in Fletcher & Livingstone, a bond and financial brokerage firm. Like many sports-minded young men of his era and class, he was involved in many sports, as player, official, and executive. At various times he played amateur hockey, refereed in the OHA, served on the Ontario Rugby Football Union executive committee, and served as assistant sports editor of the *Toronto Mail and*

Empire. What interested the NHA men was that he was a winner: as the manager of the amateur Toronto Rugby & Athletic Association hockey club, he had owned the OHA senior championship for the past two years (1913 and 1914). The NHA clubs hoped his knowledge of the Toronto amateur scene, as well as his competitiveness and persistence on the ice, would translate into success for the professional game. While "Livvy" was indeed full of ideas and had energy to burn, when his combativeness and guile carried over into the boardroom he became a lightning rod for conflict that would have lasting consequences for the association.[83]

Hockey at Work

By 1916 it had been forty-one years since the *Gazette* had reported on "a game of Hockey" at Victoria Skating Rink, and few would have predicted that in that time it would have become the most popular winter sport in Canada. Hockey had plural varieties in the Canadian, British, and American hinterlands, but the version that came to dominate the others was the one refashioned in the metropolis of Montreal, adapted to indoor play, modified with technology, organized with rules, supported with commerce, fused with middle-class aspirations, and then reexported with enthusiasm. While this Montreal game gained complexity and structure as it spread, it provided a variant that fitted an urban niche provided by skating rinks and also a social niche provided by the middle classes, which were growing and recreating in this period.[84]

In retrospect, the 1875 game marked not the birth of a new sport but the arrival of that sport in an urban environment in which it would begin to quickly evolve from a traditional game of play into a serious social event and then a profit-making commercial activity. In the decades that followed, assertions of control over the sport's meaning and purpose in North American society engendered a process of divergent and congruent development. Yet even as the sport became segmented along geographic and social lines and produced a variety of game forms in the few short decades after 1875, it was the Montreal game that persisted, developed, and grew into the model (and countermodel) for all others.

Hockey as an institutionalized sport had a distinct set of fathers in the nineteenth-century amateur and voluntary organizations of Montreal.

Anglophone bourgeois Montrealers became masters at making sport and games do cultural work. They initially used the new game for camaraderie and entertainment, but also as part of their project to demarcate social and ethnic boundaries and elaborate a national identity in modern industrial society. Paradoxically, their organizational impulse actually facilitated adaptation to commercial activities and helped the sport spread socially and geographically, thus making the amateur organizational form the basis for the commercial one. There are parallels in nonsporting organizations. Mary-Anne Clawson notes how nineteenth-century fraternal organizations, which attracted small businessmen looking for social support, soon became "entrepreneurial organizations that operated so as to maximize membership growth and financial profit or stability." There was also an irony, because sports clubs were at least partly seen as a physical tonic to the negative effects of "overcivilization," an antimodern response to the feminization and mechanization of society. Yet it was the same men who applied the tools of industrial commerce to its exploitation and modernized it. Jackson Lears referred to this process as "the ambivalence of antimodernism," where antimodern protest furthered, as much as it checked, what it protested.[85]

Translating the sport over social, cultural, and geographic borders required simplification, rationalization, and standardization. The tools of commerce—money, entrepreneurship, and organization—made it possible. Organizing to meet these demands produced pressure on the institutions of hockey to reduce transaction costs and transform the game from not-for-profit *play* to profit-making *product*. In doing so, they refashioned traditional roles into modern industrial ones: player-members became remunerated contractors, club executive members became entrepreneurial promoters, and spectators became customers. Individual entrepreneurial drive also led to hockey's transformation by commercial institutions aimed at satisfying new consumer demands for entertainment and leisure products. Changing social and commercial conditions were the context for this commercialization process, which engendered cultural conflict that had to be reconciled, particularly on the question of professionalism. In relatively quick fashion, then, Montrealers had hockey performing commercial work as well, and this mode found purchase well outside the city among other classes of players and other audiences with similar needs and desires. Although it would be decades before it was referred to as such, we can say that the Montreal game had been so integrated into the social, cultural, technological, and economic fabric of the modern industrial economy that in a sense, it too had become "industrialized" and distinct from less commercial varieties.[86]

Just as the North American economy was growing in scope and variety, so its sporting activities proliferated, ranging from purely recreational informal games emphasizing participation to highly organized competitive events where winning was the goal. Because of its success, the Montreal game became the preferred and dominant pattern for the commercial-industrial mode of hockey represented by the NHA and its professional kin, the IHL and PCHA, but there continued to be other hockeys that responded to different social, urban, ethnic, and economic meanings. Even in Montreal at the turn of the century, the elite hockey at the Victoria Rink was not the only game in town, and gentlemen still got together to play shinny outdoors at the MAAA grounds. The main alternative was the elite amateur model represented by leagues like the OHA, which continued to nurture the noncommercial player and the implications thereof, the most evident of which was the segregation of the game along the lines of skill (professional versus amateur) and age levels (amateur hockey for the young and paid hockey for adults). The formation of the Canadian Amateur Hockey Association in 1914, which was composed of provincial and regional hockey associations such as the OHA, solidified what would become Canadian hockey's modern hierarchical form. That a man like William Northey, a scion of the MAAA but also the lord of the Montreal Arena, was prominent in the CAHA's foundation speaks to the continuities between the two. These were lessons for the push into the United States, where the scope of the Montreal game's dominance was still to be determined, and also to the rest of the world, where hockey was also beginning to take a firm hold.[87]

Commercialization also made the Montreal game a highly mobile one. The technology of artificial ice, the medium of newspaper coverage, the remuneration of players, and the availability of capital made it possible to quickly enter markets far from hockey's "natural" winter homes in the St. Lawrence and Ottawa Valleys. From Vancouver and Portland on the West Coast to Toronto and New York in the East, hockey was no longer restricted by climate, only by capital and consumer markets. This expansion had important implications for the future by removing limitations on future growth but also loosening commitments to existing urban markets and communities. Within the constraints of schedule and distance, it could be expected that clubs and leagues would move to those markets with the size to generate the largest revenues, if not willingly, then forced by competition from rivals. Elite commercial hockey had failed to persist in the hinterlands of Michigan and northern Ontario, as well as in Manitoba and the Maritimes, and the success of the PCHA clubs and some NHA clubs was far from ensured. As the successful clubs became concentrated in bigger cities and arenas, they also attracted a different sort of entrepreneur, the sports promoter, who was often of a much different class and ethnicity. (By 1916 the Montreal clubs were run by a French-speaking Irish Catholic, George Kennedy, and a German Jew, Sam Lichtenhein.) Such men saw sport clearly as a business, albeit not *only* as one, and they displaced the community patrons who had run the club on a nonprofit basis. Indeed, the clubs whose primary affiliation had been with their communities were now becoming "franchises," entities that did not exist without affiliation with a league. And the league's interests were not synonymous with the interests of the individual club, let alone of the community, even though ethnicity and community were central identities of the club brands.[88]

Using the model of baseball's major leagues, the Montreal-centered elite hockey leagues themselves had helped stratify the hockey institution and restrict access to the professional game by outsiders. Not all of the baseball borrowings worked unambiguously well for hockey—the multigame road trip was abandoned in 1913, then later resurrected—but the structure appeared sound. It would be further tested by both internal dissension and outside challenge, and in the longer term it remained to be seen whether the incorporated league (NHA), the syndicate league (PCHA), or some other model would prevail. One element seemed common to all: a symbiotic relationship with the major urban ice palaces, which needed regular events hosting thousands of spectators to thrive and could be counted on to help fend off competitors. The close relationships between league, clubs, and rinks seemed destined to become tighter.[89]

Aside from the constant challenge to compromise with each other, the final major hurdle for the elite clubs to overcome was the implication of commercializing players. It required limiting league access to clubs in those larger markets with greater arena capacities to provide the needed revenues for paid rosters and adhering to business principles that stabilized the system, especially rules for player movement, including waivers (which kept players from being sold outside the league) and the option clause (which bound a player to a single club). The success of the hockey league model of the St. Lawrence clubs was reflected on the ice, where the professionals captured permanently the Stanley Cup, the national symbol of hockey supremacy. It also seemed to have distinct advantages for geographic expansion, and the test would be success in the Toronto market, where competition from OHA senior clubs and their unpaid amateurs needed to be overcome.[90]

2

A Reorganization

1917–1923

The first entry in the National Hockey League Minute Book that sits in the Hockey Hall of Fame records the first meeting as Thursday, 22 November 1917. Held at the Windsor Hotel, with representatives of four clubs from the NHA and Frank Calder, in the minutes Calder explained that the meeting had been called "at the suggestion of the Quebec Hockey Club to ascertain if some steps could be taken to perpetuate the game of Hockey." After a discussion, Tommy Gorman of Ottawa moved that "the Canadien, Wanderer, Ottawa and Quebec clubs unite to compose the National Hockey League." This motion carried, and the representatives further agreed to use the NHA "rules and conditions governing the game of hockey." The league thus reconstituted, the meeting admitted William Northey, the manager of the Montreal Arena Company, who was appearing on behalf of the Toronto Arena Company, the operator of the Arena Gardens. Northey announced that should a four-club league be formed, he was empowered to enter a team on behalf of Toronto interests. Fortuitously, Mike Quinn of Quebec was willing to withdraw his club from the league, subject to suitable arrangements being made to dispose of its players. This move was achieved when the other clubs agreed to buy them for seven hundred dollars and divide them among Ottawa, the Wanderers, the Canadiens, and Toronto. The meeting then elected the new NHL directors, including a Toronto representative to be named later. Quinn was elected honorary president and Calder as both president and secretary, at a salary of eight hundred dollars, "on the understanding that there could be no appeal from his decisions." Thus was the NHL born.[1]

It sounded both congenial and quick—Calder later casually called the creation of the NHL "a reorganisation"—but these simple minutes appear to gloss over conflicts and compile decisions that had already been taken over a period of days, and perhaps weeks, before and after 22 November. News reports in the *Montreal Daily Star* certainly offer a different version that suggests this meeting was simply preliminary and the decisions tentative, serving mainly to set in motion the rumor that a new league had been formed (under a name the *Star* had already predicted before the meeting took place). Since the dissolution of the NHA ten days before, the professional hockey clubs no doubt wanted to keep hockey customers aware that a new league was in the offing, but before it gained form the clubs would have to resolve the Quebec and Toronto question marks. The decision was expected by Monday.[2]

It seems unlikely the *Star* had it so wrong, and it is most probable that the negotiations with Quinn continued and were finalized over the weekend, and it was on Monday, 26 November 1917, that the new league was officially announced, to include Ottawa, the Canadiens, the Wanderers, and Toronto. Unlike the NHA, the NHL would have only one administrator, Calder, who would now combine the roles of president, secretary, and treasurer and exert a greater influence than his predecessors. As expected, within a week, the Toronto Arena Gardens syndicate was understood to have struck a bargain, "without any fighting," with Eddie Livingstone for his controlling interest in the Blueshirts. The Arena Gardens proceeded to organize a team under the direction of Hubert Vearncombe, the company's auditor. But the fight was far from over. The Montreal press reports failed to mention that Livingstone had filed suit against his fellow owners, alleging a conspiracy to deprive him of his franchise.[3]

While it did seem unfair, everyone would have recognized that the shutting out of Livingstone was consistent with the evolution of organized commercial hockey to that point. Almost all of the NHL's predecessors were born out of club conflicts over the adaptation of hockey's rules, organization, and expansion, and sacrificing one club for the benefit of the rest was the most common reason of all. This time a war would be fought in southern Ontario, first in Toronto and then in Hamilton, and against a background of the First World War in Europe, which put pressure on player availability. In its battles the NHL would further refine its form, adjust its administrative rules to reduce conflict, change its playing rules to appeal to new audiences, and continue expanding south into new markets.

The Reformation

The NHA owners were happy to be rid of Livingstone, but did not intend to abandon Toronto, despite the generally disappointing lack of financial success of its clubs. After a half decade, whether named the Torontos, Tecumsehs, Ontarios, Blueshirts, or Shamrocks, NHA clubs had struggled to fully establish professional hockey in the Queen City, where the amateur principles, rules, and local loyalties of Ontario Hockey Association clubs held sway over athletes, organizers, and spectators. Once his club was admitted to the league, Eddie Livingstone had brought a new vision—that the future of the Toronto market depended on reduction to one NHA club representative—but despite his track record of success at amateur level, the owners had been loath to buy into the idea.

The problems began two years earlier, before the 1915–16 season, when Livingstone, the Shamrocks' (formerly Ontarios) owner, took matters into his own hands and bought the other Toronto club, the Blueshirts, from Frank Robinson. Livingstone was reluctant to sell his Shamrocks, wanting instead to force the league to contract to only one Toronto club, so he delayed selling the franchise and instead emptied the Shamrocks by moving players to the Blueshirts. It was a risky play for an owner who had been in the league for only a year, more so since he failed to ingratiate himself with the other owners. The Ottawa club seemed ready to give up entirely on Toronto, with T. P. Gorman reasoning that "it is a hotbed of O.H.A. enthusiasm and newspapers there have never given the professional promoters a fair show." After tussles back and forth over leases at Arena Gardens, the other owners seemed to accept the fait accompli and took back the Shamrocks franchise. The season began with only one Toronto club, making the NHA a five-club league.[4]

As Livingstone had hoped, the reduction to one Toronto club focused spectator attention on a single team, but the eastern clubs complained about traveling expenses for single games in Toronto. Eliminating a club also relieved some of the pressure of players enlisting in the military, but

since many enlisted men were still playing hockey as part of their training in Toronto, an innovative solution was proposed—to allow the 228th
Battalion (Northern Fusiliers) team to join the league. With the entry of
the 228th, the league could maintain two clubs in Toronto and keep its
enlisted players in the league through transfers to the battalion club. The
only risk was that the unit would be sent overseas before the end of the
two-month season. To hedge against this possibility, like the other NHA
clubs the 228th posted a $3,000 bond with Ocean Accident and Guaran-
tee Corporation to ensure its appearance at all games. This bond was to
indemnify the other clubs for the loss of gate revenues should it leave. And
so for the 1916–17 season, the NHA loaned the Shamrocks franchise to the
228th, but it turned out the idea was much too clever by half and it wound
up setting the stage for the association's dissolution.[5]

As usual, player disputes were at the root. Livingstone wanted to retain
Duke Keats, a Blueshirts player who had joined the 228th, but the battalion club threatened to pull out of the NHA if he did. And Kennedy and
Lichtenhein threatened to throw out Livingstone if the 228th left. Ottawa
also disputed Livingstone's rights to Cy Denneny, a star whom Ottawa
wanted to help address their own wartime attendance woes. Confronta-
tions escalated, from offers of buyouts to threatened expulsions to physical
assaults. Matters finally came to a head in February 1917 owing to the bad
press the 228th was getting for playing professional hockey and not paying
bills to Toronto merchants. On 8 February military authorities in Ottawa
ordered the battalion to Halifax, from where it would sail to join the Canadian Expeditionary Force in France.[6]

With only Livingstone's Blueshirts left in Toronto, the other clubs now
faced an expensive trip to Toronto to play against an owner they had come
to dislike intensely. They met at the Windsor Hotel the next day to consider the 228th withdrawal. Livingstone did not attend (he was hindered
by a painful boil on his neck) and had arranged for NHA president Frank
Robinson to represent his club and present his idea for a five-club schedule
to finish the season. This request was summarily rejected, and Robinson
could not prevent the other owners from going a step further. Secretary
Frank Calder was instructed to write to Livingstone, informing him that
his club was being left out of the schedule entirely. Furthermore, the owners

wanted Livingstone not only to agree to suspend for the season but also to sell his franchise before 1 June. In the meantime, the other clubs intended to avail themselves of his players, who would be returned to the franchise at the end of the season, presumably to help Livingstone sell it. To add to Livingstone's troubles, the Arena Gardens, his club's home ice, refused to turn over the proceeds of the last game ($700) and then charged him $480 for defaulted games and practice times for the rest of the season.[7]

Perhaps made hesitant by Livingstone's threat of legal action, or wanting to temper press criticism, the other NHA clubs backed off a little in the next few weeks, getting Robinson to write to Livingstone, reinstating him as a member in good standing of the NHA. Livingstone went ahead anyway with a suit against the association and his fellow owners, claiming damages resulting from cutting him out of the schedule and dispersing his players. According to his claim, the 11 February resolution was "invalid, illegal and unconstitutional," and he wanted it rescinded, his club readmitted, damages paid, and the other clubs restrained from forming a club without including him. He also demanded their bonds with Ocean Accident and Guarantee Corporation be forfeited to him! In their statement of defense, the NHA owners showed they had received some sage legal advice by rescinding the decision to force Livingstone to sell the Toronto franchise, but otherwise they denied any liability.[8]

The principals simmered over the summer, and it became clear in the fall that while travel expense to Toronto was a legitimate issue, Livingstone was the main problem. The other NHA owners were also prepared to sacrifice the goodwill of the association to get Livingstone out. In October, with the season fast approaching, they asked Livingstone to agree to suspend operations for the upcoming season, setting 26 October 1917 as the deadline for responding. By 23 October the *Montreal Daily Star* was predicting the dissolution of the NHA, and the report suggested personality conflicts were being used to mask the cost issue and to allow the league to contract. Before the deadline, the NHA got its answer: Livingstone would retain his franchise and his players and "fight to a finish if necessary."[9]

In the meantime, Lol Solman, the manager of the Arena Gardens, insisted on Toronto being part of the league, and his Montreal investors brought pressure to bear on the NHA club directors while he strong-armed

Livingstone. Soon it was announced that Livingstone would relinquish control for the coming season in favor of the arena's management. He would transfer his league shares to the Arena Gardens to be held in trust, along with the player contracts, and there would be a mutual division of profits after the 1917–18 season. The arena undertook not to trade, sell, or release players without Livingstone's consent and promised to return all player contracts to him after the season was over.[10]

It was wise for the NHA to help the arena ensure itself an NHA tenant, but the owners were still not sure a five-club league was desirable. Five clubs meant one club was idle every game night, which reduced gate receipts. If having four clubs was the next best option and Toronto was not on the scaffold, either Quebec or the Wanderers was the other likely candidate to take its place. The possibility of a Canadiens-Wanderers merger was voiced, but all eyes seemed to converge on Quebec as the club that needed to fall on its sword should the new Toronto owner be found acceptable.[11]

That outcome was not assured. The long-delayed league meeting finally took place on 10 November, but notwithstanding Livingstone's willingness to let the Arena Gardens run the club, the *Montreal Daily Star* reported that "no one was apparently satisfied that there had been a change in the Toronto control." The other owners wanted Livingstone out, completely. And if he would not leave, then everyone else would. Lichtenhein moved, seconded by Kennedy, "that owing to the 228th Battalion Hockey Club having dropped out and this association remaining with an odd number of clubs, this association finds it impossible to operate with 5 clubs and as no club desires to withdraw, it be resolved that this association suspend the playing of the usual schedule of games for the season 1917–1918." The *Montreal Daily Star* reported that, after the meeting, the club directors acted "as if they had attended a funeral, and the customary gaiety was gone. Anyone unfamiliar with the doings of sport promoters would have surely come to the conclusion that it was all up with Pro Hockey for next winter." To people in the know, however, the sad faces were masks. Elmer Ferguson of the *Montreal Herald* called it for what it was: "an excellent exhibition of camouflage." The *Star* concurred, predicting that another meeting would soon be held to draw up a schedule, maybe under a new name, to operate for the duration of the war, a new association that "it would not at all be surprising might have Frank Calder, the present Secretary of the National Hockey Association as its President."[12]

Within two weeks, the predictions came true with the formation of the National Hockey League. As in 1898, 1905, and 1909, a new league had been reconstituted from the bones of a predecessor to recombine the elite clubs of central Canadian professional hockey and exclude others. The question was how long the latest version would last.

Conflagrations

The civil war seemingly resolved, almost immediately the Great War made itself felt. The institution of conscription in Canada and the United States in 1917 delayed the opening of the PCHA season, and did the same to the new NHL on account of the need to coordinate schedules for Stanley Cup play. The ensuing player shortage hurt the Wanderers hardest. Having just lost star Sprague Cleghorn to a broken leg, Lichtenhein decided the dispersal of Quebec's players to the other clubs was unsatisfactory, and just before the season opened he demanded *all* of Quebec's players for himself. Calder and the other owners offered alternatives, but the issue was still smoldering when, on 2 January, a literal conflagration engulfed the Westmount Arena, home of both the Wanderers and the Canadiens, and burned it to the ground. Attributed to faulty wiring, the fire started in a dressing room and caused the boilers and ammonia tanks to explode. The Wanderers lost $950 worth of equipment and the Canadiens $1,000 worth. The Canadiens shifted their subsequent games to the small east-end Jubilee Rink on St. Catherine St. East, but Lichtenhein's Wanderers refused to move unless they got player help as well. Their manager, Art Ross, was as pessimistic as his boss. Not only was their fan base in Westmount and the western (English) end of the city, but the club was already in dire straits: "We are badly in need of players and unless we receive help from the other clubs we cannot make a race in the showing for the title." Citing the lack of playing material, Lichtenhein wrote to the league, asking to withdraw his club from competition.[13]

At an emergency meeting on 3 January, the NHL directors discussed the Wanderers' situation. Lichtenhein's request was tabled for further consideration, perhaps in the hope he would reconsider, but delay was just prolonging the inevitable, so Calder pulled out a three-club schedule that was quickly adopted in case it was needed. Two days later, the Wanderers defaulted on their game in Toronto, and it was. In a rather harsh move, the Wanderers' franchise was terminated outright and the club fined $500. To help keep the remaining three clubs afloat, the league implemented a revenue-sharing measure that divided all the playoff gate receipts among each club equally after expenses.[14]

The clubs limped to the end of the season but benefited from Toronto's surprising playoff run, which culminated in the Stanley Cup victory against the Vancouver Millionaires and made the club quite profitable. At the end of the season, the Gardens paid Livingstone his share of the profits, $13,000, but refused to return the player contracts. True to form, in July Livingstone filed suit for breach of contract, seeking the contracts and monetary damages of $20,400.54 plus interest, the true amount he felt was due under the 9 November 1917 agreement. The Arena Gardens' defense was rather disingenuous. It argued that the agreement had never been executed since the NHA had ceased operating soon afterward and that Livingstone had never actually transferred his NHA stock or the player contracts. Boldly, the Gardens accused Livingstone of "fraudulently and wilfully suppressing" the information that the NHA had been suspended! Without the NHA shares and player contracts, the Arena Gardens had thus been "compelled" to form its own team, the Arena Gardens Hockey Club of Toronto, and operate it in the new NHL.[15]

With his lawsuits moving through the courts, Livingstone took the initiative and followed hockey tradition by creating his own new league, the Canadian Hockey Association. His partner was Percy Quinn, who had a long hockey pedigree as a Montreal Shamrocks player, manager of a NHA Toronto team, and brother of Emmett Quinn, the former NHA president. In June Percy bought the dormant Quebec NHA franchise from Mike Quinn (no relation) for $4,000 and renamed it the Shamrocks. It was not clear what Percy Quinn thought he had purchased—an NHA or an NHL franchise—and Quinn did not announce whether he planned to play it in the CHA. The questions were raised by NHL owners even as Quinn and Livingstone set about acquiring rink space for the upcoming season, trying to tie up the major ice sheets in Toronto (Arena Gardens), Ottawa

(Dey's Arena), and Montreal (Jubilee Rink). Livingstone and Quinn reasoned that if NHL clubs were shut out of their home ice, they would have to come to the table and make a deal.[16]

In September the board of directors of the moribund NHA reconvened to keep the corporation in good standing for the duration of a lawsuit against Ocean Accident and Guarantee Corporation, which had refused to pay out the 228th Battalion's $3,000 forfeiture bond. Livingstone used the occasion to attempt to oust Calder as acting president of the NHA, but failed because the NHL-affiliated clubs dominated the meeting. Still unsure of Quinn's motives, the NHA/NHL owners declared Quinn's Quebec franchise to be good only for the NHA, not the NHL, but they left the door open to an NHL application. Then they voted to formally suspend the NHA. Given its continued corporate existence, however, it was easier said than done.[17]

Meanwhile, the NHL firmed itself up for the upcoming season by confirming its club participants. At the October annual meeting, the Toronto Arena Hockey Club turned in its temporary franchise from 1917–18 and was granted a permanent one. With this transaction, any legal connection to Livingstone was severed, and with the Arena Gardens in the NHL camp so was Livingstone's chance of getting access to the Arena Gardens. Turning to the Quinn-to-Quinn franchise transfer, the directors may have been unsure about Quinn's motives, but either out of the need for a fourth club or else in an attempt to subvert the CHA, they sanctioned it conditional on the franchise operating in Quebec for the 1918–19 season. For good measure, Percy Quinn was elected a director, along with George Kennedy, Charlie Querrie, and Martin Rosenthal for Ottawa. Despite the provisional acceptance of Quinn, in the absence of his commitment to put Quebec on the ice, the papers reported that the NHL would operate as a three-team league once again.[18]

The CHA was also counting on Quinn's club in Quebec, along with a club in Montreal and two in Ottawa, one run by E. P. (Ted) Dey, the owner of the Ottawa rink, and the other by Montreal interests. As for Toronto, while the club was shut out of the arena there, the *Toronto Daily Star*'s anonymous source (likely Livingstone) assured that the CHA had players "tied up to a contract that will bind them."[19]

The inclusion of Ted Dey in the CHA's plans was surprising. When Ottawa had cast the deciding vote to end the NHA in September, Dey and Tommy Gorman had represented the club at the meeting, having taken over the club for the season. The longtime guiding interests behind Ottawa elite hockey, Martin Rosenthal and Llewellyn Bate, had been feeling hard-pressed by economic conditions in the fall of 1917 and had wanted to suspend operations. Faced with the loss of his major tenant, Dey formed the Ottawa Hockey Club to run the Senators under the umbrella of the Ottawa Hockey Association. After the 1917–18 season, he looked for more control over the club, and the NHA/NHL/CHA confusion gave him the opportunity. The September NHA meeting put him in contact with Livingstone and Percy Quinn, and over the next few weeks he met with them and sold Quinn an option to lease his Laurier Avenue rink. (Tellingly, he did not cash the twenty-five-dollar check Quinn gave him for the option, rendering the enforcement of the contract questionable.) Dey told Rosenthal and the other Ottawa Hockey Association owners to find an alternate playing venue, and when they could not they capitulated to Dey, who assumed full control of the Senators. A new company was formed, the Ottawa Arena Club, with only two owners, Dey, the president, and Gorman, the secretary-treasurer. It was a big promotion for Gorman, who was the sports editor of the *Ottawa Citizen* and had been initially hired to publicize the club.[20]

With the Senators secured, Dey committed Ottawa to the NHL and allowed Quinn's option to expire (a surprise to Quinn, who thought he had a binding contract for ice). The support was timely, since a CHA-affiliated promoter had succeeded in signing a lease for ice at the Jubilee Rink in Montreal, pushing Kennedy's Canadiens out. But without Ottawa (and Toronto), the CHA was still far from viable.[21]

The challenge from the CHA prompted the NHL owners to tighten their own contractual relations. They directed Calder to redraft the constitution and draw up a five-year agreement, committing the clubs "to play their respective teams together under the jurisdiction of the National Hockey League." Calder was also appointed for a five-year term, and postwar plans were discussed for a new arena in Montreal to replace the Westmount. To help Kennedy, Dey and Querrie proposed a motion that the Canadiens be given 15 percent of the net gate receipts in Ottawa and Toronto for traveling expenses, for one year. To help Toronto, generous terms were offered for the payment of the franchise fee, which had not even been discussed three weeks earlier in the hurry to admit the club. The payment terms were as follows: five thousand dollars, to be paid in installments of 50 percent of all net gate receipts of home games (more than seventeen hundred dollars), with the fee paid never to exceed 50 percent of the club's net profits in any year.[22]

Generous terms, however, were only for members and were not offered to Quinn after his allegiance came into the open when he filed suit against Dey for breach of contract over the option to lease the Ottawa rink. The next day Calder suspended the Shamrocks franchise. On the eighteenth Quinn and Livingstone embarked on a trip to Ottawa, Montreal, and Quebec to buy players for their new league.[23]

A bidding war for players seemed imminent, so it was fortuitous for both sides that the shooting war in Europe ended with an armistice on 11 November, and with it came the prospect of enlisted players being released for the coming season. When demobilization did not proceed as quickly as expected, it was the upstart CHA that had a hard time finding players. Livingstone failed to recruit the legendary mercenary hockey star Newsy Lalonde and also Eddie Gerard, the captain of the Senators. Adding further insult, Livingstone was simply ignored when he tried to get his former Toronto players back, notifying Corb Denneny, Reg Noble, Harry Cameron, Harry Meeking, Ken Randall, Alf Skinner, and Jack Adams that he intended to exercise his option on their services (pursuant to the option clause in their 1917–18 contracts). Instead, the arena signed them all, and Livingstone had to resort to the court, this time suing the Arena Gardens; Charlie Querrie; the Toronto manager, Hubert Vearncombe; the club manager; and even the players individually.[24]

Livingstone got more bad news from his ongoing suits. His appeal of an adverse decision in his case against his fellow NHA owners was rejected. Referring to the NHA constitution, the court agreed that clubs had the power to leave one club out of the schedule, and "the evidence demonstrated that this was the only arrangement that could be carried out, with any reasonable hope of avoiding financial loss to the majority of the members and players." Timing the moment, Calder threw Quinn an olive branch to separate him from Livingstone: the NHL would welcome Quinn back if he asked "within a reasonable time" and if he came "without an encumbrance." Quinn did not take it up.[25]

Livingstone continued his strategy to entangle the NHA and its owners in "a legal mesh," as the *Toronto Daily Star* called it, this time by trying to resuscitate the NHA. (The *Star* added that any victory might be Pyrrhic; while the professionals fight, "the fans are lining up behind amateur hockey, and the pro clientele is being shot to pieces.") Calder had said an NHA meeting could not be called until the clubs each paid a two-hundred-dollar assessment to help the league defend itself from Livingstone. Yet on the strength of his control over the NHA franchises of Toronto, the Ontarios, and the Quebec Shamrocks, Livingstone was able to call a meeting of the dormant association for 10 December 1918 at the Windsor Hotel.[26]

The meeting took place on the eleventh and was "one of the stormiest in the history of Canadian hockey." All Livingstone's nemeses, even Sam Lichtenhein, appeared to defend their interests. Percy Quinn was elected chairman unanimously, but his claim to a vote was disputed since Quebec's NHA shares had not been transferred to him. Calder argued the meeting was illegitimate because none of the clubs had paid the two-hundred-dollar assessment. The eastern clubs, even Lichtenhein, who had no prospect of ever making a cent out of the NHA, offered to pay the assessment if the other clubs would also do so. In counterattack, Livingstone and Quinn claimed Kennedy was not entitled to vote because he no longer owned a full-share position, and they trotted out Fred Barbeau of the Brunswick-Balke-Collender Company, a maker of billiard tables and other manufactured goods that had somehow become the owner of 12 of the Canadiens' original 50 NHA shares.[27]

The meeting held a vote on Kennedy's status, but the corporate nature of the NHA confused this issue as well. Following corporate principles, the three western club shares controlled by Livingstone and Quinn, plus the Brunswick shares (162 shares), were the majority, but under the common league governance principle of "one club, one vote," the two sides were tied three to three (Kennedy was allowed to vote for himself). As chairman, Calder broke the tie and voted that Kennedy should stay. In the course of discussions, Kennedy called Quinn a liar, whereupon the meeting dissolved into a shouting match. Their point made—the league would not be revived—Calder and the eastern clubs' representatives left. The western clubs nevertheless decided to continue the NHA and elected new officers. Livingstone went back to Toronto claiming complete victory, contrary to what he called "the lying reports from Montreal." He talked up the merger of the CHA and the NHA, his plans for clubs in Hamilton and Kitchener, and his expectation that the PCHA would now recognize the new league.[28]

The NHL clubs made it a point of holding their next meeting in Toronto a few days after the NHA kerfuffle, making it the first time the NHL had ever met outside the Windsor Hotel in Montreal. In the lead-up to the meeting, Calder again tempted Quinn, saying the league preferred a four-club format and it was Quinn's last chance to say he wanted in. Quinn did not show, so the NHL directors agreed to continue with the three-club league, "until such time as there were sufficient players available to make up a fourth club." A schedule was adopted to begin a week later, on 21 December.[29]

On the other side, there was no way the CHA (or NHA) was going to operate for the 1918–19 season. For all Livingstone's bluster, the players did not believe the league was sound, and the rink owners were not coming through, either. With only the Jubilee ice locked up and blocked in Toronto and Ottawa, the CHA would not function. The Hamilton and Kitchener franchises were equally evanescent, and Percy Quinn now realized he was on the losing side. Looking to save some money, if not some dignity, he sent an emissary to Calder, proposing that the NHA be revived and that he take up Livingstone's interest, "lock, stock and barrel." But with no written proposal, and with the start of the season just days away, it was too late. The NHA was condemned.[30]

Zero-Sum Game

In the short term, Livingstone may have been happy to restrict his activities to the courts and not on the ice, since the new league was soon plagued with problems. The discharge of hockey players from the military created competition for the services of the star players and drove up salaries. The three NHL clubs tried to operate under the old salary limit—five thousand dollars for nine players—but soon exceeded it. There was some contract fudging, but Ottawa simply admitted it was impossible to keep their stars for less.[31] In Toronto the stars were trying to get out of their contracts completely, and the state of play and the atmosphere of abuse at the Mutual Street rink even prompted referees Lou Marsh and Steve Vair to resign. Calder talked them back, but then had to deal with rumors of match fixing—specifically, that Kennedy's Canadiens had "laid down" for the Toronto club at the last arena game. (It turned out these "serious charges against pro hockey" were being spread around by someone using King Edward Hotel stationery, a pointed reference to Livingstone, who headquartered there.) The arena club just limped along until near the end of the season, when it dropped out with two games to play, leaving the NHL with only two active clubs, Ottawa and the Canadiens. Calder moved up the playoff schedule to compensate, but the bad news continued. When the Canadiens went west to play Seattle for the Stanley Cup, four players and Kennedy were hospitalized with the Spanish influenza, and Joe Hall, one of the star players, succumbed. Then, in June, the Canadiens home, the Jubilee Rink, burned to the ground.[32]

These developments were inauspicious to say the least, but entrepreneurial ambition was there to overcome them. George Kennedy teamed up with a local horse racing promoter named Thomas J. (Tom) Duggan to build the new rink that Montreal needed. The Mount Royal Arena would not be a Westmount rink, however, but would be located on the south side of Mont-Royal Avenue between Clark and St. Urbain Streets, in the heart of the east-end Plateau area of Montreal, a primarily French Canadian and Jewish working-class neighborhood. Duggan found investors to erect the building quickly and cheaply. Its small size and lack of an artificial ice-making plant sent Montreal back to the natural-ice era, but at least the Canadiens had a home to return to in January 1920 after opening the season on the road. Duggan also applied for an English NHL club to join the Canadiens in his new arena, but at the fall 1919 meeting the NHL directors were disinclined. They tabled his application, along with a weak Toronto application from Art Duncan, a returned 228th Battalion player.[33]

The owners had their own plan for Toronto, where they wanted to get a new club separate from Arena Gardens, which was still threatened with judgment in the Livingstone litigation and not prepared to own the Toronto franchise directly. In December Calder, Kennedy, and Gorman went to Toronto to drum up interest and found that Charlie Querrie, the Toronto manager, and some local amateur promoters and former players were interested in taking the club. The NHL still wanted a franchise fee of five thousand dollars, but Hubert Vearncombe also had to be paid off for his interest. After a two-day negotiation session, Vearncombe agreed to take two thousand dollars, and the new group of owners agreed to pay a further franchise fee of five thousand dollars to the league as revenues allowed. The move was just in time to get the club, now christened the St. Patrick's Hockey Club, ready for the upcoming season. The new group was optimistic, and at least they could get players, having recently signed four players who had been banned by the OHA for being paid amateurs.[34]

Returning to Quebec City was also a priority, and after Percy Quinn's Shamrocks franchise was officially canceled a new one was granted to Mike Quinn. (Remembering that Mike's last attempt had ended up in Percy's control, this time it was conditional: "In the event of his discontinuing or losing control of his franchise rights in any manner said rights shall revert to the National Hockey League without any recompense whatever.") Quinn started out with optimism and renamed the club the Quebec Athletics, but was soon having the same problems as during the war, namely, poor attendance exacerbated by an inability to acquire amateur players to improve on-ice performance. Quinn had a few established stars, such as Harry Mummery and Joe Malone (who would be the league's top scorer in 1919–20), but he complained to Calder that he had been dealing with about thirty players, offering them "ridiculous salaries and yet [still] cannot secure them." In January the other clubs had to loan players to the team to strengthen them for the season, and attendance was still weak, ranging from a poor two thousand to a paltry eight hundred per game. Without improvement, Quebec did not seem long for the league.[35]

That season the clubs also adopted a new constitution. It was still based firmly on the old NHA constitution, but in a signal change the club representatives were now to be known as league "governors." No longer the "delegates" of the amateur organizations or the "directors" of a corporation, as governors the NHA owners assumed a title that was empty of legal or commercial status yet still suggestive of authority. It also hinted that there might be no future move to incorporate the NHL, understandable given the problems caused by the NHA corporate form.[36]

In 1920 Livingstone's litigation was also being rewarded. Chief Justice Falconbridge found in his favor in both *Toronto Hockey Club v. Arena Gardens* suits, although he dismissed the claims against the players themselves. The judge ordered the rink to pay more than twenty thousand dollars (plus interest) and deliver the player contracts, a serious blow to Arena Gardens that prompted a management shake-up. At the June annual meeting, the company elected a new slate of officers and directors, with none other than Percy Quinn appointed as managing director.[37]

With his colleague now in the catbird seat at the major Toronto ice venue, it seemed Livingstone's litigiousness would pay off in ice for the 1920–21 season. The CHA had new life and a new international ambition. Almost immediately, Livingstone announced a reorganization with at least four teams, "and an international flavor to the association is more than a possibility." In September he and Quinn embarked on a buying spree. The *Toronto Daily Star* reported that the "Livingstone-Quinn combination" had already raided NHL camps and that it would innovate by using the amateur OHA rules that were more familiar to the Toronto crowd, especially the strict offside rule that did not allow any forward passing. The NHL clubs were an obvious target, but so was the PCHA, and the quest for players would know no limits as long as the Patricks adhered to their agreement with the NHL. The league would be more southern than the NHL, with two teams in Toronto (Torontos and the Shamrocks), one in Hamilton, and a fourth in the United States—possibly Cleveland, Detroit, or Boston. In October Livingstone and Quinn talked about the possibilities of New York, Philadelphia, and Pittsburgh.[38]

As usual, the crux came down to control over Toronto ice, and here Livingstone and Quinn got an unwelcome surprise, and one full of irony. The arena declared bankruptcy—either from the debt burden of the Livingstone judgment or to avoid paying it—and management was wrested from Quinn's control and put into the hands of a receiver. Now it was unclear who would get the ice. Under his rights as a creditor, Livingstone sued to remove the receiver, but as the case moved through the courts, the NHL went on the offensive in a proposed CHA expansion location.

American expansion might have appeared speculative, but Hamilton was a known hockey quantity, a hockey market that was home to the reigning OHA senior champions, the Hamilton Tigers, and soon to be the site of a modern new rink. Bordered by Barton, Bristol, Sanford, and Wentworth Streets, the Hamilton Arena would be centrally located and a good fit for NHL purposes, seating forty-five hundred for hockey (seven thousand with standing room). It also had press accommodations and a big clock like Toronto ("a fine way of keeping the crowd interested") as well as an electric signboard to post scores of out-of-town games. The whole venture was backed by Abso-Pure, Ltd., a local ice company, and local notables, including the president of the Canadian Westinghouse Company (a branch plant of the American firm). The arena was to be managed by Percy Thompson from Abso-Pure.[39]

In the zero-sum game the two leagues were playing, getting ice in the Hamilton Arena was important both as a block to Livingstone's own Hamilton expansion plans and as a crucial ice alternative for the St. Patrick's club, should it be shut out of the Arena Gardens. Reports of Hamilton receiving a CHA franchise were made in September 1920, but by then the NHL had already laid the groundwork with the local newspapers and the arena directors. The *Hamilton Herald* suggested that the CHA was weaker than it initially appeared, and when the Hamilton Arena directors met, it was "practically decided" that the NHL would be invited. Mike Quinn's failing Quebec franchise was expected to revert to the league and its players shipped to Hamilton. Sure enough, on 3 November, Calder announced that the Quebec franchise would be moving to Barton Street and that St. Patrick's would also operate there, if necessary. Percy Thompson said that Hamilton was committed and would operate an NHL team "if it costs the backers a hundred thousand dollars."[40]

When it was reported that another CHA attempt to obtain ice at Dey's Rink in Ottawa "had been foiled," Livingstone appeared corralled once again. His last hope was Arena Gardens control, but on 10 December a judge ruled that the appointment of a receiver had been justified under the circumstances. He questioned Livingstone's motives and suggested that the Toronto Hockey Club had been acting not as a creditor, but to obtain exclusive control over the arena for hockey. Only if Livingstone's lease for the arena with Quinn was valid did the receiver have to honor it. Almost immediately, the receiver announced that it was the St. Patrick's club that had the contract, and after it and the various amateur clubs were satisfied, there would be no more ice for the CHA. Livingstone was in denial and in a letter to the editor maintained that he alone had the professional rights at the Arena Gardens and would operate three teams there in the upcoming season, with practices to commence "this week." When the winter came, the NHL started up on schedule on 22 December, but the CHA aborted once again.[41]

It was the NHL that was making progress, although its enthusiasm for expansion was not as unanimous. There was a last-minute appeal from two Quebec Bulldogs directors to keep the franchise in Quebec (it was refused), and Tom Duggan applied for another Montreal franchise (it was tabled, "pending the first vacancy in the League"). Kennedy dissented in approving the Hamilton franchise, likely in protest over Duggan's application being delayed, and he also proposed uniform price scales across the league and revenue sharing of gate receipts. The other governors were not interested, but Calder was authorized to assess profitable clubs at the end of the season to cover the losses of other clubs, and to this revenue redistribution duty he was also given extensive powers over financial transactions on behalf of the league. It was a signal that any expansion would have to be mindful of the changing financial implications for the clubs.[42]

". . . Went to See a Slaughter . . ."

Now approved as a member, the Hamilton Professional Hockey Club set about organizing under the ownership of a group of local small businessmen led by Percy Thompson, including Andrew Ross, the proprietor of Ross Garage & Wagon Works; William Yates, a local contractor; and Robert B. Harris, the secretary-treasurer of the Herald Printing Company, publisher of a local newspaper. As was the practice in other NHL rinks, Thompson appointed local sportswriters and sportsmen to fill the minor official roles, including Patrick Jones, the sporting editor of the *Hamilton Herald*, as scorer; Tommy Moore, the sporting editor of the *Hamilton Times*, as goal judge; and a former goalie for the Hamilton Rowing Club Hockey Team, as the other goal judge. Like the St. Patrick's, the club borrowed its nickname from the local champion senior OHA club, the Tigers.[43]

The on-ice staffing was more challenging. Moving a club did not mean the players would move too. The NHL season was only three months in duration, and the days of large contracts for stars that justified the sacrifice of a local off-ice job or business obligations had not yet returned. As in the past, this arrangement meant several players chose not to report to training camps, and the other clubs' efforts to trade players to Hamilton ran into problems. Goldie Prodgers was traded by the Canadiens to Hamilton but did not want to go unless he was assured he would be the manager, and when Harry Mummery was traded to Hamilton the next year, it was speculated he might not come because he had recently been promoted to railway engineer. Thompson personally contacted every Quebec player and also targeted local amateur players, but mostly he had to rely on the generosity of the other three clubs. On 9 December Thompson signed Joe Matte and received news that Prodgers and George Carey would report, but the league's top goal scorer, Joe Malone, would not come, as he had a thriving skate-making business in Quebec that he had to attend.[44]

Nevertheless, Thompson got players, and when the new Hamilton Tigers opened their inaugural season on 22 December it was reported to be in front of a "very fair-sized crowd" at the arena (at least according to the *Herald*, one of the club's owners). For a new team the modest reception was not surprising, but it also became apparent that the Hamilton spectators had to be educated about the professional NHL game itself. Babe Dye, a former OHA star, had been loaned from the St. Patrick's for the game, but here is where much of the familiarity ended. The professional game was different, and with this first expansion in almost a decade, the NHL would have to work on persuading the Hamilton customers to become fans by promoting its stars and modifying some of its rules to appeal.[45]

With its strict offside rule, the OHA amateur game emphasized individual rushing skills, whereas the NHL's modified offside rule allowed forward passing in the center-ice zone, which put the emphasis on what were called "combination" (passing) plays. The professionals were "systematic" and "deliberate" in their attacks and kept harassing the goalie; in comparison, the amateurs "make weak efforts to get rebounds." The professionals were also less violent than their reputation, and fans were reportedly "disappointed because they went to see a slaughter and didn't see anything of the kind." Responding to spectator ignorance of the professional rules, in January the *Herald* printed the NHL playing rules and pointed out the differences, which also included the ability of goalkeepers to sprawl to make saves.[46]

Drawing fans to the rinks was also helped by advertising stars, but when Dye returned to the St. Patrick's and with Joe Malone still in Quebec, the Tigers were lacking in candescence. The plan to aid them showed the continued fragility of the league. St. Patrick's and the Canadiens both sent two players each, but Ottawa hesitated, agreeing only on 30 December to send Sprague Cleghorn and Harry Broadbent. Both Ottawa players refused to report, even when threatened with suspension. (Broadbent had an off-ice job in Ottawa he was reluctant to give up, and one might speculate the players had the tacit support of the Ottawa club.) Matters came to a head at a stormy meeting at the Prince George Hotel in Toronto on 20 January 1921, when Ottawa asked for permission to have Cleghorn returned to Ottawa. The other governors would not agree, and Kennedy even reportedly threatened to drop out of the league during the dispute. Since St. Patrick's and Hamilton backed him up, it looked like Ottawa might be the club that found itself alone. Cleghorn was reinstated on the promise that he would go to the St. Patrick's for the rest of the season to help them out, after which he could return to Ottawa. Broadbent never did play for Hamilton, and his rights were eventually returned to Ottawa.[47]

Help for Hamilton did come in the person of Malone, who arrived in the first week of January, in time to play against Ottawa in a pair of his own "Joe Malone"–brand skates. Thompson expected the star's arrival to produce a record crowd, and sure enough, before game time only one hundred reserved seats remained. Fifty-five hundred customers eventually attended, and when Malone scored the Ottawa players had to "hold their hands over their ears to shut out the din." The big crowd may have been helped along by reduced ticket prices. At the start of the season the tickets ranged from 80¢ for standing room to $2.25 for the best seats, which was the same for the senior amateur OHA games. By the time of Malone's arrival, some seat prices had been reduced to 55¢, suggesting either that Thompson was trying to create a crowd for the event or that he had been forced to modify the ticket scale midway through the season to attract spectators.[48]

Nonetheless, with a bona fide star and the growing appreciation for the distinctive rules that made the game faster and more sophisticated, NHL hockey was making a positive impression in the Steel City. Less impressive was the physical play that began to appear more frequently, or at least began to be remarked upon by the *Hamilton Herald*, a no doubt biased source. In contrast to earlier in the season when the game was perceived to be less violent than expected, by mid-January a *Herald* editorial warned that the professional hockey boom in Hamilton was threatened by "deliberate rough play." It singled out the St. Patrick's as the worst offenders, with players Cully Wilson and Ken Randall "the real 'bad-men' of hockey," and the paper warned the NHL that referees would have to be stricter in Hamilton. The Toronto-Hamilton rivalry almost certainly biased the analysis, as did the *Herald*'s ownership interest in the club, and it also reappeared when Newsy Lalonde came to town with the Canadiens and butt-ended Joe Malone in the face and then his teammate Harry Mummery slashed a Tigers player in the head. Thompson protested to Calder, and the *Herald* warned: "THAT SORT OF ROWDYISM WILL NOT BE TOLERATED HERE." The paper called for the Hamilton police to take action in the future if Calder did not. The *Herald* reprinted an editorial from the *Brantford Expositor* that also got into the act, commenting that Lalonde's behavior "disgraces hockey as a national sport in this country" and urging the NHL to take action: "The time for 'cleaning up' the many shady and dirty plays in hockey has come, and it certainly would not be out of place to start in the National Association."[49]

While civic rivalries may have been at the root of some conflict, others were embedded in a perception that the professional game was undisciplined when compared to the amateurs' play. In January the governors fined Ottawa $500 when its players skated off in the middle of their 26 January game in Montreal after a disputed goal. In the aftermath it was announced that the NHL had also decided to use the OHA penalty rules the next winter in an effort to reduce rowdy behavior. That fall they implemented the OHA rule of no substitutions for penalized players and no deferred penalties. Every man who was penalized had to serve time immediately in the penalty box, leaving his team undermanned. The minor penalty was reduced from three to two minutes, the major foul assessed at five, more serious offenses at ten minutes without substitution, and a match penalty for deliberately injuring another player. While accepting this OHA disciplinary regime, other rules that differentiated the amateur and professional games were also reinforced: the rules on offside play, accidental kicking of the puck, and rebounds from goalies were rendered more flexible to reduce stoppages and speed up the professional version. If there were to be amateur discipline, it would not be at the expense of the professional pace.[50]

The NHL was also negotiating its place with its rivals for playing talent, current and future. In September 1921 the NHL held a special meeting with Frank Patrick, president of the PCHA, to renew the PCHA-NHL agreement over the "World's Series" (that is, the Stanley Cup series) and also to discuss the relationship with a new western professional league. After the war the nominally amateur "Big Four" league had begun paying players at salary levels that began to threaten the PCHA's ability to recruit from its main source, prairie amateurs. Frank Patrick had gone on the offensive by writing to the attorney general of Alberta that the clubs were not amateur but semiprofessional and paying salaries even higher than the professional PCHA. After an investigation by the Alberta branch of the Canadian Amateur Hockey Association, the Big Four was forced to professionalize. It changed its name to the Western Canada Hockey League (WCHL) and signed a one-year agreement with the PCHA to end the player raiding. The purpose of Patrick's trip to Montreal was to include the Alberta league in a new PCHA-NHL agreement. The NHL governors appointed Patrick to act as their representative to meet with the Alberta directors to discuss details. In the fall the NHL governors ratified an agreement with the WCHL, bringing it into the emergent major league system that coordinated player distribution and prevented salary escalation.[51]

Ill with the residual effects of influenza, George Kennedy had been represented at the meeting by Frank Calder, and when on 19 October

1921 Kennedy died, the Canadiens franchise was put up for sale. This time Calder represented unnamed Ottawa interests in the sale. Tom Duggan, Kennedy's promotions partner at the Mount Royal Arena, had been serially thwarted in his applications for an NHL club and was eager to retain his major tenant. But both Duggan and Calder's principal lost out to a triumvirate of local promoters—Leo Dandurand, Joe Cattarinich, and Hilarion (Louis) Létourneau—who bid eleven thousand dollars.[52]

Dandurand and Cattarinich were the driving forces behind the new club, part of the generation of sports entrepreneurs who had been able to turn part-time activities into full-time business propositions. Both were involved in lacrosse, hockey, and other sports: Cattarinich had tended goal with the Canadiens in their inaugural 1909–10 season, and Dandurand had refereed for the NHA as well as being one of the founding members of the Canadian Amateur Hockey Association. The two went into real estate and tobacco wholesaling together under the name "Catta-Léo," but with the postwar boom, sporting ventures soon dominated, particularly gambling. Cattarinich and Dandurand ran the betting concession of the Kempton Park horse racing track outside Montreal, and in 1919 they secured a lease on the Delorimier track. They developed the bookmaking business and expanded into the United States with American partners; by mid-decade they owned the Dorval course on the Island of Montreal and controlled tracks in Ohio and Pennsylvania. After the purchase of the Canadiens, they focused on hockey and betting and moved their operations to the Canadiens' office in the Windsor Hotel. They also made a Quebec cabinet minister, Athanase David, president of the Canadiens, an appointment that burnished the social and cultural reputation of the club, although it was an honorary position. At the 1921 NHL annual meeting where the purchase was confirmed, Dandurand was elected governor for the Canadiens, and it was he who was to be the hands-on managing director for the next fourteen years.[53]

The November 1921 annual meeting was also the first not held under the shadow of Livingstone and the CHA, and the governors took the time to revise the rules, on ice and off. The league competition would forgo the split schedule used since 1916–17 (a Livingstone innovation) and return to the season-long competition, with the first- and second-place clubs playing off for the championships, this time using the same format the PCHA used: a two-game total-goals series. In other business, the governors formally adopted the OHA disciplinary rules, ratified the agreement with the WCHL, and refused an application from former Wanderers player Riley Hern for a new club in Montreal. Calder was reelected president and his salary raised to twelve hundred dollars (with a bonus if the season was successful financially), and the O'Brien Cup, inherited from the NHA, was reconfirmed as the league's championship trophy. Another legacy of the NHA, the league constitution, was also changed at the meeting. Loaned players could no longer be recalled after 5 February of any season, and Section 9 was revised so that unanimous consent of all clubs was required to admit new members. Acknowledging the turnover in the league, another five-year agreement was signed at this time. The St. Patrick's had signed on to the old November 1918 agreement, but the new accord bound Hamilton and the new Canadiens owners. It confirmed the governors' satisfaction with a structure that paired a constitution setting out the rules with a separate agreement that joined the clubs to the league and to each other.[54]

"Tied Up for Life"

The Livingstone disputes had conditioned the NHL's structure and also pushed it to expand to Hamilton, where it modified its rules to appeal to the fans of amateur hockey. The difficulties placing players in cities without a strong professional tradition also led the league to refine outstanding issues regarding the distribution and mobility of labor. These questions included confirmation of a waiver system that kept players within the league, introduction of protected negotiation lists for amateur players, rigid enforcement of the option clause to keep players under contract, and, not least, shrewd manipulation of the intransigence of amateur organizations to limit player options.

The 1921–22 season was a generally successful one at the gate, except in Hamilton, and throughout the year the main agenda item at league meetings was player help for the Tigers. The efforts were complicated by the general recalcitrance of Hamilton players as well as the stinginess of the other clubs. Additionally, there were accusations of tampering (negotiating with players already under contract to another club) and also disputes with the PCHA over reserve lists.[55]

The importance of maintaining the ethnic character of clubs was also a factor. At this time Ottawa and the Canadiens came to an agreement over French Canadian players in the Ottawa area. The Canadiens had maintained the right of refusal over French Canadian players since the early days of the NHA, and while Ottawa players were primarily English Canadian, the Ottawa area had a significant French Canadian population from which it could draw not only players but also customers. Yet the Senators rarely had any French Canadian players or staff and seemed to be generally unsuccessful in appealing to that market. Belatedly, they tried to make up for it by agreeing that the Canadiens could still approach any new French Canadian players in Ottawa, but the Senators could name exceptions before 1 November each year.[56]

Identifying potential amateur recruits was also a priority. Percy Hambly of St. Patrick's recommended that each club be allowed to reserve the services of six amateur players each year in addition to those professionals under contract. This proposal established the principle of the "negotiation list" and was the first attempt by professional clubs to control the mobility of nonprofessional players. (The list was not made public, and it is not clear how effective it was at constraining amateur opportunities at this early stage.) At the annual meeting, further modifications were made to the constitution concerning waivers and player contracts. To prevent a reoccurrence of the situation where Dandurand tried to sell a fading star (Newsy Lalonde) to a club outside the league, Querrie proposed that the waiver price be raised from five hundred to fifteen hundred dollars and that any club refusing to waive a player be required to take delivery of the player at that price. Dandurand had also tried to use another player, Aurèle Joliat, a suspended amateur, and in response his fellow governors added a clause requiring a vote of the board of governors before a player suspended by any other amateur or professional league would be allowed to play.[57]

Another key plank in the player-control structure was the option clause. Unlike the baseball reserve clause used by the American and National Leagues, hockey's option clause had never come under legal scrutiny. An opportunity might have arisen during the Livingstone lawsuit over player contracts, but his case actually depended on the *legality* of the option clause. Livingstone's conspiracy charges were argued as standard torts, rather than framed as manifestations of anticompetitive (antitrust) behavior, since Canadian competition law was relatively weak compared to the American, and in any case did not include service industries like hockey. Indeed, a by-product of the Livingstone litigation was tacit acceptance of the league's option clause by the courts. In its 1924 decision in *Toronto Hockey Club v. Arena Gardens*, the Ontario appeals court seemed to accept the legitimacy of the option clause:

> There is . . . a custom, amounting practically to a rigid law in the professional hockey world, that, notwithstanding that a playing contract may be for a limited period, such as one year, or two years, the player is nevertheless not wholly free to make a new contract with whom he pleases at the termination of his contract. The number of professional hockey clubs being limited and all being banded together in one league or association, a player, though legally free to contract elsewhere, cannot do so without the consent of the club holding his expiring contract. Any attempt at independence may result either in his finding himself out in the cold and unable to get employment as a hockey player, or in any other club which employs him finding itself in difficulties with the other members of the league.

The court cited the evidence of a Toronto player, Frank Heffernan, who agreed that he was "tied up for life," but the lack of criticism of this "rigid law in the professional hockey world," which might have been considered an undesirable restraint on trade, suggests that the hockey industry was considered special and implicitly able to make its own laws.[58]

In some cases, the NHL allowed modification to the standard player contract, but even for stars the option clause was rigidly enforced. Frank (King) Clancy's contract with the Ottawa Senators for the 1923–24 season was typewritten (not printed), but clearly standard and contained an option clause (#10) reserving Clancy's rights for the next season. It also had a handwritten "no-trade" clause in the margin, something only a star like Clancy could demand, but he was still bound by the option clause and did not have the freedom to play for a club other than the Ottawa Senators.

One player who tried to challenge the clause was St. Patrick's goaltender Vernon (Jake) Forbes. He sat out the entire 1922–23 season as a result and was shipped to Hamilton at the end of the season for his intransigence.[59]

The distance of the leap from amateur to professional play also circumscribed player freedom. For an amateur player, jumping to the paid game was a big decision since it could rule out a steady year-round day job that often came with playing amateur hockey. In some cases, the salary for a three-month season professional stint (possibly in a distant locale) had to compete favorably with twelve months of paychecks. (Even many professionals were tied to jobs and businesses in their club town, which complicated movement to places like Hamilton.) During the war salaries fell far from the levels seen in the heady days of the ECAHA and did not match expectations. Mike Rodden considered the stipend to play with the Toronto Arenas to be "ridiculously small" (all the players made between $450 and $900 for the season) and recalled that one player was offered $900 for the last half of the 1917–18 season, but chose dental school instead. After the war the salaries rose so that in the early 1920s, the average player seems to have made $1,200–$2,000 per season and a few stars more ($3,000 for Newsy Lalonde). This salary compared to the average Canadian manufacturing job in the first half of the decade, which was stagnant at a little less than $1,000 a year.[60]

For those players who could afford it, amateur principle was also a consideration. As an incentive, professional teams offered a cash bonus to sign a contract, in effect a bounty to offset the player's relinquishment of his amateur status. The professional club owners could also take advantage of the draconian policies of powerful amateur bodies like the OHA, which were in the habit of banning players for life. Once a professional commitment was made, a player was forever excluded from amateur play (in any sport under control of the CAAU). The NHL owners acquired many players from the amateur ranks owing to this rule, and its threatened application allowed Leo Dandurand of the Canadiens to acquire one of the great star players of the league, Howie Morenz.

Morenz was a star player from Mitchell (and later Stratford), Ontario, and came to Dandurand's attention after playing a match in Montreal with a Canadian National Railway (CNR) team from Stratford. Dandurand asked Lou Marsh and Mike Rodden, Toronto sportswriters who moonlighted as NHL and OHA referees, to keep an eye on Morenz and scout his abilities. They were evidently impressed, and after the season Dandurand and Riley Hern visited the Morenz home in Stratford. They had a hard time convincing Morenz's father that turning professional was more valuable to Howie than finishing his apprenticeship at the CNR and playing amateur hockey in Stratford. When Marsh told Dandurand that he had seen Morenz and his father in the company of Paul Ciceri and Charlie Querrie of the St. Patrick's club, Dandurand sent Canadiens manager Cecil Hart back to Stratford, and on 6 July 1923 Hart paid Morenz $300 up front and got him to sign a three-year contract for $1,600 a season, with the stipulation that Morenz be allowed to report as late as the end of December in order to complete his apprenticeship. Still, Morenz reconsidered and a month later returned the money and the contract. He wrote to Dandurand that "several reasons of which family and work are the most to consider" made it "impossible to leave Stratford." He apologized for the inconvenience he had caused and hoped Dandurand would accept the returned contract "in a Sportsmanlike way." Dandurand would not. Sensing interference from the Stratford amateur club, which wanted to keep its star, he sent Morenz a ticket to come to Montreal to discuss the matter. In the interval, Dandurand contacted W. A. (Billy) Hewitt of the OHA and told him that if any of his members (that is, Stratford) encouraged Morenz to repudiate his contract, then Dandurand would make known certain information that "would make the Ontario amateur authorities go red in the face," no doubt a threat to publicize common amateur practices of paying players. When Morenz arrived at the Windsor Hotel, there ensued a wrenching scene in which both he and Dandurand were apparently reduced to tears. The Canadiens owner listened to Morenz's plea but told him that if he did not play in Montreal, he would never play professional hockey at all. Dandurand also had the backing of Hewitt and the OHA, so in the end Morenz honored the contract, and he soon emerged as one of the brightest NHL stars, destined to shine far beyond the rinks of southwestern Ontario.[61]

The Cartel: Cooperation and Flexibility

By the early 1920s, the elite clubs in central Canadian hockey had reorganized and restructured, adopting a cartel form that helped reconcile club
conflicts, subordinate players, reduce competition from outside the league,
and appeal to consumer demands. It is noteworthy that after four seasons,
the NHL had still not acted to incorporate, as had the NHA. While limited
liability corporations were the norm for multiple-shareholder businesses,
the form did not seem to suit the sports league. During his deposition
related to the (failed) litigation against Ocean Accident and Guarantee,
Calder was asked whether the NHA was a commercial corporation and
a moneymaking concern. He answered no, saying that it was "a sporting
organization which is incorporated for the purpose of giving it powers
that it might not enjoy as a non-incorporated body." Belying the NHA's
corporate charter, he also clarified that its primary purpose was not even
to carry on business for the profit of its shareholders and declare divi-
dends. Evidently, even Calder understood that the commercial corporate
form was not ideally suited to the constitutional organization of a cartel,
which had no definition in commercial law other than as a conspiracy
against consumers. Furthermore, formal incorporation had done nothing
to ensure club compliance in the NHA and had in fact rendered Livingstone's ouster more difficult and caused complications in the dissolution
of the NHA that Livingstone had exploited. With the benefits of incorporation now questionable, in the ensuing years the NHA's successor would
be open to exploring alternatives. For the time being at least, the NHL
would rely on the constitution and term agreement to bind the clubs to a
common fate and reaffirm an associative mode, the cartel, which emphasized cooperation and flexibility.[62]

The cartel had many advantages, on both the supply and the demand
sides of the hockey product. It rendered operations of the clubs more
economically efficient by coordinating the games and setting rules. As a
cooperative mechanism between a limited number of producers of elite
professional hockey in central Canada, it successfully prevented competitors like Livingstone from emerging as viable competitors. It also acted as
a partner in a national agreement that coordinated with the PCHA and

WCHL to control a larger national market for professional hockey labor. In addition, the cartel form was an essential element of the hockey product because it exploited the tension between the local and the national markets. Clubs were branded with city names to appeal to local markets, but the league was branded as "national," even when it was more accurately a regional circuit. Thus, the cartel served customer preference to identify with the national (best) version of the national game, and at the same time reinforced civic loyalties. It was a careful balance: while the Canadiens were to stay culturally homogenous, another proposal in 1921 to divide up central Canada into exclusive territories for club recruitment was not pursued. As the league expanded over new borders, retaining the local character of clubs, especially the players, would be increasingly difficult.[63]

Though flexible, the cartel form was not indestructible. Like its ancestors, the NHL was born out of internecine and external threats that had destroyed its immediate predecessor. In the NHA personality conflicts had been exacerbated by the domestic effects of war in Europe and showed that the league had to be careful about whom it admitted as a member. Yet there were also advantages in the organizational peculiarities of the league form that helped it constrain those members. Livingstone had sought remedy in the courts, but his confidence in tort law and legal solutions was misplaced. While he won his case against the Arena Gardens for breach of contract and one of the appeal court judges called the conduct of Arena Gardens "utterly dishonest and despicable," he lost the suit against his fellow NHA owners. As one judge pointed out, investment in a league depended "to a large extent upon whether or not the owner of a particular team was *persona grata* to the other members, and the owner might find himself for personal reasons suddenly excluded from the league and the value of his team immediately destroyed." So comity trumped legality in a cooperative venture like professional sports. Livingstone also failed in the other essential relationship: maintaining access to ice. Keeping the rink owners onside, especially the ones with artificial ice plants, was a significant barrier to entry to rivals (or defectors), and the NHL clubs used this fact to great advantage.[64]

It is ironic that Eddie Livingstone gave the NHL both a reason to exist and an incentive to survive. His aggressive tactics forced the league to continue to expand in an uncertain environment and to grow and confront the challenge of selling professional hockey in markets dominated by strong amateur clubs. In so doing, the league was pushed to find ways to distinguish the professional NHL game from the amateur by its rules, its speed, its skill level, and its stars. In this sense, the expansion was perhaps premature, but it also reignited a preexisting southward ambition that was evident in the prewar NHA. And the 1920s would be an opportune time to expand, for in the northeastern United States sport was becoming a spectacle, and the NHL men would have to decide if they would join the show.

3

Transplanting the Clubs

1923–1926

I t was an international event. The most famous arena in the world, Madison Square Garden (MSG), was reopening on 15 December 1925 and featuring the rebirth of hockey in New York City. Gotham's dozen daily newspapers were full of detail on the new stadium, the novel Canadian sport, and the man who seemed to be behind it all: George L. (Tex) Rickard. In only a few short years, Rickard had become the most famous sports impresario in America, a man whose name drew spectators all by itself. For this reason, it was no surprise that the National Hockey League game was promoted as "Tex Rickard's All-Star Americans" versus "Les Canadiens of Montreal." Rickard knew that most New Yorkers did not understand the sport, so he gave them what they did understand—a novel game, a patriotic sheen, and Tex Rickard. With his assistant John Hammond, he sold the New York public on professional hockey's northern origins, its speed ("the fastest game on earth"), its exotic appeal (French Canadian players), and its serious commercial importance (the star of the Canadiens, Howie Morenz, was paid as much as a baseball player). The pitting of Americans versus Canadians invited nationalist passion, and Rickard tailored the decor and the music to highlight it. More astutely, he encouraged New York scribes such as the *Herald-Tribune*'s W. J. Macbeth, a Canadian and former sports editor of the *Montreal Herald*, to whet appetites for hockey's "promising reputation . . . hinting of bloodshed and ambulance bells and trephining operations." (Trephining was a colorful way of describing brain surgery.)[1]

These features could be expected to attract the readers of the New York popular press, but Rickard's other innovation was making sport palatable to "society." One of his tactics was attaching a philanthropic tether, and this game would be a charity event for the Neurological Institute of New York (perhaps another trephining connection). The charity angle gave local high-society hostesses an excuse to throw dinner parties for the *New York Social Register* elite before coming to the Garden for the 8:15 p.m. face-off. It also allowed the shrewd Rickard to charge higher prices because charitable tickets were tax exempt. And Rickard did not forget to include his political friends, who had been essential to the success of his urban sports enterprises. In addition to the current New York City mayor, John Hylan, who dropped the puck for the opening face-off, Rickard also invited Mayor-Elect Jimmy Walker to present a trophy to the winner. Renowned as "Beau James" for his personal style, Walker's contribution was much more substantial than that: while a New York State senator, he had introduced the 1920 bill to legalize prizefighting in New York, thus preparing the ground for Rickard's arrival and the Garden's renaissance.[2]

Rickard's marketing was as polished as his political acumen, and the newspaper coverage focused on the high-class patrons who arrived for the game, writing that the Garden lobby looked like "the foyer at the opera," with "fashionably gowned women there in furs and jewels." The Governor General's Foot Guards Band from Ottawa and the band of the United States Military Academy at West Point marched through the streets of downtown New York to city hall, the Neurological Institute, the Canadian Club, and finally the Garden, where they led the teams onto the ice, surrounded by box seats and balconies festooned with "bunting of red, white, and blue and gold and blue and light blue and white," and where the "Stars and Stripes mingled with the British flag" under a flood of white lights. Besides the New Yorkers and Canadian expatriates who filled the rink, fifteen hundred spectators came by train from Canada for the game; the delegation included Frank Calder, Athanase David (the president of the Canadiens), several members of Parliament, and the entire Montreal Maroons team, who were on their way back from a game in Pittsburgh. The Foot Guards took up "God Save the King" and West Point "The Star-Spangled Banner," and then Rickard, Hammond, and Tom Duggan accompanied Hylan onto the ice for the ceremonial face-off. When the puck was dropped and the game began, history was made: the full house of seventeen thousand was the largest crowd ever to see a hockey game, and thousands more could hear the event broadcast over radio station WJY.[3]

At intermission the audience was diverted with fancy and acrobatic skating demonstrations by the Canadian pair Norval Baptie and Gladys Lamb as well as Charlotte and Petersen from Chicago. When the game was over, Walker presented another novelty to the victorious Canadiens, the Prince of Wales Trophy, donated for the occasion as the new symbol of the NHL championship in the reflected glory of the popular British royal. Prize in hand, the Canadiens joined the Americans and the assembled dignitaries after the game at the posh Biltmore Hotel, where the Canadian Club of New York hosted a ball featuring the military bands and the popular orchestra of Paul Whiteman, known as the "King of Jazz."[4]

By entering New York, the NHL was coming to a city of spectacle, the economic and cultural capital of the United States, and the most populous city in the world. After a brief postwar recession, American personal incomes grew rapidly in what one scholar has called "the first truly modern decade." Abetting that modernization was swift adoption of technologies such as the automobile, electricity, and the radio. These items transformed American consumption patterns, and recreational activities like traveling, music, the movies, and professional sports became major businesses. It was the Jazz Age, but it was also the Age of Play, the Golden Age of Sport, and the Age of Sports Heroes. Even a traditional and already popular sport like major league baseball saw attendance grow 43 percent from 1919 to 1924 on the back of Babe Ruth's Herculean home run hitting. Boxing shed its working-class, vulgar, and illicit roots and attained mainstream appeal. College football and country club sports like golf and tennis also saw a resurgence of interest with their own stars, such as Red Grange, Bobby Jones, and Bill Tilden. The promise of profits also brought infrastructure, with millions invested in stadiums and facilities to welcome the crowds.[5]

The elite Canadian hockey leagues had been slowly pushing southward from the St. Lawrence and Ottawa Valleys for more than a decade, and American expansion had been on the agenda since the early days of the NHA, but if the push was going to happen, it had to come soon. There were questions that needed to be answered, however. Could hockey overcome existing political, economic, and cultural barriers and provide the cultural appeal and economic substance in an American marketplace that was becoming crowded with leisure products? Could the NHL successfully transplant its brand of the game and supplant an indigenous American version, or would a competitor, amateur, or professional outmaneuver it? And by engaging the American market, how much adaptation and change to the rules and organization of the "Canadian" game would be required?

Duggan's Designs

Despite Rickard's prominence, the New York opening was really the realization of another man's scheme, one whose role in NHL expansion is often understated. It was Tom Duggan, the thwarted Mount Royal promoter, whose initiatives in Boston and New York had led to the successful NHL penetration of the United States. While Rickard was the face of the club for promotional purposes, the New York Americans Hockey Club was owned by Duggan and his American partner, William V. (Bill) Dwyer, and it was certainly Duggan who took the most satisfaction from the success of the event. What had started as a desire to fill up empty dates at his Mount Royal Arena in Montreal had culminated in his partial ownership of two NHL clubs in the biggest sports markets of the United States and his participation in the biggest night in American hockey.[6]

After the repeated refusals of his applications for a new NHL franchise and his failure to buy the Canadiens in 1921, Duggan had become more creative. First, he suggested moving the Canadiens to Quebec City, which would open up a spot for his English Montreal club. Receiving no support for this proposal, he set his sights on the United States, where amateur hockey was seeing a postwar renaissance. Duggan persuaded his former rival, Leo Dandurand, to present a plan for US expansion before the NHL governors in January 1923. Despite being American himself, Dandurand seems to have been a reluctant pioneer, understanding that involving American capital would inevitably raise the cost of players to Canadian NHL clubs. Yet the alternative might be worse: an independent US league that would have the same effect on the player market and also relegate the NHL to a subsidiary status. And such a league might be in the offing if the United States Amateur Hockey Association (USAHA), which was growing and already draining the Canadian amateur talent pool, decided to become overtly professional. Dandurand discussed these issues with his fellow club owners, and they approved Duggan's designs in principle, giving over to Calder the power to negotiate the terms. The task was far from simple. Despite their agreeing to an option, the NHL clubs were reluctant to spend more in traveling expenses and skeptical about the availability of playing talent. Still, if Duggan could get agreements with rinks in New York and Boston, the NHL men could be convinced.[7]

On 13 February 1923 Duggan paid two thousand dollars for options on franchises in any two cities from a choice of New York, Boston, or Brooklyn. The options expired on 1 June, and within days of the deal Duggan was negotiating for ice in the office of George V. Brown, the manager of the Boston Arena. Financed by Henry Lapham, a Boston industrialist and president of the Boston Athletic Association (BAA), the arena was new (erected in 1920), seated 5,000 (7,000 with standing room), had a 220-by-90-foot ice surface, and could also be used for track meets and boxing bouts. It was an ideal building, but Duggan got his meeting and little more. Afterward, Brown told the press that Boston was "not ready" for professional hockey. His resistance was understandable. The arena was already home to one of the most successful city hockey leagues in the United States as well as hosting several clubs in the USAHA. Brown himself ran the Boston Athletic Association club and was a prominent figure in the hockey league, which had been formed in 1920 and effectively controlled elite amateur hockey in the US Northeast, with ambitions further afield. Its brand of amateur hockey was also very lucrative: in 1923 the arena had hosted 300,000 fans for seventy-two evening games, an average of 4,167 per game. Near full capacity already, Brown did not see any need for professional hockey. After all, higher-cost professional players would just cut into the profits.[8]

Duggan went looking for allies and found Bernard Tansey and Arthur Duffey, two writers from the *Boston Post*. Duffey introduced him to Charles Francis Adams, the owner of a New England grocery store chain and a prominent figure in local amateur hockey circles. Adams had managed a local amateur club before the war and, more important, was now a director of the Boston Arena. The business opportunity of professional hockey intrigued Adams, and he took up Duggan's cause. In short order he succeeded in changing Brown's mind and getting the arena to offer Duggan a contract for ice. Part of Adams's pitch was the threat that a rival arena might emerge to serve a professional team, an idea that probably originated with Duggan. The tentative deal guaranteed the arena 35 percent of the gate and a minimum of one thousand dollars per night, with the balance going to Duggan, who would be responsible for paying all expenses. After Duggan had netted fifty thousand dollars for himself, he was to give a half interest in the club to the arena. But before everything could be confirmed, the NHL added a hurdle: to justify the road trip from Canada, Boston could not operate as the sole American club for the 1923–24 season. Duggan offered to operate a franchise in Philadelphia, but this notion was rejected. As there was as yet no suitable rink available in Brooklyn, Duggan now needed New York to make Boston happen.[9]

At least New York had a long hockey tradition, stretching back into the nineteenth century. Participants were drawn from the same commercial and professional classes as in Montreal, as well as from the city's social and economic elite, who learned the sport through preparatory school and college play and continued the game in private clubs with artificial ice, like Manhattan's St. Nicholas Rink. The American Amateur Hockey League persisted as a local league from 1896 to 1917, with clubs from the New York Athletic Club, St. Nicholas Club, Brooklyn Crescents, and the Skating Club of Brooklyn, and promoters also regularly invited Canadian elite teams to town for exhibitions, thereby introducing New Yorkers to stars like Fred Taylor, Art Ross, and Newsy Lalonde. After a break owing to the First World War, interest in the sport renewed, but if hockey was to become more than a curiosity and aspire to be as popular as sports like baseball, it needed to move beyond the precincts of the privileged and into arenas where it could be viewed by the masses. Fortuitously, 1920s America was providing just the environment for such a transition, with growing urbanization, national media, and a booming economy that were creating interest in sport, with New York City at the center.[10]

The institution that crested the new wave of sports spectatorship was one of the first American buildings constructed for the urban mass consumption of leisure, Madison Square Garden. The current Garden, the second edifice to go by the name, was a beaux arts Manhattan landmark designed by architect Stanford White and built in 1890 with seating for eight thousand and amenities that included a concert hall, a theater, a restaurant, and a roof garden café. By 1920, however, the building was becoming increasingly decrepit and losing money for its owner, the New York Life Assurance Company. Nonetheless, it led the vanguard of the postwar resurgence in sport, particularly boxing, which had attracted a sports promoter par excellence, Tex Rickard, who had been the organizer of the first "million-dollar gate" boxing bout between Georges Carpentier and heavyweight champion Jack Dempsey. Armed with a ten-year contract to manage events, Rickard joined with John Ringling, of Ringling Brothers and Barnum & Bailey Circus, to take over the famous venue and resuscitate it as a mecca of indoor entertainment.[11]

Rickard and Ringling had ambitious plans for the Garden, but they knew that even with weekly boxing bouts and the five-week circus, there would be many "dark" nights. Rickard went looking for other suitable events, and in 1922 Rickard gained the assistance of Colonel John S. Hammond, a West Point graduate who had met Rickard while serving as a military attaché in South America. When Duggan came knocking in February 1923, Hammond saw hockey as a natural fit and was instrumental in getting Rickard onside, on the condition that Duggan pay to install an artificial ice plant. In March 1923 they agreed in principle, with the understanding that the renovations would make hockey for the 1923–24 season near impossible. They planned on starting up the next year, although it would require Duggan to get an extension in his options.[12]

Promise in hand, Duggan hurried back to Boston to confirm arrangements, but the mood had changed once again. When he met with Brown and Adams at the BAA offices, they had cooled to the NHL idea. The arena's main revenue generator was its USAHA club, and directors were now unsure about risking it for an untried professional hockey venture. Brown announced that contract talks were suspended until Adams had "personally investigated the hockey situation in Canada." Adams and Duggan left that same evening for Montreal, where Calder and the NHL owners apparently persuaded him that the NHL was a desirable partner. Satisfied, Adams reported back to Boston that it would be to the advantage of the Boston Arena to give Duggan a contract for the use of the arena, but despite these assurances Duggan saw that "the hockey situation was boiling" and that he was still a long way from knowing a Boston NHL team would have ice to play on, and when.[13]

The arena's hesitation and push for due diligence may have been prompted by the other power in the USAHA, Roy Schooley, the league's secretary-treasurer and manager of its two Pittsburgh clubs. Schooley was a Canadian former OHA referee who had moved to the United States before the war to work in journalism and politics. As publicist for Pittsburgh's Duquesne Garden, he worked to build up elite hockey in the Pennsylvania city, which had a storied hockey tradition stretching back into the nineteenth century. The Garden was central to that history, an old converted car barn with eight thousand seats that was used as a theater, sports arena, and indoor skating rink and had served ably as the home ice of the clubs that formed the first professional hockey leagues. During the First World War, it was used almost exclusively for skating and hockey, with many Canadian teams visiting to play exhibition matches, and the Friday- and Saturday-night games came to attract thousands of spectators. Hockey boomed again after the war, and to take advantage Schooley formed the USAHA with George Brown and William Haddock, the sheriff of Allegheny County and a prominent Pittsburgh sportsman. The USAHA model was simple: serve the burgeoning demand for hockey in northeastern and midwestern American cities with teams built from Canadian amateur stars lured south with munificent offers of off-ice employment (in other words, shamateurism). It worked. Schooley spent money lavishly, mining the elite Toronto-area OHA clubs to bring to Pittsburgh stars such as Lionel Conacher, Roy Worters, Harold Darragh, Hib Milks, and Hal (Baldy) Cotton. By 1923 he was icing both the Yellow Jackets and the Hornets, each competing in one of the USAHA's two divisions. In Duggan's analysis, through the USAHA Schooley and George Brown controlled amateur hockey in the United States "on a big scale."[14]

Just like the Boston Arena, the Duquesne Garden was doing well with the USAHA, and the arrival of the professional game was a threat to its lucrative business. Schooley and Brown engaged allies to ward off the NHL incursion, including prominent politicians, publishers, and other sportsmen. It soon emerged that the group was taking advice from none other than Eddie Livingstone and Percy Quinn. Duggan found out the group was telling Tex Rickard to avoid the NHL and have nothing to do with Duggan, as no one in Boston would do business with him. Duggan got Adams to accompany him to New York to repudiate the antiprofessional message. At the Garden, Adams conveyed the results of his own Montreal investigation and told Rickard and Hammond he was "firmly convinced that the only League that they should play with was the National Hockey League, because they were giving the brand of sport that the public was paying to see." Duggan felt so indebted to Adams for his intervention that he impetuously offered him the Boston franchise at cost, on the condition that the arrangement with Rickard came through.[15]

Back in Boston, however, the arena directors had now hardened their resolve against professional hockey. As a short-term solution, Adams asked that Duggan allow him to operate the franchise in Brooklyn instead. Duggan said he would try to convince the league, but with the June 1923 deadline on his options fast approaching, he first had to work with Dandurand to get the options extended to 30 September. Duggan continued to lobby the arena directors to change their decision and at the same time solicited architectural drawings for a new Brooklyn rink. It was no coincidence that the designer he chose, George Funk, was the architect of the arena and also a director. His persistence and Adams's influence finally paid off. In the summer of 1923, the Boston Arena directors once again agreed in principle to a contract for ice. Without a New York ice plant, however, the earliest the teams could play would be 1924–25, and so Duggan would need the indulgence of the NHL governors on yet another extension.[16]

Choosing Alternatives

As Duggan pursued the bright prospects of American expansion on their behalf, the league governors dealt with the dimmer future of the Ottawa Senators. The club performed well on the ice and had finished in first place the last two seasons, but it was starving for resources, even petty ones: in January there were complaints about the poor condition of Ottawa's goal nets, and the club was instructed to buy new ones. In May the team's triumph over Edmonton in the Stanley Cup series was dampened by its dire financial situation. Pessimistic about the club's future, manager Tommy Gorman agreed to let the Canadiens sign his star, George Boucher, if Ottawa proved unable to operate in the upcoming 1923–24 season.[17]

It would be bad if Ottawa elected to suspend operations, but what the other governors feared even more was the older threat, defection. Once again, rumors of another "outlaw league" were afoot, suggesting the involvement of American interests, perhaps Livingstone and maybe even Duggan. The NHL owners needed to present a common front, and Ottawa, as the reigning NHL and Stanley Cup champion, had to be bound tightly to the rest. After a lengthy discussion at the May meeting, the league governors proposed to reaffirm their 26 November 1921 league agreement by adding an addendum that they would "not in any way ally ourselves with any rival organization or take any steps detrimental to the National Hockey League under penalty of expulsion." Gorman, ominously, refused to sign. Until Ottawa was on its feet financially, all allegiances were apparently up for reconsideration.[18]

Ottawa's problems were rooted in the small capacity and lack of artificial ice at Dey's Arena, which was owned by Ted Dey, also the club's controlling shareholder. Another group was erecting a new Ottawa Auditorium with artificial ice and seating for six thousand plus standing room, but Dey was understandably reluctant to let go of his club and major tenant. For obvious reasons, the other NHL owners wanted the club in the new, bigger rink. And given the Livingstone and Quinn precedents and the constant threat of external competition, there would be limits on how much Dey's rights could take precedence over the common good. When the summer of 1923 passed with no hint of a move, in September more pressure was applied. The governors warmly received a franchise application from the Ottawa Hockey Association, the former owners of the Senators, now under control of Frank Ahearn, the main backer of the new auditorium. When the governors tabled the application for further consideration, Dey got the message that his options were now constrained. He could move his club to the auditorium, sell it to the Ottawa Hockey Association, or take the risk of being frozen out entirely. Dey sold his majority of shares to Ahearn, with Gorman remaining a minority owner. At the next league meeting, Gorman moved that Calder prepare a new five-year agreement to be presented for signature at the annual meeting in November. This time Gorman signed.[19]

Tom Duggan left the September 1923 NHL meetings with another option extension from Calder, his second that year. Realizing his plans for a new rink in Brooklyn were overly ambitious, Duggan focused on putting clubs in the Boston Arena and Madison Square Garden for the 1924–25 season. In December he traveled to New York, ostensibly to look for a suitable rink. Taking a page from the Rickard book, Duggan garnered significant press coverage for his trip, declaring his ambition to encourage schoolboy, college, and amateur club hockey in the city as well. Rickard was still interested, and they discussed again a retrofit of the Garden for the 1924–25 season. By February Rickard's own promotional machine was getting into gear with the message that professional hockey was coming to New York in the fall. Frank Flournoy of his staff wrote to Duggan that the New York press was buzzing: "All of our local papers picked up the hockey story and carried it pretty big. Some of them put a two column head on it and some of them are still carrying it today." Duggan used the publicity to maintain pressure on the Boston Arena. He told the *Christian Science Monitor* that it was Boston engineers making the floor of Madison Square Garden into a two hundred–by–eighty-foot rink and that all that was needed was George Brown's signature to include Boston in the new professional league. In addition to the existing formation of Ottawa, Toronto, Hamilton, and Montreal, Duggan speculated two more might be forthcoming in Chicago, Cleveland, Detroit, or Pittsburgh.[20]

The *Monitor* report suggests Duggan's ambitions were growing, and with the mention of new American cities, it was not always clear that "the new international professional league" Duggan was speaking of was necessarily even the NHL. (Sportswriters often referred to it as the "International Hockey League.") Suspicions that there were other formations possible were heightened when Charles Adams arrived at the NHL meeting in February 1924 with a companion, and Adams asked if some arrangement could be made to include his new friend in the circuit. Calder proposed that the visitor be admitted, and Eddie Livingstone stepped into the room. The governors' reactions can only be imagined, but the minutes note simply that a lengthy discussion ensued. It was pleasant enough that

Livingstone was invited to come back with a more definite proposal the next month. Then the governors moved to the next item on the agenda, Tom Duggan's report, which evidently indicated enough progress to confirm the governors' trust. They voted to extend his options yet again, to September 1924.[21]

Duggan needed the time. Back in Boston, to Charles Adams's frustration, the Boston Arena directors were continuing to vacillate. The arena required a new balcony, and the directors were deferring their final decision on the NHL franchise until the estimates were in. It was a delaying tactic: Duggan's ally George Funk wrote in February that all the directors were now lining up against Adams's professional hockey proposal in principle, feeling that the amateurs were doing well enough and that when they wanted professional hockey, they would do it without the NHL. Furthermore, Funk warned that "Schooley, Haddock and Brown" would fight NHL-brand hockey and intended to persuade Rickard in New York to get into professional hockey through them instead. Funk recommended that Duggan use direct action and civic rivalry to his advantage:

> With all these things in view, it seems that the strongest thing that you can do to help your own personal cause is to get tied with Rickard just as tight and as soon as you can. I look upon the New York proposition as the keynote [sic] of this whole thing. For instance, if professional hockey starts in New York and is given to the public in New York, it will force the Boston crowd to get in it all the quicker, as they cannot continue to dish out amateur hockey in Boston when the public is getting professional hockey in New York. Furthermore, Rickard is a logical man in New York and if you are tied up with him, this amateur bunch will be licked. Do not expect Mr. Adams to accomplish too much at the Arena because he has a great deal of opposition, and anything that you do in New York will only be of great assistance to him in bringing it about in Boston.

If New York was the keystone to professional hockey success, then Duggan had to make sure the NHL was Rickard's preferred brand.[22]

Soon Duggan received a letter from Hammond, inviting him to a meeting on 14 March, the purpose of which was "to discuss the establishment of a great hockey league and to determine the advisability of making the league continental, to include Canada, or solely American with international finals with your great Canadian teams." Hammond told Duggan his advice would be greatly valued and lured him to the meeting with the promise of "further data relative to the cost of installation of a rink at the Madison Square Garden, operating expenses, [and] methods employed in obtaining franchises and the purchase of players." It seemed likely that Duggan would be involved in bringing hockey to New York, but Hammond's ambiguous letter suggested the NHL might not be.[23]

Before the meeting, Schooley and Livingstone and their group had the chance to make their pitch to Rickard, but he seems to have decided rather quickly on an NHL affiliation. The NHL was, after all, a proven professional product. He announced afterward that a conference would be held the next week in Montreal, "after an important hockey match," to perfect arrangements for hockey in the Garden, as part of a league to include New York, Boston, and Pittsburgh, in addition to the existing NHL cities. Rickard was now even "more enthusiastic over the plan . . . than when [it] was first broached to him several months ago," and he proposed that the season culminate in a "world's series" in New York. He also envisioned a restoration of the glory days of the old St. Nicholas Rink, with college, amateur, and schoolboy games played alongside professional contests in the Garden, fitted between the Garden's boxing bouts and other events. It all could start as soon as November, since plans for the ice plant were nearly complete.[24]

The Montreal conference took place on 18 March. The "important hockey match" was the opening game of the Stanley Cup series between the Vancouver Maroons and the hometown Canadiens, who featured one of the rising stars of the game, Howie Morenz. Adams attended, and Hammond came on behalf of the Garden after Rickard was summoned to appear before a US Senate committee. (Rickard was being investigated as part of a larger inquiry into the Justice Department and its attorney general, Harry Daugherty, who were suspected of taking kickbacks, bootlegging, and, in association with Rickard, illegally distributing the Dempsey-Carpentier fight film. Rickard was indicted two months later.) In Rickard's absence, nothing definite could be decided, but the Americans had the opportunity to meet with Calder, the NHL owners, and also Lester and Frank Patrick of the PCHA, and it was understood that a six-club international NHL was definitely in the works.[25]

One week later the Canadiens were Stanley Cup champions, and the NHL governors were flush with optimism about the American venture, and also with cash—the playoffs had produced a surplus of two thousand dollars for each club. The governors discussed the prospects of more American clubs in addition to the ones in New York and Boston. As might have been expected, Eddie Livingstone did not appear with any new proposal. Adams later revealed to Duggan that he and Livingstone were no longer partners and that he suspected Livingstone was behind a recent franchise application from the Toronto Granite Club, which the St. Patrick's had vetoed: "Undoubtedly if such is the case, Mr. Livingston [sic] was behind the scenes, and after having been defeated in his recent American plans is coming around to the situation that was so generously offered him at the meeting of the league which I attended. I feel that his interests, if in any way they are not for the best interest of all of the league members, should not be considered further." Livingstone clearly expected no consideration; true to form, in April he announced the formation of another international hockey league, likely in concert with Schooley and his associates.[26]

The March 1924 meetings in Montreal were a turning point that ensured NHL expansion would happen. Afterward, Adams fully committed to the NHL and set out to solidify the relationship. He wrote to Calder that he was satisfied any prospect of a Livingstone league had "been sidetracked by the eastern rink interests and that they are all agreed that the league to support and play the game with is your organization." Writing to Duggan asking for an update on the New York negotiations, Adams reported that he had been approached by two different interests wanting to buy his franchise. He had refused, but it was clear the winds were changing in Boston, and the NHL was finally getting the fair breeze. Adams suspected the sudden interest in the professional game was amplified by a scandal that had just blown up over the USAHA playoffs the previous weekend. Schooley's Pittsburgh team had allegedly thrown a game against the arena's BAA club so that the playoff series would return to their home ice and swell the Duquesne Garden gate receipts. Adams noted that the

newspapermen "have been very open in their criticism of the way amateur hockey is conducted from the Pittsburgh headquarters. This lends
strength to all the arguments that I have used and undoubtedly is a point
in our favor." Adams wrote to Calder that the Pittsburgh amateur scandal was a "black eye" for amateur hockey and that people were coming to
recognize that professional hockey was "on the level." Flattering Calder,
he wrote that it was contributing to "a wonderful reputation that your
league is enjoying and I have no doubt that your attitude in these matters
has material bearing on the conduct of hockey in the league." Adams also
revealed that the Patrick brothers had come to Boston the year before and
warned that "it would be for our best interests to keep out of professional
hockey." He speculated that the only possible reason for this statement was
that they "did not exactly relish the idea of the National Hockey League
further strengthening [the NHL's] already strong position in the East."[27]

The attempts to discredit professional hockey had failed, and instead
amateur hypocrisy had been revealed. The effects were immediate. Since
the scandal had broken, Adams had conversed with the president of the
Boston Arena and now felt "absolutely sure that after this season [1924–
25], you will find us in pro hockey." Adams explained to Calder that the
Boston Arena now had "nothing but friendliness toward the professional
hockey situation," but that since the arena had earned more than three
hundred thousand dollars for amateur hockey in the season just ending,
the directors hoped to have one more like it to bring it out of debt, at which
point they would change their policy to allow professional hockey. The
scandal had clearly made the arena directors more amenable, as had the
prospect of USAHA rivals the Pittsburgh Yellow Jackets joining the NHL,
in addition to endemic rumors about the construction of a new and larger
Boston rink to house the NHL club. Whatever happened, Adams assured
Calder, "you will find my personal interest and the Boston franchise cooperating with the desires of your present franchise owners."[28]

Professional Ascendance

The about-face in Boston showed that the NHL's brand of professional
hockey had at least two virtues. One was the simple promotional advantage of being able to bring the best players to Boston on a regular basis.

The other was an ethical superiority when compared to the hypocrisy of American elite amateur hockey. The Pittsburgh playoff scandal had laid bare the difficulty in applying the amateur ethos to profit-making clubs: a club that subscribed to the moral authority of amateurism to prevent the incursion of commerce had now fixed a game for commercial advantage. The BAA actually fired its whole team after the Pittsburgh incident, but the bad press worsened when one of their players sued the club for non-payment of salary, claiming players were being paid between five hundred and twenty-two hundred dollars for the season. Club representatives and George Brown issued denials, but were ridiculed in a nationally syndicated column. W. O. McGeehan wrote sarcastically that, in Boston, an amateur was defined as "an athlete who does not sue when he is not paid off."[29]

The irony was that it was the fully commercialized professional game that was more, as Adams put it, "on the level." In the aftermath of the Black Sox scandal in 1919, in which baseball players took bribes to throw the World Series, it was hard for professional sports to make any claims to moral purity, but the professional hockey clubs did take the perception of the integrity of their game very seriously. (In the past they had sued those individuals who had suggested that games were being fixed.) Yes, professional players were paid, but it was an aboveboard commercial transaction, in contrast to those players who finagled jobs off the ice and followed perhaps the law but certainly not the spirit of amateurism. It certainly looked suspicious when Leo Dandurand tried to lure Lionel Conacher to the Canadiens from the amateur Yellow Jackets with an offer of more than five thousand dollars per season and Conacher chose to stay put in Pittsburgh.[30]

Schooley did not capitulate, but floated the idea for a new semiprofessional league to include Pittsburgh, Cleveland, New Haven (Connecticut), and Boston. It seemed to have a chance when Duggan announced in April that the Boston Arena was trying to hold off NHL hockey for one more season in an attempt to wring out another year of amateur revenues. Schooley went to New York to convince Hammond that, instead of forming a Garden amateur league, he should place a team in Schooley's proposed semiprofessional league. This gambit died soon after when the Boston Arena directors refused to participate, and Adams predicted Schooley would soon be replaced as USAHA president.[31]

Writing to Calder, Adams pointed out that the main practical deficiency of Schooley's semiprofessional proposal was that amateur players would not "consider the lengthy absences from business that such a circuit would make necessary." He also expressed his doubts about the suitability of the Boston Arena: the total seating was only thirty-eight hundred for hockey, and the cost of balconies, which would add only eleven hundred more seats, was prohibitive. The interest in hockey had prompted plans for a new Boston rink—one proposal was for an exposition building seating fifteen thousand—but without this option, "under these conditions, the best possible plan would be to operate professional teams in New York City or Brooklyn the coming season." Adams requested Calder's assurance that if the Boston Arena refused ice and the Boston franchise had to be placed in New York or Brooklyn the coming season, there would be no objection to transferring it back the following season. He evidently got it, and later that month Hammond wired Duggan that he had met with Adams and they had agreed the franchise would be placed in Brooklyn for 1924–25, with terms to be arranged.[32]

The American promotion of professional hockey was now in full swing, but not necessarily under NHL control. New franchises—real and potential—were being bandied about without any consultation with the existing club owners. Trying to sort it out, Calder asked for clarification of the relationship between Adams and Duggan and between the Boston, Brooklyn, and New York franchises. Adams informed him that he would be buying the Boston franchise at Duggan's cost, but that the franchise was to be used in New York this year and Boston the next. He suggested that Boston and New York should even get two teams each to reduce travel costs and fit the schedule better, but realized that some NHL owners might be getting cold feet. Leo Dandurand had been in New York and was said to have changed his mind, being now "not absolutely in favor of the international idea." But what Dandurand and the other owners did recognize was that hockey fever was spreading across the US Northeast and the threat of a rival league was always an unwelcome possibility if the NHL did not press its first-mover advantage and stymie those individuals with the capacity to create one.[33]

In the meantime, New York became the focus of attention. In June 1924 the Garden's landlord, New York Life, presented an expected eviction notice to Rickard, to be effective the next summer on 1 August 1925. Rickard was prepared and announced that a new Garden would be built on Eighth Avenue between Forty-Ninth and Fiftieth Streets, just off Broadway and north of Times Square and the theater district. There he planned a stadium seating twenty-five thousand—almost double the capacity of the old Garden—with the facilities to host skating, hockey, boxing, horse shows, six-day bicycle races, circuses, automobile shows, and industrial exhibitions. With typical forward-looking optimism, he let it be known that already the New Madison Square Garden Corporation had "purchased the New York and Brooklyn franchises in the National Hockey League for international contests" and also two New York franchises in the USAHA. His plan was to promote hockey in the old Garden through special events in the winter of 1924–25 and then move the ice-making equipment over to the new Garden for the next season.[34]

Although it was supposed to be secret, Rickard also let it be known that his ambition was to establish "a string of sport and amusement arenas in several of the largest cities of the country." Perhaps inspired to this possibility by the emergence of chains of movie theaters in this era, which themselves had followed the pattern of department stores and grocery store chains, Rickard went looking for locations. Just the month before, he had announced his intention to purchase the Philadelphia Arena, capacity seventy-two hundred, for hockey. And on 5 July, when Duggan officially applied to Calder to transfer his franchise options to the Brooklyn Hockey Club and the New York Hockey Club, he also made an application for an additional franchise on behalf of the Philadelphia Arena. Despite his claims that he would be the owner "after several minor details have been adjusted," in the end Rickard did not succeed in acquiring the Philadelphia Arena, but his idea for a chain of arenas stocked with NHL hockey clubs was now publicly known. The question remained: should Rickard's ambitions be taken seriously?[35]

At the July NHL meeting, Duggan's Philadelphia application was tabled, as was one from the Ravina Rink in Toronto, and most of the time was devoted to sorting out the situation in New York. Options on franchises were changing hands and promises were being made, but no clubs were being formed or players acquired, and the 1924–25 season was only months away. The governors sent Calder to visit Rickard and Hammond in New York, where it transpired that there might not be any club taking to the ice in New York in the fall. Lack of ice was the main problem, and time was getting short on the decision to renovate the Garden's floor to accommodate the necessary brine pipes. For obvious reasons, Duggan was getting cold feet about renovating the old Garden for only one season. In August he told Funk that, to justify the investment, he needed a bond of two hundred thousand dollars from the old Garden to guarantee that he would also have a place in the new Garden the season afterward. The Garden refused to post the bond and proposed waiting until the next year to outfit the new building. It was not a good sign. In late August, still with no clubs in the making, the NHL club owners started to get apprehensive and asked Adams what he intended to do. When the issue came to the table at a 31 August special meeting, Calder was instructed to carry out the agreement with Duggan "as it stands," implying that the options would either have to be paid for as agreed or would be allowed to expire. There would be no more extensions.[36]

Then Duggan had a stroke of luck: Boston suddenly reappeared as a possibility for the fall. On 29 August George Funk wired Duggan that he believed "pro hockey can be put over in Boston if handled right" and invited him to Boston after Labor Day, warning him "not [to] let anyone know" he was coming to town. Duggan and Funk met with an unnamed director of the Boston Arena who said he would take up the matter with the others. Five days later Duggan had his contract for ice, along with an agreement with Adams to operate the Boston franchise for the first season on a fifty-fifty profit-sharing basis. He informed Calder that New York would have to wait for the new Garden to be ready in the fall of 1925, but Boston could begin play that very season and requested that the league authorize the transfer of the Boston franchise to the Boston

Hockey Club and the New York franchise to the New York Hockey Club, Inc., subject to both assuming responsibility for the balance due on the franchise fees. Then he went to Boston to finalize arrangements, taking along NHL referee and former star and Hamilton Tigers coach Art Ross as the first manager of the new club, to be known as the "Bruins."[37]

The NHL governors approved the franchise transfers but refused Duggan's request to defer payment. Patience exhausted, they insisted that Duggan pay six thousand dollars by 1 November, three weeks' time. Adams paid for Boston, Duggan borrowed money to pay for New York, and Calder transferred the franchises. After almost two years of negotiation, the National Hockey League was going international.[38]

Expansion Achieved

There was still the problem of schedule balance. American expansion had been contingent on two clubs starting play in order to justify the trip south, and without the New York entry, another was needed. Ironically, the expansion project that Duggan had led after being thwarted in bringing a new English Montreal club to the Mount Royal Arena wound up encouraging the granting of just such a franchise—but not to Duggan. And to add further insult, the club would be housed in a new building in direct competition with his own.

Over previous seasons the NHL governors had received several applications for new franchises, mainly in Toronto and Montreal, but for various reasons had refused them all. The governors seemed comfortable with a single club in Toronto (implicitly confirming Livingstone's judgment), and further Toronto applications were consistently vetoed by the St. Patrick's under a principle of territorial exclusivity that seems to have become part of an NHL club's franchise rights about this time. In Montreal there seemed to be more general support for the resuscitation of a franchise to claim the allegiance of the English community, albeit not one owned by Duggan. Since the incineration of the Westmount Arena in 1918, Montreal had been left wanting a west-end rink, and without it hockey had moved east from its Westmount Anglophone roots and ended up at Canadiens games in Duggan's smallish Mount Royal Arena. In doing so, the audience had also drifted down the social hierarchy and was now nurtured by men who promoted hockey alongside boxing and wrestling to the working-class Montreal audience.[39]

With hockey becoming mass entertainment, it would never return to the exclusive domain of well-to-do English Montreal, but an entrepreneur came on the scene who could bridge both English and French cultural differences and capital markets. By virtue of his birth into a prominent French Canadian family from Quebec's Beauharnois district, and his marriage to the daughter of Henry Timmins, the wealthy owner of northern Ontario gold and silver mines, Donat Raymond was a rare breed—a French Canadian with access to English Canadian capital. The Timminses had a long hockey history—Henry had been a member of Montreal HC, and his brother Noah had backed Haileybury in the NHA—and Raymond himself loved horse racing and had owned the winner of the 1914 King's Plate thoroughbred race. His business expertise was in hotel management, and with his brother he had bought Montreal's Queen's Hotel and, in 1922, the Windsor Hotel, the city's most prestigious. Over the next decade, he became a respectable figure in the financial and industrial company boardrooms and used to political advantage as a fund-raiser for the Liberal Party, which resulted in a Senate appointment in 1926.[40]

Around the time of the Windsor purchase, Raymond also began discussing a new west-end rink project with William Northey, the former manager of the Westmount Arena. Using a refrain familiar to North American urban audiences, the promoters sold investors on the civic virtues of the project in addition to its economic prospects and enlisted notables like Sir Edward Beatty of the Canadian Pacific Railway to write letters of solicitation appealing to community spirit. By the summer of 1924, $406,000 had been raised, and alongside Raymond, Northey, and Henry Timmins, the new Canadian Arena Company (CAC) listed as shareholders many of the prominent names in Montreal business and finance, including Kenneth Dawes, E. R. Decary, Sir Charles Gordon, H. B. MacDougall, A. D. MacTier, Herbert Molson, C. E. Neill, J. K. L. Ross, R. J. Magor, Thomas Arnold, J. W. McConnell, Gordon Cushing, and Sir Herbert Holt (one of the richest men in Canada). The site chosen for the new building, to be known as the "Forum," was an entire city block on the west side of downtown, bordered by Ste. Catherine, Atwater, St. Luke (later Maisonneuve), and Lambert-Closse. The size permitted seating for more than eight thousand and up to ten thousand with standing room. It went up swiftly, in 159 days, and was ready for the fall of 1924 and the beginning of the NHL season. But who would play there? The Canadiens were obviously interested, despite a new six-year lease with Duggan's Mount Royal Arena, but the owners of the Forum almost certainly expected to house a new English Montreal club of their own. Projects the size of the Forum were not done purely on speculation, and with the extensive connections of the investors, the promise of an NHL club had surely been part of the deal.[41]

Sure enough, in August the CAC applied for a new Montreal club. To perpetuate the perception of an arm's-length relationship with the rink as well as accentuate the English nature of the club, the new club's president was Wanderers club founder James Strachan. At the NHL meeting in October 1924, Tommy Gorman of Ottawa moved that the CAC franchise application be approved for a fee of $15,000. The *Gazette* noted with surprise that Dandurand had seconded the motion, but his reasons were simple: first, the Canadiens co-owner saw the promotional benefit of a new crosstown English rival, and, second, a deal was struck for his Canadiens to receive $10,000 of the franchise fee "as recompense for the splitting of their exclusive territory." Percy Thompson of Hamilton and Gorman voted against the split, but Calder cast the deciding vote to give the Canadiens the money. At the annual meeting that followed, the Montreal Professional Hockey Club, Ltd., along with the Boston Professional Hockey Association, Inc., were formally admitted to the league. James Strachan was elected governor for Montreal and Art Ross for Boston.[42]

Before the 1924–25 season, the clubs also fortified the league by locking in Calder with a five-year contract and themselves signing a new ten-year league agreement to prevent defection or the formation of competitor circuits. Since five-year agreements had already been signed in 1918, 1921, and 1923, the league agreements were having a hard time keeping up with the growth. There was more to come. Even before a New York team hit the ice, Rickard was so convinced of the commercial promise of hockey that he sent Hammond to the November NHL annual meeting with Duggan, Garden lawyer Eugene L. Garey, Frank Carroll of Pittsburgh, and three franchise applications in his hand: a second team for the Garden in New

York, another for Philadelphia, and a third for Duquesne Garden in Pittsburgh. The latter was supported by Henry Townsend, a former mayor of Pittsburgh and now the superintendent of public properties, and James Callahan, a local lawyer. There was a lengthy discussion that should have made it obvious that Rickard was behind at least two of the applications, but the governors seemed to accept it and granted them at $15,000 each, requesting only that the applications be made separately.[43]

Pittsburgh and Philadelphia had been recommended before, but the New York franchise seemed a surprise—it was not Duggan's franchise but an additional one for the Garden—and Duggan had not only declined his right to veto it but supported it. The genesis of this odd situation was in the peculiar arrangement that finally dictated the arrival of professional hockey in New York.

Changing Clubs

Duggan and Rickard had come to a formal agreement on bringing an NHL franchise to the Garden for 1925–26, but the terms were one-sided and highlighted Duggan's desperation to get into the Garden. As the owner of the NHL franchise for New York, Duggan was to organize and capitalize a corporation called the New York American Hockey Club, Inc., to which the Garden agreed to rent its rink for fifteen to twenty-seven nights each year and provide up to four hours of practice per week without charge. The "Americans" agreed to pay $500 per game night to cover all rink expenses other than heat, lights, and ice, including the cost of ushers, ticket sellers and takers, rink attendants, police protection, and equipment. Duggan also agreed to pay for half of the cost of the new Garden refrigeration system, the total cost estimated at $80,000. That was all before the actual lease fee, which was set at half of the gross gate. Furthermore, half of the net profits of any event held outside the Garden (that is, presumably from any away games, including playoffs) were to go to the Garden, which was guaranteed at least $50,000 per year out of the agreement.[44]

The claim on revenues outside the Garden was unusual in itself, not to mention the requirement to put out for the ice-making equipment, but that was not all. Duggan also agreed "to use his best efforts, energy and influence in effecting the acquisition" by Madison Square Garden of its own NHL franchise. In other words, Duggan waived his territorial right to veto a Garden franchise and was obliged to help his landlord obtain one of its own. And until the Garden's own franchise became reality, Rickard would have a special role to play with the Americans, not just as primary promoter but also as ostensible owner. The agreement stipulated that "the public relations . . . may at all times be subordinated [to Rickard] and the relations of Tex Rickard shall at all times and in all public advertising, announcements, press items and the like be featured . . . it being deemed and declared desirable by the parties . . . that the HOCKEY CLUB may appear to be American-owned and under the personal direction of Tex Rickard." Rickard was fully aware that he was a brand that could sell a product, and in all likelihood he named the club himself in order to maximize the patriotic dimension of the marketing message. Indeed, the Americans' contract indicates Rickard's vision was national in scope and extended well beyond New York. While the Garden agreed not to become interested in any non-NHL club, it reserved "the full right to be interested financially or otherwise in any other manner in any or all of the clubs or franchises of the National Hockey League." Congruent with Rickard's dream of a string of Gardens, the ownership of several NHL clubs to play in them was being reserved as a viable future option.[45]

Duggan finally had his own NHL franchise, but until he paid for the Garden's ice plant, it was in name only. The terms going forward were certainly unfavorable and would be a sore point for years to come for him and any future partners. If Duggan had any doubts, he did not show them and instead distracted himself with preparations. He hosted Rickard, Hammond, and others at a game at the Mount Royal Arena on 18 February, and they pored over plans for the new Garden, which promised to be impressive. Madison Square Garden III was to be designed by leading theater architect Thomas Lamb, and though smaller than Rickard's early estimates, the new arena was still huge, with 16,138 permanent seats and 6,000 movable. It would be the biggest rink in the biggest city in North America, and it was coming with NHL hockey as a main attraction. The financing was equally impressive: $2.5 million in mortgage bonds and 256,054 common shares, a portion to be distributed to existing Garden shareholders, whom Rickard called his "six hundred millionaires." As usual, this statement was hyperbole. Headed by Richard S. Hoyt of Hayden, Stone & Company, a New York investment house, it was mainly him and five others—George Herbert Walker, Edward S. Moore, Matthew C. Brush, R. Roland Harriman, and W. Averill Harriman—who provided the bulk of the money and controlled the Garden through a voting trust. Rickard raised the balance by selling memberships in the Madison Square Garden Club for $1,000 each (these were his "millionaires").[46]

The Boston deal was a sweetheart by comparison. The Boston Arena Company would provide ice for games, preferably on Mondays, plus one hour per day for practice. Unlike in New York, the rink would pay for the ticket sellers and takers, a band, and attendants, as well as provide dressing rooms for the club, the officials, and its visitors. It would also provide a press agent, although Duggan and the club were to pay his $25 weekly salary. The arena also paid for the insertion of extra seats. (This move reduced the ice surface by approximately 23 percent, from 220 by 90 feet to 190 by 80 feet.) As rent the rink would accept a graduated scale, receiving $1,000 per night if annual gross receipts were under $70,000, plus half of any receipts from $70,000 to $100,000, and 30 percent if revenues were more than $100,000. Compared to the New York deal, it was a much more generous contract for the hockey club and no doubt owed its fairness to Adams's seat on the arena board.[47]

Less satisfying were Duggan's negotiations with Adams over the ownership of the Boston franchise itself. In his haste to satisfy league deadlines, Duggan had transferred the franchise to Adams without a firm agreement in hand. When it came time to negotiate a price, Adams seems to have become more and more pessimistic about the profit-making potential of the club and reduced his offers incrementally. After months of haggling that deteriorated their relationship, Duggan took the matter to court. In the absence of a written agreement, the judge sustained the original one-year fifty-fifty profit-sharing understanding, and when Adams claimed the club had lost money on the season, Duggan got nothing.[48]

In the meantime, the Bruins were busy selling professional hockey to Bostonians. Art Ross, the former star player, coach, referee, and now manager, became the evangelist, aided by two fictional French Canadian characters, Joe LaPorte and Jules Levesque. Ross "spread the gospel of professional hockey throughout eastern Massachusetts," dining out on LaPorte and Levesque "habitant" stories designed to appeal both to English-speaking New Englanders and to the descendants of French Canadians who had immigrated to the textile towns of Massachusetts in the late nineteenth and early twentieth centuries.[49]

Aside from its ethnic flair, just as in Hamilton the professional game had to be distinguished from the familiar amateur game. With the Bruins lacking stars, the club's publicity focused attention on visiting players like Howie Morenz and Aurèle Joliat of the Canadiens. As did their Hamilton peers, Boston sportswriters noted the superior skills of the professional players, the different rules of play, and the greater physicality. They saw that the professionals were faster and more efficient skaters (attributed to the fact that they were "earning their living at the game") and that forward passing, which was limited in amateur hockey, sped up the game considerably. The first Bruins game against Montreal on 1 December 1924 was fast and rough, with "the most rugged body checking that Boston fans ever have seen." Opening night featured none of the marching bands or associated spectacles that Rickard would introduce a year later, but the game did feature one innovation. While attendance in the arena was sparse, the audience was potentially much greater since Adams had arranged to have all the Bruins' home games broadcast in their entirety over radio station WBZ (Springfield and Boston), with play-by-play by Frank Ryan of the *Boston Traveler*. In the short term, since the crowds inside the arena failed to meet expectations, almost immediately Adams announced a reduction in ticket prices ranging from 16 percent to 30 percent, bringing them down to $2.75 for a reserved seat and $1.10 for standing room. The *Boston Globe* noted that fans still had to be "cultivated" to the prices, which were higher than they had paid for amateur hockey.[50]

The shortage of marketable stars illustrated that the availability of players for the new clubs had been a legitimate concern about expansion and had been foreshadowed by the troubles stocking the Hamilton Tigers. Announcing the new Montreal franchise in October 1924, Frank Calder admitted the club owners "were reticent regarding possible player shifts," but the Montreal club at any rate seemed to have little difficulty getting players. Although the club was unable to acquire the Wanderers name for the club (Lichtenhein apparently wanted $5,000 for the rights) and became known simply as the "Maroons" after the color of their uniforms, it was one of the few assets the club did not succeed in buying. Senators stars Clint Benedict and Harry Broadbent, as well as St. Patrick's veteran Reg Noble, became Maroons, and the club also had success turning amateurs. Burly defenseman Dunc Munro, star and captain of the amateur Toronto Granites who won the 1924 Olympic gold medal, was signed for a salary that made him one of the best-paid players in the league in his rookie year and included the franchise for game programs at the Forum, which brought his estimated annual income to $20,000. Through Munro, the Maroons tried to entice the top scorer of the Olympic team, Harry Watson, to join the club, but Watson was one of those players who still refused to forfeit amateur status, even when in his case the contract was rumored to total an unheard-of $30,000. Adherence to principle became rarer, as salaries and signing bonuses more easily overcame amateur reluctance to jump to the professional game.[51]

In Boston it was another story. The Bruins got players, but they were not very good, and unlike Canadian cities they could not draw upon any high-quality local talent. It immediately began to tell on the ice. By the end of December, the club had suffered eleven straight losses, and a special league meeting was called to discuss assistance. The other clubs offered some help, but even with the acquisition of Ottawa star defenseman Lionel Hitchman, Boston finished the season with only six wins out of thirty games.[52]

Even established clubs felt the pressure. Competition for players was growing and demanding new capital requirements from the owners of the existing clubs, and it soon became apparent some were unable or unwilling to keep in the game. The St. Patrick's owners were the first to bail out. At the December 1924 special meeting, the governors approved the transfer of Percy and Fred Hambly's shares to the deep pockets of gold mining magnate J. P. (Jack) Bickell, the president of McIntyre-Porcupine Mines, the centerpiece of the northern Ontario gold rush, and movie theater impresario Nathan L. Nathanson, the managing director of Famous Players, a Canadian theater chain and distributor of Paramount films. These two men had been convinced of the moneymaking opportunities of hockey by Charlie Querrie, who survived the change of ownership and retained his St. Patrick's shares and his job as manager. Nathanson proved a quick study on the challenges of operating an NHL club and with Hamilton's support requested a special meeting in January to propose a salary limit as a solution to the increasing competition for players.[53]

Like the St. Patrick's, the Senators were undergoing an ownership transition—for the third time since the league had formed. The Frank Ahearn and Tommy Gorman partnership had soured, and the pair were disagreeing over an offer from Gorman to buy out Ahearn's interest. The governors gave Calder the power to take any action to bring about a resolution, and he pressured the Ottawa men to come to a resolution. It was agreed that Gorman was to get $20,000 in cash, half of the 1924–25 season's profits, his remaining salary, and half of Ottawa's split from the NHL capital account, including the Boston and Montreal franchise fees. With the sale, Ottawa came under control of a single owner for the first time. Gorman took his money south and two days later signed on to manage the Americans in their inaugural season.[54]

The Canadiens were also considering jumping to a greener—or, rather, colder—pasture. During the successful Stanley Cup campaign in 1923–24, the mild weather caused postponement of games at the natural-ice Mount Royal Arena. As a result, the club only broke even. In spite of the lease with the Mount Royal and Dandurand's personal relationship with Duggan, the club was sorely tempted by the artificial ice and big capacity of the new Forum. To forestall the move, Duggan agreed to install an artificial ice plant, but when it was not ready for the opening of the 1924–25 season, William Northey paid him $1,000 to let the Canadiens play their opening game at the Forum. After that contest, the club returned to the Mount Royal, which it filled for the rest of the 1924–25 season. The lack of extra capacity cost the club unrealized profits, and Duggan promised plans for a complete reconstruction that would raise capacity to twelve thousand, making it larger than the Forum. In return Dandurand agreed to play in the new arena for fifteen years and commit to buying some bonds to finance the construction. In a plea to outside investors, Duggan made an ethnic appeal, soliciting the support of the French Canadian investment community in particular "to subscribe generously to these debentures in order to permit our race to conserve its identity in professional hockey, where we have figured prominently for several years." The new arena was to cost $650,000 and begin construction in the spring of 1926, but despite the appeal to ethnic pride, it never got off the ground. In October 1926 the Canadiens offered a cash payment to break the lease and move to the Forum. When the Mount Royal management refused the compensation, the Canadiens left anyway and the arena sued. For the Canadiens, it was a small price to pay. In the 1926–27 season, they soared to the top in league attendance, with the other Forum tenant, the Maroons, a close second.[55]

Change was coming in Hamilton as well. After several seasons at or near the bottom of the league, by the 1923–24 season professional hockey was resonating with the crowds through the Tigers' superior on-ice play. There were still persistent problems—the fans still needed to be educated about the professional rules, and Percy Thompson spoke about the need to convince more amateurs to turn professional—but at least the player-quality problems had been overcome. Helped by the arrival of the Montreal and Boston expansion clubs, the Tigers were soon out of the basement in the standings and in first place for the first time. Evidently, Hamilton was maturing as a professional hockey market, and the spinning turnstiles were already prompting talk of a new arena or, at the very least, a renovation to increase seating, similar to the one recently done at Toronto's Arena Gardens. As if on cue, the optimism was suddenly deflated by news of a player revolt. The Hamilton players had always been demanding, and now they were seeking to change the established labor practices of the hockey business.[56]

Player Precedents

With two extra clubs, the NHL had added six more games per club for the 1924–25 season, bringing the total to thirty and extending the season by three weeks to just over fourteen weeks, the longest to date. More revenue for clubs and rinks, however, did not necessarily mean more for players, as contracts were for the season and the number of games was unspecified. This arrangement led to dissatisfaction. After clinching first place at the close of the regular season on 9 March 1925, the Hamilton players demanded extra payment for participation in the playoff series, either

$200 cash or a prorated portion of each player's salary. Their captain, Wilfred (Shorty) Green, argued that while the player contracts did not specify the number of games in the regular season, the postseason NHL playoffs were not part of the player contract and should be remunerated separately. The idea was not unprecedented. The issue of remuneration for extra games had come up during the NHL's first season and also two years before, when St. Patrick's players (including Ken Randall, now a Tiger) had demanded—and received—$175 each to take the ice for a game. This time would be different. After meeting with the players, Percy Thompson stated categorically that the club would "absolutely not pay the men $200 each" and referred the matter to Calder, who promised an iron hand.[57]

The players garnered some sympathy in the community, even from the *Herald*, whose sportswriter (and arena off-ice official) P. J. Jones pointed out that Shorty and his brother Red had signed two-year contracts based on twenty-four-game seasons, not thirty. When Thompson responded that most players had received new contracts that year, when thirty games was understood, the players brought up a new grievance—that they had not received a "Christmas remembrance" (a bonus) like players on other clubs. As Shorty Green saw it, the fundamental issue was the changing commercial value of hockey players:

> The players have played the game on the ice all year. They have given of their best. And they're playing the game right now in this crisis. It isn't a matter of sportsmanship at all. It's money, and we feel that we have a perfect right to be paid for work done. Professional hockey is a money-making affair. The promoters are in the game for what they can make out of it and the players wouldn't be in the game if they didn't look at matters in the same light. If we weren't producing the kind of hockey to draw the crowds we wouldn't be paid accordingly. Why, then, should we be asked to play two games merely for the sake of sweetening the league's finances?

The players were fully aware of the commercial implications, but also sensitive to public opinion. They had considered the fans in their timing, wanting to resolve the issue before the first playoff game, but Green also wanted the fans to be aware that, despite the "threats and abuses" taking place behind the scenes, the players "refuse to be intimidated." Staying true to his word, Green did not back down, even after being called on the carpet by Calder in Toronto.[58]

To end the rebellion, on 16 March Calder suspended the Hamilton players as a group and instead of paying them $200 fined them the same amount. He said it was a question not of bonuses but of adherence to the contracts, which did not restrict the number of games to be played but limited only the period of time in which they could be played—from "on or about 1st of December to on or about 30th of March." Calder admitted the Hamilton club could have yielded, but "to have acceded to the players' demands, however, would have established a precedent which would have been seized on for years to come. The majority of the club members of the National League are directly interested in large capital tied up in hockey rinks and arenas—investment which must be protected." As Calder saw it, the league interest remained paramount, and it was his personal duty to protect a club against any inclination it might have to make exceptions that might set undesirable precedents for the rest. To make his point, Calder declared Hamilton ineligible for the playoffs, leaving the Canadiens–St. Patrick's playoff to determine the league champion.[59]

The player strike deprived Hamilton of its first championship season on the ice, but also revealed weaknesses in the club's management, not only by its handling of the players, but also in its overall commitment to continue professional hockey in Hamilton. On the same day that Calder announced the suspensions, a rumor surfaced that the Tigers' owners were negotiating for the sale of the whole franchise to the owners of the new York franchise, although one Hamilton co-owner, Andrew Ross, stated to the *Hamilton Herald* that while all the current players would be sold (presumably because of the revolt), the intent was to roster the club anew. Ross denied the club itself was for sale and pointed out that the strike had actually renewed the campaign for a much-needed new rink, but another owner revealed that if the right offer was made, the franchise could go too, and in an interview Tex Rickard said negotiations were under way and a deal expected that would soon bring the Tigers to New York. Helping his cause was yet another rumor of a new US-only professional league. With this threat in the air, pressure was maintained on the NHL governors to grant Rickard a second franchise in New York, and the NHL owners would in any case have to be careful not to turn the Garden into a rival and find themselves outflanked entirely.[60]

When the governors met after the 1924–25 season ended, Duggan's New York Americans franchise was formally approved and Gorman elected to the board as its governor. The *Montreal Herald* reported that the Garden's decision to join the NHL, while expected, had thus destroyed "one of Eddie Livingstone's new League bubbles." But the new league talk was probably just "a smoke screen thrown up by the Pittsburg [*sic*] aspirants, in order to get free admission into the N.H.L." Whatever the case, Calder was authorized to negotiate with the Pittsburgh applicants. He was also confirmed in his control over the fate of the Tigers when the governors endorsed the fines and suspensions meted out and left the players' futures in Calder's hands. Despite the demands of the new American clubs, who were desperate for talent, it was Calder who would decide if and when the recalcitrant Tiger players would hit the ice again. The new economics of the international NHL would determine where they would play.[61]

League Reform

With the rapid addition of new clubs, the turnover in existing clubs, and the prospect of future expansion, the relationship between clubs had also to be addressed. A rules committee was formed to revise the playing regulations, and at Dandurand's request the Canadiens' right of first call on French Canadian players was reconfirmed, but the main discussions concerned revision of the league agreement binding the clubs and a reconsideration of the legal form of the league.[62]

The ten-year agreement signed 2 September 1924 had been obsolete almost from its signing. At that time, the question of returning to the incorporated form of the NHA was discussed, and Calder was appointed, along with Redmond Quain, the Ottawa club's lawyer, to look into the league's options. Quain and Calder applied for Dominion (Canadian) incorporation in December 1924 under the name of "The National Hockey League, Limited," likely to test whether the institution could be made to conform to the league's special requirements. Quain modified the boilerplate clauses of the standard form to adapt them to the nature of a cartelized sports league. While the company's purpose was standard—to "promote, operate, conduct and carry on the game of ice hockey"—its share structure was not. This corporation had only eight shares, and the number could be increased only by "a resolution passed by at least two thirds of the votes cast at a special general meeting called for the purpose." Quain's modifications were trying to provide for a league-expansion mechanism, and furthermore the document's reference to eight "members" was an obvious attempt to equate shareholding with league membership. Unlike in the NHA, the shares were not designed to be divisible, and there would be no shares given to outsiders in order to avoid situations like George Kennedy's problematic sale to Brunswick-Balke-Collender.[63]

These modifications raised no eyebrows with the Dominion Corporations Branch, and the letters patent were duly issued on 24 December 1924. Quain probably had them on hand at the 11 April 1925 special meeting, where he and Calder found that their efforts had been for naught. Perhaps it was too complicated, perhaps the governors knew that expelling Livingstone was made more difficult by the existence of the NHA's corporate body, or perhaps the owners were simply more comfortable with the existing term agreements. Whichever the sentiment, after a full discussion the governors decided not to proceed, and instead a committee comprising Calder, Quain, Strachan, Dandurand, and E. L. Garey was struck to draft a completely new club agreement, constitution, and bylaws.[64]

Among other things, the committee would have to consider the new binational environment in which the league was now operating and the new characters involved. At the first NHL meeting in the United States, held on 26 September 1925 at the Biltmore Hotel in New York City, Percy Thompson announced the sale of the Tigers' player contracts to the Americans for $75,000. The governors agreed to ratify the sale on the condition that the Hamilton franchise would only be considered inactive. The governors assured the Duquesne Garden representative that his application for a Pittsburgh franchise would be favorably received at the annual meeting. With business completed, the NHL governors and newspapermen left for a dinner banquet featuring famous speakeasy owner Texas Guinan and her dancing girls.[65]

The evening's entertainment had been arranged by Tom Duggan's new partner, William V. Dwyer. "Big Bill" was a type of owner the NHL had never encountered before. While sports promoters like Rickard and Duggan and racetrack gambling concessionaires like Dandurand and Cattarinich were often seen to be operating on illicit margins, Dwyer was an outright criminal. He was not a rarity, or even a new breed, however. His involvement in hockey was emblematic of the close connections between sports, criminal activity, and urban politics that had been developing in major American cities since the late nineteenth century. These networks had strengthened after the 1919 ratification of the Eighteenth Amendment, which effectively banned the manufacture, sale, and transportation of intoxicating liquors. Opportunities suddenly appeared for enterprising hustlers, especially in New York and Chicago, to produce or smuggle beverage alcohol to parched consumers recovering from the economic jitters of the postwar recession and learning how to make money and spend it on leisure. Entrepreneurs like Dwyer bought breweries, paid off officials, and began deliveries. By 1924 he was known as the "King of Rum Row" and was awash in millions of dollars and looking to spend it. He invested in racetracks and nightspots like the Stork Club, and at some point he met Tom Duggan, who shared Dwyer's interest in horse racing and was not worried about Dwyer's reputation as long as he had money to invest. In June 1925 Duggan convinced Dwyer to put up most of the money in return for a part of the Americans: $10,000 for the franchise, $75,000 to purchase the Hamilton club assets, $40,000 as the club's contribution to the ice installation in the Garden, plus expected seasonal operating expenses of more than $160,000 (for that expensive Garden lease!). To his detriment, due diligence was not his strength, and Dwyer was seemingly unaware of the strict conditions of the deal Duggan had made with the Garden—a deal that put all the risk into the club's hands but most of the profits in the Garden's pockets and required him to nurture his own competitor. When Dwyer did find out, he was "thunderstruck."[66]

After returning to Montreal for the annual meeting, the governors got down to business, organizing future expansion and further refining the rules, continuing a process begun years before to make it faster and more offensive minded. The Pittsburgh application from Duquesne Garden was approved for a fee of $15,000, this time unanimously, and two applications for franchises for Chicago were tabled for further consideration, including one from Rickard's lawyer, E. L. Garey. The playing rules were modified to enforce discipline, bring more precision to the timing of periods, speed up the game, and limit defensive obstructions. Strengthening earlier amendments, any player with two major fouls was to be cautioned by the president and suspended after a third. To enhance speed, a rule was adopted calling for a face-off if the puck ever stopped moving while a player was "ragging the puck" (that is, keeping possession without moving the play forward). Goalie pads were limited to twelve inches in width and an anti-defense rule enacted to prevent more than two defenders from being in their own defensive zone when the puck was up the ice.[67]

The perceived desires of American customers drove the changes. They were seen to appreciate speed and physical play, as well as the "scientific play" that professional hockey offered, in contrast to the amateur college game that prevailed in the United States. This discourse of science was also prominent in baseball, where in the 1920s low-scoring "scientific" or "inside" baseball contests of base running, tactical hitting, and pitching began to be seen as retrograde and reflective of the earlier "deadball era" and were being replaced by a preference for the high-scoring style of Ruth and the Yankees, who depended on power hitting and home runs. In hockey "scientific" was applied to combination play (passing) but was preferred over the individual rushing style of the amateurs, who were prevented from forward passing. Nonetheless, players like Howie Morenz were known for their exciting end-to-end rushes, so professional hockey essentially had it both ways—the excitement of the individual rush and the sophistication and flow of the forward-passing game unhindered by whistles.[68]

There was also some debate over whether the clubs themselves should be constrained in their management of player costs. The governors agreed to limit playing rosters to twelve players and reserve lists to fourteen after 31 December of any year (twelve players under contract and up to two inactive players who might "refuse to report or are held under previous contracts which they refuse to fulfill"). There was more resistance to the imposition of a salary limit. Nathan Nathanson of Toronto proposed that no club be permitted to have a salary list exceeding $35,000, except the new US clubs—New York and Pittsburgh—which would be permitted to spend up to $45,000 for two seasons only. The meeting minutes noted that this motion was "unanimously carried," but Hammond requested that his protest against the adoption of this measure be recorded. He obviously wanted the freedom to spend even more.[69]

The rest of the 1925 annual meeting was served over to modifying the constitution wholesale. Despite the move onto international ice, the name "National Hockey League" was confirmed, as were the objects of "the fostering and furtherance of the game of hockey," which broke subtly from the baseball-inspired precedent of the NHA. A provision was added that confirmed club territorial monopoly rights: "A franchise shall not be granted in any city where a franchise already exists without the consent of the club operating such existing franchise." Rights over players were also strengthened, with amateurs who attended tryouts placed on a club's reserve list and all notices of release or transfer of player contracts to be made on an official form.[70]

The most detailed addition was to the powers and prerogatives of the board of governors. Governors now had to be club officers to sit on the board, which would render judgment on any disputes over league rules, and also on behavior "prejudicial to the good repute of the game of hockey." This change suggests the board saw itself increasingly (or already) as the governing body for the entire sport. And there was more. The board would hear disputes and appeals of the president's decisions, with its decision to be final, and "under no circumstances [would decisions] be reconsidered, reopened or inquired into by any subsequent Board." Furthermore, "nor shall any recourse be had to law, under penalty of forfeiture of franchise." (No more Livingstones would presume to sue.) From now on, the NHL board of governors would brook no superior legal authority, not even the law of the land. Like the elite baseball leagues, hockey's dominant league was now beginning to assert itself as a quasi-legal institution.[71]

Stars, Patriotism, and Exotic Appeal

Now that the Americans were finally on their way, Tex Rickard could begin "reviving for New York the practically extinct game of hockey," as the *New Yorker* put it. Supported by a three-man publicity staff, Rickard applied his skills at wooing consumers. Like many Americans, Gothamites had taken to commercialized leisure after the war with a passion and did so supported by the wealth of the country's biggest city. They were eager for more. Rickard used the same techniques he had applied to his boxing promotions: creating a sensational media event, promoting the sport's stars, promising violence, involving high society as well as low, inviting women to join the men in the audience—and stirring a little nationalism into the mix.[72]

What people were most interested in were stars, sports celebrities whose exploits provided leisure-time diversion. Star making was an important feature of twenties modern sport consumption, and Tex Rickard was a prime proponent. Leveraging what hockey tradition there was, Rickard introduced the new Americans captain, Billy Burch, as a larger version of Hobey Baker, the legendary American college hockey player. For those spectators not familiar with the game, Rickard borrowed the reflected star power of athletes from other sports: Burch was "the Red Grange of hockey" or "the Babe Ruth of hockey." Being American born, Burch was a rarity in the game, and Rickard made sure prospective fans knew about Burch's humble birth in Yonkers, New York (just north of New York City); his recent receipt of the Hart Trophy as the league's most valuable player (MVP); and his large three-year contract worth twenty-five thousand dollars.[73]

Rickard also used his own star power. In November he organized a visit of sports scribes to the Americans' training camp at Niagara Falls to see Burch and his teammates. When the journalists arrived, Rickard decided to take advantage of the new advances in photojournalism, which featured faster cameras and flash photography. Giving them a picture to go with their stories, Rickard donned skates and pads, and, still chomping his cigar, he stepped onto the ice in the garish new star-spangled and striped Americans uniform to fight "a duel upon the ice" with Colonel Hammond. Since Tex could not skate, it was a short-lived contest, but the photographers ate it up, and afterward Rickard, Hammond, and Duggan spent the rest of the session talking up the game to reporters to get them excited about the inaugural season.[74]

With Madison Square Garden undergoing finishing touches, the Americans opened the season on the road against their expansion rival, the Pittsburgh Pirates, a team built with the bone and sinew of Roy Schooley's USAHA champion Yellow Jackets. It was a competitive squad, with Harold Cotton, Roy Worters, Harold Darragh, Duke McCurry, and, not least, the great Canadian amateur star Lionel Conacher, who signed at a reported salary of ten thousand dollars per year. Under coach Odie Cleghorn, the Pirates won their first two games on the road before opening at home at Duquesne Garden against the Americans, who showed that their change from Tiger stripes to stars and stripes had not affected their skills. The red-white-and-blue silenced an abusive Pittsburgh crowd by beating the Pirates in overtime. Continuing on the road, the Americans lost to St. Patrick's but soundly defeated the Canadiens at the Mount Royal Arena and then got set for the return encounter.[75]

Before the Americans made it back to Manhattan for their home opener at the Garden, they suffered a casualty, albeit not one that threatened their play. The day after the season started, Bill Dwyer was arrested in a raid on his immense liquor-smuggling operation. According to the *New York Herald Tribune*, authorities had figured out that Dwyer was "the biggest single figure in the underworld of bootleg finance," with an operation that "practically controlled the entire supply of imported liquor which found its way into the country from the Atlantic seaboard." Dwyer made bail, but his legal troubles meant he would not have time to pay much attention to his new investment. In June he got off relatively easy, sentenced to two years in a federal penitentiary for bribing a coast guard official.[76]

On the opening night he helped pay for, no one missed Dwyer, and under the deal with the Garden the real focus of attention was Rickard, who made the opening night a glorious success. Would it have a lasting impact? The *New York Times* was hopeful: "New York's hankering for virile and bruising pastime" appeared to have "found a realization in hockey." The paper noted that many of the enlightened were female: "No game has enlisted so many supporters of the more attractive sex as hockey." Others were more skeptical, their gaze no doubt unclouded by a Rickard pay packet. The *New Yorker* reported that in one "heavily fur-coated box," the talk had not been hockey but "mostly about horses and bazaars." At the next game attendance was much lower, and the upper galleries, where "most of the money is made," were empty, exerting "a deadening effect on all but the vitally interested." Although it did not help that the Garden had not really been designed with consideration for the sight lines to the ice and there were many obstructed views, a month after the opening the novel game was still sustaining good crowds. It seemed hockey in New York was on its way.[77]

Rickard was not complacent and used a variety of techniques to keep up interest. He emphasized patriotic imagery and on Hammond's advice maintained the Canadian tradition of playing the national anthems before every game, not just restricting them to special occasions. The practice eventually spread from the Garden to other cities and other sports. He also added aboriginal exoticism to the mix, billing Americans player René Boileau as "Rainy Drinkwater [from] Caughnawaga Indian Reservation" near Montreal. In similar fashion, Rickard arranged to have Joe LaFlamme, the so-called Wolf Man of the North, mush seventeen hundred miles from northern Ontario to Manhattan behind eleven huskies (four of which were reputed to be domesticated timber wolves). After being escorted the length of the island to city hall, LaFlamme met Mayor Walker, who did some mushing on his own before facing the puck at the Garden. LaFlamme performed between periods, as "Drinkwater witnessed the game from a tepee in the back row." Among these Canadian "celebrity" events, Rickard sprinkled the usual stars of the American firmament: both Babe Ruth and Lou Gehrig "faced" (dropped) the puck for ceremonial face-offs, as did movie stars Humphrey Bogart and George Raft.[78]

Besides stars, patriotism, and exoticism, Rickard also sponsored technical improvements in the presentation of the game itself. Responding to criticism that the ice surface was "coffee-colored" and looked "more and more like a big cake of maple sugar the mice have scratched up," Rickard got to work. To get rid of the "dirty and disturbing brown," Rickard had the ice painted white after a half inch of water was frozen and then added another inch of ice, producing a surface "nice and white." With paint, colorful star-spangled uniforms, and intermission entertainments, Rickard improved the spectator experience without affecting the game itself, but his touch was not so light when it came to his next change—eliminating the heavy fur coats in the audience.[79]

Expecting cool temperatures, spectators sported furs and stoles at the inaugural game, but audience members in the mezzanine soon discovered it was warm enough to doff their winter wear entirely. The heat produced comfortable spectators but slow and sticky ice and warm humid air that exhausted the players, who were used to near-zero or subzero and relatively dry conditions at ice level. Afterward, players complained that the rink had been much too warm—midsummer warm. Although there were initial adjustments back to the colder side after their complaints, the issue carried over into the next season, culminating in a lawsuit that showed clearly how far the game product was being modified for the New York audience.[80]

Rickard claimed that while the ambient temperature in the first season had averaged 70 degrees Fahrenheit (21° Celsius), during the next season he had reduced it to 53–55°F (12–13°C). Tommy Gorman, the Americans' manager, wanted it at 40°F (4.4°C), claiming that otherwise it "depletes [players'] physical powers and slows up the game to the extent that interest decreases." Compared to Canada, "where the game is played under the usual winter conditions prevailing at such time," the Garden play was slow and the game "not as interesting as it should be." Some Americans players were losing eight to ten pounds during games, and Gorman believed every Americans loss at home was attributable to the heat. The Americans' record seemed to support him. In Hamilton the Tigers had led the league, but playing as the Americans with the same core of players the next season, they finished fifth, winning only four of fifteen home games. (Since the heat should have also affected visiting teams adversely, it may be that other environmental effects, like New York's nightlife, were factors.) In any case, after the Garden made a small concession, the injunction was withdrawn in January, but the relative warmth of the Garden was commented on for years afterward.[81]

For Rickard and Hammond, these concerns were minor. Professional hockey was taking off in the Garden, and Hammond began exploiting other levels. First, he reorganized elite amateur hockey to fill the vacuum created by the dissolution of the USAHA. With George Brown he attempted to create an Eastern Amateur Hockey League, which was to take the place of the eastern branch of the USAHA and include two clubs from Boston and three from New York. The western division of the USAHA, which did not compete in cities with NHL clubs, split off and renamed itself the Central Hockey Association, with clubs in Minnesota (Duluth, Eveleth-Hibbing, Minneapolis, St. Paul) and Canada (Winnipeg and Sault Ste. Marie, Ontario), but even these clubs were not immune to northeastern US hockey fever. (In November Hammond invited the Soo club to move to New York to play, but the club declined.) And the Colonel was not yet done with NHL hockey. The Americans were doing well enough for the Garden to justify immediately implementing the plan to arrange its own club.[82]

Gravitational Pull

The rapid growth of interest and capital investment in professional hockey in the US Northeast (particularly New York City) was exerting a strong gravitational pull on players and clubs from areas of traditional hockey popularity. By virtue of its seating capacity alone—almost twice the capacity of any other NHL rink—Madison Square Garden began to shift the playing field of the league itself. The Garden's capacity for seventeen-thousand-person sellouts gave the New York club a financial advantage that augured a move of player talent southward and of player salary scales upward, salary limit or not. American capital seemed to portend the relegation of Canadian clubs to a lesser status, perhaps even to the point of forcing clubs out of the league. After the move to New York, the tension between a stasis pattern and a growth agenda, which often pitted Canadian against American clubs, grew even stronger.[83]

To address the emerging imbalance, the Canadian NHL clubs had successfully installed the salary limit, and now they proposed baseball's model of revenue sharing, with the visiting club getting a share of the gate receipts. The alliance the Canadian clubs wanted already looked to be compromised when the Canadiens club would not support the idea. Dandurand and Cattarinich were rumored to be considering moving the franchise into an immense new stadium planned for Chicago, from where they might be able to pay the high salaries themselves.[84]

The Chicago idea was part of the pressure to expand the league even further and could not be dismissed out of hand. If NHL clubs did not satisfy the burgeoning interest in professional hockey, another league might try to take existing clubs with it. At the end of December 1925, Calder reported franchise applications from Brooklyn, Chicago, and Detroit interests, and he called a special meeting for mid-January to consider them. By the day of the meeting, Jersey City was also in the running. The governors tabled all the applications for the time being, but action would soon have to be taken. The Brooklyn application pushed Hammond to declare that the Garden (not the Americans, note) had exclusive rights to the city of New York, which included Brooklyn, and that he intended to exercise its promised franchise. This premature announcement caused some confusion, particularly since Hammond was both the president of the New York Americans and the vice president of the Garden, a situation that had led many to understand that the Garden owned the Americans.[85]

Predictably, the prospect of the Garden being the owner of "another" NHL franchise brought forward talk of "syndicate hockey." Syndicate leagues like the PCHA, which had allowed a single owner to control one or more teams, had significant advantages from an administrative point of view, but were also prone to accusations of match fixing and for this reason were generally frowned upon by the sport press, which acted as a proxy for consumer sentiment on the subject. If there was no competition between clubs off the field, how could there be legitimate competition on the field? The Patrick brothers had had to defend their PCHA from these exact charges and also counter criticism that the movement of players from team to team was designed to favor one club over another. The NHL practice was congruent with the mode of professional baseball, which prevented ownership of multiple clubs on the grounds that it destroyed public confidence in the integrity of the sport. The separation of club interests was also extended to the relationship between the clubs and their home rinks, especially when there were two clubs calling a rink home. In 1924 the Canadian Arena Company had tried to keep its control over the Maroons quiet, presumably so as not to be seen as biased against the Canadiens.[86]

Sensitive to the issues, Rickard stepped in to finesse the situation by putting distance between the Garden and the Americans. On 5 February Eugene Garey incorporated the New York Giants Professional Hockey

Club, taking the name of the popular local National League baseball team (and also the recent National Football League entry). A week later Hammond resigned as president of the Americans to head the new club, being replaced by New York deputy fire commissioner Joseph Hannon. The message was clear: the Garden would have no more say in the operation of the Americans. With the interests officially divided, Hammond went to the 14 February NHL meeting at the King Edward Hotel in Toronto, expecting to obtain a franchise for the Giants, but also prepared for opposition. Obliged to do so by his contract with the Garden, Tom Duggan supported the Garden application. As if on cue, a rumor began circulating that if the Garden were not satisfied, a rival league might appear under Rickard's direction—possibly an exclusively American league comprising those new cities that had become interested as a direct result of hockey's success in New York. If the NHL owners felt threatened by rival-league rumors, or felt obliged to honor quickly their November 1924 commitment to give the Garden a franchise, they did not show it. Instead, they tried to take advantage of Hammond's hurry. The governors proposed that if Hammond were to give visiting clubs 5 percent of the gross gate of the Garden games to offset their travel expenses, they would let him have his franchise immediately. Doubtless annoyed, Hammond agreed to consider the idea.[87]

A week later Eddie Livingstone reemerged and played his old tune, announcing the formation of an International Professional Hockey League with two clubs in New York, two in Chicago, and one each in Buffalo, Toronto, and Detroit. This time the NHL governors simply ignored him, being too busy considering a raft of inquiries from Buffalo, Detroit, Cleveland, and Chicago. They felt comfortable enough to more than triple the franchise fee to fifty thousand dollars and require an accompanying pledge to build a suitable rink, all in order to prevent frivolous applications. This stipulation put off some, but not the one from Patrick L. (Paddy) Harmon, a Chicago six-day bicycle race promoter and roller-skating rink owner.[88]

Paddy Harmon had money and plans for a new building—a giant Chicago Stadium—that needed an NHL franchise to fill it. If not his own club, it might be the Canadiens, whom he had been tempting with a move to the Windy City. Harmon soon found out that his stadium plan—ironically modeled on Madison Square Garden—conflicted with a proposed

Chicago link in Rickard's chain of Gardens. By announcing his new Chicago Stadium in January 1926, the Chicago entrepreneur stole Rickard's thunder, and within weeks Rickard was in Chicago arranging for his own Chicago Madison Square Garden and making plenty of disparaging remarks about his competitor. In April Rickard too announced the erection of a building, seating more than twenty thousand, to break ground in two weeks' time and be complete by December 1926. Chicago was in for a stadium fight, and the NHL would be in a position to anoint the victor.[89]

Expansion dominated the agenda at the April 1926 semiannual meeting, and the Canadian owners used the issue to move their own interests forward. Over the previous weeks, the governors had negotiated a revenue-sharing agreement that provided 3.5 percent of the gate receipts to every visiting club for all league games. Hammond had successfully argued for the principle that revenue sharing should apply to all clubs and not just New York, so while the Garden would still pay more than the other clubs because of its capacity, the rate would apply to all clubs, all games, and all rinks. In return, Hammond got his assurance that the Garden franchise, now to be called the Rangers, as in "Tex's Rangers," would be admitted at the annual meeting in September.[90]

With revenue sharing and the Rangers settled, Calder, Strachan, and Dandurand formed a committee to interview franchise candidates in Chicago, Detroit, Jersey City, and Philadelphia. Other applications from New York, Chicago, Cleveland, Philadelphia, and five from Detroit were tabled. When the semiannual meeting resumed two weeks later, on 1 May, the clubs disagreed on whom to accept. Disagreed is an understatement. Until now, Rickard had been represented at NHL meetings by Hammond, but the stocking of his Gardens was worth the promoter's personal attention. He arrived in the meeting expecting "a nice friendly gathering with everybody on the best of terms," but when some clubs dissented against Chicago and Detroit being admitted, Rickard "suddenly jumped to his feet and declared: 'There will be hockey in Chicago no matter what you do'" and then intimated he would "break" the NHL if he were thwarted. The lines were drawn, with Nathan Nathanson of Toronto leading a group that included the Canadiens, Senators, and Americans against the Maroons, Boston, and Pittsburgh, who backed Rickard. The *Chicago Daily Tribune* reporter predicted two leagues would be the result, with the proexpansion Rickard loop being led by Frank Calder.[91]

After more rancorous discussion during which Nathanson and Rickard got into a shouting match and threatened to build a rival facility across the street from the other's rink, the governors adjourned. The next day they finally came to an agreement to admit Chicago and Detroit, but then could not agree on which applicants. The Chicago choice was between Paddy Harmon and Huntington (Tack) Hardwick, who both had New York backers. Harmon was allied with Duggan, and Hardwick was an employee at Hayden, Stone & Company, the New York brokerage that had helped put the Garden financing together, so he was really a stalking horse for Rickard (though he initially denied it). Of the five Detroit applications, the most prominent were one from a man named Hardy and one from Rickard's favorites, Paul R. Bierer, the part owner of the Fairbairn Hotel, and Morris Friedberg, a prominent Detroit jeweler, who proposed a new auditorium in Detroit (perhaps a cloaked Detroit Madison Square Garden). The Nathanson group supported Harmon and Hardy and the Rickard group Hardwick and Bierer-Friedberg. After two days of meetings, the clubs tried to compromise, but Duggan still refused to approve the new franchises because he apparently wanted *four* new clubs admitted—Detroit, Cleveland, and two in Chicago. (He probably realized that he could not forestall a Rickard-backed Chicago franchise, so he wanted Rickard to have competition.) Since the constitution required unanimous agreement on expansion, until he relented no one at all could be admitted. The other clubs served notice they would get around this provision by amending the constitution two weeks hence to allow for majority rule on the issue. Meanwhile, confident they would prevail, both the Hardwick and the Bierer-Friedberg groups acted to acquire players. Fortuitously, but not coincidentally, Frank Patrick announced that he had a whole lot for sale.[92]

The Patricks' PCHA had struggled in the postwar era and merged with the WCHL in 1924 to form the Western Hockey League, but it played only two more seasons, as eastern and American developments continued to exert pressure on salaries and player availability. In May 1926 Lester Patrick told newspapers that he and his brother had known for months that the PCHA and WHL could not last, given the "exuberance" of the

East for hockey and "the desire of American financiers to get in on the ground floor," as well as "the big increase in salaries paid by the National Hockey League." Except for Vancouver, the western Canadian urban centers were all small (less than one hundred thousand in population), and with annual club revenues ranging from forty-four to sixty-five thousand dollars, it meant WHL clubs could not compete with the market potential of the large American centers. In the spring of 1926, the Patricks tried to shift the Canadian Prairie clubs to San Francisco, Los Angeles, and Oakland, but the deal fell through. Faced with a bleak future for the league and expensive repairs at their own Vancouver Arena, the Patricks and their fellow WHL owners decided to get out while they still had assets to peddle.[93]

With Art Ross's assistance and Charles Adams as guarantor, on 2 May the Patricks sold Tack Hardwick fourteen players, mostly from the Portland Rosebuds, for one hundred thousand dollars and the day afterward sold the entire Victoria Cougars club (including the services of the coach, Lester Patrick) for the same amount to Friedberg. Aside from the Saskatoon Sheiks, who negotiated their own fate (many wound up with Rickard's Rangers), the players from Edmonton, Calgary, and Vancouver supplemented the Portland-Chicago and Victoria-Detroit deals. In return for helping guarantee the Hardwick and Friedberg payments, Charles Adams acquired seven players for his own Bruins. The other owners thought Adams was taking unfair advantage and argued that under the NHL-WHL agreement, all the players should have been available to all NHL clubs through waiver procedures, but the dispute was put on hold as the clubs met to resolve the more immediate question of Chicago and Detroit expansion.[94]

At the 14 May meeting, the governors circumvented the Americans' obstruction by amending the constitution so that expansion would require the assent of only two-thirds of the clubs. The Canadiens and Americans voted against the constitutional change, but it passed. The governors then immediately accepted Tack Hardwick's Chicago application and one from Detroit, but in a surprise it was not Bierer-Friedberg, or even Hardy. The new Detroit franchise went to John C. Townsend and Wesson Seyburn of the Detroit Winter Palace, Inc. Seyburn was a real estate developer and financier and the son-in-law of John F. Dodge of car-making fame. They were backed by a syndicate of elite Detroit moneymen affiliated with the Detroit Athletic Club, so the group was probably much better financed and connected than Bierer and Friedberg. It is possible that the governors wanted to spite the Bierer-Friedberg interests for purchasing players before the Detroit franchise was granted, but it is more likely that Rickard had switched horses midstream.[95]

At any rate, with the expansion mechanism fixed and the two new clubs admitted, the governors signed a new league agreement on 15 May 1926 that included the Garden's renamed New York Rangers Hockey Club, Inc. The document explicitly bound the clubs to each other for fifteen years and provided for damages to be paid to each club and the league in case of a breach, up to ten thousand dollars each. Out of pique, Duggan initially refused to sign, but did so by September, along with the new franchise holders, the Detroit Hockey Club, Inc., and Chicago National Hockey Team, Inc. With the Adams-brokered deal with Friedberg now undone, Frank Patrick tried to sell the players to the new Detroit franchise holders for the same price, but they wisely held out over the summer and eventually got the Cougars players at a significant discount.[96]

Defensive Expansion

Despite conflicts among owners and the promise of more to come, the NHL had transplanted its brand of elite professional hockey into the United States relatively quickly, successfully extending the scope of the cartel—and, more important, maintaining its coherence. Yet even though the league's American expansion seemed to be an aggressive move on its face, at heart it had been a defensive maneuver that followed the existing pattern of southward expansion from the St. Lawrence Valley cities, which was meant to prevent competition from other leagues like Livingstone's (no matter how evanescent) or ones more substantial that were backed by American capital. The league's ambivalence to the process is embodied by the agency of Tom Duggan, who was given risk-free options to ascertain whether there was any real American interest in NHL hockey. Indeed, much of the credit for the successful foray into the United States can be given to Duggan, and by successfully bringing the NHL to Boston and Madison Square Garden he did much to fashion its international fate.

Through Duggan and others, the league exploited existing and often over-lapping business networks (sports, journalism, horse racing, boxing, and crime) to establish its game. In retrospect, it was imperative that the NHL gain access to the New York market. Not only did entering the Garden trip the decision in favor of the NHL in Boston and give it credibility across the Northeast, but selling Rickard also brought onside a man who had the ambition and wherewithal to create a viable rival organization.

At the root of the NHL's success, however, was the rise in sports spec-tatorship. American economic growth in the twenties meant the game was sown on fertile ground, and rising American income levels spurred demand for new leisure activities and sports. Hockey was not the only sport to explode in the early 1920s, but it was certainly one of the most rap-idly successful. It had shown that even an imported brand could resonate with American consumers both economically and culturally by emphasiz-ing elements of novelty and diversion, stars and sensationalism, and speed and physicality. It was also crucial that other sports and entertainments, especially boxing, pushed development of the needed infrastructure—are-nas with artificial ice—that made hockey viable in large markets, irrespec-tive of climate. In contrast, even a domestic American product like the professional National Football League, born in 1922, was relatively less successful at differentiating itself from its amateur analogues and mak-ing the move to larger cities. Professional basketball was also slow to take advantage of the arena boom, and another eligible sport, indoor soccer, failed utterly to do so.[97]

The appeal of hockey was arguably part of a more profound cultural attraction, as it and other sports seem to have provided some of the mean-ing of modernity for North American consumers. At a symbolic level, not only did the obsession with sports and its "stars" fill leisure time, but the athlete as public hero, as Ben Rader has argued, also provided "a com-pensatory cultural function . . . [that] assisted the public in compensating for the passing of the traditional formula of success, the erosion of Vic-torian values, and feelings of individual powerlessness." For Americans, the prime form of this compensation had been baseball, but in the 1920s all manner of sports arrived as complements. Hockey provided heroes both exotic (Howie Morenz) and American (Billy Burch) and tapped into the paradox of modernity, where traditional elements survive and thrive in modern society; hockey was at once scientific and technological, thus modern, but also violent and passionate, thus premodern.[98]

At the commercial level, hockey filled a seasonal void, providing a regular winter pastime for audiences and commercial events for the traditional weak spot in the seasonal sport calendar. It expanded into the vacuum and made year-round sport obsession possible. Hugh Fullerton of *Liberty* wrote that "America has found a new sport to fill in between baseball and football and make a complete cycle of thrills." Customers were responding. Damon Runyon of the *New York American* wrote in March 1926 that ice hockey had "shown the greatest increase in public interest in the past year." That fall Burris Jenkins of the *New York Evening World* wrote that, in New York, the sport had taken "better hold on the public than football." With the addition of the Rangers, the *New Yorker* expected hockey to "leap into prominence as the greatest attraction of the season." By the next winter, the promise was being fulfilled. One writer observed that "hockey is threatening to harness, in the winter months, the tremendous energy that would be wasted during the summer if it were not for baseball." Al Wilson of the *New York Evening World* made a common parallel, seeing hockey "assuming the proportions of organized baseball," with teams all over the United States, even as far as California, and it was fast becoming America's "national winter sport."[99]

Rickard also made sure hockey appealed to all social classes. At the Garden "good quality high hats were in evidence," and hockey gained "the Garden's most socially gifted coterie" aside from the horse show crowd. And high-hat or cloth, none seemed put off by the body checking; it may have been the most attractive aspect. Opposing players were said to be enraged at the sight of Canadians wearing star-spangled New York Americans uniforms, and the resulting conflict made for "good hockey." Even fighting was appreciated. After a pair of players were sent off after a bout and then resumed fisticuffs on the penalty bench, the *New Yorker* writer opined that "all this comes under the head of good clean fun, and one spends a truly sporting evening."[100]

American market success meant profound changes for the formerly all-Canadian professional hockey business. Penetrating and growing the

American market required greater capital requirements for all clubs, and so Canadian franchises like St. Patrick's moved into the hands of investors with deeper pockets, into arenas with more seats, and into cities with bigger populations. This expansion was evident to Percy Thompson, who said that after Boston and the Maroons came into the league, he knew the Tigers' days were numbered, as "the game was getting too big for Hamilton to handle it" with its mere thirty-eight-hundred-seat arena.[101]

Frank Calder was a central player in negotiating the changing business model, the one who brokered the tradition of the older Canadian clubs with the innovation of the new American entries and almost certainly kept the cartel from disintegrating at key moments. He guided playing-rule changes, constitutional modifications, revenue sharing, and salary limits to adapt and accommodate the league members and maintain order in the cartel, even as the members themselves used the threat of dissolution or the formation of a rival league to achieve their goals.

The demise of the WHL, the NHL's only major rival, was a result of the NHL's American expansion, but also the means to make it work. Dissolving WHL clubs removed the one bottleneck to growth by freeing up the extra players needed to expand from seven to ten clubs in only one season. Obtaining these elite players thwarted the possibility of competition, both from within and from without. Yet it also magnified the shift of the elite clubs from smaller cities to bigger metropolises and also from North and West to South and East.

While economic at root, the geographic shift was perceived in national terms, as it also corresponded with a movement from Canadian cities to metropolises in the United States. Contemporaries feared it might be irreversible. The *Montreal Daily Star* noted that with six American and only four Canadian clubs in the NHL, the requirement of only two-thirds agreement for expansion implied the Americans could determine policy, possibly to unilaterally expand the league against Canadian club opposition. In a *Maclean's* article entitled "Will U.S. Cash Cripple Our Hockey?" Charles Good speculated that big-league hockey might disappear from Canada and be monopolized by Americans in "Tex Rickard's league." Good did see a bright side: for many years, Canada had imported a large portion of its entertainment from the United States—music, vaudeville, movies—and now "a natural reciprocity has set in." The fear was that Canada's unique contribution to American culture would soon move beyond its control. Good predicted that Ottawa, with its medium size and low ticket-price scale, would soon follow Hamilton's fate and that, despite the ironbound league agreement, the American clubs would split from the Canadian. After all, he reminded his readers, "something of the kind occurred at the formation of the professional hockey league as at present constituted."[102]

For their part, American owners defended their motives and saw the future more optimistically. Charles Adams wrote to the sports editor of the *Montreal Daily Star*, challenging the idea that Canada would lose professional hockey and the NHL owners would do nothing to stop it: "From the time of my entry into NHL affairs I have never once, I hope, wavered in my loyalty to that body which was entirely Canadian in its traditions and its development. . . . Every substantial Canadian city within a territory that can be successfully traveled by the balance of the league, should always be represented, and as far as I am concerned, they always will [be]." The man who was at the focus of these fears, Tex Rickard, tried also to reassure, telling reporters that the sport had entered a new phase in which scale was the central feature but nationality still an essential marketing ingredient: "Hockey is out of the hole-in-the-corner class and must be promoted and planned on a big scale, and Canadian teams must be kept in to give it an international flavor. . . . It is a game of great and wonderful possibilities, and within five years it will be drawing more money than boxing." All that was lacking were ambition and boldness. Rickard warned that "some of your [Canadian] owners are narrow and small. They talk like children. They are against every suggestion to widen the game, particularly as concerns the United States." Like it or not, the NHL had been pulled into the United States and into the orbit of the premier sport impresario of the day. And the sport fitted well, justifying investments in the new indoor forums of sport like the new Madison Square Garden, where it provided regular income between boxing bouts over the winter and provided a complementary business form that could be imitated by new arenas popping up across the American Northeast.[103]

Al Wilson of the *New York World* did not deplore the shift from Canada to the United States, but saw danger in one aspect of the game that had a negative connotation in American sport: syndicalism, "the 'sport crime' charged with the ruin of the Pacific Coast League." According to Wilson, Rickard's intention to build other Gardens threatened to revive this model, but "thankfully" the other NHL governors "balked at his proposal to sponsor Chicago and Detroit and other cities" and would not allow him the Rangers until he surrendered control of the Americans. Wilson was right to look closely at Rickard and his plans, but Rickard was not the first or the only one to think about the synergy of rink and club and the value of horizontal integration. The Montreal and Toronto Arenas had been an early example of a similar strategy and the Duggan-Harmon connection a contemporary one, but for impact Rickard had no peer. Indeed, it might be argued that Rickard's adoption of hockey for the Garden was the event that ignited the start of the evolution of the civic arena into the modern network of multipurpose arenas.[104]

Writers like Wilson were worried about the competitive defects of multiple club ownership, but centrally owned syndicate hockey had another defect. It hindered the marketing of a club as being a local institution worthy of civic support. In another modern paradox, audiences wanted national stars celebrated in the media, but they also wanted to see players as local representatives, and the cartel league's individually owned clubs within a national framework was the most effective accommodation of these wants. The outstanding question was one of scale—could the league accommodate all the cities that now wanted in? The NHL itself was growing so fast that it seemed reasonable that soon Philadelphia, Cleveland, or Buffalo could be added and the circuit split into two sections on the major league baseball model.[105]

While influenced by American capital and culture, the expansion of the NHL also resulted in Canadian-rules, fully commercial, professional hockey becoming the dominant industrial mode of hockey in the United States. The American semiprofessional "shamateur" model (also a quasi-Canadian import) was relegated to the second tier when it was unable to adapt as quickly to the commercial growth of the sport and tied up in its own hypocrisy. In comparison, fully commercial professional NHL hockey was seen to offer honest, clean competition to consumers and a labor pool uncomplicated by amateur ethics. Yet while the NHL brand was ascendant, it was not the only brand, and by selecting from among the best markets, the NHL left others open, perhaps to be filled with alternate products. The next stage would be the development and subordination of these other markets so that the NHL could position itself as the major league and continue to mold the North American industry in its preferred image.

4

Creating a Major League

1926–1929

At the NHL annual meeting in the fall of 1926, the governors met to resolve the residual ill will over the distribution of Western Hockey League players in the spring and dubious deals still being made up to the time of the meeting. As the only club not sold wholesale by the Patricks, the stars of the Saskatoon Sheiks were in special demand. Frank Ahearn of Ottawa made a deal to buy the rights to Bill and Bun Cook directly from Saskatoon club management, but then Conn Smythe, the manager of Tex Rickard's new Rangers club, intercepted the players on their way east to Montreal (where they were going to meet with the Maroons!) and convinced them to sign with him. Several other players were in a similar tangle. At first, the only agreement was that Charles Adams's acquisition of seven WHL players for his Bruins had been particularly self-serving. By ignoring the interleague agreement on waivers, Adams was encouraging an undesirable element in a sports cartel—competition between clubs for players. But when the governors nullified his deal, the Boston owner saw it through a national lens, calling the Canadian owners "small-time operators, unable or unwilling to spend real money." He was likely even more displeased when the committee formed to redistribute the players comprised three men from Montreal: Frank Calder, James Strachan, and Leo Dandurand. Adams threatened a lawsuit until the others backed down and let him keep his players, but in the course of the discussion Cattarinich apparently sent Dandurand out for a certified check to prove to the American owners that the Canadiens at least had a lot of money to throw around and were not small-time. The national cast to league governance boded ill, especially as a binational divide was beginning to be reflected in diverging financial strength.[1]

With somewhat more comity, the governors turned to the challenges of growth, adapting the league and product to its new geographic and temporal scope. The NHL continued to emphasize speed and borrowed the more generous PCHA offside rule, moving the blue lines farther away from the goals to allow more free space for forward passing in the attacking zone. The number of games was boosted from thirty-six to forty-four and the regular season stretched from mid-November to the end of March (almost nineteen weeks), an extension made possible by the league-wide use of artificial ice. With ten clubs—four Canadian and six American— schedule making was made more challenging, and a new system was required. Some thought ten clubs unwieldy and that the NHL should follow the baseball model and divide into two leagues, but instead the league divided itself into two sections, the Canadian and the American (to balance them out, the Americans had to play in the Canadian section). National divisions made a virtue of the NHL's unique national rivalries for marketing and organizational purposes. The new schedule had clubs playing six games against section rivals and four against the others, which both reduced travel costs and created more parity (and rivalry) by having the generally weaker American clubs play each other more. Divisions also addressed the problem of the Stanley Cup. Without a worthy successor to the WHL, the Stanley Cup challenge conditions were modified so that the NHL could internalize the cup series. Though not explicitly designed to do so, the existence of two sections allowed the league to retain a semblance of the challenge tradition by having them compete in a playoff for it, while effectively making the cup an NHL trophy.[2]

Another area of friction was Calder's direction of the cartel. With its new international scope, the NHL was moving inexorably beyond the control of its original Canadian clubs and entering into the American sports capital mainstream, where ambitious entrepreneurs had their own designs in mind. Calder's strong hand in Montreal was resented by some (Adams especially), and he would need to nurture the idea that his abilities were—and would continue to be—necessary to the maintenance of the NHL's position. In the short term, this situation meant accomplishing two things: the successful organization of other leagues into a hierarchy under NHL control geared to reducing player-acquisition and training costs and the subordination of individual club interests to the cartel's. The league's own durability would owe much to the member clubs finding it increasingly prudent to accede to Calder's direction and to trust that in the long run, his executive powers would save the clubs from the costs of expensive conflicts, both internal and external. The next decade would see many difficulties arise in negotiating these processes over a national border that separated different economic and cultural environments, and the pressure would only increase to revise rules, revisit revenue models, rebalance the relationships between the league and its members, and forestall competitors.[3]

Despite the disputes they had caused, the NHL governors must have recognized that the new playing talent placed the league in an enviable position. Besides fortifying existing club rosters, the new players facilitated the creation of three American franchises that would now be able to start play in the fall. Establishing new clubs in Detroit, Chicago, and New York in turn solidified control over the largest indoor ice facilities in the major urban centers of Canada and the United States, from Montreal to New York and from Boston to Chicago. With the most elite players and the largest major cities, the NHL was in a position to become the hockey equivalent of baseball's major leagues. It was up to its members to assert the league's power over any pretenders and consolidate its status.

Making the Minors

In the mid-1920s NHL hockey was becoming the dominant elite brand, facilitated by its high profile in the major sports markets of the American Northeast and Midwest. Americans were beginning to take hockey seriously, both as spectators and as investors. Syndicated columnists hyped the sport to consumers, and arena operators as far away as California began to incorporate leagues into their business models and invite NHL teams to play exhibition games. There were no million-dollar gates like boxing, but hockey could generate revenues in a way that the circus, six-day bicycle races, and the occasional musical evening could not—weekly, consistently, and throughout the winter months. With the boxing title fights now being held in outdoor stadiums where attendance could be maximized, the indoor arena was becoming hockey's domain. At Madison Square Garden, the arena Rickard and Ringling built for boxing, during the 1925–26 season almost a half-million tickets were sold for hockey.[4]

In 1926 the demand for elite hockey heated up in the northern United States. As soon as the new NHL franchises were announced in May, the *Detroit Free Press* reported on the future plans of the disappointed applicants, noting that "Detroit can have a professional hockey league all of itself if the flock of promoters who have signified their intention of operating clubs here next winter go through with their announced plans." E. P. Strong announced he had been offered a franchise in the International Hockey League ("whatever that may happen to be," editorialized the *Free Press*), and B. C. Whitney announced plans for the transfer of the Sault Ste. Marie (Ontario) Greyhounds to Detroit to represent the city in the Central Hockey Association (CHA), the professional successor to the western section of the USAHA. The McCreath-Townsend interests announced they were going to play professional hockey next winter, "whether awarded a National league franchise or not," and Charles S. King and his colleagues were importing "a flock of hockey players to play in a minor professional league in western Ontario, in the event that the OHA refuses to grant playing certificates to touring players." The promoter of that league was none other than Eddie Livingstone.[5]

None of these announcements was news to the NHL owners, but the question was how to exploit the strong demand for their own product without also diluting it. The first problem was league size. In this era sports leagues tended to have fewer than ten teams, mainly for economic and logistical reasons, namely, the availability of viable urban markets within feasible travel distances. For this reason, the NHL men knew they could not yet span the entire continent or even become much denser in their current geography. Yet the experience of decades of competition from professional and amateur rivals suggested that hockey's popularity would not be limited to the NHL brand for long. Entrepreneurs would not wait, and if the NHL did not expand, then others would offer substitutes. Some degree of market division was needed, and the solution was for the NHL to become involved in the formation of new leagues, preferably subordinate ones.

Another major obstacle hampering the expansion of elite hockey was the availability of high-quality players. While the WHL's demise had solved the short-term problem by shifting most of its players directly to the NHL, there was no assurance that the NHL would be the only destination of elite players. Only by controlling player supply, development, and distribution would the NHL owners be able to thwart potential competitors. To do so, they would need to determine the nature of the new interleague relationships and push the burgeoning American hockey market to develop according to NHL rules, under NHL hegemony.

Managing the transition from amateur hockey was also essential. Up until 1926 most professional players had come directly to the NHL clubs from the ranks of the elite Canadian amateur teams, especially clubs in the Ontario Hockey Association. The professionals had used the "signing bonus," a lump-sum payment in return for turning professional, as an up-front incentive to players to forfeit their amateur careers, but there was an inherent risk involved: the player might not make the professional club roster, and the club would lose its investment. What was needed was a system that mitigated these risks, a system that allowed players to turn professional and train for eventual NHL play without having to start out in the top league: in other words, a circuit of professional clubs "minor" in status to the "major" league NHL. While amateur clubs still dominated in Canada, especially in Ontario, the US amateur tradition was less entrenched, and there might be opportunities to establish professional teams in smaller northeastern cities and even in the NHL cities themselves. A minor league system would kill two birds with one stone by fleshing out a player-development system and satiating American demand for hockey at the same time.[6]

As usual, hockey had a baseball model to follow. Since the nineteenth century, professional baseball had been stratified into a league hierarchy that by 1911 was calibrated into AA, A, B, C, and D leagues. Minor league clubs served small to medium-size markets while serving as a development environment for potential major league players. At first, the minor league clubs were independent entities that controlled the contracts of their players, so they were often in conflict with the major leagues concerning the "draft" provisions that allowed higher-level clubs to force lower-level clubs to relinquish players upon payment of standard fees. In response to this resistance, after the First World War the innovative manager of the St. Louis Cardinals Branch Rickey began formalizing a prewar practice of "farming" out major league prospects to minor league clubs. So that the major league club would have control over the players, Rickey bought parts of minor league clubs and established formal player-development agreements, thereby lowering reliance on the draft and increasing the major league club's control.[7]

In 1925 Frank Patrick predicted the emergence across Canada of leagues graded by skill level, along the lines of the baseball industrial model, but until hockey had an outright professional level below the NHL, PCHA, and WHL, senior amateur hockey clubs from the OHA took up the player-supply function and were just as reluctant as baseball's minor leagues to play servant to a major league master. Though it might be trotted out as a justification for independence, amateur principle had little to do with it, as by the 1920s the most successful OHA clubs had come to be run along commercial lines and they competed in the marketplace with the NHL for the same players. Besides an off-ice job, the amateur clubs also held as their trump card the fact that once a player had "made the jump" to the professional level, he would be hard-pressed to regain amateur status. (There were also many more amateur teams to play for.) On the other hand, amateur players held a stronger hand than their professional brothers. Because they did not sign binding commercial contracts (or an option clause either), they were free to "sell" their services from season to season, subject only to certain residency requirements. Just as the elite clubs at the turn of the century had learned, mobile labor was a threat to financial stability, and soon enough the elite amateur clubs would be pushing for the revision of amateur codes to accommodate remuneration and other features short of overt professionalism to help bind their players.[8]

Leo Dandurand of the Canadiens saw an opportunity in the convergence of elite amateur and professional interests. After the expulsion of several senior clubs from the Quebec Amateur Hockey Association in January 1926, Dandurand met with James Strachan of the Maroons to discuss accommodating the ostracized in a new professional "B" league that would serve as a training ground for the NHL and include teams from all NHL cities. By March, concurrent with NHL expansion discussions, Dandurand's gaze shifted south to new rinks in the US Northeast. Solid attendance at exhibition games played by the Americans and Bruins in Providence, Rhode Island, showed the promise of the sport in that city and others like it. With this thought in mind, Dandurand allied with George Brown, who was now apparently regretting being the mere landlord of a Bruins club becoming profitable at the expense of the arena's amateur hockey operations. Together with Hubert Milot, a former classmate of Dandurand and one of the owners of the new Rhode Island Auditorium, they spoke to Charles Adams, Judge Dooley of Providence, Albert Geiger of Providence and Boston, and a representative of Colonel Hammond to gauge their interest in forming a new professional circuit. After the meeting they told the press that a new league would be in the offing.[9]

Various configurations of this new "American Hockey League" were discussed, with clubs expected in New York, Providence, Montreal, and Boston and possibly New Haven, Connecticut; Springfield, Massachusetts; and Newark and Jersey City, New Jersey. (Frank Ahearn was offered one hundred thousand dollars by unidentified Jersey City interests for his Senators so they could be moved.) George Funk, the arena architect, wrote to Tom Duggan that he had high hopes the new league was to be "in every sense of the word, a big league on a par with the National Hockey League, and it was not to be a feeder [league]." Within days, however, Charles Adams was clarifying that the league should be subordinate to the NHL. Dandurand also confirmed that he too would not have anything to do with it unless there were "ironclad" agreements with the NHL and stated that the NHL did not intend to allow any new leagues to challenge its major league status.[10]

The other partners had different ideas. Brown, Geiger, and Dooley did not relish subservience to the NHL and believed that Boston could support two major professional teams and Providence one. George Funk was also onside, and his letter to Duggan reveals how convoluted NHL interests were becoming: Funk proposed that Duggan shift his "proposed Chicago team" (presumably Paddy Harmon's NHL bid) to the new circuit to make it "a big league" and put it "on the map." Then Duggan could also swing "the second New York team" (was this club the Americans or the Rangers?) into the league, which Funk speculated could include Philadelphia, Detroit, or Buffalo. In Funk's view, the existence of a second major league would also not hurt the NHL, but would provide "honest-to-goodness competition" in each city, where both clubs could be fully patronized if the clubs played "good, honest and hard hockey." Funk predicted the new league would draw, but only if it could get players.[11]

This new league-formation talk involving NHL owners lends important context to NHL internal discussions over expansion in the summer of 1926. Along with the Central Hockey Association's proposed expansion into the US Midwest, Dandurand's northeastern league was certainly in the background at the showdown expansion meetings of 1–2 May, but the refusal of Dandurand, Adams, and Hammond to support major league ambition meant it had little chance to rival the NHL. If that was not enough, the NHL's acquisition of most of the WHL players effectively consigned the new northeastern professional league to a subordinate status. Without stars, it could not aspire to be a major league. Albert Geiger saw the writing on the wall and wrote to Calder in June, announcing the new league's official formation but assuring him it would not try to compete but instead would offer NHL clubs a place for some of their reserve players. He pointed out that Adams and Hammond approved of the venture in this form, and Adams would be personally supporting the Boston club. With this format established, over the next few months Calder helped Geiger organize the new Canadian American Hockey League (Can-Am) as a model of a minor league in the NHL's image, with NHL rules, standard player contracts, and binding interleague affiliation agreements.[12]

Next to make the transition were the top OHA senior clubs. The prospect of continued NHL expansion and US minor league growth was already luring OHA players, and many OHA clubs were considering outright professionalization as the only means to retain their rights over players. In June, after the OHA began to strictly enforce residency rules, seven clubs broke away. Geiger had hoped to convince them to join the Can-Am, but travel costs to New England militated against it. Instead, the OHA clubs formed their own circuit, the Canadian Professional League, with teams from London, Windsor, Hamilton, Stratford, and Niagara Falls. They elected as president Charles King, the Windsor owner (and failed Detroit NHL franchise applicant), who told Calder the new clubs intended to act as "affiliates" of the NHL.[13]

So in the fall of 1926, at the same time that the NHL governors were resolving their own expansion plans, four new professional leagues were accepted as affiliates of the NHL: the Canadian American Hockey League, the Canadian Professional League (Can-Pro), the Central Hockey Association, and the Prairie League, a western Canadian successor to the WHL. Calder summed up the NHL position: "We are willing to cooperate with minor league clubs, but will not consent to entertain them as competitor [sic]." Their lower status was made clear by the NHL's right to draft players from them, and it would begin to do so the next season. Problems were still envisioned—particularly how to ensure players moved up the chain, how to negotiate territorial rights between leagues, and how to contain minor league ambition—but the important thing was that the professional leagues had now been stratified to provide a framework for orderly elite player movement. It helped that in the press, Calder was beginning to be seen as hockey's equivalent of baseball's commissioner, "the final judge of all disputes among the minor league and clubs." Other added bonuses were the number and distribution of US clubs, which promised wider exposure for the sport and for the time being sated American entrepreneurial ambitions. (Despite Dandurand's initial involvement, no Montreal club ever joined the Can-Am, and the cradle of hockey remained the domain of Canadiens, Maroons, and elite amateurs. After all, there was no threat of American professional incursion in Montreal.)[14]

Later in the 1926–27 season, when the Can-Am looked at awarding a Brooklyn or New York franchise, Calder warned Hammond that "the whole scheme . . . is a step in the direction to raise the Canadian-American League to major league proportions." Hammond agreed that "any effort to build an arena and place the Canadian-American League Club in New York City [is] an unfriendly act and detrimental to our interest." The statement can be read ambiguously, but in this case "our interest" seemed to include both the NHL and the Madison Square Garden. It had not always been so, but, like Dandurand and Adams, Hammond and Rickard were becoming content to identify their business's primary interest with the NHL as the major league, under Calder's leadership.[15]

Livingstone's Last Play

The next major challenge to NHL hegemony took place at the margins of the league's new footprint. Despite ambitious architectural plans, in the fall of 1926 the new Detroit and Chicago clubs still did not yet have major arenas in which to play, or even exclusive control over the temporary ice accommodations they leased. They also had competitors for customers in markets that were new to elite hockey. Aside from the franchise fees, this factor was the price the new NHL clubs had accepted for entry into the major league. It would be up to the local investors to try to make the business work by controlling the major arena facilities and subjugating any competitors.

In Detroit the franchise took the name of the Victoria Cougars club that formed its backbone. Now led by Charles Hughes, the secretary of the Detroit Athletic Club, the Cougars expected to join the minor league Detroit Greyhounds in a new rink by February 1927, but in the meantime started the season at the Border Cities Arena across the St. Clair River in Windsor, Ontario. It helped when the Greyhounds suspended operations for the season, meaning one less competitor for hockey spectators, but that season the Detroit Cougars' version of NHL hockey failed to attract many fans from either side of the border. (It did not help that Detroiters had to ferry across the river and then take a taxi to the game and reverse the process on the way home.) The opening night against the Bruins on 19 November was in front of a capacity crowd of six thousand, mostly Canadians, and it was to be the season high point. In 1926–27 the club attracted an average of only two thousand customers for home games and generated only $81,494 in gate revenues, losing a similar amount on the balance sheet. Jack Adams, a Cougars player, later remembered that the team got booed even when it won, as "most of the fans who attended the Detroit games came from Windsor—and they came just to see the Cougars get 'killed' by Canadian teams. . . . A simple case of border city rivalry." Windsorites also had their own new Can-Pro club to root for,

Charles King's Hornets. (King's failure to win the Detroit franchise might have been a blessing in disguise.)[16]

In Chicago it was a similar story. With Rickard's Garden only in the planning stages, the new NHL club arranged to play in the existing Chicago Coliseum, which had to be retrofitted with an ice plant. As in Detroit, the franchise ownership had quickly evolved. As soon as Tack Hardwick acquired the franchise, if not before, he had been looking to unload it and successfully enticed Major Frederic McLaughlin, the president and chief stockholder of Manor House Coffee Company and W. F. McLaughlin & Company. The major was a renowned sportsman with interests in thoroughbred racing and boxing, and even though he had never seen hockey played before he was looking for something less physically demanding to replace his other hobby, polo. With several other Chicagoans he initially pledged $95,000 (to Hardwick's $105,000) to cover the franchise fee ($12,500), the player contracts, and the artificial rink apparatus in the floor of the Coliseum. Impetuous and competitive by nature, McLaughlin dove into the new sport and had soon acquired the majority of the shares of Chicago National Hockey Team, Inc., installing himself as president, Lucius P. Ordway as vice president, and John J. Mitchell Jr. as treasurer. He even named the club the "Black Hawks," after the US Army's Eighty-Sixth Division in which he had commanded the 333rd Machine Gun Battalion. As McLaughlin set out to introduce big-league hockey to Chicago, Hardwick quietly faded from the picture, but the man everyone knew had been backing him, Tex Rickard, soon appeared at McLaughlin's side to preside over the first use of the Coliseum ice. Rickard was maintaining the link so he would have a tenant for his Chicago Garden.[17]

Chicago presented a marketing challenge. Like New York, the Windy City had a hockey tradition, albeit sporadic, dating from the late nineteenth century, but, in the words of Frank Schreiber of the *Chicago Daily Tribune*, "hocky [sic] has been a dead sport in Chicago for the last ten or 12 years." McLaughlin seemed to be following Rickard's recipe, if not his direct guidance, in selling hockey with class distinction and patriotic sentiment. He asked Calder for a Canadian opponent and decided to produce the inaugural Black Hawks game as a gala social affair. This time it was members of the Junior League, an educational and charitable women's organization, who sold game tickets to the society crowd, with the profits going to support two local charities—the Visiting Nurse and Infant Welfare Societies.[18]

The opening game against the St. Patrick's was played in front of a substantial crowd of eight thousand, and the game was reported at length in the social pages of the *Tribune*: "Society rubbed the sleeves of its gold brocaded evening wraps and its immaculate dinner coats against the checked suits of the sporting element . . . and apparently liked it." The consensus dress code was "warm and serviceable garments," but in the crowd there were many shirtfronts and hatless women clutching their cloaks. One of the most prominent was the major's wife, the former Irene Castle, a renowned dancer whose glamorous pose in an immense white fox collar graced the newspaper's photo page. As in New York, society seemed hooked, albeit in smaller numbers. The novelty faded quickly, and the Black Hawks dropped to four thousand in attendance for the second game and then averaged only thirty-three hundred for the rest of the season. In the NHL expansion class of 1926, the Black Hawks were ahead of the Cougars but far from matching the Rangers, who were riding the coattails of the Americans and soon averaging more than seven thousand spectators per game.[19]

Like the Cougars, the Black Hawks initially expected competition from a local minor league club, in this case a representative of the American Hockey Association (AHA), the new name of the Central Hockey Association, the midwestern successor of the USAHA. The previous spring, the CHA clubs had agitated to professionalize the league in the face of player raids from NHL clubs and, after the failure of the WHL, poised themselves to step into the former's territory. To that end, they even appointed Frank Patrick to represent them in negotiations with the NHL. The NHL's acquisition of most of the WHL players tempered the CHA's aspirations, but that it continued to desire to be on a par with the NHL is evident in the agreement made in September. The two leagues agreed to use William Foran to settle their disputes, no explicit mention was made of the CHA's minor status, and it was the only league eligible for a "world series" with the NHL, should one take place. By fall the CHA's ambition was reflected in its expansionary name change, and the newly minted AHA added its own new Chicago and Detroit clubs to the existing franchises in Duluth, Minneapolis, St. Paul, and Winnipeg.[20]

To this new potential for friction was added another, older, irritant. As early as August, Calder had begun to suspect that Eddie Livingstone was hiding behind the CHA-AHA screen. Though Livvy denied it, when the AHA was officially announced, the Chicago franchise had his name on it. For months, he had been organizing the Chicago Cardinals, signing players and conducting training camp at the Mutual Street rink in Toronto. More crucially, he had already arranged to share the Chicago Coliseum with the Black Hawks. Within days of confirming his suspicions, Calder told AHA president Alvin Warren that Livingstone was persona non grata and that the recently signed agreement with the NHL, under which the AHA hoped to operate, was under threat. Warren immediately wrote to Livingstone, asking him to sign an agreement that would have limited his franchise to one season only. Livvy refused. Fearing NHL reprisal, Warren began asserting that Livingstone was no longer a member of the AHA, spreading a message to that effect around Chicago and directing it in particular to Charles R. Hall, the president of the Chicago Coliseum, likely hoping it would filter through to McLaughlin and Calder. The rumor was insufficient. In December Calder voided the interleague agreement, declaring the AHA an "outlaw" league (it would no longer be party to the interleague agreement with the NHL and other minor leagues). This revocation meant AHA player rights were no longer protected, and soon after Calder decided that two of Livingstone's Cardinals players belonged to the Black Hawks and the Can-Pro Windsor Hornets. Calder's offensive did not prevent Livingstone from putting his team on the ice anyway, and it was the Chicago market that would decide his fate.[21]

In a city that was new to the game, both Cardinals and Black Hawks struggled to attract fans in their inaugural 1926–27 season. Black Hawks captain Dick Irvin remembered the first season as "an uphill fight" for customers, with the players being "supplied with hundreds of tickets, to distribute in shops and offices, free, as a means of stimulating interest in the game, and attracting folk who might become customers. Often, when I left half a dozen tickets in a store, I would be asked: 'What is this hockey?' for there was very little background for the game, which was almost entirely new, and played by athletes completely unknown in Chicago." This strategy of "papering the town" with tickets was a time-honored tradition that served both to introduce the sport and also to generate an audience big enough to create excitement at the rink for those spectators who did pay. Still, the crowds were not forthcoming. Livingstone cut his ticket prices but McLaughlin followed suit, and since Livingstone's pockets were not as deep, he soon ran into financial difficulties. In March McLaughlin began actively inducing Cardinals players to break their contracts, even as Livingstone's resolve dissolved and he announced his intention to sell his last-place Chicago Cardinals to a local syndicate. To add insult to injury, the other AHA directors refused to sanction the proposed sale. In spite, Livingstone canceled the upcoming Cardinals game against Alvin Warren's St. Paul club and then abruptly closed up shop.[22]

After the season was over, Warren proposed a new AHA-NHL agreement that would see hockey divided into three levels—major, intermediate, and minor—with the implication that the AHA would sit in the middle category. McLaughlin wrote that the AHA was being "very stiff-necked about coming into organized hockey," and Calder also seems to have seen the AHA proposal as rather presumptuous, standing by as Art Ross of the Bruins raided the Winnipeg AHA club for players. Within a month the fear of further raids and escalating salaries drove the AHA clubs to accept affiliation with the NHL as a minor league and to accept Calder's authority over any disputes. As a last condition, the NHL agreed to sign only after the AHA had, in Calder's words, "officially severed connections with [that] lunatic" Livingstone. Dutifully, the AHA directors canceled Livingstone's franchise outright and in September signed the AHA-NHL agreement. True to form, Livingstone later filed a lawsuit, charging a conspiracy between the AHA, the NHL, and McLaughlin to steal his players, oust him from the Coliseum, and eliminate his club from organized hockey entirely.[23]

Eddie Livingstone returned to Toronto, and it must have been cold comfort for him to know that, as innovator and as antagonist, he had done so much to shape the NHL's form and scope. In many ways, it was he who had forced the NHL out of its central Canadian shell and into a greater continental marketplace just in time to take advantage of the blossoming

American sport culture. Livingstone was left behind, and he retreated to amateur hockey, never again to irritate the NHL or even to return to the professional game.[24]

Minor Discontents

Dissatisfaction with minor league status was not limited to the ambitious AHA owners. The Can-Pro and Can-Am clubs were also feeling acutely the limitations of their subordinate position. The October 1926 affiliation agreement had included a draft by the NHL clubs on their clubs at a price of five thousand dollars per player. Implementation was delayed for a year, and in the meantime NHL clubs simply purchased players for cash and took advantage of the ability to lend players to minor league clubs without passing them through NHL waivers. These transactions caused several problems for the minor league clubs. First of all, loan arrangements usually had no time limits, so players could be recalled at any time. Also, any cash sales to NHL clubs ran the risk of competitors getting the player first, via the minor league's own waiver rule. Finally, the waiver price kept a ceiling on the sale price of a player contract, as did the NHL draft fee; together, these costs effectively capped the profits a minor league club could make by selling player contracts. In one instance, the Detroit Cougars reneged on an offer to buy player Larry Aurie outright for seventy-five hundred dollars and instead drafted him for five thousand. When a dispute arose over this transaction, the other advantage accruing to the major league club became obvious: Frank Calder was the arbitrator who decided the issue.[25]

When the time came to renew the affiliation agreement in June 1927, the NHL responded to the minor league complaints by adding a clause limiting player loans to before 15 February and requiring a minimum loan period of three weeks without recall. The Can-Am president, Charles Clapp, and his club owners had some other changes in mind, namely, a restriction on Calder's arbitration prerogative and acknowledgment of Can-Am club territorial rights to protect the league from future NHL expansion. Calder rejected these proposals, and Clapp protested that Calder seemed to figure that "the strength of your league is sufficient to tell us what we shall do without considering the fact of co-operation." What the proposed new deal showed was that the NHL was not deaf to minor league complaints and would make some efforts to conciliate, within limits.[26]

Calder's role in keeping the minors subdued is hard to underestimate. Although his power was based on NHL club control of the major hockey markets and he was nominally under the direction of the league governors, Calder often acted as an equal to club governors and had considerable discretion. It was an authority that had its roots in the early years of the weak four-club league, but Calder tried to maintain it as the league grew. Supremely confident in his position, he was not averse to putting it on the line to force a vote of confidence in his favor, and what he could not accomplish through persuasion at board meetings, he could often do through the great control he exerted as the only executive officer and day-to-day administrator of the league. After all, the governors came to only a half-dozen meetings during the year, usually as a part-time diversion to their main business affairs, whereas Calder's new office in the Castle Building at 1410 Stanley Street in downtown Montreal was the beating heart of the hockey cartel, serving as the clearinghouse of information and administration and the main connection point to all its clubs and affiliates. There was some resistance. Charles Adams was emerging as a regular Calder opponent, coming to see the president as an autocrat who represented, or at least defended, the parochial ways of the Canadian clubs, particularly in regard to playing rules. And he was not alone. Within months of his own initiation into the NHL, Frederic McLaughlin also began to bridle at the president's direction.[27]

Before joining forces to fight Livingstone in Chicago, McLaughlin and Calder had waged their own battle behind the scenes. It transpired that, as a condition of their franchises, the Chicago and Detroit franchise recipients had consented to waive the right to market exclusivity (territorial rights), leaving the way open to the NHL awarding another franchise in their cities. This situation was news to McLaughlin, and he refused to acknowledge that any waiver existed when Calder asked him to confirm it a few months into the 1926–27 season. When Calder insisted, McLaughlin sought legal advice and argued that it was Hardwick personally—and not the Chicago club—that had acceded, if there had been any agreement at all. He also asserted the waiver was unconstitutional after the 15 September 1926 NHL meeting, when the constitutional bylaws on territorial rights had been amended and no limitation on the full rights of Detroit or Chicago was made. In his letters to Calder, McLaughlin lashed out at the NHL presidency itself, criticizing the "autocratic" nature of the position as, "from a business point of view, absurd." McLaughlin declared that it was the club owners, who were "putting up their money and risking their capital for the sake of developing hockey," who should be setting policy, "and this kaiser, or czar, attitude should surely by now be recognized as out of date." Undeterred, Calder kept at the issue of the waiver, asking Hardwick to confirm that the consent had been "made as part of the assets of" the Chicago club. When Hardwick would not, Calder threatened to "cancel" Hardwick's association with the club, perhaps an attempt to nullify retroactively the granting of the franchise itself. The dispute ended somewhat abruptly when, at a February 1927 meeting, the governors agreed to rescind both Detroit and Chicago waivers and to treat all clubs as equals in territorial rights.[28]

The initial motivation behind the waivers may have been to allow two-club cities (after all, Montreal was already a success and New York was proving to be), but Calder's pursuit of McLaughlin at this time seems odd. Given the poor Chicago attendance and the AHA competition, it was unlikely the league wanted to place a third professional club in Chicago right away. One might speculate that the second franchise may have been destined for Paddy Harmon, who was still intent on building an arena, but more likely it was for Tex Rickard, who may have envisioned two NHL franchises in his Chicago Garden, on the New York pattern. Certainly, the waiver situation brings to mind Duggan's acquiescence to a second team in New York. After initial affinity, McLaughlin did not seem to be getting along with the Madison Square Garden people, and if Rickard wanted confirmation he would be able to put a team in his new Chicago rink, he could conceivably have pushed Calder to confirm the waiver. (Why Calder did not have a copy of the waiver, or the minutes did not record it, is another interesting question.) However, at the same time Calder was also seeking information on Chicago's share structure to verify there was no interlocking ownership of clubs, and he may have been looking for a persisting Rickard-Hardwick connection to the club. It is possible, then, that the pressure on McLaughlin was actually directed *against* Madison Square Garden interests, possibly by the Canadian clubs wanting to keep options open in Chicago. Given the convoluted interests at this time, clear motives are difficult to discern.[29]

Calder's authority was further challenged a few months later during the 1927 Stanley Cup playoffs. This time McLaughlin was in the president's corner. After an on-ice brawl in Ottawa, Calder fined five players, suspended Hooley Smith of Ottawa for a month, and expelled Billy Coutu of Boston permanently from the league for attacking the referee. Calder confided in McLaughlin that he expected "every string will be pulled in certain quarters" to have his ruling set aside. This time McLaughlin agreed with the scope of presidential prerogative and replied that, if Calder's ruling were to be overturned, "I will admit that as a League it is a dismal failure and should be done away with." The unnamed puppeteer was Bruins owner Charles Adams, and though he did not succeed in having the ban reversed, McLaughlin remained his boardroom opponent. After being outdone later that spring over an amateur recruit, McLaughlin wrote, "I do hate to see that Boston outfit constantly get away with murder, and hope some day . . . to stage a little private murder of my own." In any case, he was "pretty certain to always be in the opposite direction" to Adams.[30]

The postexpansion NHL had introduced a new set of ingredients, and though a mutable stew of loyalties and simmering feuds continued to roil, the mixture seemed to work well enough for Calder to remain the presiding cook. There were certainly few complaints from the owners when he extended his authority into the affairs of the minor leagues. The retention of the Stanley Cup also allowed Calder to tread into the bailiwick of the cup trustees. After the first game of the 1927 Stanley Cup series ended in a tie and the Boston Arena ice was considered too poor to continue after one overtime period, Calder ruled that there would be no sixth game, "because it might arouse public criticism." He decided that if the two clubs were still tied after five games, the championship would be shared. That neither William Foran nor P. D. Ross, the cup trustees, seems to have been consulted is telling.[31]

Expansion Effects

As the NHL was realigning the institution of hockey in accordance with the interests of its clubs, there was worry over the uneven business performance across the league. Disparate club attendance numbers (and revenues) were serious enough to temper enthusiasm for more expansion. During the 1926–27 season, average club attendance was more than 120,000 (more than 5,000 per game), but Pittsburgh (45,000, 2,045 per game), Detroit (48,000, 2,182 per game), and Chicago (73,000, 3,318 per game) were objects of concern.[32]

New buildings would hopefully solve some of the capacity limits, as well as provide modern amenities to attract spectators. In March 1927 Frank Calder laid the cornerstone for the new Detroit Olympia, a red-brick Romanesque polygon with a capacity of 11,500 for hockey, situated on Grand River Avenue and McGraw Street. Though located in a residential district, the location of the Olympia was otherwise perfect, being three miles from Detroit's business district and a half mile from its center of population on a major thoroughfare and at the intersection of two major electric streetcar lines. The designer was Charles Howard Crane, a renowned movie theater architect whose work was already prominently featured in Detroit and across North America. Crane's Olympia was state of the art, with the largest indoor ice-skating rink in the United States (242 by 110 feet) and ice that could be installed in six to eight hours and removed in less than four.[33]

In Chicago no ground had yet been broken, but both Harmon and Rickard rinks still seemed to be in the offing, so there was no fear of a future capacity shortage; in the meantime, McLaughlin was grudgingly absorbing the deficits. Pittsburgh was another story. Having started with great promise from its USAHA roster, the Pirates were now the worst on-ice performer, and there were few sincere prospects of a new rink to replace the old Duquesne Garden. Pittsburgh expansion now looked like a mistake, and it could be that a change of venue, of ownership, or of city was the only long-term solution.

The weakness of the expansion markets was to be expected, but more disquieting were attendance woes in established hockey markets like

Ottawa and Toronto, whose clubs rounded out those teams with fewer than 100,000 in attendance. (Ottawa averaged 3,716 customers per game and Toronto 4,500.) After a season dominating the other clubs on the ice, Ottawa had just won its fourth Stanley Cup since 1920 with stars like King Clancy, Cy Denneny, and Alex Connell, but most of the American clubs proved to be poor draws at the Ottawa Auditorium, and local spectators often seemed to prefer local amateur teams to the professional Senators. In order to compete, Ottawa's tickets were the cheapest in the league, and the management had even reduced the price scale further, halfway through the 1926–27 season, to little effect. In February Ottawa owner Frank Ahearn concluded that twenty-two games were too many for the Ottawa market to sustain, and the club began arranging for some games to be played in big American rinks the next season.[34]

The Toronto club was similarly anemic at the gate and even worse on the ice, finishing at the bottom of the Canadian section in 1926–27. The manager, Charlie Querrie, suggested winning was the solution and told the *Ottawa Journal* that, if his team had Ottawa's superior record, "we could sell out on season tickets alone." He was being optimistic. The St. Patrick's club also competed with the popularity of local amateur hockey and was still playing in the outdated Arena Gardens. Though the Mutual Street rink was only sixteen years old, even when full it was still too small to make the same profits as the new American rinks, which were twice the size. Toronto did have two advantages Ottawa did not. One was an urban population base of more than a half million—more than three times the populace of the nation's capital—and the second was an ownership change in February 1927 that promised new capital, new energy, and a new building.[35]

After the fractious summer meetings of 1926, Toronto co-owner Nathan Nathanson seems to have tired of fighting Rickard and the American clubs. Rumors circulated of a St. Patrick's sale, possibly to a Philadelphia or Montreal group. Spurred by the possibility the club might move, a local syndicate stepped in, and on Valentine's Day of 1927, the Toronto Maple Leaf Hockey Club, Ltd., took over the club for a reported price of $160,000. The *Toronto Daily Star* initially reported that Nathanson and J. P. Bickell would retain a small interest, but while Bickell still held his position and would become the new president, Nathanson was out entirely, having decided that the worry over players was no longer fun.[36]

Unnamed in the publicity was Conn Smythe, the driving force behind the Toronto Maple Leaf syndicate. Smythe was a local quarry owner and also an amateur hockey manager who had been hired and fired as the first Rangers manager just the year before. He was only a minor shareholder in the new Toronto organization, but it was he who at Bickell's urging had gathered the investors—mainly local magnates in mining, brokerage, construction, and manufacturing—and for his efforts was appointed managing director of all aspects of the club's operations. To burnish the club's image, Smythe arranged for Great War flying ace Lieutenant-Colonel William G. (Billy) Barker to be the first chairman of the board. As manager Smythe retained the indomitable Charlie Querrie, who had survived all the Toronto ownership changes since 1918, and appointed Frank J. Selke, a successful amateur and minor pro coach, as his assistant. In addition to the name change, Smythe also designed a new crest featuring a maple leaf on the front, a symbol that Smythe thought "meant something across Canada" owing to its association with the First World War and the last Canadian Olympic team uniform. (It was also similar to the uniform of the minor league Toronto Maple Leafs baseball team.) The next season the hockey club adopted a blue and white uniform with a blue color scheme very similar to the colors of Smythe's old amateur squad from the University of Toronto.[37]

The month after the St. Patrick's sale, Smythe's former boss Tex Rickard revived his dormant Philadelphia plan. This time it was more ambitious than ever. Flush with cash from two highly profitable years at Madison Square Garden, Rickard discussed more Gardens in Philadelphia, Pittsburgh, and Detroit and the possibility of buying the NL New York Giants to obtain access to the Polo Grounds as an outdoor venue for boxing. Rickard was coy about his plans for a eighteen-thousand-seat, $5 million Philadelphia stadium, saying he had not expected them to come to light, but felt sure that "there is little danger of a slip now before I have another great arena under my direction." Besides the usual attractions, the rink would feature a hockey team, but it would be "owned and supported by Philadelphians," for Rickard was "unalterably opposed to syndicate hockey." He was said to be looking forward to the addition of a club in Cleveland and a twelve-club NHL for the next season, but as in Chicago the scope of Rickard's vision seemed finally to be exceeding his capacity to execute it.[38]

For a brief moment, Cleveland did actually seem a possibility, but the brakes were being applied on expansion. In mid-March 1927, when the league governors met at the Waldorf-Astoria Hotel to arrange the playoffs, rifts between current clubs curbed the enthusiasm for new applications. The New York Americans complained about the unwieldy schedule and that the Rangers got first look at all visiting clubs to New York. Others pointed out that the American clubs had to travel more than the Canadians, but a suggestion for ending play between league sections (and thus reducing travel) was resisted, as it would mean the popular Canadiens and champion Senators would not be seen in American cities at all. Furthermore, the players themselves were becoming envious of Canadian-American salary differentials (American clubs paid more), to the point that an attempt at unionization was being rumored. Given these problems, Calder expressed his personal opinion to the *New York World* that "it was high time that the National League set a limit upon its franchises." The governors agreed, and for the last two seasons of the decade, they focused on modifying the game for existing audiences and trying to ameliorate the revenue and attendance disparities between clubs that had been brought about by rapid expansion.[39]

Refining Forms

Thanks to the growth of the NHL and the minor leagues, hockey was making continued headway into sports consumer consciousness of the late 1920s, particularly via New York, the media and cultural center of the United States. This progress was helped in no small measure by the performance of the Rangers, who won the Stanley Cup in 1928 after only their second season. Hockey's potent combination of novelty, speed, danger, and physical play attracted fans to the game and readers to newspapers, where on most days during the season a hockey story would be featured in the banner headline on the sports pages of the major dailies. But American spectators were also frustrated. On the ice, offside whistles stopped play regularly. Off the ice, the organization of the schedule was seen to confuse fans who were used to the baseball format, where the regular-season games produced a league champion. Press commentary conveyed this criticism, and the NHL governors felt pressure to adapt the Canadian heritage of the sport to the American marketplace in order to continue the brand's growth. Continuing the refining process that had long been part of the league, they experimented with playoff structure, rules, and the financial relations between clubs.

The owners started with the playoffs. This idea was a professional hockey innovation originated to keep fan interest high throughout the season, even when their club was not leading the standings, but one that had taken on increasing importance as an additional revenue stream. After the 1924–25 season, Charlie Querrie summed up their importance to the bottom line: "I'll wager that there is not a team in the league that made $10,000 this season. Hamilton for four years finished last, and for three years lost money, and only the play-offs helped them out. Canadiens won the world championship last year and made less than $5000, while this season Montreal, Boston, and Ottawa lost money."[40]

Now that the Stanley Cup competition was an intraleague affair, the NHL governors could decide on a new format for revenue sharing that included both league playoffs and cup play. Traditionally, all the NHL clubs had shared intraleague playoff receipts equally after expenses, with the interleague Stanley Cup series receipts being divided only by the players (after deductions for expenses). In 1925–26 the governors changed both traditions. They relinquished the principle of equal distribution of playoff revenues and decided that only the league itself and the clubs participating in the playoffs would share in the receipts. The net proceeds were to be divided with 20 percent to the winner, 17 percent to the runner-up, 13 percent to the third-place club, and the rest going to the league. The players would now be paid from a $25,000 pool that was independent of gate receipts.[41]

For some reason, the pool system proved unsatisfactory, and the next year the system returned to the old practice of sharing net receipts with the players. The rosters of the two cup finalists got 45 percent of the net receipts of the first three games of the best-of-five finals, on a sixty-forty split. (While this arrangement seemed to shortchange players in a longer series—and benefit the clubs—the restriction was almost certainly to prevent any incentive among the players to prolong the series unnecessarily to boost their share.) In that year, 1926–27, players on all six teams shared receipts ranging from $3,837 to the Chicago team, a quarter-final loser, and $11,099 to Ottawa, the cup winner. Although it sounded impressive, when divided by the number of games played, the shares per player (assuming twelve players per club) were similar, ranging from $104 per game for a Canadien, who played only two playoff games, to $185 per game for a Senator, who played eight and won the cup. As the player's salary was for the regular season only, this bonus was their entire postseason pay, and since many players made more than $100 per regular-season game, it might not be much of a premium above their regular-season rate (although it was an opportunity to make more money). Furthermore, the amounts were also much lower than in the NHL-WHL years. For example, in 1924 Ottawa players had received $600 each just for the two games of the cup finals. So while salaries had gone up after expansion, they were being offset by reduced postseason remuneration.[42]

The logic, marketing appeal, and complexity of the playoff format itself also came under scrutiny. In the last season of the WHL, 1925–26, the format was simple: the second- and third-place finishers played off for the right to play the first-place club for the NHL championship and the right to play in the Stanley Cup against the WHL champion. For the next season, with ten clubs in two sections and no WHL, the governors followed the same process within each section: second against third, with the winner playing against first, and these winners facing off against each other for the cup (with all series decided on a two-game, most-goals-scored basis). This setup worked well for 1926–27, when Ottawa, the best regular-season team, won the cup, but in 1927–28 there were complaints because even though the Canadian section was much stronger, it was the Rangers—with only the fifth-best regular-season record—that had taken the cup. So in September 1928, a new solution was agreed upon: cross-sectional playoffs. These playoffs might have been fairer, but they were far from simple. Immediately after the regular season, the section leaders would play each other in a best-of-five series "to determine the championship of the N.H.L." Concurrently, the second-place teams would play a two-game, most-goals series, and the third-place teams the same, with the winners to play each other in a best-of-three series for the right to meet the NHL champion and play for the cup. The logic of following league tradition by determining an NHL champion before the cup competition seemed sound, but it confused many fans, especially new American devotees. Canadians understood the two-step process of a league playoff followed by a Stanley Cup competition, but most Americans were accustomed to the major league baseball practice of having league champions determined by regular-season standing only and then a single best-of-seven World Series. The New York sportswriters, as representatives of the American sports Everyfan, were particularly critical of the new hockey system, which seemed to emphasize postseason over regular-season play. John Kieran of the *New York Times* suspected that "the idea seems to be to make the regular season of comparatively little importance and make the post-season play the main show." He predicted the result would be "loafing" during the regular season, and he warned that the fans might catch on and refuse to attend regular-season games. His solution was that hockey should follow the baseball tradition by creating two separate leagues with only one playoff.[43]

Indeed, the need to sustain regular-season interest had to be balanced with revenue considerations. With the growth in the number of playoff games and the reduction in player share, playoff receipts were becoming a nice addition to the club (and rink) bottom line, and it was too much to expect that the clubs might pare down and rationalize the system to fewer games. The two-section format also helped boost regular-season interest by creating intrasectional and national-flavored rivalries, which also spilled over into the playoffs. The decision to reemphasize a distinct "NHL championship" before Stanley Cup play also helped validate the regular season, as did giving greater financial incentives to the clubs to make the playoffs by placing first to third in their section.

Another way to generate interest among customers and incentivize both teams and players to high performance was the creation of subsidiary contests with trophies as prizes. From 1927–28 the regular-season Canadian and American section leaders were awarded the O'Brien and Prince of Wales Trophies, respectively, before the Stanley Cup competition. But there were also other trophies representing intracity rivalries, like the Kendall Memorial Cup fought over by the Canadiens and Maroons and the West Side Merchants Association Trophy between the Rangers and Americans. Individual awards were given to local star players, often by local businesses, but league-wide awards also multiplied, with or without official league sanction. The Hart Trophy, donated by the father of Canadiens manager Cecil Hart for "the player judged most useful to his team during the season," was awarded from 1924, and the next year Lady Byng, the wife of the Canadian governor general, gave a trophy to be presented to "the fairest and most sportsmanlike player" in an effort to reduce the rough play that she perceived was becoming a detriment to the game. After legendary Canadiens goalie Georges Vézina died in 1926, his club presented a trophy in his memory to the best goalie in the league. These three persisted, while others, like the trophy donated by Paul Whiteman, the famous bandleader, for the league's top goal scorer, and the Greyhound Cup, given by the bus company for the league's MVP, fell by the wayside.[44]

Competition for trophies could stimulate fan interest and player performance, but did not address the widening income gap between clubs, which could also be addressed through league revenue policy. As the 1927 Stanley Cup winners, Ottawa's players received bonuses and the club extra home gates, but it still ran a deficit and Ottawa management concluded that the NHL needed to revise the visitor's share of regular-season games so popular draws like the Senators could better monetize their road appeal. Frank Ahearn sent Redmond Quain to make Ottawa's case at the September 1927 semiannual meeting, and the lawyer listed several reasons for Ottawa's weakness. Some of the problems were unique to Ottawa, including its small market and the growth of skiing as a recreational activity, but others related to the state of the NHL on-ice product, in particular the "dilution" of quality of play and the general lack of hockey tradition among the new (read: American) clubs. Quain argued for assistance on the basis that Ottawa's "hockey history and name make it a valuable asset always as a visiting team." He proposed revising the visitor's gate share along the lines practiced in baseball, up from the present 3.5 percent to 15 percent of the road gates. The other governors were disposed to help the champions and initially agreed to an upper limit of 10 percent, but at the suggestion of John Hammond they decided to form a committee to determine the exact number. Unfortunately, over the next few months sympathy evaporated, and when the committee of Calder, Dandurand, Hammond, and Adams returned its report in December, it recommended maintaining the 3.5 percent rate. Exasperating Ottawa even more, the governors also abolished the salary cap of thirty-five thousand dollars and increased the waiver price from twenty-five hundred to five thousand dollars, moves that would certainly raise club operating costs and make the NHL game even more expensive to play. All Ottawa could do was renovate its auditorium to attract more customers and transfer more games south, including two to the new Olympia in Detroit.[45]

The American clubs and the stronger Canadian clubs did feel real pressure to change the financial regulations, but they agreed to modify the on-ice rules more readily. Before the 1927–28 season, the rules committee recommended changes to encourage goal scoring, reduce stoppages, and discourage tie games, which were not a satisfying conclusion for many customers (especially Americans used to baseball). Most notably, the offside rule was modified. The ice was divided into three zones (defending, neutral, and attacking, from the perspective of the team in possession of the puck), and forward passing now allowed for defending teams in their own end and for both teams in the neutral zone (although forward passing across the zone lines was still banned). (See fig. 1) Goalie leg pads were reduced from twelve to ten inches in width to reduce their profile in the net, and goalies were prohibited from traveling more than four feet with the puck. To keep play moving, goalies were allowed to pass the puck back with their hands, and any rebounds would not now be considered offside passes. Also, there would be a penalty for picking up the puck or deliberately clearing it out of play, but kicking the puck was now allowed in the neutral zone and by defending teams. The overall goal of these changes was to increase scoring, provide a definite game result, and reduce whistles—all in order to appeal to spectators who were seen to be less appreciative of the subtleties of the "scientific" and combination (passing) style of play that had prevailed.[46]

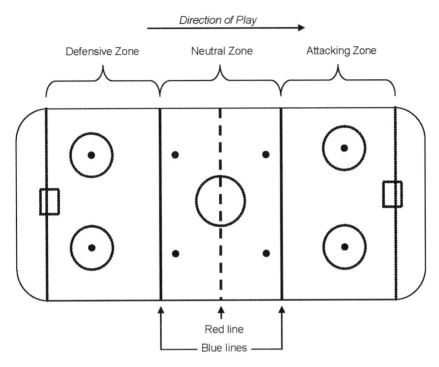

Fig. 1. NHL rink showing zones and lines, 1943–44.

Despite opposition by Ottawa, the Maroons, and Toronto to forward passing in the defensive zone, the rule remained, and it did result in fewer stoppages and more consistent officiating. Yet even with the rule changes, scoring in the 1927–28 season went down again, to only 3.8 goals per game from 4.0 the season before (likely because the defense now had the advantage of forward passing, but attackers did not). And even with a new ten minute sudden-death overtime period, the number of tie games more than doubled, from thirty-six to seventy-four. Players also tempered the pace of the game, to the point that in the fall of 1928 a committee was formed to report on solutions to "stalling" and a rule introduced requiring the puck to be kept constantly in motion and prohibiting passing back to delay the game. These changes were also ineffective.[47]

Midway through 1928–29, with scoring still in a trough (scoring ended the season at 2.9 goals per game), matters came to a head. In February

1929 the governors discussed widening the goal and instituting a penalty shot, and referee in chief Cooper Smeaton acknowledged in the press the motivation: the governors "were aware that low-scoring was one of the handicaps of the game, from an American point of view, [and] there was every disposition to take into consideration the public's demand for more tallies without destroying the essential action or zest of the play." Perhaps to make the best of a bad situation, Calder created another statistical category for his weekly release of scoring statistics and attendance figures: details on goalie performance, including shots stopped, saves made, and save percentage. Although it does not seem to have persisted, it was a means to make the best of the lack of scoring by encouraging customer appreciation of the defensive aspects of the sport.[48]

In some desperation, the governors used the last game of the 1928–29 season for an experiment, with the Rangers and Pirates trying out new rules that allowed forward passing in the attacking area (provided the players were onside going over the blue line), kicking of the puck by any player (except into the net), and prohibition on the goalie holding the puck for more than three seconds. The experiment was deemed successful, and the next fall at the September 1929 semiannual meeting in New York, the rule experiments were confirmed and the offside rule loosened even further, with forward passing within a zone permitted (but still no passing between zones). Crucially, attacking players were no longer required to be behind the puck carrier (onside) as the puck crossed the blue line into the attacking zone. In addition, Smeaton instructed his staff to bear down on the rules and see that every foul drew a penalty, especially for holding and deliberate attempts to injure.[49]

The 1929–30 season began with the high scoring expected, but with less effect on the pace of the game. There were fewer whistles, but it was even more evident that the players had depended on regular stoppages for respite from the action. Without regular breaks, they simply stalled and played more defense in order to recuperate. Nonetheless, according to the *New York Times*, "there was nothing in the opening night combat to arouse doubt that the revised rules have done excellent service in removing the game's most criticized features, namely, the halting of play and the paucity of goals." The Pittsburgh press was also positive, and Art Ross of the Bruins was happy because he had primed his players to thrive under the new rules. In Canada the reviews were generally less enthusiastic: the Toronto fans were "not impressed," and the Montreal press thought the rules generated "great excitement" but it was an open question whether the "wild scramble" that ensued was still hockey. On-ice strategy was being upended: an attacking player could now stand anywhere on the ice and not be offside, and it was joked that players like Nels Stewart of the Maroons and Cooney Weiland of the Bruins were setting up "light house-keeping" at the side of the opposition goal crease.[50]

One-quarter way into the season, the 3-goal-a-game average of the previous season had exploded to 7. It was too much. Dandurand and Smythe rallied support for a resumption of the requirement that all attackers at least be onside going over the blue line, and the other governors agreed. Dandurand defended the reversal by saying that "the league should not be swayed by the fanciful ideas of a few, whose main objects are to create added interest every year by making changes to the rule book." The *New York Times* noted that "the governors wished to tame the game only a little," and the tempering of the rule so that no attacking players could precede the puck into the opposing defensive zone seemed reasonable when the season continued on its high-scoring pace (the season finished at 5.9 goals per game). And the willingness of the NHL to innovate was appreciated, with one writer later noting that "tampering with the rules of any game is a favorite American pastime," and he appreciated that "the element engaged in promoting professional hockey was eager to cater to the American public."[51]

The Weak Links

Restructuring playoff incentives and tinkering with the on-ice product did little to overcome the fundamental weakness of poor clubs in small-capacity rinks. Over the course of the 1927–28 season, it was apparent that while most of the league was improving, some teams were still lagging badly. The Maroons, Canadiens, Rangers, Boston, and Detroit led the league in average attendance, with Pittsburgh, Chicago, Ottawa, Toronto, and the Americans in the bottom half (see fig. 2). Measuring by gate receipts showed the same pattern, and the American clubs were much better revenue generators per spectator than the Canadian. This prosperity reflected the ability and willingness of American spectators to pay more, but also the different competitive circumstances of Canadian and American clubs. Canadian clubs had competition from high-quality amateur clubs who could provide a cheaper substitute, whereas in the American cities there were fewer direct substitutes for elite hockey.

If trends continued, it seemed that Canadian NHL hockey might soon be restricted to Montreal. Moreover, the American clubs were increasing rink capacities even further. It was a new building that was behind the Cougars' rise, and in their second season, the first at the Olympia, gate receipts jumped 250 percent and attendance almost tripled, to 142,000. In the spring and summer of 1928, there was more news of rink construction in other cities. Stalled in Chicago and Philadelphia, Rickard planted

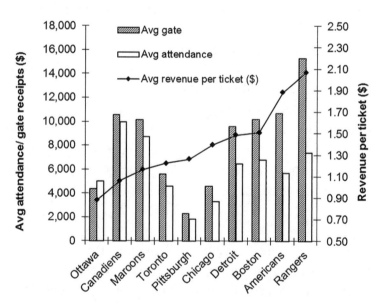

Fig. 2. Average NHL gate receipts, attendance, and revenue per ticket, 1927–28. No currency adjustments have been made as the Canadian and American dollars were at par in this era.

another Garden in Boston. He convinced the Boston & Maine Railroad to incorporate a new "fight auditorium" into their renovation plans for the downtown North Station, and the new Boston Madison Square Garden was designed to sit right on top of the railway station itself. The four-million-dollar building would hold 15,000 for hockey, almost equal to its namesake, and the spectators arrayed in the three tiers would take in many of the same events—boxing, the circus, horse shows, and NHL hockey. Although the Boston & Maine would own the building, a twenty-five-year lease gave Rickard's Madison Square Garden–owned operating company the exclusive right to promote all events. The new board was stocked with New York Garden representatives: Rickard, William Carey, Richard Hoyt, and Tack Hardwick as chairman of the executive committee. Charles Adams was also a director, no doubt to confirm the tenancy of his Bruins. He did not need much convincing. Averaging nearly 7,000 fans per game over the 1927–28 season at the arena, the Bruins were bursting at the seams and eager to move to the bigger Garden.[52]

In Chicago, however, Rickard was being trumped. Despite attempts to waylay Harmon, after what the *Tribune* called "three years of intermittent ballyhoo interrupted by periods of quiescence," he was finally getting his Chicago Stadium off the ground. Adding to Rickard's chagrin, the building would be bigger than either of his Gardens (seating 19,034) and also cost much more ($7 million). Even the pipe organ was to be the largest six-manual type in the world. In addition to his main partners, Sidney and Harold Strotz, Harmon had convinced several more deep-pocketed and prominent Chicago sportsmen to finance and sit on the board of the Chicago Stadium Corporation. Two of these men were Frederic McLaughlin and John Mitchell of the Black Hawks, the building's expected tenants, but there were many other representatives of Chicago's business elite, including a new resident of Chicago recently arrived from New York, James Norris, the president of the Norris Grain Company, a brokerage house.[53]

In the fall of 1928, with construction proceeding in Boston and Chicago, the NHL governors met behind closed doors on 23 September to discuss the more pessimistic Pittsburgh situation. Owner Henry Townsend had died in 1927, the Pirates' attendance was low, and there was no real prospect for a new rink. A change was needed. Several parties made proposals, including Tom Duggan, who was continuing his promotional efforts in Chicago (in association with Harmon) and also in Buffalo, where he was said to be behind the new Can-Pro franchise. Surveying the American hockey landscape, Duggan had earlier in the year identified a move to Cleveland as a solution to the Pittsburgh problem. When Philadelphia entrepreneur Irwin P. Wener obtained an option on the Pirates in January 1928 with the intention of moving the club to Philadelphia, Duggan and Cleveland promoter Tom Downes convinced him that the club would prosper more in Cleveland since Sunday hockey was permitted there. Wener agreed to give Downes an option to buy the club for $275,000, expiring 5 March 1928, and Downes and Duggan began promoting the idea of the NHL franchise coming to Cleveland to play in a new arena.[54]

Duggan's sales pitch embodied his assessment of the best business strategy for a new NHL club. To bring hockey to Cleveland, Duggan argued that "the first step to be taken would be to invite a group of prominent men, (Both socially and financially) to organize for the purpose of financing and socially dressing the sports arena." But they searched in vain for a local investor to take part. At the NHL meeting in March 1928, the NHL governors refused Wener permission to transfer his option to another party, instead asking Calder to arrange its disposition. By fall, despite James Callahan's assurances to the contrary, there were persistent rumors that the Pirates would be moving, and Cleveland was mentioned once again. Two weeks later the shoe dropped with the news that the Townsend family had sold majority control of the club to Benny Leonard, a former lightweight boxing champion. Callahan stayed on as president and, along with others, maintained a minority position, while Leonard became treasurer and Callahan's brother Charles club secretary.[55]

It was unclear why Leonard became interested in the Pirates, and almost certainly he was not acting entirely on his own. Leonard had retired from the ring in 1925 reportedly with a million dollars in the bank, but he knew nothing of hockey other than what he might have picked up incidentally with his connections to the sports promotion networks centered on Madison Square Garden. It was rumored that the money behind the Pittsburgh purchase actually belonged to Bill Dwyer, recently paroled and returned to control of the New York Americans. It was certainly curious that Dwyer and Leonard shared the same lawyer, Joseph Shalleck, who was a director of the Americans and appeared with Leonard and the Townsends at the signing over of the club. Whether Dwyer was the principal investor or not, Leonard was the public face of the Pirates and the Duquesne Garden. At first he played to his strengths, speaking about boxing promotion. He noted that hockey was eating into the boxing audience and speculated that, far from being complementary, the rise in hockey popularity might be one of several factors contributing to boxing's wane. To Leonard's way of thinking, what the two sports had in common was the need to keep prices low enough so that the "gallery gods" in the upper-level inexpensive seats could afford to attend. At only forty-five-hundred capacity, however, Duquesne Garden was much too small to sustain his goal of a modestly priced fifty-cent ticket, and Leonard told the press he planned to enlarge it and build a new arena.[56]

As a hockey man Leonard quickly ran into trouble. Within weeks of his takeover, the entire Pirates team refused to sign their contracts and held out for more money. He eventually cajoled most into returning, but his stars—Jack Darragh, Baldy Cotton, and Roy Worters—would not budge. Frank Calder had to step in and threaten that anyone without a contract by 30 October would be suspended, which got Darragh and Cotton to sign, but Worters still held out. To help break the impasse, Bill Dwyer offered up Americans goalie Jim Miller and twenty thousand dollars for Worters, but Calder made it clear he would still refuse to reinstate Worters unless he was under contract to the Pirates at the time of a trade. James Collins of the *Washington Post* pointed out that Calder was trying to avoid the dangerous precedent of selling holdout players, which could give the players more power over where they played.[57]

Dwyer threatened legal action unless the governors overturned Calder's decision and reinstated Worters, but in a meeting at the Waldorf-Astoria in New York in December, with Callahan and Dwyer out of the room, the governors upheld Calder's decision unanimously. Seeming to emphasize the point, after Callahan and Dwyer returned, Conn Smythe moved that Calder's contract be extended another five years. Knowing he was beaten, Dwyer even seconded the motion. Actually, the severe shortage of goalies had already forced Calder to allow Worters to play for the Americans in a game, and the feeling was that he would soon reinstate him and allow the trade now that he had ratification from the governors. Calder pronounced himself satisfied that the principle that players under suspension should not be traded had been upheld, and with his authority confirmed he magnanimously allowed Worters to play.[58]

Aside from serving as a good example of Calder's ability to stand on principle in the face of owner opposition, the Worters dispute also confirms the likelihood of a less than arm's-length relationship between the Americans and Pirates. By extension, it also suggests a resuscitation of the latent ambition harbored by Duggan and Dwyer to control multiple NHL clubs and arenas. As we have seen, Duggan had been actively continuing hockey and arena promotional efforts in Chicago, Buffalo, and Cleveland. For his part, Dwyer had briefly threatened to try to gain control of Madison Square Garden itself after returning from prison. It was not clear how serious this idea was—it never did pan out—and he may have been simply targeting the Garden as leverage to revise the Americans' onerous lease conditions, but the Leonard-led Pirates may also have been part of a more ambitious scheme.[59]

The strongest syndicate threat was still Rickard's realm, which was expanding. In November 1928 the Boston Madison Square Garden opened on Causeway Street. It was considered an engineering marvel, built over a former arm of the Charles River and poised directly on top of the North Station tracks, a distance of twenty-two feet from arena floor to station floor. Designed by Funk & Wilcox, the new coliseum could seat 14,500 for hockey and 18,000 for boxing, making it the second largest in the league by capacity after Madison Square Garden, at least until Harmon's giant Chicago Stadium made its appearance. On opening night on 17 November 1928, more than 17,000 fans mobbed their way through the gates for the game against the Canadiens, confirming the pent-up demand for Bruins hockey that the arena had not been big enough to satisfy.[60]

Like the Mount Royal Arena several seasons before, the Boston Arena would not let its NHL tenant go without a fight and sued for breach of contract, asserting the Bruins had one more year left on the lease. Litigation dragged on through the season, but, irrespective of ethics, the Bruins had certainly made the right financial decision. Attendance in 1928–29 jumped 97 percent to 249,000, and gate receipts were up 92 percent to $477,130. The *New York Times* reported that the club made $200,600 in *net* profit that year—an incredible 42 percent of its gross revenues. The Bruins were never going back, and in September the Boston Arena and Garden came to a truce that divided the city's sporting event market. The Bruins and Can-Am Tigers could move to the Garden permanently, and in return the Boston Arena would have exclusive right to the popular local amateur and school activities, as well as public skating. It was worth it to the Bruins. In 1929–30 they continued to lead the league in gate receipts, grossing $502,136—over $100,000 more than even the Rangers, the next highest.[61]

Rickard's Gardens were central to achieving this augmented level of revenues, but in January 1929 the dream of a continuing linking together of a chain of profitable Gardens across the US Northeast perished, interred with the man himself. On a trip to Miami to open a greyhound track and arrange a title fight, Rickard suffered an attack of appendicitis and died of infection. Jack Dempsey, the heavyweight boxing champion, accompanied the body back to New York, where it lay in state in the Garden. Calder and Dandurand represented the NHL as honorary pallbearers.[62]

Paddy Harmon also came to the funeral (perhaps to confirm his rival was really gone) and took advantage of the occasion to talk up a new hockey league. The Black Hawks were reluctant to nest at his stadium, and Harmon was cranking the new-league rumor mill in an attempt to put pressure on the other NHL clubs to bring McLaughlin in line. McLaughlin was certainly aware that, if they would deign to use it, Harmon's giant new arena in Chicago would send the Hawks soaring to the same revenue heights as the Rangers, Americans, Cougars, and Bruins, but he was also aware that the devil was in the lease details. And with Livingstone's Cardinals having given up the ghost, the Black Hawks were the only hockey tenant to be had, and despite the club's debts McLaughlin could afford to press the advantage and take his time negotiating with both the Coliseum and the Chicago Stadium. (Although he had been an initial investor in the stadium, he had left the board and could now act solely in the hockey club's best interests.) Negotiations soon bogged down just like stadium construction, which was plagued by the union unrest that characterized corruption-rife Chicago. In November James Norris, a stadium board member, asked Frank Calder to arbitrate. It is unknown if Calder took up the role, but by Christmas the parties were still at an impasse. Putting the pressure on, McLaughlin announced plans for his own rink, a twelve-thousand-seat building to be located on Chicago's North Side. At a cost of $750,000, McLaughlin's stadium would have been a very cheap building, which suggests the proposal was not very serious. Harmon retaliated with a threat to create a rival hockey league, and this idea was what he was trotting out at Rickard's funeral. Both threats were dubious, but with no lease, and with the stadium still unfinished anyway, the Black Hawks were forced to play their home games out of town, mostly at Detroit's Olympia. In February Black Hawks manager William J. (Bill) Tobin wired Calder that the club planned to return to the Coliseum in the fall, as it did not anticipate "deals of any kind with Harmon and Norris and [the] Stadium."[63]

As part of his bid to obtain an NHL club, Harmon had offered to buy Ottawa, and he was not the only interested party. In January 1929 Ottawa's Frank Ahearn announced that he had three offers for his stake and formally notified Calder that the club would be moving to the United States. Whether Ahearn ever thought he would actually have to sell, by the midway point of the 1928–29 season he was projecting a loss of $20,000–$40,000 for his club, so it looked increasingly likely. Ahearn denied rumors Ottawa would start peddling its remaining stars, but also warned that it was the Canadian clubs that would suffer most if Ottawa were forced to drop out. If Ahearn did not bring it up again directly, his request for subsidy was still in the air, but Calder told the *New York Times* that "in his opinion the league would not consent to such a move" (increasing the revenue sharing).[64]

In a letter to Fred McLaughlin, Calder made clear his ideological opposition to any revenue-sharing proposal modeled on baseball, such as Ottawa favored. He argued that "a club with a lesser constituency might sit back and lose all initiative, knowing that it would be taken care of anyhow." McLaughlin disagreed. In his view, "a chain is only as strong as its weakest link, and the present N.H.L. is beautifully designed to make weaker the weak links. . . . I consider it important that the N.H.L. should decide once and for all whether it is composed of enemies or allies. Is it

composed of ten teams each of which is constantly trying to do the other
in the eye, or of ten teams trying to promote each others [*sic*] sporting and
financial welfare? My own impression is that the former is the case, and
that the latter would elicit cries of raucous laughter at any league meeting."
McLaughlin was highlighting the tension that sustained the league cartel
form, between individual club competition in local markets at one pole
and collective support at the other. It goes without saying that his own
preference for collective solidarity fed his own club's interest, insofar as an
Ottawa move might be to Chicago—and into Harmon's stadium as a competitor to the Black Hawks. Furthermore, Chicago was still far from flush
(the previous season it had only barely passed the $100,000 mark itself)
and so would likely benefit from any support schemes.[65]

In Ottawa Ahearn saw the balance as one between commercial self-
interest, on the one hand, and patriotism and civic pride, on the other.
Even with offers said to be as high as $250,000, Ahearn found reasons on
both counts to keep the team in Ottawa. He and his father, Thomas, an
electricity and traction magnate, were heavy investors in the Ottawa Auditorium, and retaining the Senators as the anchor tenant was a good business decision. The price for a local sale would be nowhere near as high as
the highest bid from outsiders, but it was a discount Ahearn was willing to
accept in order to keep the club playing in "the Aud." At an Ottawa Rotary
Club dinner in February, Fred Burpee, president of the Aud, announced
the rink would buy the club and that the Senators would remain in Ottawa
for another season at least. Frank Calder was in attendance and told the
guests, "The team cannot live on tradition and sentiment. In the last analysis it depends on the people of Ottawa whether the team remains or not."
Later, at a shareholders meeting, Burpee revealed the price, $125,000, and
the future options: operate in Ottawa, operate in an American city, or sell
to the highest bidder. The shareholders decided to continue in Ottawa.[66]

To finance the purchase the club offered five thousand shares at $25
each, but even in the heady investing environment of early 1929, the stock
sale did not go well. In April Burpee got an extension from Ahearn and
revised the offer, but with the shares still not selling, the auditorium
instead issued $125,000 of its own 7 percent preferred shares, which had
the advantage of a guaranteed dividend rate and first call on real assets.

Even then, Ahearn could not be fully paid off, but the transfer of control happened anyway. In the fall he was replaced as president of the Ottawa Hockey Association by William Foran, the Stanley Cup trustee, along with a new slate of directors. Now it was Foran's turn to plead Ottawa's case for revenue sharing to the other clubs. In a letter circulated before an NHL meeting, he again argued for implementation of the baseball model. This time Foran wanted to increase the visitors' share as high as 20 percent if necessary. Once again, he provided Ottawa's numbers showing the power of the Senators as a road draw and the weakness of reciprocation, indicating that Ottawa generated away revenues of two to five times its home gates; once again, the governors delayed a decision, only later convening a committee to study the matter. In the meantime, Ottawa's debts mounted. Calder refused the club's request for its share of the league's equity account (its cash reserves) in order to pay off Ahearn.[67]

In February the committee reported back, recommending a new solution: the creation of a National Hockey League Joint Relief Fund. A half percent of the existing 3.5 percent visitors' share would go into the fund, and upon application a club could receive a subsidy of up to half its deficit, subject to an audit of its operations by the other clubs. This charity plan was not the long-term structural adjustment Ottawa was looking for and was inadequate at best. Using the previous season's gate-receipt totals (1928–29), the pool would have been about $11,335 (0.5 percent of the league's gross gate of $2,266,944), of which approximately $400 would already be Ottawa's own contribution. Even with no sharing (with Pittsburgh, for example), the most Ottawa could then expect was half of a deficit up to $20,000 or so. Most important, the amount was in no way guaranteed and depended on a committee's determination of an appropriate figure. It was far easier for Ottawa to try to make up the difference by arranging for games in American venues, and in 1929–30 the club scheduled two in Atlantic City, New Jersey; two in the Detroit Olympia; and one in Boston. NHL hockey was leaving Ottawa a few games at a time.[68]

The International Hockey League

Having made the international leap to take advantage of the rabid American interest in sports in the 1920s and to thwart competitors, the NHL owners were now committed to making their transnational enterprise work. To do so, the governors committed themselves fully to the idea of a single major league, setting aside ideas of dividing the NHL or allowing minor leagues to rise to equality. Controlling the elite player market after the demise of the WHL was an advantage that the NHL would not easily relinquish, and if necessary force would be exerted, as in the case of the AHA, which was treated as an "outlaw" until it accepted its subordinate status. It was a strategy that would have to be used again soon enough, but the preference was to co-opt potential competitors using the benefits of affiliation, getting them to function as training grounds within a new "organized" hockey-industry hierarchy. The league owners also accepted that the cartel had to convey the image of separately owned clubs—whatever the reality—and rejected a hybrid syndicate model that might have come had more of Rickard's Madison Square Garden–controlled Gardens been built. Below the surface, there was room for multiple interests as long as they did not become too public. In the new decade new relationships would lead to new disputes, indicating the issue was not yet completely or comfortably resolved, and overseeing it all was still the main referee, Frank Calder, who had successfully brought the minors into line and continued to weather his own conflicts with his employers.

Besides cartel rules, the Canadian clubs also accepted change in the rules on the ice to make the product work in the United States, particularly the redefining of offside rules for American audiences to make hockey quite literally a game of greater forward progress. Designed to appeal to audiences unfamiliar with the game, it emphasized speed and uninterrupted play and now demanded new fitness levels and new strategies such as switching lines of players as play progressed. (NHL player and coach Dick Irvin later recalled that "it was the total legalizing of the forward pass in 1929 that opened up hockey.") When combined with the physicality of the game and the promise of violence, hockey presented a distinct and novel product to the entertainment marketplace. America, as Leslie Roberts of *McClure's* phrased it, "came in curiosity and remained to yell" at a sport that "seemingly . . . has everything that the sports-loving public holds dear—speed and skill, blood and brain, beef and science . . . [and a] battle-cry of speed and goals." The success of clubs like the Rangers, on and off the ice, showed that it could become a natural fit as an American sport as well. Except for the later permanent introduction of the red line during the Second World War, with relatively few changes by 1929 the standard of twentieth-century professional hockey had been set for the ensuing decades. And over time it would increasingly influence and transform the amateur and international games.[69]

NHL brand hockey attracted both working and wealthier classes to some degree. In New York Rickard had enticed the upper crust, but the bulk of the audience, as one might expect, reflected the ethnic diversity of the New York area (with the exception of the near-total absence of African Americans). Women appear to have been a good portion of the audience. In February 1929 Calder claimed that 40 percent of fans were women, and the percentage was going up. According to Roberts, this growth was an advantage of playing at night, when "husbands and wives, stenographers and boyfriends, and society buds escorted by young men in dinner coats came to witness the proceedings." Charles Adams contended, "Hockey fans are the most rabid of sports devotees. In no other sport can be found such blind, intense and unceasing loyalty. Their team can do no wrong, and the other team with few exceptions, can do no right. The men are bad enough, the women are worse."[70]

With the NHL now a success in the United States, at the gate and on the ice (the Rangers won the Stanley Cup in 1928 and lost the first all-American final to Boston in 1929), the question was whether Canadian clubs would continue to accept and adapt to the changes needed to continue to participate in the binational league. A split into two leagues (Canadian and American) along the successful model of baseball's NL and AL would likely have produced uncertain effects on the Canadian clubs and the quality of play. Once Canadian stars had received the high American salaries, there was no reason to think they would return home for mere patriotism's sake. So the Canadian clubs had accepted the binational form with its compromises and risks, because for many clubs it seemed worth it. By dint of leases in facilities in the most important North American urban sport markets, control over the best players through the option clause, and priority over the championship trophy (the Stanley Cup), the

Canadian-born NHL was consolidating its hegemony over a North American sport spectacle.

Growth and internationalization were also contributing to a perception that the nature of the enterprise was changing. Certainly, the scale had grown. American expansion had changed the cost picture significantly—the average salary had grown three times—but this increase was outpaced by revenues. The Hamilton Tigers club had gate revenues of $35,448 in 1920–21; seven years later its descendant, the 1927–28 New York Americans, made almost seven times that amount ($235,466). Franchise values kept pace. Charlie Querrie noted the great appreciation in franchise fees (from the "pay-as-you-can" $5,000 Toronto franchise in 1918 to the $50,000 demanded from Detroit and Chicago in 1926) and also the franchise purchase prices (from the $11,000 paid for the Canadiens in 1921 to the $160,000 paid for the St. Patrick's six years later). For Querrie, the enterprise had changed in magnitude, and also in character, which he framed as the difference between sport (the traditional activity) and business (the modern): "In 1919 professional hockey was more of a sport than it is to-day. With big expenses and large investments it is one large business now." This expansion had national implications: "It will not be many years before all the large centers of the United States will have rinks seating . . . 20,000 people and it will not surprise us if Montreal and Toronto are the only two Canadian cities which will be in the big league."[71]

With Ottawa weakening, it seemed Querrie's prediction might soon come true. The Senators' difficulties were representative of the price being paid for the NHL's American expansion—a pressure on weaker clubs to adapt to the new model of larger payrolls, higher costs, and larger arenas or else be set adrift. The governors of the ten-club major league were leaving much of the collective sentiment of the preexpansion era behind in favor of more club independence. In the international NHL, clubs like Ottawa could not now depend on the kindness of other clubs, and market realities would be allowed to take precedence over national or civic loyalties as revenues grew and the league's viability as a whole became more ensured.

In his study of the NHL in this era, historian Bruce Kidd asks why the Canadian NHL owners did not "act to protect their interests"; in other words, why they did not band together to prevent American domination of the NHL? His answer is that owners like Tommy Gorman and Percy Thompson "were so deeply imbued with the ethos of competition that they were unable to contemplate any significant undertaking" of this kind. Underpinning this interpretation is an assumption that Canadian club self-interest could not include affiliation with Americans in a binational league. Yet the Canadian clubs were doing very well with American affiliation, with the exception of Ottawa. And Gorman and Thompson were more managers than owners and could be expected to be less idealistic, while the important governors like Ahearn and Dandurand, and even Smythe, clearly *did* think along national lines and continued to do so into the next decade, later even contemplating the idea of a Canadian league. Furthermore, while Kidd notes that the 1920s was a decade of American takeover of Canadian companies, he does not consider that hockey as an export product, and the wages and remittances of hockey laborers, could have actually been of net benefit to the Canadian economy. Contemporaries like Linde Fowler of the *Boston Transcript* saw this aspect:

> The antipathy in Boston to professional hockey (not inconsiderable) had its counterpart in Canadian circles. They were not so sure across the border that they wanted their national game established in the United States.
>
> They had visions, some of their leaders, of big populations to build up great hockey patronage in American cities; they had visions of increased prices for tickets, increased financial resources to overbid them for their own Canadian stars. They were not far astray on those visions. What they don't stress strongly enough in their disgruntlement, those who wail the loudest, is that it is still a Canadian game; that American dollars are going into Canadian pockets and spent, in very material measure, in Canadian communities.

So while NHL expansion changed the economic game, it was still not obvious that it was detrimental to the Canadian game. The economic transformations wrought by American capital would need even more accommodation in the decade ahead, as would the tension between the cultural meaning of NHL hockey in Canada and its meaning in the United States. It was hoped that the continuing popularity in both countries would bring convergence.[72]

Before any harmony, there would be challenge. The end of the first wave of NHL expansion was punctuated by two deaths. Tex Rickard's demise truncated his dream of a chain of arenas forming an interurban circuit of circus shows, boxing bouts, six-day bicycle races, and NHL hockey games. The next year Tom Duggan, the man who had sold Rickard on hockey (and may have been trying to emulate his strategy), also died, at his home in Montreal. Unlike Rickard's, Duggan's departure provoked little commentary in the sports pages. Baz O'Meara of the *Montreal Daily Star* paid modest tribute to Duggan's vision and his prediction that hockey would be the "greatest attendance-getter of all sports in America before many years." It was only years later that Elmer Ferguson came closer to acknowledging Duggan's impact when he wrote that it was Duggan, "lovable, financially careless but clever and imaginative . . . who was responsible for the great international edifice that is today the National Hockey League—Tom, and no one else." This hyperbole ignores many other people who played important roles—Adams, Calder, the other owners—but does highlight how the essential involvements of Duggan, Rickard, and Eddie Livingstone have often since been elided in the history of the NHL. While US expansion would have likely happened without Duggan or Livingstone, it might not have been successful without the timely encouragement of Rickard and Madison Square Garden, which allowed it to benefit from the sport-friendly 1920s and get firmly established before the Depression came. Richard's string of NHL clubs planted in American Gardens had to come to pass through the exploitation of hockey, boxing, horse racing, journalism, business, and even illicit gambling networks, allowing the NHL to thwart competition—professional and amateur—and quickly tie together a chain of the largest indoor arenas of both central Canada and the northeastern and midwestern United States in order to become a dominant international hockey league. In retrospect, the deaths of Rickard and Duggan were harbingers of the end of a golden age of arena promotion that made the NHL. With the league now having survived Canadian infancy to attain American majority, the question was whether it could remain united in the face of impending widespread economic crisis, continuing internal dissension, and the ever-present threat of external competition.[73]

1. Early hockey thrived in the clubhouses of the middle classes, who could afford recreation in facilities like this Quebec City rink. With its low boards and lack of seats, the rink space was oriented to participation, not spectatorship. In the undated picture, a seven-man hockey team poses for a "bully," an early version of the face-off that persisted in field hockey, one of ice hockey's predecessors. (J. E. Livernois fonds/Library and Archives Canada/PA-024066)

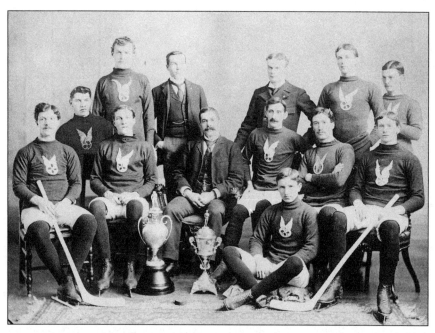

2. The popularity of hockey among Montreal sports club members led the formation of teams graded by ability and age, and their seasons were commemorated in the studios of society photographer William Notman. As an affiliate of the Montreal Amateur Athletic Association, the 1897 champion Montreal Hockey Club intermediate team pictured here was stocked with scions of Montreal's elite commercial classes, including Norman Dawes, who later ran National Breweries and whose brother Kenneth became an investor in the Montreal Forum. Towering above the others is the teenage son of a prominent grain broker, James Norris, who would later muscle his way into the National Hockey League, renaming the Detroit club the Red Wings and giving it a new crest based on the winged wheel of the MAAA. *Front row*: J. McLeod. *Center row, left to right*: A. Hough, A. Locke, A. Cameron, G. Hamilton, F. Bickerdike, and C. Bourne. *Rear row, left to right*: S. Fernie, J. Norris, A. MacKerrow, G. James, N. Dawes, and A. Waud. (A. N. MacKerrow fonds/Library and Archives Canada/PA-124967)

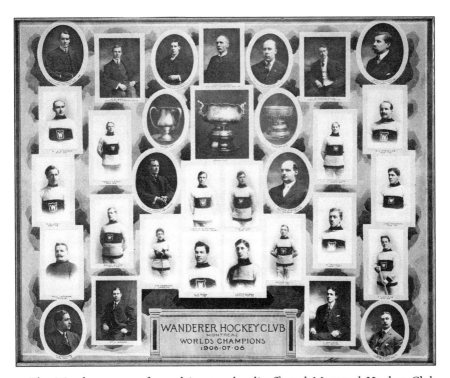

3. The Wanderers were formed in 1903 by disaffected Montreal Hockey Club amateur players who joined the new club with the understanding that they would be paid to play. The new Wanderers became the dominant Montreal club in the first decade of the twentieth century and were at the center of the major evolutions of the elite leagues up to the formation of the NHL in 1917. This montage of head shots contains both the business minds who organized the new club, like James Strachan and William Jennings, as well as the star players, like Art Ross and Lester Patrick, who were paid to win on the ice. Between 1906 and 1908, the club was the main holder of the prestigious Stanley Cup (denoting the "World's Champions"), but in this 1908 image the cup cedes centrality to the Arena Cup, donated by the main Montreal venue for professional hockey, the Westmount Arena, for the championship of the Eastern Canada Amateur Hockey Association. (Thomas Patrick Gorman fonds/Library and Archives Canada/C-080072)

4. Magnats de Hockey Promoteurs de la Ligue Internationale (Hockey Magnates Promoters of International League), *La Presse* (Montreal), 11 February 1924. Partly to keep other hockey entrepreneurs like Eddie Livingstone at bay, the NHL had felt pressure to expand southward. Sometimes interests got mixed up. At this meeting at the traditional venue, Montreal's Windsor Hotel, the board of governors discussed the pending expansion into the United States. They had invited the new Boston owner, Charles Adams, to come and were probably surprised when he brought along their old foe, Eddie Livingstone, whose very ouster had prompted the formation of the league in the first place. They listened politely to his proposals and had their photo taken, but did not follow up. Livingstone did not give up, however, and would reemerge a few years later to challenge the NHL in the US Midwest. *Back row*: Leo Dandurand (manager of the Canadiens), Charlie Querrie (manager of Toronto), Percy Thompson (manager of Hamilton), Paul Ciceri (Toronto), Dr. W. T. Hand (Hamilton), and Percy Hambly (Toronto). *Front row*: Andrew Ross (Hamilton), Charles Adams (Boston Arena), Frank Calder (president of the league), E. J. Livingstone (Toronto), and T. P. Gorman (manager of Ottawa).

5. Canadian Arena (the Forum), St. Catherine Street, Montreal, 1924. Arenas had a crucial part to play in the development and expansion of professional hockey. At the time it was built, Montreal's Forum was a state-of-the-art building that typified the urban multipurpose facilities that were emerging to respond to consumer demand for sport in the 1920s. Conveniently integrated into urban transportation networks—note the electrified Montreal Tramways Company tracks out front—the Forum was a profitable venue where English and French Montrealers of all classes could see their favorite professional and amateur hockey teams. Just like its predecessor, the Westmount Arena, the Forum management kept close ownership ties, formal and informal, with the NHL clubs. (McCord Museum MP-1977.140.18.2)

6. Though finishing with the fifth-best regular-season record, the New York Rangers won the Stanley Cup in 1928 after only their second season in the league. The club, originally to be named the Giants, was quickly changed to the Rangers, as in "Tex's Rangers," in tribute to the impresario of Madison Square Garden. In this picture the Rangers show off the Stanley Cup to New York mayor Jimmy "Beau James" Walker. As a state legislator in 1920, Walker had been the sponsor of the Walker Law, which legalized boxing in New York State and paved the way for the revival of Madison Square Garden under Rickard's stewardship. On John Hammond's advice, Rickard picked hockey to fill the dark nights between fights and the circus, and it was to be the financial savior of the Garden during the Depression. *Left to right*: Alex Gray, Bill Boyd, Leo Bourgault, Frank Boucher, Bill Cook, Colonel John Hammond, Lorne Chabot, Mayor Jimmy Walker, Taffy Abel, Lester Patrick, Murray Murdoch, Patsy Callighen, Bun Cook, Harry Westerby (trainer), and Paul Thompson. (Underwood & Underwood/Photography Collection, Miriam and Ira D. Wallach Division of Art, Prints and Photographs, The New York Public Library, Astor, Lenox and Tilden Foundations)

7. Violence was part of the appeal of hockey, but on occasion it resulted in serious injury. In a game at the Boston Garden on 12 December 1933, Eddie Shore of the Bruins blindsided Irvine "Ace" Bailey of the Maple Leafs and knocked him unconscious. The Leafs' Red Horner, Shore's intended target, then knocked Shore to the ice in retribution. The picture shows the immediate aftermath, with Bailey on the ice at left (beside Charlie Sands, #16), having suffered a life-threatening head injury, and Shore being attended to on the right (on the ice in front of Joe Lamb, #10). After several harrowing hours and days, it became clear Bailey would survive, but he would never play hockey again. Two benefit games were played in his honor, the second being the first league all-star game, one of many institutions hockey borrowed from baseball. (Courtesy of the Boston Public Library, Leslie Jones Collection)

8. The central body of NHL administration was the board of governors, which was composed of club representatives (usually owners) who met regularly to set policy and resolve disputes over players, revenues, schedules, rules, and regulations. At this meeting in Chicago on 13 May 1934, the public news was the announcement that the Ottawa Senators would move to St. Louis. Behind the scenes, the Canadiens looked to sell and the Americans tried to find new financing for the cash-strapped club. The Rangers representative was absent, likely owing to the recent boardroom takeover of Madison Square Garden engineered by John Hammond and financed by new Detroit owner James Norris. By the end of the decade, Norris would have connections to four of the seven NHL clubs. *Front row*: Leo Dandurand and Joe Cattarinich (Canadiens), Frank Calder, and Redmond Quain (Ottawa). *Back row*: Fred McLaughlin (Chicago), James Strachan (Maroons), Bill Dwyer (Americans), James Norris (Detroit), Charles Adams (Boston), and Conn Smythe (Toronto). (© Bettmann/CORBIS)

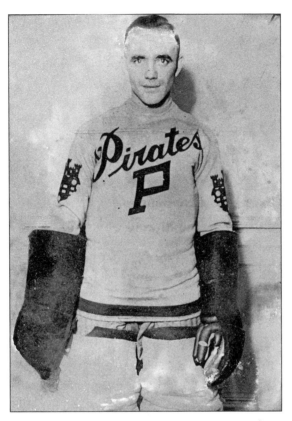

9. Roy "Shrimp" Worters began his NHL career with the Pittsburgh Pirates in 1925–26, and later he became a star for the otherwise lackluster New York Americans. Despite his short stature (five foot three), he was an effective player, and in 1928–29 he became the first goalie to win the Hart Trophy as the league MVP. Upon retirement in 1939, Worters spoke of the challenges of professional hockey labor. Aside from the long apprenticeship, low pay, tough training, physical injuries, emotional stress, and lack of job security, not least was the option clause that tied a player to his club "indefinitely" and prevented him from achieving his full market value. (Library and Archives Canada/Mikan no. 3685876)

10. As the son of W. A. Hewitt, the sport journalist and longtime Canadian
Amateur Hockey Association executive, Foster Hewitt had a head start in the
world of sport media. After a decade at the *Toronto Daily Star* and its radio station, in November 1931 he became the first director of radio—and play-by-play
announcer—for Maple Leaf Gardens. Hewitt's *General Motors Hockey Broadcast*
originated from a "gondola" perched five stories above the ice and became part of
the Gardens' business model, as well as establishing the NHL, the Maple Leafs,
and Hewitt himself as national brand names. From 1935 the show was sponsored
by Imperial Oil and became informally known as "Hockey Night in Canada,"
later helping strengthen the argument that NHL hockey was essential to morale
during the Second World War. This image shows him advertising General Motors
in the *National Home Monthly* (1933).

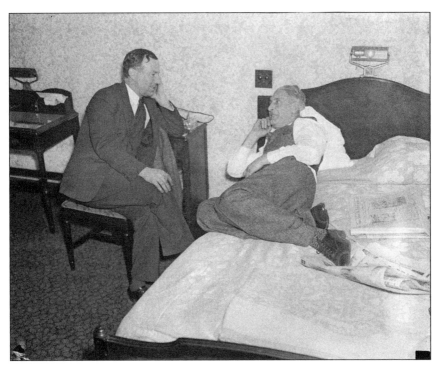

11. Two Westmount boys, Lester Patrick and Art Ross, shown here in 1935, remained central to the NHL into midcentury. Art Ross was the most petulant personality in a league full of fractious owners and later wrote a letter that lambasted his fellow governors and Frank Calder. Along with his brother Frank, Lester Patrick innovated the PCHA as a rival to the NHA, providing competition and then players. He went on to run the New York Rangers and had a clear understanding of the novel appeal of the game. When asked to consider banning fighting, he said it would be like "throwing gold out of the window." (Courtesy of the Boston Public Library, Leslie Jones Collection)

12. Conn Smythe embodied hockey's—and wartime society's—ambivalence to the Second World War. On the one hand, he wanted to limit the effect of the war on Maple Leaf Gardens operations by lobbying against wartime taxation measures, and he was eager to use Canadian monetary policy to suppress competition from US leagues. At the same time, Smythe enlisted in the artillery at the advanced age of forty-five, demanded a combat assignment, and was to be later wounded in the invasion of Normandy. Upon his return to Canada, his criticisms of government conscription policy set off a political crisis, but he also lobbied to have men released to play for the NHL. Here Smythe is pictured ca. 1941 with Leafs coach Hap Day (*far right*) and several Maple Leafs players, including Wally Stanowski (*far left*), who got caught up in the politics of Canada's wartime manpower system. (F223-3-2-4, photo #10, Archives of Ontario)

13. Bobby Bauer, Milt Schmidt, and Woody Dumart (*left to right*, ca. 1945–46) formed the Boston Bruins' high-scoring "Kraut Line." In January 1942 "the Krauts" joined the Royal Canadian Air Force and were often renamed the "Kitchener Kids" for the remainder of the war. Like the other American teams, the Bruins lost many of their players to military service and the vagaries of passport requirements and wartime manpower policies. (Courtesy of the Boston Public Library, Leslie Jones Collection)

14. From his office in Montreal's Sun Life Building, the founding president of the NHL, Frank Calder, helped guide the league's clubs and also kept a guiding hand on the many strands of hockey outside the league. His touch could be light or heavy as the situation demanded, but his first priority was always to the NHL as the major league, and his commitment was total: recovering from a heart attack in 1943, he died in his hospital bed while working on league business. His successor, Clarence Campbell, eventually concluded that the league Calder had fostered was "a rather unique sort of organization." (From William Wood, *The Storied Province of Quebec, Past and Present*, vol. 3)

5

Becoming "the Big Thing"

1929–1935

On 12 November 1931, Maple Leaf Gardens opened in Toronto with a fanfare not seen since the introduction of NHL hockey in Manhattan six years before. Despite a recent worldwide economic downturn that was most acute in North America, Conn Smythe had succeeded in building the largest indoor arena in Canada as a new home for his Maple Leafs. Along with more modern amenities and a seating capacity almost double the size of the Arena Gardens on Mutual Street, Smythe had also installed a new broadcasting booth high above the ice. Suspended from the rafters in this "gondola," the Gardens' director of radio, Foster Hewitt, broadcast the first home game under sponsorship of McLaughlin-Buick and General Motors Products of Canada (GM). The *General Motors Hockey Broadcast* was heard by thousands of listeners outside the arena over stations CFCA and CFGW, and General Motors promised that all Maple Leafs home games that season would be broadcast for "out-of-town fans, or those not lucky enough to secure seats at the Maple Leaf Gardens."[1]

At the inaugural game, there were still empty seats, but Smythe was confident that the Gardens would soon fill up and that radio would have a part to play. Despite the broadcast range being limited to the city of Toronto, and being only occasionally linked to small networks in southern Ontario or back to Montreal for Maroons and Canadiens games, the seventy-five-minute shows gained immediate popularity, and well outside NHL cities. In the fall of 1932, after only one season, the producer of the show wrote that pressure was building from western Canada and the Maritimes to send the hockey broadcast across Canada, even though "when this feature was undertaken, no one ever imagined that those sections of the country would have any particular interest in National Hockey League games played in Toronto." Responding to the demand, in January 1933 GM set up a national network of twenty stations across the country, and Hewitt began welcoming listeners with the greeting: "Hello Canada, and hockey fans in the United States and Newfoundland." The next month, a telephone survey estimated the audience at more than one million listeners for one Saturday-night game, from a national population in 1931 of just over ten million (although with the high-powered stations of the era, not all were necessarily tuning from Canada, but reached as far south as Kentucky). By the next February, a Montreal survey determined that, of listeners at home using radios, 74 percent were listening to the GM broadcast.[2]

The transmission of regular-season games across the continent was a first for North America, and it was soon apparent the broadcast was extending the potential market for NHL hockey by educating listeners from regions where the sport itself was often unknown. Listeners were intrigued, writing in to ask "if blue lines were hurdles, whether a puck looks like a basketball, and whether sticks resemble tennis rackets." In areas where hockey was a popular activity, the game broadcasts began to have a profound social effect. There were reports that lodge and missionary meetings were breaking up early to listen in, and the final game of the 1932–33 Boston-Toronto playoff series was heard by "almost the entire population [of Ontario]. . . . Motorists who were out late that night told of seeing whole streets of lighted houses at half-past one in the morning." For good reason, the Canadian Radio Manufacturers Association soon concluded that GM hockey broadcast stickers in their showroom windows were "the best display material it can get to help its dealers sell radio sets."[3]

General Motors decided to acquire the rights to Saturday-night Montreal Forum games as well, but only sent the Leafs' broadcasts to the national audience. The Canadian Arena Company initially refused to permit the broadcast of Forum games in both English and French, so the Maroons and Canadiens were heard across North America only if they were playing in Toronto. The rest of the time, they were restricted to the province of Quebec. The Senators were an afterthought. Having turned its back on the medium except for a brief game broadcast experiment in

1923 and local on-air promotions in 1932–33, the club asked only that the broadcast be kept out of Ottawa when the team was playing at home. It was a fateful decision, for in a decade in which the Canadian clubs would all feel under threat, radio was emerging as a potential savior and an essential part of the business model of successful NHL clubs.[4]

In these early years of the 1930s, the disparities between clubs— between Canadian and American, large market and small, rink owned and independent—would become exacerbated as the Depression wore on. First, the league was challenged in the Midwest by an upstart American Hockey Association and would be forced to accommodate ambitious outsiders like James Norris. Financial straits would put clubs and arenas into difficulties with their markets, with each other, and with Frank Calder. The resolution would see the loss of old partners and the gaining of new ones, as the league tried to find the right relationship between clubs, rinks, and markets—all without losing what had already been achieved.

"Outlaw" League

It turned out that Maple Leaf Gardens would be one of the last in the line of the large indoor multipurpose arenas before the Second World War. Two years before there had been warning signs in Chicago, a drama in the NHL's first expansion phase that saw the last serious threat of major league competition, but also signaled the end of the NHL's rapid growth.

In March 1929, Paddy Harmon finally opened his Chicago Stadium at 1800 West Madison Street on Chicago's West Side. The massive structure could seat more than nineteen thousand for hockey and add another sixty-eight hundred seats for boxing. "The main hall," the *Chicago Daily Tribune* reported, "is a vast circle of seats, wooden chairs painted red [and] no posts to obstruct vision." Twelve great steel girders supported the roof, and there were three balconies, with separate entrances for each level of seating, thus keeping the audience socially stratified by ticket-price scale. The mammoth custom-built pipe organ was said to have the volume of a twenty-five-hundred-piece military band, and it shook the building to its foundation when all of its 3,675 pipes were put into service. But Harmon's stadium did still lack one very important element—a hockey tenant. The opening event was not an NHL game but a prizefight, and the event seemed less a celebration than a eulogy. Though the title bout between Tommy Loughran and Mickey Walker had raked in a seemingly impressive $175,000, it was considered disappointing, a pale imitation of Rickard's million-dollar gates in New York. With the high expenses and carrying costs of the building, Westbrook Pegler of the *Washington Post* observed that the stadium looked like it had been overbuilt and its owners would be principally engaged in managing the losses.[5]

Harmon was understandably desperate to get a hockey club into his building and fill dates. After negotiations with the Black Hawks staggered along to nowhere over the 1928–29 season, Harmon went looking for help. In the spring of 1929, he consulted Joe Cattarinich and Frank Patrick and talked about several options: buying the Pittsburgh Pirates, importing Pacific Coast amateur clubs to play as a civic league, and even inviting in AHA clubs. None of these ideas panned out, and when Major McLaughlin decided the Black Hawks would play the 1929–30 season in the Coliseum, Harmon's personal position weakened. In November, after thousands of tickets to a six-day bicycle race went unsold, stadium investors saw red ink on the horizon and to stem the tide ousted Harmon as the president and general manager. They replaced him with Sheldon Clark, a local sportsman and vice president and general manager of the Sinclair Oil Refining Company and the man who had replaced McLaughlin on the stadium's board of directors.[6]

The coup had been percolating for months at the instigation of James Norris, whom Harmon had ironically convinced to invest $600,000 in the stadium, which gave enough common stock to effect control. Norris, the scion of a Great Lakes shipping family from St. Catharines, Ontario, had grown up in Montreal and attended McGill University, playing hockey briefly for the MAAA intermediate team. After moving to the United States, he started up Norris Grain Company in 1908 and by the 1920s had built it into one of the most successful grain brokerage companies in North America. Norris then began to indulge his passion for playing sports—particularly squash, boxing, and hockey—and also investing in them. He especially liked arenas and owned shares in Rickard's Madison Square Garden in addition to his stadium stock. But above all, it soon became evident that the former Montrealer's main goal was to win a Stanley Cup.[7]

The rationale for pushing out Harmon was related to boxing politics—the other directors told Harmon he was "bull-headed" in negotiations, had quarreled too much with the boxing commission, and had overpaid fighters—and after his removal Harmon suspected Norris changed allegiance during a visit to Madison Square Garden. It did appear that Harmon had been removed at least partly to facilitate a closer relationship between the Chicago Stadium and the Garden, but Norris seemed primarily disappointed that no lease agreement had been achieved with the Black Hawks. Harmon refused to countenance a deal that would have given the club a Sunday-afternoon slot at near cost. A few weeks after Harmon was let go, the stadium directors approved what the *Tribune* described as "an unusually advantageous contract" (three years at $4,500 a night), with the writer suggesting that the directors had virtually let McLaughlin dictate his own terms.[8]

In their first season at the stadium, the Black Hawks' gate receipts almost tripled to $282,350, and attendance more than doubled to 186,920. As Irene Castle McLaughlin recalled, before long "it was very difficult to get seats and impossible to get a box unless you were a member of the social elite. The boxes were taken by the season—as at the opera." Her husband's patience had paid off, but he did not let his guard down. After the season was over, McLaughlin resisted the stadium request for new lease terms and also refused to consent to its request for another NHL franchise in Chicago. Frustrated, Norris pursued another strategy: if McLaughlin and the NHL would not let him into the cartel, he would try to break in from the outside.[9]

The AHA had always coveted a club in Chicago, but the post-Livingstone agreement with the NHL protected McLaughlin's territorial rights. That deal also contained another provision that rankled—the draft that allowed NHL clubs to take the AHA's best players. Led by Tulsa's Walter Whiteside, a Minnesota millionaire who built the Tulsa Coliseum to house hockey in 1928, the AHA clubs began to pressure for changes, but harbored their major league ambitions for the moment. The NHL agreed to restrict the draft to alternate years, but after the deal foundered when the International Hockey League (IHL, the renamed Can-Pro League, not to be confused with the league that operated 1904–7) would not give its consent to the changes to the interleague agreement, the AHA owners again considered deaffiliation from the NHL and began fishing for new partners in cities like Toronto.[10]

Then Norris stepped in. He helped a former Black Hawks manager, Thomas J. Shaughnessy, negotiate to buy the AHA Minneapolis Millers and on 23 May announced that either it or a new AHA club would be placed in Chicago. In July the AHA duly granted another franchise for Chicago, to play as the Shamrocks. It was supposed to be a secret meeting, but the press reported on it, noting that AHA officials "did not believe" the action would mean war with the NHL, even though it seemed to be a clear violation of the interleague affiliation agreement, which was set to expire in less than three months' time. Since the AHA owners also granted another franchise to compete with the IHL in Buffalo, they had effectively announced the AHA's rejection of NHL hegemony and the end of affiliation.[11]

When the affiliation agreement expired, Calder stated that the midwestern league's action in putting clubs in Chicago and Buffalo without the consent of NHL clubs "was a direct challenge to organized hockey." As a result, the AHA had outlawed itself and had "cut off itself and its members from any player deals or other transactions with clubs in the National, Canadian-American, International, Pacific Coast, and California Hockey Leagues." Calder warned all minor league clubs to sever relations with the AHA and told players and on-ice officials that they would be "barred from organized hockey" if they signed with AHA clubs. The message was bold: the NHL determined hockey law and controlled its application, and there was no legal "organized" existence outside its purview.[12]

William Grant of the AHA resisted any notion that the AHA was in the wrong. He responded that the establishment of the Shamrocks had not violated the agreement and that the AHA (now styling itself the American Hockey League) was within its rights not to renew the agreement. The AHL clubs simply no longer supported the "unjust" draft or Calder's position as commissioner of hockey. However, as "responsible business and professional men," the club owners intended to "respect the rights of other leagues as regards legal contracts." They would respect contract law, but not NHL authority.[13]

For the rest of the 1930–31 season, the conflict remained civil and localized. Although the option was available, none of the player raids that had prevailed in hockey wars of the past were yet launched. Aside from a brief dispute over the rights to player Gord Brydson, the other NHL clubs probably saw it as a phony war. Even McLaughlin was not really suffering—despite the new competition and harassment from the stadium management, who favored the AHA club, his gate receipts were up—although he did admonish Calder for not publicizing the blacklisting of AHL players, claiming the Chicago press "did not even consider that a war existed."[14]

That would change soon enough.

Move or Build

Chicago was becoming a hot spot for hockey, but other NHL cities were beginning to lag, even relative to the unfavorable general economic conditions. Serious thought needed to be given to the viability of markets and the investment of infrastructure needed to exploit them properly. The main options were to sell or move clubs or else to commit to building new rinks.

In October 1930 the governors agreed to allow Benny Leonard to shift his Pirates club to Philadelphia and change the name to the Quakers. The league's referee in chief, Cooper Smeaton, resigned to take up the managerial reins.[15]

Benny Leonard had long been looking to sell the club. In December 1929 he was reportedly in Texas trying to start up a minor professional hockey league. The owners of the new IHL Cleveland Indians were interested, but it was later reported they were advised by the NHL to wait for a lower price. So in the spring Leonard gave an option on the Pirates to Lincoln Dickey of the Atlantic City Auditorium. When it was learned that Dickey intended to move the club to Cleveland, it complicated NHL relations with the IHL and the deal was not approved. Instead, Philadelphia was chosen as a more viable option. While at more than two million in population the City of Brotherly Love did have twice the market size, there was not much else to recommend it. The Quakers would play at the Philadelphia Arena, a rink located in a poor district of the city and just as old and confined as Duquesne Garden. Because the rink was small, the

Quakers expected a capacity crowd for their opening game, but even that goal turned out to be too much to hope for.[16]

In Ottawa the 1929–30 season showed improvement at the gate, but at the end of the season club secretary Clare Brunton still predicted a loss of $25,000. Furthermore, only $50,000 of the $125,000 auditorium preferred-share subscription had been taken up, and until Frank Ahearn was fully paid off, he still had a claim on the club's assets. Ahearn asked Calder to tell the other governors that all sales of Ottawa assets—including player contracts—had to have his personal approval. As it geared up for 1930–31, the Ottawa club was only stumbling along, still heavily subsidized by the auditorium. A rumor began circulating that the Senators' star attraction, Frank (King) Clancy, was on the auction block. All the clubs were interested, but it was Conn Smythe of the Leafs who won the bidding. (Since the Leafs were almost as strapped for cash as the Senators, Smythe had to supplement the amount authorized by the Maple Leafs' board of directors [$25,000] with two players and $10,000 of his own money from a winning racetrack bet.) Soon afterward, Ottawa also sold three other popular Ottawa-raised players to the Quakers—Allan Shields, Wally Kilrea, and Syd Howe. The money received in return went a long way toward keeping the Senators afloat, but Ottawa was mortgaging its future. By the end of December, the club was for sale once again. The auditorium hoped to keep it in Ottawa, filling its seats, but the time for making conditional sales was passing, and the price ($200,000) was high in an economy sliding into depression.[17]

Ahearn could still pick his poison, however. He rejected an investment by Charles Adams on the grounds that "American control . . . would . . . be just too bad for the three Canadian clubs in the NHL. That would make a 7 to 3 vote, no matter if Ottawa played here or in Timbuctoo. It doesn't very much appeal to me, because I feel that it would not be long before Canadians would be at a disadvantage in hockey compared to the present position." The best prospect was Chicago, where stadium management could still use another club to fill the cavernous arena that was dark on many nights. Norris and Shaughnessy were willing to offer $225,000 if they could move the club to Chicago, but McLaughlin again stonewalled the plan by insisting on his territorial rights. To aggravate matters, McLaughlin raided the clubs of Norris's colleagues in the "outlaw" AHL.[18]

Ottawa and Philadelphia kept bleeding, and the 1930–31 season was an utter failure for both. With its player sales, Ottawa could no longer even count on winning on the ice and finished in last place in its section. With the club struggling under a $70,000 deficit, William Foran resigned as president. The Quakers finished the season with one of the worst records ever seen—four wins and thirty-six losses—and lost $90,000. Attendance was even worse than the Can-Am Philadelphia Arrows, and the Quakers and drew only fifteen hundred spectators to a game in March. At the 26 September 1931 annual meeting in Detroit, the governors allowed the Ottawa and Pittsburgh-Philadelphia franchises to suspend operations for the upcoming 1931–32 season. According to the *New York Times*, the reasons were clear. Ottawa's expenses had been forced up with the addition of the American clubs, and the population base was the smallest of all the NHL cities. Philadelphia had failed to thrive under the "triple handicap" of a small rink, a losing team, and "a city which had not yet developed a large body of hockey fans." After the Ottawa and Philadelphia players were distributed in a draft to the other eight clubs, Ottawa received $25,000 as a lease fee for its players, and the league endorsed the club's $28,000 Bank of Montreal commercial note. Philadelphia got similar consideration, and both clubs retained full rights and privileges as members of the league, including seats on the board. It remained to be seen whether either could resurrect.[19]

Now down to eight clubs, to compensate the league schedule was increased from 44 to 48 games per club, but there was still a drop in total games, from 220 to 192. Even more worrisome was that some of the clubs that remained were not looking much stronger than the ones that had suspended their schedules.[20]

When Conn Smythe's syndicate assumed control of the St. Patrick's in 1927, the goal was to increase capacity and revenues and make the Leafs a winner on the ice. The club was trying to compete with local amateur leagues like the senior OHA, which was packing the Mutual Street Arena at a time when the professionals could not. Smythe implemented marketing changes, such as a preseason training camp as a publicity event to bring attention to the new Maple Leafs and displace amateur hockey news. In Toronto Smythe could take advantage of what clubs like the Senators did not have—a relatively large urban population and a large pool of local capital. Toronto was beginning to rival Montreal, Canada's industrial center, in both size and economic power. As such, Smythe's club was better positioned to compete in the new NHL economic model, which required larger markets and more capital to finance player salaries and travel expenses. It also required larger rinks to obtain the needed revenues. In July 1927 Smythe agreed to a five-year lease at the Arena Gardens in return for an expansion of 950 seats. If the club sold out 5 games of the 1927–28 season and receipts exceeded $150,000, the Mutual Street rink would even build extra seating galleries in return for a ten-year lease agreement.[21]

In the fall of 1927, Smythe also followed another American practice by initiating the regular radio broadcasting of home games. Four years before, during a period of early content experimentation, the owners of the Arena Gardens had agreed to allow CFCA, the *Toronto Daily Star* radio station, to broadcast its hockey games, including one NHL game on 14 February 1923. However, the Gardens required that all seats be sold out for a game before it could be broadcast, and since the club was not selling out, there were few other broadcasts of St. Patrick's games. Despite the worries of the Gardens' directors about the effect on attendance, Smythe pushed for radio and likely cited the experiences of the Boston, New York, Chicago, and Detroit clubs, which had used it to stimulate local interest in the game. Smythe also compromised. Following the practice used for amateur games, only the third period of games would be broadcast, so as not to discourage walk-up sales. Being initially free, the broadcast garnered no direct revenue, but Smythe soon found there was a benefit to having announcer Foster Hewitt promote the sale of game programs over the air.[22]

In Smythe's second full season at the helm, 1928–29, the Leafs saw a 31 percent improvement at the gate, reaching $180,087. Despite packed houses, this amount was still lower than clubs with bigger rinks and ranked seventh in the league. With the Arena Gardens rink bulging at the seams,

Smythe concluded that the Leafs needed much more seating capacity than even a renovated rink could provide. He began beating the drum for a new building, rallying support in the press and the financial community and targeting investors big and small. Once again, the project was promoted to investors with an appeal to their "civic duty," with a Canadian national twist. The eleven-page prospectus conveyed the message that the future of Canadian hockey was also at stake:

> Most hockey fans can remember a few short years ago when the National Hockey League was eking out an extremely precarious existence and struggling to introduce the game in the United States. . . . It is estimated that already over thirty millions of dollars are invested in franchises, equipment and buildings, the latter used largely for hockey. This city and province is the cradle of the game; each year sees stalwart young athletes skate out for the first time into the arena of fame. Canada may well feel proud of her sons, amateur and professional, who have popularized hockey in the United States and abroad, and incidentally have done much to advertise our country.

Smythe pointed a finger on the paradox of NHL expansion: the great success of the league was pulling it out of its Canadian "cradle." Putting it in stark terms for prospective investors, the Maple Leaf club was being presented with a choice—to give up major league hockey entirely, operate as cheaply as possible and sell off players, or build a new arena. Montreal, Boston, Detroit, and Chicago had all built new rinks in recent years, and "Toronto dare not lag behind." Smythe cited the major boost in attendance and gates that could be expected by moving into larger accommodations—Boston had improved by 92 percent at the gate, Detroit by 58 percent, and Chicago by 89 percent. The prospectus also listed an eminent board of directors of the new Maple Leafs Gardens, Ltd., including some of the most prominent names in Canadian business: Aird, Gooderham, Birks, Laidlaw, Tory, and Samuel. Smythe expected these names to impress small investors as well as large, and even women were targeted, albeit patronizingly in the prospectus, which stated: "The Maple Leaf Management particularly encourages the ladies to take up small holdings in the company."[23]

To overcome the reluctance of financial backers made skittish by the economic depression, Smythe tapped into the social capital of the Canadian financial establishment. When several businessmen canceled their subscriptions and Sun Life Assurance threatened to renege on providing a mortgage, Sir Edward Beatty intervened and convinced Sun Life to live up to its promise, playing a crucial role, as he had done for the Forum seven years earlier. Smythe also promoted through popular channels. He had his assistant, Frank Selke, feature the arena plans in a special issue of the Leafs hockey program, which Foster Hewitt then promoted over the air. They sold ninety-one thousand copies, fifty-nine thousand more than expected, and the stock selling was renewed. Even then, the general financial market funk meant sales were not brisk, and the project went ahead only with last-minute subscriptions that included Selke convincing some of the tradesmen to take part of their pay in Gardens shares.[24]

Smythe hired the prominent architectural firm of Ross and Macdonald, the builders of the Royal York Hotel and Eaton's College Street department store, and incorporated several features that showed his appreciation of the innovations in 1920s American arena architecture, including trussing that allowed unobstructed views and a modern heating system that allowed the audience to shed outerwear when viewing the game. For the location, Smythe considered several options, but convinced Eaton's to sell his company a centrally located piece of property on the northeast corner of Church and Carlton Streets, not far from the Mutual Street rink and right on the College Street streetcar line. Smythe got the land for less than its market value, after calming the fears of the Eaton's president that "the people who attended sports events were hardly the type to whom Eaton's catered." Smythe promised quite the opposite, that the Leafs would appeal to just the sort of upmarket crowd that Eaton's wanted to have pass by its College Street windows. Like Rickard's Garden, Smythe's Gardens aspired to attract a high-class audience. Although there is no evidence that the Gardens actually had a more affluent audience than the Mutual Street rink, through pricing, a smoking ban, and dress codes in the higher-priced sections, Smythe did try to construct a class-stratified spectator environment, no doubt inspired by the Arena Gardens and Madison Square Garden precedents. Indeed, on opening night, the *Toronto Evening Telegram*

featured a cartoon that suggested Smythe had adopted the new temperature regime: "In the good old days one would wrap up warm to attend a
hockey game. . . . BUT— . . . Last night the ladies and gentlemen could not
have been more comfortable in June." Unlike at Madison Square Garden
six years before, however, there do not seem to have been any complaints
from players, indicating either that the temperature was still brisk enough
or that it was by then an accepted norm.[25]

With few other construction projects to compete with for workmen,
Maple Leaf Gardens took only four months to build over the summer and
fall of 1931 and was easily ready for the Leafs' opener on 12 November. Even
with the depressed economic conditions, Smythe's $1.5 million rink that
seated 12,500 for hockey and 16,000 for other attractions came through
on the promise of its NHL cousins with its added capacity and increased
ticket scale. Leafs revenues rose 76 percent to $355,931, now second high-
est in the league. After the inaugural season, attendance dipped, but the
Gardens had already put the Leafs in the league of the big American clubs
and, more important, kept them in the NHL. Perhaps galvanized, perhaps
envious, in December 1931 Leo Dandurand of the Canadiens announced
his own new amphitheater in Montreal, but with economic conditions
worsening it did not seem likely to succeed.[26]

Norris Gets In

Though it was unevenly felt in 1931, the economic downturn in Canada
and the United States was beginning to have a profound effect on consumer spending, with consequent effects on NHL gate receipts. The
drastic fall in consumer demand led to business failures, job losses, and
further consumption reductions. Civic economies with a heavy reliance
on consumer durables experienced rampant unemployment, and Detroit's
automobile industry was devastated. Even Ottawa, whose economy was
anchored by government employment, felt the effects, which contributed
to its club suspending operations. In 1931–32 every club lost more than 25
percent at the gate, and the league as a whole fell 33 percent on average.[27]

Such substantial revenue losses threatened the clubs but also their
rinks. Entertainment became a luxury and the palaces of the golden age
of sport were soon tarnished with losses, but weakness and failure could

also present opportunities. A man like James Norris, whose successful speculations in the grain market would make him one of the richest men in the United States, could take advantage. If he waited long enough and pushed hard enough, his dream of an NHL club might become available for a song, if not through the front door of a club purchase, then through the back door of arena bankruptcy.

First came the pushing. In the lead-up to its second season as an "outlaw league" (1931–32), the AHL and its clubs took more liberties. In September Shaughnessy of the Shamrocks signed promising Quebec amateur Paul Armand, who was reserved to the Canadiens owing to his French Canadian heritage. In response, Calder threatened the players directly. In October he refused to reinstate three who had played in the AHL and publicized the policy that "players now under contract or option to clubs in organized hockey who play in any outlaw organization will be permanently debarred."[28]

The Chicago fight began to get nasty as the stadium dispossessed the Black Hawks of their traditional Tuesday and Thursday dates, forcing them to Wednesdays and causing problems for the entire NHL schedule. Then the Shamrocks showed their equally strong drawing power by opening to twelve thousand fans at the stadium in November 1931—the same attendance as at the Black Hawks' opener. Civility was also fading fast. McLaughlin initially agreed to play a charity game against the Shamrocks with the proceeds to go to the Joint Emergency Relief Fund, one of many charitable organizations that had sprung up to wrestle with massive unemployment. Later, likely at Calder's direction, McLaughlin now declared the game impossible owing to the AHL's outlaw status. By February he was even less inclined to cooperate when it became apparent that the combination of the Depression and Shamrocks competition was putting a big dent in Black Hawks attendance.[29]

In the fall the AHL attacked on another front by filing an official challenge for the Stanley Cup. The trustees were ready to indulge it, and William Foran wrote to Grant and Calder saying the challenge would be accepted. While McLaughlin for one "could not conceive of the trustees of the trophy permitting it to go by default to Tulsa or Kansas City," the possibility of losing the cup caused an abrupt change in NHL strategy, from passive aggression to active disruption of the AHL. McLaughlin lured away two players from the Tulsa club, on the grounds they were not being paid. On 1 February the NHL board of governors partially lifted its ban on outlaw players, a move that seems to have been made to facilitate its own raiding. Calder then said he would allow the NHL to forfeit the cup rather than play the champion of the outlaw AHL. The governors supported his position. Foran warned that, while the trustees were still friendly to the NHL, they would have to take back the cup if the NHL did not at least negotiate. Foran probably well understood the NHL position (recall he was recently the Senators' president), and so he suggested the NHL consider playing before the start of the next season. After meeting with Calder in Montreal on 25 March 1932, he announced that although there was not enough time to stage a series this season, the AHL was still eligible to compete for the trophy. This suggestion did not resolve the issue, but effectively postponed it, which allowed the NHL to continue its own lucrative playoffs and continue its campaign to disunite the AHL clubs before it came up again.[30]

The AHL was certainly suffering. Minneapolis had withdrawn after the 1930–31 season and Buffalo midway through the next. The St. Louis Flyers club was the major success story, playing to crowds of up to twelve thousand at their arena, but if left standing alone it might be tempted to look to the NHL. Tulsa and Chicago were also solid, being backed by Whiteside and Norris, respectively, but the AHL owners must have known that Norris's real interest all along was the NHL. Without him, they had little chance as an independent entity. Even McLaughlin saw the play for what it was, and he wrote to Calder that he had no objection to Norris coming into the league, as long as Tom Shaughnessy was kept out. McLaughlin expected that if Norris knew that he could have a club in the NHL by sacrificing Shaughnessy, there would be "a speedy parting between the two."[31]

As it had been two seasons earlier, Ottawa appeared to be Norris's likely entry point. After the one season of suspended operations (and respite from financial losses), Frank Ahearn had rejoined the Ottawa board of directors and gone looking for alternative franchise locations. Still motivated against moving to the United States, he proposed instead to share the new Maple Leaf Gardens as a cotenant. The auditorium would keep half the club, and Conn Smythe, Joe Cattarinich, and James Strachan (representatives of the other Canadian clubs) would own the other half. In Ahearn's mind, this setup would maintain "the Canadian end of major league hockey" and "would stop the menace of American control." The deal foundered when Smythe demanded a sixty-forty split in favor of the Gardens and a per season guarantee of one hundred thousand dollars. Any patriotism Smythe might have felt in saving the Senators was diluted by his business sense.[32]

At the annual meeting in May 1932, it began to look like Ottawa might not have to move at all. Only three clubs had revenues that exceeded their expenses, and the rest were now seeing the value of a revision of the league revenue-sharing and cost-control models. The Olympia, the Detroit owner, had actually succumbed to its bondholders the previous summer, burdened as it was with the lowest attendance in the league and its Olympian mortgage payments. It was now represented at the meeting by August Pfleiderer of the Union Guardian Trust Company, who was duly elected governor.[33]

The governors conceded that league-wide economy measures were desperately needed. The playing roster was cut from twenty to fourteen (including goalkeepers) and the payroll to seventy thousand dollars per club, with an individual player limit of seventy-five hundred dollars. The governors agreed not to draft any players (thus saving draft fees), and Charles Adams recommended that the clubs dip into the league's equity account and declare a dividend on the surpluses of the previous two seasons. The governors also considered a new franchise application from James Norris, this time for St. Louis. There was a long discussion, no doubt about the prospects of ending the AHL insurrection, but in the end the spirit of parsimony decided the matter—railroad expenses would be too high if the league extended that far to the southwest.[34]

At this meeting Charles Adams also moved that the league headquarters be relocated to Detroit during the playing season. His motive is not clear, but reducing the power of Calder was probably at the root, as was making a point about the American club majority. The clubs divided along national lines when the proposal came to a vote, and the motion failed when Dwyer abstained. The discussion seems to have further aggravated

Frank Ahearn, who gave his sentiments free rein in later correspondence with Calder, writing that he was "damned if I want to see the team [Ottawa] go across the border" and warning Calder that "Adams & Co. would be hard masters." He might not have included James Norris in the company, for the same day the *Chicago Tribune* reported Ahearn had announced that Norris would buy Ottawa, although Norris denied it.[35]

Ahearn then decided that reviving the Senators in Ottawa was a civic and patriotic duty. When the Bank of Montreal loan came due in July, Ahearn convinced his father to assume responsibility for it. In August he wrote to Calder that he would have to "shoulder the white man's burden again," and by September he was back as president. Having convinced the players to take a salary cut, just as Ottawa's civil servants had recently done, Ahearn put the Senators back on the ice.[36]

Denied in Chicago, Ottawa, and St. Louis, Norris found his way in through Detroit by offering to take over the bankrupt Olympia and its club, which had changed its name to the Falcons in 1930. The receiver could not sell the team during the period of foreclosure, but an arrangement was made whereby Norris was allowed to take over interim management. In October 1932 he renamed the club the Red Wings and gave them a new emblem, a design marrying the winged wheel of Norris's old club, the Montreal Amateur Athletic Association, with a modern automobile tire as a gesture to Detroit's main industry. In the summer of 1933, he acquired the arena and club free and clear after the company missed a debt payment and Union Guaranty foreclosed. Joining him were his twenty-six-year-old son, Jimmy, and an associate, Arthur M. Wirtz, a Chicago real estate entrepreneur.[37]

Norris was finally in the NHL, but his entry was not without friction. In the summer of 1932, Ottawa and Pittsburgh both anticipated returning to the league, and Detroit was depending on four of Ottawa's players. To compensate for returning them, Norris wanted to bring his Shamrocks stars to Detroit, but McLaughlin and the Canadiens wanted those AHL players to whom they had asserted their rights. Over the next few days, the Canadiens compromised, but McLaughlin would not. To make the deal happen, Norris had to give up two players to the Black Hawks. It was a small price for his acceptance into the league.[38]

With James Norris now ingratiated, the AHL's will to fight on was broken. Within the month the warring leagues came to a new agreement. The AHL would vacate Chicago, admit to minor league status, and return all players claimed by NHL clubs. It also dropped *League* in favor of *Association*, became subject once more to the NHL draft, and agreed to respect the territorial rights of the other leagues.[39]

While the NHL club bosses were happy with the reduced competition, their players were not. The demise of the AHL's major league aspirations solidified the salary cap, and it was further reduced to sixty-five thousand dollars per club. The players did not take it lying down. In October Calder was confronted with a gaggle of holdouts—Frank Boucher and Earl Seibert of the Rangers, Hooley Smith and Archie Wilcox of the Maroons, Lorne Chabot and Harold Cotton of the Leafs, and Reg Noble of Detroit. The clubs gave Calder the power to suspend holdouts if he thought the terms of the contract were fair, a rule meant to intimidate, but one reporter suggested many of the players might welcome the opportunity for arbitration, as Calder was perceived as fair-minded. However, Calder used the extra leverage, and within a few weeks all were signed save Seibert, who was duly referred to Calder for official action "under the new league policy covering 'persistent holdouts.'" After a meeting in New York with the player and his club, Calder suspended him. Lacking any alternative employment option, Seibert signed a few days later. With the resubordination of the AHA to "organized hockey," the NHL and minor league affiliates were once again protected from raiding, and there was nowhere else for a player to ply his trade. Seibert and the others had to take the contract terms and salary offered or else leave professional hockey entirely.[40]

That fall, when a revived Western Canada Hockey League requested professional affiliation with the NHL, the Memorandum of Agreement they signed showed the full extent of the integration of the professional hockey business. Essentially, the agreement created a "cartel of cartels" under the hegemony of the NHL. The main parties included the NHL, Can-Am, IHL, AHA, and the WCHL, with the California Hockey League and a reborn (minor league) Pacific Coast Hockey League as additional signatories. All leagues agreed to respect each other's reserve lists of players under contract and agreed that the president of the NHL would resolve all player disputes. Clubs had territorial rights to their cities, except where two franchises already existed, and all leagues would use a uniform player contract (which could be modified), a standard Form of Transfer, and a standard Agreement for Assignment. The leagues would decide playing rules themselves. This arrangement seemed egalitarian save for two clauses in particular that encapsulated the NHL's major league status: all non-NHL clubs could dispose of players to NHL clubs without passing through waivers in their own leagues, and each NHL club had the right to draft one player from any other non-NHL club at a price of five thousand dollars. In this way, elite players were to be forced to the top league for a flat fee, and the costs of getting them there were reduced through standardization of fees, forms, and procedures. Furthering the NHL monopsony was the requirement that all leagues respect each other's player suspensions and that no club deal with any club outside the agreement. It went without saying that outlaws would not be tolerated.[41]

Fissures

The conflict in the Midwest was officially over, although bad blood persisted between McLaughlin and Norris over the Chicago Stadium lease (Norris openly rooted against his tenant even when they were not playing Detroit). In this situation and other conflicts arising over rules, Calder stepped in as a mediator, but in so doing he became a focal point for club disaffection and his position came under threat.

In October 1932, after a meeting with the Chicago Stadium mediated by Calder did not produce the compromise he was seeking over playing dates, McLaughlin declared his intention to return to the Coliseum. Sidney Strotz, the stadium president, claimed this announcement was simply a pretext to obtain a rent reduction and pointed out there would be no playing date conflicts now that the Shamrocks were gone. McLaughlin and Strotz offered and counteroffered various percentage-scalable rental proposals, with Strotz finally putting on the table a five-year deal at a flat 37.5 percent of the gate plus a payment of one hundred thousand dollars to McLaughlin if he would waive his territorial rights and allow a second NHL franchise in the city. Evidently, Norris still wanted a Chicago NHL club. McLaughlin refused and asked Calder and Charles Adams to negotiate any deal on his behalf as long as it contained the prospect of breaking even. Both were unsuccessful, and even Adams was forced to admit that the Bruins, the most financially successful club in the league, could not operate under the terms being offered to McLaughlin.[42]

While the capacity of the Coliseum was small (variously estimated at five to eight thousand), the Black Hawks had exceeded that number only five or six times in the cavernous stadium the season before, so McLaughlin felt he could make up any loss in capacity by saving on the rent. When the Black Hawks opened to seven thousand customers on 13 November, it was below the twelve thousand of the last season, but well above the season average and, most important, enough to keep the club in the black. The next week the stadium threatened a lawsuit for breach of contract. The parties renegotiated, and in November a deal was finally reached to have the Black Hawks finish out their season at the stadium. Details were not forthcoming, but it seemed to favor McLaughlin, being certainly less than forty-five hundred dollars per night and not involving any waiver of territorial rights. Norris and Strotz had relented, unwilling to let the behemoth stadium stand empty with the bills piling up. Any deal was better than none.[43]

How much satisfaction McLaughlin took from this victory is unknown. He seemed embittered after the battle with the AHL and Norris and resigned from the NHL board of governors, sending Black Hawks business manager Bill Tobin in his stead. He stayed engaged at the club level, however, and dove into a pet project to form an all-American-born roster. He also kept the carousel of Chicago coaches moving by hiring Tommy Gorman midseason to manage his third NHL team.[44]

McLaughlin's resignation, though to be temporary, showed cracks in the harmony of the league, fissures that were aggravated by financial pressures. Yet over the 1932–33 season, the main points of conflict at board meetings remained the traditional ones: rules and their enforcement. One of the main issues was the persistence of so-called defensive stalling—the various tactics used by players and coaches to slow down the play and control the game. Skilled offensive-minded teams like the Bruins wanted these tactics limited and the practitioners punished. After one game against the Americans featured particularly egregious examples, Charles Adams ordered his Bruins to throw the puck down to the other end of the ice as often as possible in the next game against the Americans in New York, and they did so, dozens of times. The game was a farce, but it prompted the reaction Adams had hoped for. Calder telegraphed the other governors to get approval on a rule calling for an automatic offside to be called on the first instance of this "icing" of the puck and a face-off in front of the goal of the offending team on the second.[45]

Calder's impartiality was also at issue. Since the resignation of Cooper Smeaton as referee in chief in 1930, Calder had taken over referee supervision. As an economy move it made sense, but the result appeared to be more erratic officiating. In January 1933 Bruins star Eddie Shore was involved in an altercation with Sylvio Mantha during which referee Cooper Smeaton (who had returned to the job after only one season as manager of the Philadelphia Quakers) suffered broken ribs and facial injuries. Before the judgment had even been rendered, Adams wrote to Calder complaining about the officiating, particularly his perception that Calder was yielding to special owner requests for certain officials not to handle their home games. Adams called it "bad business." First, it humiliated referees, and, second, it did not distribute referees (good, bad, and mediocre) evenly to each team. Although Adams had been "rather pleased" with the officiating at the beginning of the season, he had since become "certain that the caliber of the officiating is rapidly depreciating and I believe it is due to our permitting them to be creatures subjects [sic] to the whims of various owners." Adams proposed all officials serve all clubs in proper rotation.[46]

In the case at hand, Smeaton gave the benefit of the doubt to Shore, so Calder imposed only a one-hundred-dollar fine on the Bruins star. Even this judgment Adams called "obviously unfair" and promised that "the incident is not closed." Calder refused to relent, and the situation was further exacerbated on 4 February in Ottawa, when Art Ross threatened to pull the Bruins off the ice in a dispute with officials. A week later Adams announced his resignation as NHL governor and president of the Bruins, leaving him free to criticize openly without fear of being fined by the league. He traveled to Montreal to hold court and blasted Calder in the papers, referring to the president as "our astute political head, who uses the league constitution as a shield in his own defense, but as a bludgeon when the shoe is on the other foot." At the March NHL meeting Adams confirmed his resignation as Bruins governor and nominated Robert R. Duncan, a lawyer and secretary of the Bruins, in his place. The substitution was accepted as a temporary measure, but a committee was formed to try to persuade Adams to reconsider. It would not do to have one of the most powerful NHL owners alienated from the league's board, and the reasons for his disaffection had to be addressed.[47]

While many saw Adams's action as born of his inability to influence Calder's decisions in favor of his own team, Adams explained that his main reason for leaving had been the requirement to remain publicly silent on league issues, a bylaw known as the gag rule. Even after McLaughlin returned to the board in March and the threat of a league split lessened, the other governors were keen to mollify Adams. By the time of the league meetings in May, the *Chicago Tribune* reported that Calder's player punishments had "brought him into sharp conflict with several clubs" and convinced the governors that fuller attention was required. That was an understatement; Calder's very removal was being considered. On 12 May the NHL governors met secretly without Calder at the University Club in Boston. Three of the clubs wanted Calder fired, but Dandurand seems to have mustered enough support from the others to retain his position, but a compromise was needed. When the governors met officially the next day in New York, Dandurand recommended that Frank Patrick be appointed managing director of the league and Calder's duties concerning league officiating be transferred to him. Primarily, Patrick would assume oversight of on-ice officials and enforcement of the rules, keeping in close touch with the situation around the circuit and listening to complaints. The compromise reached, Calder was reelected president, but this time only for a two-year term, a noticeable reduction from the usual five years. Calder could not help but understand the message: as the former president of the Pacific Coast Hockey Association, Frank Patrick was well qualified to succeed him, and the *Chicago Tribune* pointed out that "the establishment of Patrick as the new arbiter was interpreted as a victory for those opposing the league head." Even though he did not return to the board of governors, with Calder's power now attenuated Charles Adams was appeased.[48]

That fall Patrick promised to clamp down on rowdyism and punish violent offenders with stiff fines. The PCHA innovator also announced rule changes: the establishment of an eight-by-five-foot crease in front of the goal, the allowance of a player to stop a flying puck with his hand, and a ten-minute misconduct or match penalty for touching, holding, body checking, or tripping an official. Yet his main task was soon to deal with one of the most violent incidents in the early history of the league.[49]

On the ice the spotlight was often on Eddie Shore, whose mastery of the defensive position was matched by his physical play—he won the Hart Trophy as the league's most valuable player in 1932–33 and also held the league record for penalty minutes in a season. The glare brightened after he blindsided a Toronto player, Irvin (Ace) Bailey, in a 12 December 1933 game at the Boston Garden. Bailey hit his head hard on the ice and slipped into a coma, while Red Horner, Shore's intended target, laid out Shore in turn. As head of officiating, Patrick was called upon to decide the fate of those players involved in the fracas. Eventually, Patrick suspended Horner for six games, and after it was clear that Bailey would live, he gave Shore sixteen. Overall, Patrick was seen to have handled the matter with great diplomacy and tact, a real challenge any time Conn Smythe and Art Ross were involved in a dispute.

With Bailey's future uncertain (he would never play hockey again), the league played a benefit game for him in Boston, but Smythe complained that the amount raised was insufficient so he arranged another all-star game in Toronto. (While charitable games had a long tradition in hockey, the idea of an all-star game almost certainly originated with major league baseball's inaugural game the previous summer.) All told, $27,969 was raised for Bailey, of which $20,000 was put into a trust fund, with Smythe and Calder as trustees.[50]

Soon after the benefit game in February 1934, Patrick decided to resign from the league. It is possible that he expected to succeed Calder sooner rather than later and left when the prospects dimmed. For a man who had started and run his own league, being head of officiating was not enough, and in April he announced he had coaching offers from two NHL clubs. He chose Boston and led the team to two division titles, but was fired by Ross after the 1936 playoffs. With Patrick's resignation from the league and the distraction of the aftermath of the Bailey-Shore incident, Calder's position started to strengthen once again.[51]

Arena Trouble

From the 1932–33 season, the full impact of the Depression was felt by both clubs and the arenas that hosted them. Philadelphia did not even get restarted after its hiatus. At the semiannual meeting in October 1932, its application for readmission was rejected: the governors simply did not believe the city could support the club. Financially wiped out, Benny Leonard returned to boxing for a living at the advanced age of thirty-seven. Ottawa did return to the ice that season and was rewarded with better gates, but the crowds were still too small and by the end of the season the club was $6,300 in debt to its players and other creditors. The other clubs fared better, but still had to adjust. Toronto actually increased its ticket prices for the 1932–33 season, but after attendance flagged the club pushed them back down to 1931–32 levels for the rest of the decade. NHL attendance in 1932–33 declined only 4.4 percent, but most clubs suffered gate-receipt declines of one-quarter to one-third, so that across the league revenues fell a drastic 32 percent (see fig. 3). Spectators were still coming but paying less, as ticket prices were slashed and many free tickets distributed, with the result that revenue per customer declined from $1.47 to $1.05.[52]

As the situation in Detroit showed, lost revenues affected not only the clubs but also the stadiums, which were suffering from a general downturn in sports spending, especially for boxing. The losses threatened to force changes in ownership for those owners without the wherewithal to withstand the losses. Chicago Stadium was still struggling under the weight of its financial obligations and was not really helped by the lease compromise with the Black Hawks. In January 1932 it defaulted on its bond payments and the next year went into receivership. Just as he had done in Detroit, James Norris acquired temporary control of the stadium in the fall of 1934 and the next January bought it outright in return for an investment of $300,000. Norris put the active management in the hands of his son and Arthur Wirtz.[53]

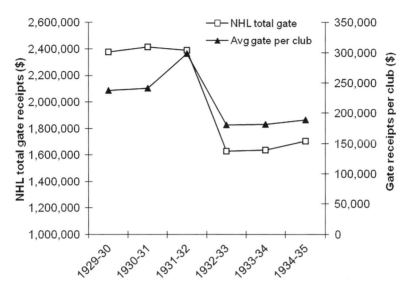

Fig. 3. NHL gate receipts, total, and average per club, 1929–30 to 1934–35.

The East Coast Gardens were also in trouble. After Rickard's death in 1929, John Hammond took over as general manager of Madison Square Garden under the direction of William Carey as president. By 1932 the Garden was suffering, even with two NHL clubs to help fill it. Revenues were down by a third, mainly owing to sagging boxing attendance. As Rickard had predicted in 1926, hockey had come to outdraw boxing within five years (actually four). In 1930 hockey brought in $2 for every $1 in boxing revenue at Madison Square Garden. By the 1933–34 fiscal year, of the 1,461,694 spectators who attended Garden events, 41 percent came to see hockey, and 30 percent saw the National Hockey League variety. Boxing was only a pale imitation of its former self, attracting only 84,944 fans to twelve bouts, a paltry 6 percent of the total tickets sold at the Garden and a drop in boxing attendance of 59 percent from the year before. With good reason Westbrook Pegler could write in the *Washington Post* that, "in the new Garden, the hot house of the cauliflower trade, the frost is on the cauliflower now." John Kieran of the *New York Times* was even more direct: "Hockey has been the financial salvation of the Garden." Without the almost $500,000 of hockey revenue in these two years, the Garden would have been in very precarious financial position, if not bankrupt.[54]

The shifting tastes and the financial strain led to changes in Madison Square Garden management. After a disagreement in December 1932 with Carey over reducing hockey ticket pricing, Hammond resigned as vice president of the Garden and president of the Rangers. Lester Patrick replaced him as vice president of the Garden and general manager of the Rangers, and Carey assumed the NHL governor's seat. Hammond's resignation was announced at the same time as the new ticket scales were revised down— from a range of 40¢ to $3 (tax included) to 40¢ to $2 (tax excluded). The reduction had the desired effect, and by mid-January attendance was up 28 percent. The directors were also unhappy with Carey, and in the summer of 1933 he was succeeded by another vice president, John Reed Kilpatrick, a renowned college football player who was vice president of the George A. Fuller Company and seems to have been groomed for the post.[55]

Exiled, Hammond went looking for allies to help him stage a shareholder coup, and one of the men he contacted was James Norris. In May 1934 Hammond announced that his group of investors had acquired the 78,883 shares of Garden stock previously held by Richard Hoyt and his associates. With this stake, Hammond could control the board. He replaced Hoyt as chairman, retook his place as president of the Rangers, but asked Kilpatrick to remain as president of the Garden proper for the time being. One of Hammond's first acts was to emancipate Madison Square Garden from its Boston appendage and cut loose the dragging weight of the Boston operating company on New York's bottom line. The Boston & Maine Railroad, owners of the Boston Garden building proper, had been agitating for the New York Garden to fully pay up its $168,000 worth of stock and also agree to a higher rental fee. Instead, Hammond went looking for buyers. Charles Adams made his interest known, but it was a group headed by Henry Lapham, the owner of the Boston Arena, that took over the Garden position. The deal had the added benefit of bringing the Boston Arena and Boston Garden under common management, and the merged entity, to be known as the Boston Garden-Arena Corporation, allowed the two major Boston venues to work in concert to attract Boston's scarce entertainment dollars.[56]

After a special charge of $148,115 was taken on the capital loss from the sale of the Boston stock and some other expenses, Madison Square Garden bounced back into the black. In August the net profit was $179,568—or 64¢ a share, compared with a loss of 22¢ per share the year before. All events showed improvement, especially boxing, but hockey still led the way with its $236,200 net profit contribution. Hammond was still not satisfied. The Garden's matchmaker had missed out on hosting the Joe Louis–Max Baer heavyweight fight, and when Kilpatrick refused to allow former heavyweight champion Jack Dempsey to take over boxing promotion, Hammond tried to remove him as president. Hammond then discovered he was at the mercy of the syndicate members who had provided his reentry into the corporation the year before. At the corporation's annual meeting on 24 September, the issue was fought out. Charges and countercharges were leveled, and the two factions presented rival slates of directors: Kilpatrick's had nine existing members and Hammond's only three besides himself, but including James Norris and Arthur Wirtz. In the end, Hammond lost a close vote, but his patron, James Norris, was named to the new board of directors, no doubt because of his strong share position. And as a man of substance who had saved two other major arenas, he was a man well worth keeping.[57]

Clubs and Rinks

With his investments in the New York, Chicago, and Detroit rinks, it was in no small measure owing to the resources of James Norris that the American NHL rinks were able to reorganize and weather the Depression. A single savior was problematic for the league because of the disfavor of multiple-club ownership and the syndicate-league form, but there was also a growing awareness that cross-ownership of club and arena was a desirable, and possibly necessary, arrangement. In the Depression hockey clubs, whose only assets were player contracts and league membership, were more vulnerable than the arenas, which at least could leverage their real estate. Furthermore, the rink-owned, or "house," clubs—Rangers, Red Wings, Maple Leafs, Maroons, and Senators—were in a much more advantageous position compared to the independent clubs, which depended on favorable lease terms to make ends meet and could not always rely on the magnanimity and financial strength of the rinks. The overlapping of interests caused problems for the league itself, which depended on harmony between club and rink. Over the next few years, the league's role as mediator between the two was tested.

Over the summer of 1934, the Boston Garden and Chicago Stadium could not agree to lease terms with their hockey tenants. Both rinks were trying to increase revenues, the latter because it was in receivership and the former because the new owners had probably agreed to pay a higher rental fee to the Boston & Maine. It did not help that Charles Adams had failed in his attempt to buy the Boston Garden and that McLaughlin and the Chicago Stadium were almost constantly at loggerheads. In the fall the Garden threatened to lock out the Bruins, so Adams threatened to play in other cities. At a twelve-hour emergency meeting at the end of September, the intercession of the other clubs resolved both the Boston and the Chicago disagreements with 35 percent rental payments. However, almost immediately the Americans and Madison Square Garden resumed their own long-standing lease dispute.[58]

Bill Dwyer's Americans had the most costly lease in the league, and in 1931 Dwyer had tried to get the Garden to renegotiate. To publicize his club's plight, Dwyer had provided the 1930–31 balance sheet to Stanley Woodward of the *New York Herald Tribune*. Woodward duly noted that while the Americans took in an impressive $292,163.25 at the gate, after expenses, including the $189,688.64 rental fee to the Garden (65 percent of gross receipts), the team posted a net deficit of almost $30,000. The rental fee worked out to $8,622 per game, comparing unfavorably to the Black Hawks' deal, which was $4,500 per game for the larger stadium. In 1932 Dwyer threatened to sue, alleging that the Americans had paid for items for which the Rangers had not contributed their share. Carey agreed to revise the lease terms in return for the Americans dropping the lawsuit, and Dwyer renegotiated a new forty-sixty split of the gross in favor of the club. For Dwyer, the timing was felicitous. As the economy worsened, Dwyer's other business operations suffered. Later that summer he was forced to sell the Brooklyn Dodgers, his National Football League club. In 1933 he lost his brewery and took a major loss on his racing operations at Tropical Park in Florida.[59]

In the lead-up to the expiration of the original ten-year contract signed with Rickard, Kilpatrick had intimated to Dwyer that a favorable new ten-year deal would be offered for 1935–36, but when Hammond regained control at the Garden, the offer was rescinded. Dwyer threatened to revive his lawsuit, so Hammond offered a new ten-year deal with concessions but including a guaranteed $80,000 per year in rent for the Garden. Dwyer refused to sign, and his lawyer recommended putting the case before Calder for arbitration. The NHL president wired the warring parties to cease fire until he could come to New York to investigate.[60]

Dwyer made some serious charges. He accused Hammond ("the mercenary militarist") of drawing up a lease with "trick" clauses and alleged he was conspiring with other arena owners to increase rentals across the board in order to force certain NHL club owners to abandon their franchises. Hammond denied it, but the Garden directors began getting uncomfortable with the suggestion that they were trying to force the Americans out and effect a monopoly over hockey in New York. One of them confided to a reporter that the suggestion was similar to one about the Garden's supposed monopoly over boxing, and the Garden directors wanted to avoid any public discussion on the topic.[61]

Hammond wanted to maintain the Garden's 40 percent share of the gate, but Dwyer did not want to pay more than 35 percent, given the drop in ticket prices that had been necessary over previous seasons. The 35 percent figure was a magic number of sorts, the compromise figure that had been applied to the Chicago and Boston disputes, and the Americans knew the precedents. Martin Shenker, the club's business manager, claimed, "You know Boston and Chicago rink owners tried the same blackjacking tactics but the league stopped them." In an all too familiar turn, rumors surfaced that Hammond was threatening to form a new league with Boston, Chicago, and Detroit. An Americans official suggested Hammond's threat was to scare Calder into adhering to the Garden's proposal. If so, it did not work. Calder moved quickly to name a committee of himself, Smythe, and Dandurand to arbitrate the issue, and by January a new contract was being drawn up that was even less favorable to the Garden. The Americans would get two-thirds of the gate and the Garden the rest. The parties signed.[62]

The financial future of the Americans was still far from secure. In addition to Dwyer's other setbacks, the Internal Revenue Service was suing him for millions of dollars in back taxes on all his bootlegging income of the previous decade. His cash position was precarious by the end of the 1934–35 season, and the tabloid *New York Daily News* reported that Americans players were threatening "to mutiny" over unpaid salaries and lack of medical care. Dwyer offered to sell the team to the Garden, but Kilpatrick refused, fearful that "if we owned both clubs it would look as if we were trying to secure a monopoly on the sport." Ever resourceful, Dwyer found a temporary savior. He borrowed $35,000 from James Norris to keep Tropical Park in operation, securing the loan by an option to buy the Americans for $150,000. If Dwyer could not pay, then James Norris would have a second NHL club in his possession.[63]

Other clubs were in even more desperate straits. The Americans may have had an insolvent owner, but at least they had strong gates and a new lease. Since the Senators had resurrected in Ottawa, Frank Ahearn was constantly denying rumors the club would be sold and moved to the United States. After a 1933–34 season that saw a new low in gate receipts—$58,798, a mere 3.6 percent of the league's total—Ahearn gave up on the city, albeit not the club. He decided the Senators would move south to play as the Eagles in St. Louis. He and Redmond Quain would retain majority ownership in Ottawa, but also encourage local St. Louis investors to participate. Probably with some relief, the league governors approved the move. The sports editor of the *Ottawa Citizen* concluded: "Much as this move is regretted by all concerned, it was inevitable. Enormous losses season after season could not be maintained and something had to be done to protect the Auditorium shareholders." The answer to Ottawa's troubles was the greater revenue potential of rinks the size of the Forum or the New York, Boston, and Maple Leaf Gardens. James Callahan in Pittsburgh also realized it and obtained the green light to revive the Pittsburgh Pirates for the next season, once he assured the governors that work on the long-awaited new Pittsburgh arena was beginning "on Monday." But when Monday came and went with no arena news, the Pirates were no more.[64]

The Eagles opened at the St. Louis Arena in the fall of 1934, hosting the cup-winning Black Hawks in the hopes of igniting a regional rivalry.

St. Louis was not virgin hockey territory, and the AHA Flyers were already flourishing there. Since several NHL clubs shared their rinks with minor league clubs, the AHA had declared it had no objection to the NHL moving to town. The Flyers' franchise holder, however, did object and greeted the Eagles with his intent to file a $200,000 lawsuit for invasion of his territory. He did not have to worry, since the Eagles never really got off the ground, dragged down to earth by paltry crowds and a punishing travel schedule. (Despite their new location, they had retained Ottawa's place in the Canadian division and its heavy commitment to games against faraway divisional rivals in Montreal, Toronto, and New York.) By January many expected the team would be split up at the end of the month and the players sent to Chicago and Toronto. This prospect was denied by the club, but within months the Eagles were selling off the last of the Ottawa stars—Scotty Bowman and Syd Howe to Detroit and Frank Finnegan to Toronto. At the end of the season, the revenue was a meager $61,258, and the club had lost an estimated $40,000.[65]

That fall Calder called an emergency meeting at the Waldorf-Astoria in New York to decide the Eagles' fate. Redmond Quain told the governors the Ottawa syndicate was no longer willing to support the club. Unlike the heady days of the expansion era, there were no eager buyers this time, and James Norris now had his club. With no alternative presented, the governors agreed to buy out the franchise, in effect paying Ottawa $40,000 for the rights to their twenty-three players, who were then redistributed, with priority given to the weaker clubs. Although the league had no obligation to remunerate Ottawa (it had not done so for Pittsburgh), Calder stated that it was "in the best interests of the league. St. Louis was unable to make a financial go of it and we did not think it was sporting to allow the Ottawa syndicate to take a loss after it had made every effort to keep going." Having resisted Ottawa's calls over the years for effective revenue sharing, it was a last sporting gesture—or gesture of sympathy—on the part of the NHL governors.[66]

Ottawa had failed miserably in St. Louis, but things were little better in Montreal, where the Maroons' and Canadiens' gate receipts combined were less than three other clubs' revenues individually (Toronto, the Rangers, and Chicago). The likely solution to this problem was a tighter relationship between the Montreal clubs and the Canadian Arena Company, the owner of the Forum, and a greater emphasis on marketing. In the spring of 1934, William Northey, who had been at the helm of the leading arenas in Montreal for more than thirty years, resigned after a disagreement with CAC directors. With dwindling attendance and revenues, the Forum looked to replace him with a promoter, and when Tommy Gorman predictably parted company with the irascible Major McLaughlin in Chicago, almost immediately he was mentioned as a possible manager of the Forum. At the same time, Northey's contemporary James Strachan was also eased out of the Maroons and replaced as president by a CAC executive officer, Thomas Arnold.[67]

Gorman was duly hired and identified several challenges. One was amateur competition: as in Ottawa and Toronto, the Maroons and Canadiens competed with high-quality local amateur hockey clubs that ate into their audience. The existence of two professional clubs magnified the problem, and with one arena controlled (Maroons) and the other not (Canadiens), a familiar conflict over lease terms arose. Another issue was the club-arena connection. Like the Rangers, Maple Leafs, and Red Wings, the Maroons were financially protected by their arena, but the Canadiens, like the other independent clubs, depended on the willingness of their own owners to sustain losses. And as Leo Dandurand was fond of pointing out, the Canadiens got nothing from ancillary revenue streams such as program sales, concessions, and radio. Dandurand and Joe Cattarinich had deep pockets from their main business, racetrack gambling, which did very well in the 1930s, but the two entrepreneurs also had a continental view of their sports interests, and keeping a money-losing club in Montreal as a public service became less and less attractive. In 1934 they even did the unthinkable, selling their biggest star, Howie Morenz, to the Black Hawks.[68]

When the Canadiens ran another deficit in 1934–35, Dandurand encouraged talk that the club would be sold to American interests, presumably to put pressure on the CAC to revise the lease. In January 1935 it had been reported that Walter O'Hara of Rhode Island had offered $200,000 for the club, but when Dandurand arrived in New York to meet him and other bidders, Dandurand suddenly reconsidered and declared the club was not for sale. Two months later, after one of the poorest financial seasons in years, Cattarinich revealed the club was contemplating selling out again, this time to Cleveland investors. The lease was the main issue—the club paid 40 percent of the gross gate to the Forum and thought this amount was too high.[69]

In May Cattarinich and Dandurand pushed even closer to the brink, giving notice to the board of governors that at the league's annual meeting they would be requesting permission to move the Canadiens or else suspend operations. The threat worked, and the club was given a new multiyear lease in the morning before the meeting. Dandurand withdrew the request to move, but the other shoe dropped in September when more than a lease revision was agreed to. He and Cattarinich sold the club for $165,000 to a syndicate directed by J.-Ernest Savard, a successful Montreal stockbroker and an associate of Donat Raymond. As president of the Montreal Exhibition Company, the owner of Montreal's baseball stadium, as well as a former owner of the Montreal Royals baseball club, Savard had the credentials as a French Canadian sportsman to make him an ideal candidate to take over the Canadiens, perhaps too ideal. Indeed, *La Presse* reported that the new syndicate, which included Maurice Forget and Louis Gélinas, "will administer the Canadiens on behalf of the Canadian Arena Company." Although its ownership was not overt, the CAC now controlled both Montreal NHL clubs. Would this solution work? Dandurand thought it might. In an interview with Charles Mayer of *Le Petit Journal*, Dandurand claimed to be still bullish on hockey. The weakened interest in Montreal was simply cyclical, he argued, and the sport would continue to grow: whereas "yesterday it was our national game, now it is the sport in the spotlight among several cultures and is played in almost all the countries of the world."[70]

A Changing Model

The economic pressure on clubs and their arenas wrought by the early years of the Depression had threatened the survival of all aspects of the league's clubs, arenas, owners, and even Calder as league president. The period also saw challenges to the league's hegemony and its dominance over the emblem of professional hockey supremacy, the Stanley Cup. In retrospect, while much credit can be given to Calder and the governors for their fortitude and commitment to finding solutions to the disparities, it was an outsider, the expatriate James Norris, who played savior. The league probably would have survived in some form without his intercession, but almost certainly after much more financial tribulation and likely the loss of the Detroit Falcons and New York Americans.

The solutions to the league's problems were found in new markets, new owners, new buildings, and new lease arrangements between clubs and rinks, but the loss of an expansion club (Pittsburgh-Philadelphia) and the oldest NHL club, Ottawa, brought up profound questions about how the NHL business model was changing. The Ottawa example made it clear that even traditional hockey markets needed a more substantial population base to sustain professional hockey and to fill the large arenas that were required to pay the travel and salary expenses of a binational league. With a new arena and a new marketing medium—radio—the Toronto Maple Leafs were surviving, but having two clubs in Montreal was looking to be one too many. Also, it was now clear that it was a substantial advantage to be vertically integrated by having the hockey team become a "house" club. In two-club cities the independent clubs were second-class tenants, and disagreements over leases also put the league itself at greater risk of instability. Ownership of the club by the rink seemed to be the way of the future. The sports editor of the *Christian Science Monitor* saw this issue quite clearly, proposing that "the ideal situation would be for the club owners to own the rink and then hockey could be operated on a basis which should give a good return to all concerned at a price which the hockey public will be able to pay."[71]

James Norris had also shown that entering the NHL cartel was expensive and required capital to force open the door. Later, he revealed he had never actually owned the Shamrock AHA club, a situation that supported the idea that his goal was always to get into the NHL. Yet Norris's money had supported the AHA rebellion, and it had taken substantial resources for Norris to acquire failing arenas in Chicago and Detroit and force his way into the league (and along the way beginning to actualize Tex Rickard's dream of a chain of arenas). With the Norris arenas co-opted into the league, the barriers to entry for other aspirants rose, as new clubs would need an adequate rink in a large city. Deep pockets were also necessary to sustain operations in trying times. Increasingly, these trends militated against the participation of smaller-scale entrepreneurs without substantial means and without a strong relationship with an arena. Charles Adams, Frederic McLaughlin, and even the Catta-Léo partnership could sustain losses, but it was becoming obvious poorer businessmen like Bill Dwyer could not. Without capital reserves, the independent clubs were vulnerable, and the best option seemed to be the Madison Square Garden model, which Conn Smythe had followed by adding wealthy backers to his own small-scale investment anchored in a larger corporate entity that owned both club and arena. Smythe was the last small player to get into the NHL game, and his Maple Leaf Gardens was one of the last big arenas for a generation. In contrast, Ottawa and Pittsburgh-Philadelphia failed to find the same investment support and were hampered by small markets, small rinks, and weak demand. As Dandurand and Cattarinich found out, the pressure on independent clubs to merge with their arenas was building. But there were two downsides to these trends.[72]

One concern was the possible intersection of ownership (or creditor) interests between the clubs themselves, a prospect that could have consequences for consumer perception of the integrity of the on-ice product. The Canadian Arena Company now controlled both the Maroons and the Canadiens. Bill Dwyer owned the Americans and since the summer of 1934 had been trying to sell the dormant Pirates-Quakers franchise to the Mellon family of Pittsburgh. But the widest reach was the grasp of James Norris, who by 1936 owned the Detroit Red Wings and Olympia, was the Black Hawks' landlord, had an option on the Americans club, and had substantial control over the New York Garden, home of both the Americans and the Rangers.[73]

As much as possible, these relationships were kept from the public, and there was also a nominal constitutional impairment against multiple ownership of clubs. With some ellipses, from Paragraph B of the 15 May 1926 agreement, one can read: "No member of the League . . . shall . . . [become] interested in the promotion, ownership or operation . . . of any hockey team other than the one representing such member in the National Hockey League." (In theory, this requirement also prevented NHL clubs from being involved with minor league clubs.) Yet while the Dwyer situation brought criticism from Calder, the principle does not seem to have been evenly applied. Recall that Ahearn seemed convinced that it was appropriate to sell the Senators to a triumvirate of Smythe, Strachan, and Cattarinich. During the Depression, compromising times required compromise measures, and it seems that, as long as they were kept quiet, these ambiguous relationships brought on by the integration of arena and club—and by the joining of arenas into networks of their own—would be tolerated.[74]

The main guide of league relationships through the decade of the worst economic catastrophe in North American history was Frank Calder, who became, with the departure of Ottawa, the last institutional connection to the founding of the NHL. Despite Charles Adams's campaign to curtail his power and perhaps remove him, by 1935 he had regained his former influence, and perhaps more. At that year's annual meeting, the governors even showed themselves keen to have him expand his authority and deal with issues of information management and control arising from issues such as Dwyer's (failed) resuscitation of Pittsburgh, the adverse publicity over the Canadiens' lease fight with the CAC, and the need to publicize league activities with the New York press. Calder was quick to note the change in attitude, and the minutes show he took time to review the history of his authority. He recalled that his initial hiring had been on the condition that "everything I do goes and that there is to be no question about it," but in 1924 this policy changed, "when the League expanded and some of the new Governors looked askance at the way the thing was conducted, and said 'What is the idea of this man having so much authority, he does things without consulting us and nobody appears to know anything but him.'" Calder recalled that after he had "clashed with one or two governors . . . authority was taken away from me"—a reference to his run-in with Charles Adams and the appointment of Frank Patrick as managing director. Now that the governors were offering more power, Calder warned them they must be willing to submit to it and to his style of using "an oilcan rather than a blackjack." The governors proved willing, and for the rest of his tenure as president, Calder suffered no more successful challenges to his authority.[75]

The other downside to the convergence of club and arena in larger markets, at least from the perspective of some Canadian observers, was the continuing shift of professional hockey to cities in the United States. By 1935 the Canadian American Hockey League had lost its Canadian clubs, and the Canadian Professional Hockey League had become the International Hockey League, with only two Canadian clubs to the Americans' six. At the same time, however, the national radio broadcasting of hockey was having a huge impact on Canadian public appreciation of NHL hockey. Foster Hewitt was becoming a national (and possibly continental) celebrity and the *General Motors Hockey Broadcast* a cultural phenomenon. In a few short years, the Maple Leafs and Smythe's new Gardens had become the flagship brand for NHL professional hockey across Canada, becoming nearly synonymous with the sport itself. Ottawa had been unwilling to take the risk of the new medium (who knows how this gamble might have changed its fate?), but there was hope the Montreal clubs could still take advantage. The widespread allegiance to the Leafs was evident when the club embarked on off-season tours with other clubs. In Barry Broadfoot's oral history of the Depression, *Ten Lost Years*, a contemporary recalled that "hockey was the thing in those days. The big thing. The Toronto Maple Leafs and Foster Hewitt on Saturday nights. Hell, he was better known than the prime minister. It was the touchstone to success, the way a kid could gain fame and a little fortune, playing for Toronto or the Montreal teams, Detroit, [or] Chicago."[76]

In the later years of the 1930s, the question of how a kid could gain fame and a little fortune would become the important one to answer. With professional hockey's labor force based in amateur hockey clubs spread across Canada, the challenge was to line up the Canadian amateur system with the voracious needs of professional leagues.

6

Integrating the Amateurs

1935–1939

In February 1935 Frank Calder agreed to sit down with Montreal French-language weekly *Le Petit Journal* to discuss the NHL and its business. Though no byline appears, the interviewer was almost certainly Charles Mayer, the paper's sports editor. Mayer had a common interest with his subject: he was in charge of NHL minor officials (scorers and goal judges) and also translated into French league press releases and issues of *Hockey*, the weekly broadsheet of short articles, statistics, and photographs compiled by Elmer Ferguson for the league to send out to newspapers. So the interviewee was also the employer, and the close relationship had been almost certainly necessary to even get the appointment. Later, Mayer would write that Calder was a solitary man who was hard to make friends with and that he did not like journalists—even though he had been one— because of their "indiscreet" questions. Despite the many trips Calder took with Mayer, other journalists, and league officials, Calder never let down his guard. According to Mayer, he was not timid, but simply modest and detesting of publicity. For this reason, the interview was a rare occasion of insight into his ideas about the larger context of the business he helped direct. For *Le Petit Journal*'s readers, Calder provided his perspective on the historic tension between the commercial and cultural considerations that drove the NHL's business.[1]

Calder told Mayer that professionalization had been the most important development in hockey since the turn of the century, and he divided the history of the sport into three stages relating to its evolution. The period up to 1912 was one of suspicion and mistrust over the rampant practice of paying amateurs, but this situation had changed when open acknowledgment of professionalism came in 1912, when a major benefit became evident: as club owners began paying their players and were able to exercise control over them, they could be assured that they would appear for the club at game time. The years from 1912 to 1924 were a struggle, as professional hockey competed with amateur hockey for a public that remained biased against the professional game, but after 1924 the public grew to accept professionalism so long as it was not seen as less honorable than the amateur ideal. Through he did not explicitly specify the significance of 1924, this period corresponded to the NHL's expansion into the United States, and he implied it was his league that had succeeded in overcoming the most common prejudices—that money was the first consideration, that all games were organized to produce the highest gate possible, and that professional hockey was a "racket" whose outcomes were fixed.[2]

Calder appeared ambivalent about the role that money played in hockey, but he argued it had been crucial to its development. Without it, he noted, the long road trips and costly arenas could not be maintained and "organized" hockey could not exist. Capital had emancipated the game from intracity and proximate intercity leagues, allowing it to shrink distances and form interregional and international leagues. Without money, the players could not be free from the necessity of off-ice employment during the season in order to travel long distances. Higher salaries also attracted the best players, and the result was better hockey. In Calder's judgment the quality of hockey play had improved immensely since 1917 and now featured more stars. Calder's only worry was that the NHL was now in "a static moment" in terms of player development, held back until a better system was created to produce high-caliber players. The key to the puzzle was the amateur, whose attitude, according to Calder, had changed. The goal now was to play in the NHL, because "professional hockey gives the amateur a higher standard of play to compare himself with. Now all amateurs, whether they perceive it or not, have the ambition to turn professional. Every boy with a hockey stick also has this ambition and he dreams of becoming a Morenz, a Joliat, a Blinco, or a Stewart."[3]

Even in the depths of the Depression, Calder's comments seemed to be becoming truer every day, owing in great part to the growing popularity

of Canada-wide NHL hockey broadcasts, which were legitimizing the professional game, and also to the continuing growth in commercial hockey
in the United States and, more recently, across the Atlantic in the United
Kingdom. Having integrated the hockey markets, as Calder suggested, it
was now up to the NHL to pave the way for the skilled and ambitious amateur players to move up to the major league, by removing the remaining
hurdles and bottlenecks in the player-supply system. To do so, the league
would have to formally integrate the amateur producers of hockey as well,
even while it continued to refine its own operations and grapple with
ongoing concerns over the viability of some of its clubs and their relationships to their arena landlords.

The Farm System

In the 1920s the growing American capital investment in hockey had
improved the financial position of professional players to the point that
Fred Edwards of *Maclean's* was prompted to ask: "Does professional
hockey hold the elements of a desirable career for the young Canadian
who is just starting business life?" With salaries averaging five thousand
dollars a season, comparable to a lawyer or physician salary (albeit short
term), the question of whether the game could be a bona fide career was
certainly a logical one. The lure of "big-time" hockey only accelerated
in the next decade, as the Depression limited traditional employment,
national hockey broadcasts legitimized the professional game, and new
opportunities proliferated outside Canada. It was not a free market for
labor, however. First of all, increases in NHL player salaries were capped
by the salary limit. Players like Earl Seibert of the Rangers and Eddie
Shore of the Bruins continued to exert pressure (Seibert made holding out
for a higher salary an annual event), but in the absence of any comparable elite league as an alternative employer, the NHL monopsony held
and exceptions to the salary limit were few. Second, by drafting from and
farming out to minor league clubs, the NHL could determine the location where a player would practice his craft. In the late 1920s and over the
decade of the 1930s, the NHL had successfully regimented the other levels
of semiprofessional and professional hockey, organizing the hockey markets through interleague agreements. In 1931 it also began to tacitly allow

direct ownership by NHL clubs of minor league clubs, as a means to exert control over minor league operations. It also began to tolerate the informal sponsorship of amateur clubs, especially of junior grade (with players sixteen to twenty-one years of age).[4]

The benefits of direct minor league ownership (or affiliation) and the sponsorship of amateur clubs soon became obvious from the player-development point of view, particularly for those American clubs that lacked proximity to the elite Canadian amateur clubs in Toronto, Ottawa, and Montreal. While Canadian NHL clubs could hold tryout camps in their home cities and depend on informal networks in their hinterlands to acquire players, American clubs needed more deliberate arrangements that tied players to the clubs early on.

Ever forward thinking, Lester Patrick recognized that the Rangers had to do something to overcome the lack of local talent, the distance from high-quality amateur play, and the difficulty in getting amateur junior players to play for American clubs given the radio-driven popularity of the Canadian clubs. Amateur sponsorship solved this problem and became the response to, as Lester Patrick put it, overcoming the preference of seventeen- and eighteen-year-olds to play for the Maple Leafs or Canadiens. Patrick's Rangers led the way in developing sponsorship into a tiered edifice that moved players along from amateur to professional play. Since 1926 the Rangers had relied on the Springfield Indians of the Can-Am League to house their prospects, but that club's suspension of operations during the 1932–33 season left the club without a farm. Taking the bull by the horns, the Garden created a new league, the Eastern Amateur Hockey League (EAHL), run by Thomas Lockhart, the Garden's amateur hockey impresario, who built it on two bases: the Metropolitan house league clubs that had been playing out of the Garden since 1925, and the nearby Tri-State Hockey League, which included clubs from Atlantic City, Baltimore, and Hershey, Pennsylvania. By 1935 the Garden had purchased the Can-Am Philadelphia Arrows (renaming them the Ramblers) and also bought their own EAHL club, the New York Rovers, thereby creating a graduated farm system from amateur to minor professional to major league. All three clubs of the Rovers-Ramblers-Rangers system played their games at the Garden, alongside a renewed local amateur New

York Metropolitan League. To access Canadian amateur talent, in the fall of 1933 Patrick inaugurated a tryout camp in Winnipeg. Since all NHL clubs held their preseason training camps in eastern Canada, the move to the West, an area Patrick knew well, was a clear attempt to get beyond the well-trampled ground of Ontario and Quebec. Finally, to evaluate the players, Patrick developed an extensive scouting staff comprising one chief scout, eight to ten local scouts on commission, and up to one hundred volunteers.[5]

The other American clubs employed similar tactics to lesser degrees. Charles Adams was an early financial supporter of the Can-Am Boston Tigers and bought the club in 1932, changed its name to the Cubs, and put his son Weston in charge. Bill Dwyer purchased the Can-Am New Haven Eagles for development purposes, and the Detroit Olympia gathered in the Olympics of the International Hockey League. Although he resisted direct ownership, even Frederic McLaughlin became a keen promoter of American hockey talent, focusing his attention on the occasional diamond produced in the rough of the midwestern AHA.[6]

With the exception of Toronto, the Canadian clubs seemed complacent by comparison, at least in terms of scouting. In the 1933–34 season, Toronto manager Conn Smythe criticized his fellow Canadian clubs for the diminishing prestige of the game in Canada, a result he attributed at least partly to the lack of player development by the Canadiens, the Maroons, and Ottawa. He encouraged them to establish a scouting system similar to the Maple Leafs', who employed five scouts, developed their players in Ontario amateur clubs, and were now at the point where they "have more players than we know what to do with." The Leafs had briefly owned the Can-Pro Toronto Falcons (formerly the Ravinas, known as the "baby Leafs") in 1928, but preferred to rely directly on the junior and senior amateur ranks by sponsoring the OHA Marlboros. From the late 1920s, the Leafs trained and financially supported the "Marlies," which produced the core of the Maple Leafs' Stanley Cup championship teams of the 1930s, with players such as Charlie Conacher, Busher Jackson, Red Horner, Alex Levinsky, and Joe Primeau. In this decade the Leafs also began an affiliation with St. Michael's College, a Roman Catholic boarding school where they could board out-of-town prospects for development and use St. Mike's academic reputation to entice parents to allow their boys to come to Toronto.[7]

The other Canadian clubs were surrounded by enough amateurs that spending additional money on faraway scouting might have been seen as unnecessary or a luxury. Ottawa never developed a formal recruitment system, and despite Dandurand's intent to form the Can-Am as a development league, the Canadiens continued to rely on local recruiting and their right of refusal over French Canadians. By 1935, ten years after Frank Patrick's prediction of the emergence across Canada of leagues graded by skill level, Dandurand admitted that the NHL's real challenge was still channeling strong Canadian amateur talent into the professional leagues through a scouting and farm system similar to the one developed by the St. Louis Cardinals in baseball. The Maroons did better, signing many of the players of the MAAA—in 1931 almost its entire Allan Cup–winning team—and employing a western representative to help stock the CAC-owned Quebec Royals, who played in the Quebec Amateur Hockey League. By the mid-decade, this system seems to have weakened, but like the Canadiens, the Maroons could depend on local talent, trades, and purchase of players. For all the NHL clubs, however, the future was a fully integrated player-development system that formally bridged the gap between amateur and professional and created a continuous process of identification, training, and promotion of hockey talent.[8]

Redefining the Amateurs

Surprisingly, given the poor economic environment of the mid-1930s, the market for hockey players was still growing, with increasing remuneration moving it along the amateur-professional continuum and also southward. The minor leagues were losing Canadian clubs and gaining American ones, and even the nominally amateur EAHL was drawing players from Canada in increasing numbers, attracting them with salaries and the prospect of moving up to professional ranks without sacrificing amateur status. The hypocrisy did not go unchallenged. The Amateur Athletic Union (AAU) of the United States, which made the rules for US amateur hockey, grew increasingly annoyed at the flagrant flouting of amateurism and by the mid-1930s was spoiling for a fight. It would culminate in open conflict in 1937, but by that time the same conflict in Canada had already changed the rules of amateur hockey and was bringing into line the principal organizations of amateur hockey with the organizing principles of the commercial game.

Pressure to retain players had been mounting on Canadian senior amateur clubs since the early 1920s. In addition to the long-standing competition from the professionals, the USAHA had been enticing star amateur players like Lionel Conacher with promises of lucrative off-ice employment. Echoing the amateur reaction in the first decade of the century, the CAHA responded by using both economic power and stricter regulations. It cut off lucrative exhibition games with USAHA clubs and then affiliated with the AAU of Canada (AAUC), a move that committed its clubs to adhering to a strict interpretation of amateurism based on five "nevers": never entering into a competition for money, never teaching sport as a means of livelihood, never receiving payment in lieu of lost time at work to participate in sport (so-called broken-time payments), never selling or pledging prizes, and never promoting an athletic competition for personal gain. The CAHA may have expected AAUC affiliation to end American player raiding (through the influence of the powerful AAU), but with further defections of senior OHA clubs and the emergence of the American-weighted minor leagues, the suction pressure on Canadian amateur clubs only increased. Indeed, in the years that followed, the American minor league clubs emerged as a bigger threat than the NHL clubs. Whereas NHL rosters required just over a hundred players in total and needed only a few dozen new players each year, the American minor leagues involved hundreds of players of wider skill levels and sourced their players primarily from amateur ranks. Ominously for amateur organizers, the popularity of the sport was still expanding in the United States, and players were discovering new opportunities in the United Kingdom as well. As had been seen before, the pressure to hold on to players, and even to financially compensate them, brought the CAHA-affiliated clubs into increasing contradiction with the amateur ethos.[9]

Even before the Depression provided economic incentive, the CAHA had tried to stem the tide in two ways: by asking for professional help and by threatening its own players. In March 1929 the association proposed that professional clubs be prohibited from signing players under the age of twenty-one. In return, the CAHA would allow professional tryouts that would not threaten a player's amateur status. A meeting with the NHL did not produce any agreement, and in June 1930 W. A. (Billy) Hewitt, the CAHA registrar, submitted the proposal again, arguing that the arrangement would help develop players "without cost to the professional clubs." Again, the NHL felt no compunction to act.[10]

The pressure continued to build. In the fall the national periodical press engaged the topic. Fred Edwards of *Maclean's*, still on the hockey beat, accused amateur hockey of being "a sham, shot through and through with veiled professionalism," and alleged various egregious violations of the amateur ethos, including the sponsoring of amateur clubs by professionals in return for the rights to players. He focused particular attention on the relationship between the Montreal Maroons and the "long on tradition but short on cash" MAAA club that had just won the Allan Cup. Edwards framed the debate in national (and colonial) terms, arguing that the amateur definition being used was "borrowed from the United States, and diametrically opposed to all British tradition." The players were "the victims of obtuse officials who stubbornly adhere to a foreign, un-British amateur definition which makes complete honesty ridiculous, encourages hypocrisy, winks at perjury, and puts rank opportunism on the back." Henry Roxborough made a rejoinder to Edwards the next month, disputing his facts and maintaining that the Canadian amateur laws were "almost identical" to many British sports definitions. But it was hard to argue against the substance of Edwards's other point—that the CAHA seemed powerless to contain the pollution, "so powerful has the spirit of commercialism and opportunism become in the past few years."[11]

To constrain the players, the CAHA appealed to their honor and restricted their geographic movement. In 1931 a CAHA Oath of Allegiance was required of all players taking part in branch championship finals, Allan Cup, and OHA Memorial Cup games. It included this phrase: "I am not under any contract or understanding to play professional hockey nor will be until after the final series is over." That this pledge obviously did not solve the problem is evident from the policy the next year, when the CAHA now required it to be taken "en bloc by the players in the dressing room and a written copy signed by each individual player." Residency rules were also used to limit the ability of players to become "tourists" and shop their services from one club to another, especially after the season had begun.[12]

Resolving the hypocrisy of "shamateurism" was also a priority, for ideological but also financial reasons. Some observers speculated that the nominally amateur Maritime Senior Hockey League would professionalize because professional players actually cost *less* than amateurs, because of the practice of offering twelve months of off-ice employment to amateurs. Various modifications of the amateur definition were proposed. Maritime delegates to the 1931 CAHA annual meeting endorsed broken-time payments, but the motion was defeated. The next year a Saskatchewan branch motion to allow professionals in one sport to register as amateurs in another was taken more seriously, and the CAHA delegates revived the debate over modification of the amateur definition at the AAUC annual meeting. An extensive debate followed that featured a discussion of the practical realities of amateurism. Nothing was changed, but liberalization was in the air.[13]

It did not come soon enough. In 1933 the CAHA acted unilaterally to allow amateurs to try out with professional clubs without permanently losing their amateur status, subject to the condition that they take no money except for expenses and that they notify their regional branch of the tryout. While the AAUC continued to dither over redefinition, the CAHA felt compelled to act owing to player emigration to the United States and increasing internal migration between elite amateur clubs. In early May 1934, President E. A. Gilroy had informed the CAHA branches, "and on at least three different occasions issued a warning through the Canadian Press," that migration of players from branch to branch was not permitted after 1 January 1934. Something had to be done if the CAHA was not to be made, in his words, "the laughing stock of the whole of Canada." At the association's eighteenth annual meeting in Halifax in April 1935, the registration committee resolved that there would be no more transfers that year, but there would be an amnesty for those players who returned to their hometowns to play.[14]

A new problem appeared that summer to aggravate the situation even further. The current iteration of the English National League, centered on Wembley and Harringay Arenas, was now placing no limitations on the number of imported players. By August English hockey clubs were already waging a full-on recruitment campaign in Canada. The CAHA issued a warning to players that they would be banned from Canadian hockey if they went to England without permission, an action that prompted a meeting with the British Ice Hockey Association in Toronto at the end of September. After a two-day conference, the BIHA representatives agreed that "no Canadian player would be permitted to play without the sanction of the C.A.H.A." When the CAHA executive decided not to grant any more transfers, the BIHA ignored the ruling and allowed twenty-two players to play anyway. (Even worse, two Canadian players were also allowed to play on the British Olympic team, which won the gold medal at the 1936 Olympics at Garmisch-Partenkirchen in Germany, Canada's first loss at the Olympics.) Canadian amateurs were also continuing to go to the United States, mostly to EAHL clubs. When the CAHA suspended them and notified the AAU, the latter refused to enforce the suspensions, despite the agreement with the AAUC. After the season was over, Billy Hewitt wrote that "so alluring was the picture painted that it appeared as if all the senior players in the Dominion had been approached by these active agents. . . . The exodus of Canadian hockey players to England, the Continent and the United States reached alarming proportions."[15]

From the CAHA point of view, the BIHA was delinquent and the AAU simply impotent. Even at home the AAUC was not cooperating with the CAHA and its attempts at amateur redefinition. An association committee was appointed to confer with the AAUC "to discover if something could be done towards broadening the definition of 'amateur status,'" but it "failed to make any headway." Instead, George Dudley, the second vice president of the CAHA, recommended the CAHA act unilaterally and begin to allow broken-time payments, to allow players to obtain legitimate employment as a result of hockey ability (that is, the "shamateur" scenario), to allow exhibition games between amateur and professional teams, and to allow professionals in other sports to play amateur hockey.

Dudley emphasized that it was the CAHA's job "to legislate for the good of hockey," but "the realities" of Canadian hockey required a broadening of the definition and the association had to "face the facts, and no longer set up one thing in our handbook and practice something else." It was time to admit that senior amateurs in particular were playing for more than "mere love." Dudley argued that the effect of a new definition would be confined to a select series (presumably the Senior A level), and residency rules could be maintained to avoid indiscriminate transfer of players. Bearing in mind that the CAHA was beset "with many problems in connection with the inroads that professional teams are making into our ranks," as well as the difficulties of the British and American "migration," Dudley was convinced that the only way forward was to "put our players on such a basis that our clubs can enter into a definite contract with them." He was not advocating that amateur clubs issue player contracts just yet, but the redefinition would free them to do so, and he hoped that the CAHA delegates would, "in a few years time . . . go further and adopt the proposals I have made." (It would eventually take four.)[16]

CAHA annual-meeting delegates asked questions of the committee members and were understandably concerned about what the new definition would do to their relationship with the AAUC. One of the committee members was Clarence Campbell, and he assured the meeting that the question had been seriously considered. The committee's conclusion was that unless the AAUC changed, the affiliation would have to be ended. This threat alarmed William Fry, a former CAHA president who was also the current AAUC president. He warned that "it would be a sorry day for [the AAUC] when it had a split with this organization which is its strongest supporter both financially and otherwise." He cautioned that "radical action [that is, redefinition] would deprive Canada of the right to compete internationally." After a debate, the motion to present the redefinition proposal to the AAUC passed. Fry called an immediate informal meeting of the union members present at the meeting and reported back that the group was friendly to the first three proposals, but divided on the fourth (regarding amateurs playing against professionals). Fry warned that the CAHA resolution was vulnerable if the AAUC rejected even one and warned about the possible influence of hockey's secession on other sports affiliated with the union. His warnings were for naught. After the AAUC rejected the CAHA's modifications of the amateur definition, the CAHA announced it would deaffiliate and go its own way.[17]

Now able to take on directly its own international relations, in 1936 the CAHA delegates agreed to ratify a new one-year deal with a new amateur organization, the Amateur Hockey Association of the United States. The AHA of US was the response of the American elite amateur leagues to their own repeated disputes with the AAU over players skipping out on contracts with the EAHL's Boston Olympics and New York Rovers. Organized at the behest of the owners of these clubs—Walter Brown (son of George) and Reed Kilpatrick of the Garden, respectively—its first president was Tom Lockhart, the EAHL president. The new American group agreed to limit Canada-US transfer requests to one player per club per year and to limit importation of players to not more than four CAHA players per team per season. With this American agreement in hand, Gilroy was authorized to enter into negotiations with the BIHA, the Ligue Internationale de Hockey sur Glace (LIHG, the international governing body), and professional hockey.[18]

In May 1936 CAHA delegates met with an NHL committee to work out an agreement. They agreed on four points:

1. the mutual recognition of suspensions
2. that there be no signing of juniors by NHL clubs without the amateur club's consent
3. that the NHL was to give notice of intent to try out an amateur player by 15 August and signing him by 15 November
4. that the CAHA was to adopt NHL playing rules

While both parties professed to be happy with the deal, several NHL governors not party to the negotiation were displeased. Thomas Arnold of the Maroons disagreed with the suspension recognitions, and Lester Patrick disliked both that provision and the second one about signing juniors. He thought the NHL was "getting very little and the CAHA . . . [was] getting everything that they want." In his mind, the NHL could take a tougher line with the association, which he called "an amateur group with no investments and a depleted treasury." At the summer meeting, the NHL clubs eventually agreed on the basic tenets, but added a board of appeal to adjudicate suspensions, consisting of one NHL and one CAHA representative, plus Calder. The CAHA initially objected to the board of appeal (given its composition, perhaps not a surprise), but not for long. With deals in place with the Americans and British, signing with the NHL fully achieved their short-term goals at least, and the CAHA signed a one-year agreement.[19]

In retrospect, the initial CAHA-NHL deal has been seen as the start of a slippery slope that, in the words of historian John Wong, put the CAHA, "for all intents and purposes, on its way to becoming a subsidiary of the NHL." Bruce Kidd suggests it was only a few short years until the CAHA was forced into "complete surrender." At the time, however, this outcome was less than clear. In his 1937 CAHA presidential address, Cecil Duncan spoke as though the association's goals had been achieved:

> The principal object of these meetings was to arrive at some satisfactory agreement with respect to the transfer of hockey players to the United States and to Great Britain, and also with respect to the signing of hockey players by the National [Hockey] League.
>
> Furthermore, I think you will admit that the agreements entered into have been of great value to our association.
>
> As a result of what took place, we were able to know early in the season the number of players that we were to lose to various other countries, and were therefore in a position to make replacements if we so desired.

Insofar as the main concern of the CAHA was defections to the United States and United Kingdom, it may be that the CAHA agreed to the NHL deal without fully appreciating its later consequences, but that judgment is hard to make. In a sense the CAHA really gave up relatively little, except an agreement to use NHL rules and an acceptance of a practice that would go on with or without their acquiescence—professional clubs signing away the best amateur players. In return, they got protection from the raiding of junior clubs, established guidelines for signing other players, and got NHL help to enforce association control over amateur players. If more proof were needed, in 1937 the CAHA annual meeting was a generally happy one. In comparison to previous years, the financial statement was "a very creditable one . . . and the [CAHA] which last year was . . . ailing, is now not only convalescent but completely recovered."[20]

Although the CAHA balance sheet may have improved, the disputes were not over. Over the next few years, the association continued to argue over amateur redefinition and residence rules, mindful of both British competition for players and charges of hypocrisy. The issues were finally dealt with after the 1940 Allan Cup playoffs, when the Valleyfield Braves senior team went on strike for their wages, arguing that their weekly pay should be continued through the playoffs. This public admission of paid amateurism pushed the CAHA to revise the amateur definition to its most simple and most defensible term: "An amateur hockey player is one who has not engaged in, or is not engaged in, organized professional hockey." It soon began allowing players to be signed to standard contracts, bringing the amateur system closer into line with the professional model.[21]

With the formalization of the relationship between the amateurs and professionals, the NHL clubs were more comfortable extending their affiliations with senior amateur clubs. In 1938 the NHL specified that member clubs could now "designate, assist and finance" one amateur, junior, or senior club in the United States or Canada. The next year this ruling was amended to allow for sponsorship of two clubs. Since senior clubs in turn could sponsor junior teams, the stage was set for the elaboration of a long supply chain that reached into the youngest strata of the Canadian amateur hockey system. Furthermore, with the CAHA now affiliated with the Madison Square Garden–influenced AHA of US, the international link was also ensured. There would still be disagreements in future, but the path to integration of the amateur and professional hockey labor markets was being turned into a highway.[22]

Taking over the Americans

As the league worked toward an ensured player supply, it was also moving to ensure club financial stability. Even with the sacrifice of Ottawa and Philadelphia and the quiet binding of the Canadiens to the Canadian Arena Company, the NHL clubs were not all on durable footing yet, especially the Americans. With a new lease in place, the club started off the 1935–36 season in bold fashion, with Dwyer claiming to have spent sixty thousand dollars on new players. His optimism was short lived. Dwyer's track investments continued to lose money, and in addition to James Norris Dwyer also began to depend on one of his own players, Mervyn (Red) Dutton, for financial help. Perhaps in recognition of his creditor status, in a sort of on-ice receivership Dwyer made Dutton player-manager of the club in October 1935.[23]

Dwyer was not without options. Flush from the sale of the Canadiens, Dandurand and Cattarinich offered to buy his club, but Dwyer did not want to sell outright. What the Montreal men probably did not know was that the club was encumbered. After a November meeting with Cattarinich and Dandurand, Dwyer went to Chicago to visit Norris, setting off new suspicions of syndicate hockey among New York sportswriters. Dwyer succeeded in renewing the option he had sold to Norris, but his price tag of three hundred thousand dollars for the club was too rich for Dandurand and Cattarinich, and they were not interested in an offer of a minority position. It still seemed likely the Americans would have to be sold to someone. By January the club was again slumping at the gate, and there were stories that games were being "papered" with free tickets to boost attendance numbers. Jim Norris Jr. attended the last Americans game of the season, sparking rumors that the club still might go to "an appointee of the Norris interests."[24]

By this time, the Americans also owed the league assessment money (5 percent from each home game's receipts went to the NHL), and the club's plight began to preoccupy the other governors. Dwyer was clearly broke and, according to some, lacking in business sense, but, unlike Ottawa or Philadelphia, the Americans at least had a viable market. Committing to sustain the Americans for the upcoming season, the governors appointed a committee under Calder to arrange the club's reorganization. Dwyer was given a deadline to pay his debts to the league and to the club's other creditors, and when he could not do so by October, Calder announced that the league would solicit a buyer. By the end of training camp in November, there was no outside interest in the club, so the governors took over formally and transferred the franchise to a new corporation, the American National Hockey Club, Inc., whose shares were owned by the other clubs. Calder sat on the board of directors as president and treasurer; Dutton as vice president; C. N. Valiquet, a league employee, as secretary; and John Banser, a New York lawyer, as a director.[25]

Dwyer was not willing to relinquish his club. His business manager, Martin Shenker, responded that because the players were under contract to the New York Hockey Club, Inc., an injunction would be forthcoming to prevent their use by the new club. Sure enough, an order was acquired from a Canadian court and served on the Americans players on 5 November in Toronto, meaning that they played the next night in Chicago under Dwyer's ownership, not the league's. Soon afterward, the two parties compromised. At an all-day meeting at the Hotel Commodore in New York, it was agreed that the American National Hockey Club, Inc., would take over the club as planned, but Dwyer would remain the governor and a club director and would have a year to pay off the debts and resume control. In February Dwyer was pushed into receivership by his creditors and by May was still in no position to regain the club. The club would remain under league management until an acceptable buyer appeared who could pay off all the creditors (among them Norris [$40,000] and Dutton [$60,000]). In the meantime, Dutton set about writing a book, *Hockey: The Fastest Sport on Earth*, to further promote the sport.[26]

Contrary to what might have been expected, there was no press criticism of the league taking control of the Americans, a move that might have been construed as a form of syndicate ownership. Indeed, Alfred Dayton of the *New York Sun* wrote that Calder's handling of the situation was "little short of a stroke of genius." League ownership was obviously seen as an acceptable, neutral proposition, unlike multiple ownership of clubs by one owner.[27]

Within the league, the Americans takeover led to a new willingness on the part of the governors to reconsider the borders between club and league, particularly the ones affecting revenues. Tommy Gorman of the Canadian Arena Company once again recommended the sharing of gate receipts, to address what he called the "economically unfair" disparity between the Canadian and US teams. The former Senators owner repeated the Ottawa refrain: the Canadian clubs were "making gates" for the American clubs, but were getting "very little in return." Gorman was particularly incensed after a Maroons visit made $15,000 for Chicago at the stadium, but the Black Hawks drew only $3,500 at the return date in Montreal. The trend was of long standing. In 1935–36 the Maroons and Canadiens had drawn together only $206,296 at home, but on the road the gate figures were more than twice as much—$479,084—for the clubs the Montrealers visited. In comparison, the disparity between home and away receipts was a net benefit to the Rangers ($90,639), Chicago ($88,647), Boston ($45,047), Americans ($38,903), and Toronto ($32,040). Other than the Montreal teams, only Detroit had been a lesser draw at home than on the road ($22,473). Even accounting for stadium size (and leaving aside the weak Montreal attendance that might be laid at the clubs' own feet), Montreal clubs were clearly superior road draws, and Gorman wanted a larger cut for them. The obvious solution was adoption of the baseball model and some measure of pooled receipts. Without this structure, he threatened, "the Canadian teams cannot exist and the league itself will collapse for the lack of Canadian background in what even the people of the United States regard as a Canadian game." As it had been when he represented Ottawa, Gorman's proposal was in vain. The Montreal clubs might be hurting, but sympathy among the governors for revenue sharing was again wanting.[28]

Gorman, who had managed in New York, would have certainly realized that the superior capacity of the American rinks was a major factor in the disparity. (In ten years the Forum had gone from the biggest to the smallest NHL rink by capacity.) The other factor was market size. Could Montreal really sustain two clubs anymore? Receipts in 1935–36 suggested otherwise: whereas the other twin-club arena, Madison Square Garden, had combined gates of more than $500,000 for its clubs, the two Forum clubs together now drew less combined than all other individual clubs except for Detroit.

Gorman made efforts to change this predicament, starting with radio. After General Motors relinquished the sponsorship rights to the popular weekly national hockey broadcasts in 1936, Gorman tried to renegotiate the deal with its successor, Imperial Oil of Canada. He pushed too hard, and Imperial dropped the Quebec network entirely. Looking for an alternate outlet, in 1936 Gorman allowed WJBK Detroit to broadcast games from Montreal, and he hired his own advertising firm to negotiate directly for airtime with the Canadian Radio Broadcasting Commission

(CRBC), whose regulatory permission was required to establish network broadcasts. There, he ran up against a reluctance to broadcast sports on Sundays. In Quebec, where the Sabbatarian tradition was much less intense, Sunday night had become the traditional hockey time; in Sabbatarian Ontario, it was Saturday night. And as Ontario went, apparently so went the CRBC, and all other Canadian listeners had to follow. Gorman eventually accepted new Imperial terms in 1937, but Toronto's first-mover advantage in national radio meant that Montreal played second fiddle for more than a decade afterward.[29]

Radio promotion could not be the only solution, however, and did not fundamentally address the viability of the two-club, one-rink model. In 1936–37 the Maroons lost $41,000 and the Canadiens $33,000, and even before the season was over there was talk the Maroons would be moving, perhaps to St. Louis but more likely to Cleveland. The sudden death in March 1937 of Howie Morenz, who had returned to play for the Canadiens, cast a further pall over Montreal hockey. That many thousands who visited his body and attended his funeral spoke to the profound cultural importance of the sport, but it was also one of the few times the Forum was filled all season.[30]

At the league meetings in May, when the governors once again refused to consider serious revenue sharing, the talk even led to discussions of an all-Canadian league. (In Charles Mayer's somewhat partisan view, it was a solution to the Canadian spectator's lack of interest in the "less interesting play" of the American teams.) Toronto would not support the idea, and instead a committee of Calder, Norris, and Kilpatrick was struck to act on "any plan to ameliorate the professional hockey situation in Montreal." The focus instead would be on the "general belief that Montreal has not sufficient population to support two clubs." Though already tried, Pittsburgh, Cleveland, and again St. Louis were discussed as possible destinations for the Maroons, showing the continued importance of market size in the governors' thinking about the crucial ingredient for long-term club success.[31]

Despite the economic doldrums, hockey in the United States had its bright spots, especially in the Great Lakes region, where Cleveland in particular offered the prospect of a large market (population of 900,429 in

1931), a hockey-friendly environment (the International League Falcons were drawing well), travel ease (it was in the geographic center of the NHL), and the promise of a suitable arena: Al Sutphin, owner of the Cleveland Falcons, was building a ninety-three-hundred-seat arena and declared his intention to bid for an NHL franchise for 1937. When the NHL would not promise him a franchise without secure financing on the building, Sutphin decided instead to recommit to his minor league partners in the new International-American Hockey League (IAHL), which was formed in the fall of 1936 with a merger of the Can-Am League and the IHL.[32]

The woes of the Forum and its clubs continued. At the beginning of the 1937–38 season, the sparse attendance was on embarrassing view when an all-star team played to hundreds of empty seats at the charity hockey game for the Morenz family, and at the end the Maroons were the only club not to see increased attendance. In June 1938 the CAC finally decided to pull the plug and asked to suspend the franchise. The other owners were reluctant and once again appointed a committee to investigate options. In August Gorman presented a plan to sell the club to St. Louis interests, but unsure the Eagles' fate would not be repeated, the governors refused this proposal. Because it was now obvious the CAC would not operate the club in Montreal, the governors relented and consented to allow the club's temporary suspension and the distribution of its players to the Black Hawks and Canadiens.[33]

The decision to retain the Canadiens over the Maroons was not an easy one, but it was predictable. Initially, there was some trepidation in the French-language press that the CAC might choose the Maroons, the club of the Anglophone community, but in the end the ethnic plurality (more than 60 percent of the population was Francophone) no doubt decided the question. Suspending one club would leave one of the two solitudes without a club, but it would be the smaller one. Also, if the Maroons could not be revived, then moving that club to the United States would be much easier than moving the ethnically branded Canadiens. In the meantime, the Forum management hoped Maroons fans would shift their allegiance to the Canadiens. Many seemed willing to do so in the fall, but many also stayed home, and with half the number of NHL games at the Forum it was five seasons before the Canadiens' gate receipts matched the combined receipts of the last season with two Montreal clubs.[34]

Stability and Optimism

As the NHL reached the end of its second decade in 1937, the governors held a dinner in New York to celebrate Frank Calder's twentieth anniversary as president of the league and to honor his role in the development of professional hockey. The tributes of the NHL member clubs were amplified by testimonials from Pacific Coast League representative Cyclone Taylor, IAHL president Maurice Podoloff, and AHA president William Grant. After dinner Calder was presented with a magnificent silver tea service engraved with the signatures of all the NHL governors.[35]

The celebration for Calder was also for the league. In two decades the NHL had risen from the ashes of its predecessor and spread far beyond Montreal to twelve cities in two countries. It thrived in only six cities, but had lasted more than twice as long as any ancestor and so the picture was of hard-won relative success. Thwarting and co-opting players, rival leagues, and shamateur challengers alike, it established itself as the only major league, subordinating all others to preside over the dominant commercial version of hockey and to exert greater influence in the noncommercial amateur world as well. However, the most important achievement was that the NHL cartel had avoided fracturing from within, remaining united and averting both failure and plausible alternative structures, either by dividing into two "national" leagues or perhaps even by becoming semisyndicalized in some form. Growing and maintaining the league across two national economies had not been easy, but overall the story was one of successful sport export. Along with amateur proponents, the NHL had modified the Montreal game to appeal to audiences beyond the St. Lawrence River markets, bringing it to areas where winter ice had previously been only a brief visitor.

The national repercussions were significant. While the players were still Canadian, the professional clubs were increasingly American, and even minor professional hockey was disappearing from Canada. Reporting on the testimonial dinner, Harold Burr of the *New York Post* predicted that in the near future, major league hockey would be restricted to the United States. Indeed, he noted there were only three major league clubs left in Canada—as he was writing, the Maroons were yet to suspend—and only one minor league club, the Vancouver Lions of the Pacific League. Burr's idea was not new, having also been voiced when US expansion took off in the 1920s, and Calder himself had bemoaned the trend away from smaller Canadian cities in the 1935 interview with Charles Mayer. Although the league had survived its tenuous early years, negotiated well the popularization of professional hockey in the United States, and endured the doldrums of the Great Depression, there had been casualties: those smaller markets, usually Canadian, whose small populations could not support a major league club over the increasingly longer seasons.[36]

Elmer Ferguson of the *Montreal Star* also noted the trend, pointing out that although twenty Canadian cities had tried professional hockey, by 1938 only Montreal (the Canadiens) and Toronto (the Maple Leafs) remained (he missed Vancouver). The lesson for him was that the high cost of big-league hockey could be sustained only by big metropolitan areas, which were mostly in the United States. And in those markets only one club could thrive, with the possible exception of New York. Major league hockey was not alone in this process, and aside from major league baseball, the rationalization of small-market teams and the movement to larger markets were also seen in the National Football League and the National Basketball League.[37]

NHL policy reflected this new reality. John Wong argues that "individual efforts determined the failure or success of a franchise. If an owner failed in his efforts to save a troubled franchise, little support could be expected from the league." This judgment is perhaps too sweeping. Although there was a change in attitude over the 1917–39 period that appeared biased to individual efforts, league intervention was by no means absent. It was the criteria for league involvement that had changed. In the league's early years, basic survival was at issue, and the league used significant revenue sharing. After 1926 the clubs applied salary limits and the 3.5 percent subsidy to encourage parity and even out costs across the league and sometimes allowed the drawdown of the league equity account. By the 1930s the league governors emphasized market viability in their decisions of whether to help individual franchises, and the revenue-sharing model now left most revenue in the hands of individual clubs and avoided any significant long-term subsidy or league-wide revenue sharing. Short-term financial help and permission to move were used, but calls for a greater division of revenues from Ottawa and Montreal went unheeded. The league did support clubs by stepping in to negotiate leases in Boston, Chicago, and New York, but these measures were to help clubs in large markets weather the Depression. Above all, the league governors clearly wanted to avoid revising the general revenue-sharing formula permanently to subsidize clubs in weaker markets. The governors were not willing to rescue the Senators in Ottawa, where the market was now unviable, or the Eagles in St. Louis, where the potential would not be realized. The same held true for Pittsburgh and its move to Philadelphia. But the insolvent New York Americans, a large-market club with solid attendance, got special consideration, showing that the new NHL business model prized market viability (and a suitable rink) above "individual efforts"—even if it meant historic elite hockey markets would be allowed to drop from membership in the cartel.[38]

The importance of hockey to the American stadiums has also been mischaracterized. Bruce Kidd writes that "it could be argued that the American franchises in the NHL survived the Depression only because of hockey's cultural, and organizational links to boxing," but it should not be. Actually, the reverse is the case. In a few short years, NHL hockey made a swift transition from novelty sport to necessary revenue stream for the large American arenas. While boxing promotion networks were an important initial connection point for American clubs (as was horse racing), hockey quickly supplanted pugilism as the bread-and-butter activity of the major civic indoor stadiums and helped these boxing venues survive the Depression. There is no evidence that James Norris saved hockey only as a by-product of an attempt to save boxing arenas; again, if anything, it was the other way around.[39]

In Canada it was somewhat ironic that while Canadian NHL hockey production was concentrating in Toronto and Montreal, popular consumption was growing across the country. Just as the sport itself had crossed climatic borders and gone international through ice-making technology, the borders of nation, city, and region were being transcended through the technological intercession of radio, which was, as Marshall McLuhan later noted, a much more intimate and immediate medium than newspapers. National radio broadcasts facilitated the greater integration of the league into the cultural fabric of Canadian society, but also played an important role in the legitimization of professional hockey in the minds of amateur players and the listening public. Frank Cosentino argues that the high profile of the Gardens and the hockey broadcast contributed to the changing attitude toward the NHL and professional hockey in general. He dates the transition from "vilification to glorification" of the professionals to 1933, the year of the first regular national hockey broadcasts.[40]

In combination with the Depression, this legitimization process had important implications for senior amateur hockey and the minor leagues. First, playing the professional game became increasingly desirable for amateur players, and talent began to shift to professional clubs, inside and outside of Canada. Second, the hockey broadcast created a national market for NHL hockey that shifted attention from local community amateur hockey (especially senior) to the professional game of the larger urban centers, the ones that could sustain the new economic scale of the NHL game. In Canada especially, the net effect was of elite hockey moving in different directions. Senior amateur hockey was to begin a long downward slide in quality and popularity in favor of the professional game and the junior hockey that fed it. Consumer attention was being drawn away from local and regional markets to an emerging national market served by professional hockey and focusing on central Canadian NHL cities, more specifically Toronto. The American pull was also powerful, since most amateur hockey was Canadian, but the professional growth was taking place south of the border.

This integration of the national market and the legitimization of professional commercial hockey in the minds of consumers and athletes in turn put pressure on the amateur strictures girding the CAHA. International competition came from UK and US leagues, as well as economic pressure that made transgression of principle a necessity for many players. These factors combined to push a modification of the definition of amateur, a process that had begun in the pre-Depression era. Responding to the demands of its elite senior clubs, the CAHA began to accept commercialization more openly. Deaffiliating from the AAUC and affiliating with the NHL served both to resolve the hypocrisy of shamateurism and to strengthen CAHA restraints on amateur player freedom and movement. Here they found a convergence of interests. The CAHA amateur clubs essentially wanted the benefits of player control (as Calder might put it, to be assured that the player would appear for their club at game time) without the price of full market participation (in other words, high salaries). So did the NHL clubs, who also wanted a controlled monopsonistic structure that guaranteed trained players would be consistently available. In return, both were willing to accept some restrictions on recruitment age and signing timing.

In the United States the establishment of the AHA of US meant US amateur hockey would be closely attuned with eastern professional interests for the foreseeable future. One of the great disappointments of the interwar years was the failure of American players to break into the NHL in significant numbers, a situation that might change with the proliferation of US amateur clubs and the support of the AHA of US. The American NHL clubs made great efforts to set up local hockey leagues and recruit American players. Boston in particular looked to college stars such as Dartmouth's Myles Lane and Harvard's George Owen to provide local content. The Americans were also keen on college men, hiring Dartmouth graduate Eddie Jeremiah in 1932, but American-developed players generally could not yet compete at the NHL level. In the short term the greatest exponent of American talent was Major McLaughlin, who was resentful of the Canadian influence on the game. In 1937 he announced plans to change the name of his club to the "Yankees" and develop an American "hockey factory" to provide American players for the club and replace the Canadians entirely. It did not pan out, and McLaughlin had to release his American players in order to compete, but it showed that the export of Canadian ideas and labor to the United States could produce negative sentiment in the United States as well as Canada.[41]

By 1939 it was apparent that a sea change in labor conditions had taken place over the first two decades of the NHL. Initially scorned in many quarters during the 1920s, professional hockey as a career became more acceptable in the 1930s, and the deal between the CAHA and NHL (with tryout provisions and an amateur reinstatement process) meant a professional player no longer sacrificed his amateur career in perpetuity. Professional pay was also increasing: in the early 1920s it was often hardly more than that of a skilled senior amateur, especially when their year-round employment was taken into consideration, but with the advent of American capital the salaries eclipsed the pay of amateurs, who were themselves enticed to US and UK clubs. Not all was to the players' benefit, however. The removal of the PCHA, WHL, and AHA as competitors for player services made the NHL and its affiliates the only professional employers, an effective monopsony. The negotiation list reserved the services of amateur players and prevented players from taking offers from multiple teams (and possibly obtaining higher salaries as a result). Salary limits could also be effectively used to maintain parity between the small-market Canadian clubs and the large-market American clubs and to keep costs under control during the 1930s. As the Depression wore on, the natural instincts of the clubs to compete to obtain better players meant the salary cap wore off, and the average payroll by 1938 was said to be one hundred thousand dollars per club (more than six thousand per player). Competition for talent was also restricted by another standard feature in player contracts, the option clause, which meant that the club did not fear losing the player, only that he would not play, something few players were in a secure-enough position to threaten.[42]

In a 1939 *Maclean's* article, former Americans all-star goalie Roy Worters gave a rare contemporary perspective of the recently retired player. He highlighted the special conditions of hockey employment: long apprenticeship, low pay, tough training, physical injuries, emotional stress, and no guarantee of employment. The farm systems were making competition for jobs much tighter, and Worters claimed that, of the 131 players in the league when he started (in 1925), only 4 were still playing in 1938–39. Contracts had also been reduced from three years to one, as the option clause "ties the player to the club that owns him indefinitely." Worters was fully aware that the contracts were "tough" and not like "in ordinary commercial life," so not much had changed since 1924 when the judge had noted that Frank Heffernan was "tied up for life." Despite this tightening control, there could be considerable room for variation and negotiation, and many owners paid bonuses above and beyond the contract requirements. Dave Trottier of the Red Wings apparently received an oil-supply contract for James Norris's Great Lakes shipping fleet as part of his playing contract.[43]

NHL players were also not fully in control of their bodies and could be sent to work to a distant minor league club, often without their consent. Although the practice was not universal, by 1939 Conn Smythe was using "two-way" contracts that specified a different salary structure for major and minor league play so he could save money. The owners also added a clause to the player contract that stipulated the club's right to use the player's likeness and signature as they saw fit and reap the benefits of commercial use.[44]

NHL paternalism did address catastrophic injuries. In 1938, as an alternative to holding an annual all-star game (as in baseball), the NHL club owners developed policies for career-ending incidents, first voting to insure players against career-ending injury and also establishing a fund for salary replacement using 5 percent of the playoff pool. Maple Leafs prospect George Parsons lost the sight in one eye and became the first beneficiary of the Injured Players' Fund. The Leafs covered his medical bills and found him a job, and the NHL supplemented his salary to bring it up to forty dollars a week, indefinitely. The league also continued to sponsor one-off charity games to generate larger sums in more tragic circumstances, such as when Canadiens coach Babe Siebert drowned in August 1939 and an all-star game was held to benefit his family.[45]

Control over the NHL's own members still presented most of the challenges. For Calder, it was an uphill battle imposing discipline on a league where the owners were responsible for some of the mayhem. His goal was not just consistency of enforcement, but also restoration of respect for the rules and the referees themselves, both of whose reputations had been suffering for years among players and owners. A game in March 1936 was a case in point. Charles Mayer wrote that it was a "burlesque" that was started by Conn Smythe, continued by the referees, and ended by the local constabulary "as usual." What was not usual was that Calder himself had been forced to intervene, hopping on the ice and telling Smythe and the referees to stop the "show." Even time was contested. In 1932

Smythe installed a "SporTimer" in Maple Leaf Gardens and began agitating for similar electric time clocks to be installed in all arenas, probably to remove the discretion of timing of period and penalties from local officials. A clock was installed in Madison Square Garden in 1935, possibly in response to Smythe's complaints, but the discipline of objective timekeeping had a long way to go to change the competitive and mistrustful culture of the NHL: Tommy Gorman claimed that even the SporTimer was "fixed."[46]

Internal conflicts were endemic, but with clubs, player relations, attendance, affiliated leagues, and player-supply channels relatively stable by the late 1930s, the prospects for the NHL looked auspicious, and it was poised to grow along with the slow recovery of the North American economy. Stability and optimism would soon be challenged, however, and over the next six years the NHL's place in North American society would be tested as never before, this time by a real war.

7

Managing a Morale Business

1939–1945

In a January 1943 Maple Leaf Gardens game program, the acting manager of the Gardens, Frank Selke, wrote an article criticizing the Boston Bruins, Boston hockey, and Boston sportswriters. He also called Art Ross a "sourpuss." The Boston manager replied to the insults with a four-page diatribe against Selke, Conn Smythe, the Toronto press, the NHL board of governors, and NHL president Frank Calder, and he did not spare his opinions. We cannot be sure Ross actually mailed the letter (a carbon copy resides in the papers of Boston sportswriter Harold Kaese), but the spirit of invective was fully in character and reflected both his short temper and his willingness to express his animosity to his fellow NHL governors.[1]

Ross's litany of grievances went back to the early years of the league and centered on his experiences in Toronto. He had been tossed headfirst into a snow pile at the Mutual Street rink by Charlie Querrie and seven Toronto policemen, been taken advantage of in several player trades with the Leafs, and even been "hit on the head with a cane" by an unnamed Gardens director.[2]

Ranting on, Ross defended Robert Duncan, who had recently taken his place as Bruins governor, and described Duncan's negative impressions of the typical NHL board of governors meeting. The governors arrived late, clutching train schedules so they could "catch the first train back, regardless whether any business had been done or not." Selke refused to vote "on any serious matter," claiming his "lack of experience." Lester Patrick had to "refer everything to his Board of Directors." Tommy Gorman was always trying to explain how double-headers of "so-called" amateur hockey did not hurt Canadiens attendance. Bill Tobin claimed the Black Hawks "were going to give all their profits . . . to charities this winter." "Bull" Jim Norris tried "to second every motion he made himself," and "Norris' hatchet man," Jack Adams, "doesn't throw hatchets according to the old Chinese custom, but throws sticks and punches at officials." But no fate was worse than "being sentenced to sit alone in the somber presence of the 'Great Silent One,'" Frank Calder. Ross had an obvious dislike of the league president, writing that the league could not hope to prosper with Calder's "appalling incompetence . . . [his] many errors of omission and commission, and . . . grossly apparent inactivity."[3]

Then it was back to Toronto. Ross caricatured the Toronto press ("the Froth Estate"), his correspondent ("Frank Sulky"), and even the legendary Gardens radio announcer ("Foster,—and how he can Hueit"). In particular, Ross was irate that Selke had refused to give a discounted Leafs ticket to a former NHL player who was now in the military; in contrast, he wrote, "Old Sourpuss has arranged that over 25,000 men in uniform here in Boston will see our games this season free of any charge whatsoever. Think that over, Stupid."[4]

The Ross rant is a rare illustration of the long-standing grudges, jealousies, and suspicions—even occasional physical assaults—that characterized owner relations behind the closed doors of the NHL cartel. The fact that the league was able to manage this kind of personal conflict showed its strength, but the coming of the world war would put it again to the test.

While scholarship on the NHL in the Second World War focuses on the degree to which Canadian hockey players may have avoided military service by virtue of their athletic or cultural status, and the degree to which this avoidance was abetted by the league, clubs, or military and civilian authorities, there has been much less discussion of the way in which the NHL itself had to reorganize its business within the new confines of wartime society. Indeed, the stress of the conflict would magnify internal rifts and patch over others as the governors struggled to negotiate the new social and economic circumstances and navigate the business successfully in two wartime societies (one of which, the United States, was not even a belligerent at the outset). The league's very survival depended on its ability to elaborate a role as a socially and economically useful business and define itself as something essential to wartime society: a booster of morale. To do so required refashioning its public image and engaging with the state in ways that had not been required before, all the while hoping that the political economy of war would allow the league to continue recovering from the Depression.[5]

Declarations

The German invasion of Poland on 1 September 1939 led to a quick British declaration of war two days later, and within the week Canada was also deciding whether to join in. On 7 September, the same day that the Canadian Parliament met to discuss its response, another emergency session was held to discuss how Canadian participation might affect the hockey business in the upcoming season. Like the politicians, Frank Calder, Conn Smythe, Jack Adams, Lester Patrick, and W. A. (Billy) Hewitt (representing the CAHA) had a British model to consider: the British Football Association and National Ice Hockey League had just suspended their operations to put their facilities at the disposal of the War Office. But there was a big difference: unlike the NHL, the British leagues did not have half their clubs located in a neighboring—and so far neutral—country.[6]

Sportswriters had already begun discussing the war's possible effects on the large amounts invested in assets and player contracts in the United States. They pointed out that many US arenas depended on hockey for survival, and so the possibility of conscripting Canadian hockey players did not augur well. Frederic McLaughlin was optimistic that the war would not unduly affect attendance or player supply, as he assumed Canada would send its regular army to the front first, but he was unaware that Canada had fewer than ten thousand regulars to send. Charles Mayer of *Le Petit Journal* presciently predicted that American—not Canadian—policy would likely be the deciding factor on hockey's continuation. He surmised the Canadian government might not want to defend sports in wartime and that even if it did, the US government might change *its* policy and no longer allow players to cross the border to work, a possible deathblow to a league whose players were almost all Canadian. These possibilities had Frank Calder making inquiries in Washington as well as Ottawa.[7]

In the face of speculation that the league might be forced to suspend, the NHL decided to carry on. Calder voiced the league's commitment to assist the government in the war effort and also started making the connection to morale: "We will just as in the last Great War [World War I] patriotically assist the government in every possible way. Any of our players who wish to volunteer will be assisted in doing so. We feel that a well-conducted sport will be of great benefit to the national morale in these days of worry and mental stress." Press reaction was positive. The *New York Herald Tribune* editorialized that the league was to be congratulated for deciding to go on with "the most popular winter sport. . . . [T]he continuation of hockey has seemed absolutely essential both to relax a nation in arms and a nation in the proximity of the terrible threat." More practically, as a preemptive move against anticipated labor shortages, the seven NHL clubs reduced playing rosters from sixteen to fifteen men.[8]

Even when the Canadian Parliament decided to declare war on Germany on 10 September, though Prime Minister William Lyon Mackenzie King spoke of full economic support, he made no immediate commitment on Canadian military participation. With no real plan for active engagement and no fear of imminent attack, the prospect of the NHL losing its players or its arena facilities faded somewhat. A decision to continue was reaffirmed at the league's next board of governors meeting on 20 September in Detroit: conscription or not, the season would start on schedule on 2 November. Of active NHL players, only Bill Cowley of the Bruins had enlisted, and, at age thirty-seven, there was little chance of his being called to serve at this early stage. By mid-October the war fever had abated somewhat. At the season opener, Calder was optimistic: "The National Hockey League, born in the dark days of the last war, has weathered many storms and it faces the future confident that time will bring victory for the allies as well as greater interest in major league hockey."[9]

The war in Europe was not the only worry; the league was still recovering from the economic effects of the Depression. Total attendance at regular-season games in 1938–39 had shown a softening in New York, Toronto, and Montreal. This slowdown may have been an effect of the so-called Roosevelt Recession, which saw a general economic downturn from mid-1937 to 1938. Without the Maroons, gate receipts at the Montreal

Forum had fallen 35 percent. Madison Square Garden had also lost spectators, and any improvement would be hampered by the trading away of the few stars left on Dutton's already too sparsely spangled Americans squad. Chicago and Detroit appeared weak on the ice, and only the Rangers, Toronto, and the previous season's Stanley Cup winner, Boston, promised any solidity. With the uncertainty of wartime, the expected shifting of the dormant Maroons franchise to another city also seemed out of the question. The governors agreed to delay their decision. Likewise, they extended the May 1926 league agreement, set to expire in 1941, until after the cessation of hostilities.[10]

The early games of the 1939–40 season brought new lows in attendance and criticism from all quarters over the state of play. Attendance was so poor in Detroit that the deep-pocketed James Norris was even said to have changed his mind about revenue sharing. The press identified several defects—low scoring, the lack of stars, and, in particular, the secretive nature of the NHL governors, "the supreme suppress agents of the age." The governors were hardly suppressing their own frustrations. Tempers boiled over in Chicago in December, with on-ice officials the target of verbal and physical abuse. In one game James Norris publicly berated referee Bill Stewart (a former referee in chief) for biased calls, and later there was a bench-clearing brawl. In the next match Mervyn Dutton "sought to attack" referee Norman Lamport, and in the next game the Hawks and Canadiens emptied their benches to engage in another mass melee. Three days later the board of governors met and legislated fines for any manager or coach who got on the ice for any reason after the game had started, and also for players who left the bench to join fights. While the player brawls were curtailed, the owners were harder to corral; only two weeks later, Ernest Savard, president of the Canadiens, called referee Frank Clancy over to the bench to remonstrate with him about a disallowed goal and finished by seizing him and giving him a violent shake.[11]

The altercations were not without publicity value, as Conn Smythe demonstrated when he goaded his nemesis, Art Ross, in a rather creative fashion. Annoyed by the unexciting defensive play of the Bruins in Toronto, Smythe placed an ad in the *Boston Daily Globe* before the next Leafs match in Boston on 19 December, promising that the Maple

Leafs would show Boston hockey fans "a real hockey club." As might be expected, Ross hit the roof and brought the issue before the board of governors, which censured both Smythe and Ross. Such internecine conflicts were not unusual—the Ross-Smythe feud and others had been going for years—and also sold tickets, but in context it did not bode well for a league already challenged by weak revenues as well as an external threat that could force suspension of operations by sudden government fiat.[12]

Foreign Exchange Control

While the long-term nature of Canada's involvement in the war was not yet evident, the Canadian government agreed to send one division of fighting men to Europe and to provide economic support to Britain. It also began soliciting orders for airplanes, tanks, and other war matériel, and the challenge became how to pay for these items while at the same time continuing the purchasing of civilian goods for a society that was as yet not ready to sacrifice its standard of living for an overseas war. Purchases of finished goods and industrial machinery from the United States combined with loans to Great Britain put Canada's foreign exchange reserves under serious strain, especially its store of US dollars. In anticipation, the government created a Foreign Exchange Control Board to coordinate foreign exchange reserves under the direction of the governor of the Bank of Canada and representatives from various federal government departments. By April 1940, with the country desperate for US dollars, all foreign exchange held by Canadian residents was required to be sold to the board, all transfers of Canadian dollars to nonresidents now needed FECB permission, and all approved transactions had to be exchanged at fixed official rates that favored the government. Furthermore, any travel to the United States required board permission, and from July 1940 US funds were no longer provided for pleasure travel to the United States.[13]

These developments had a serious impact on all cross-border businesses, and the NHL was no exception. In October 1939 Calder argued for special consideration and negotiated with the FECB to obtain exemption for the NHL on the requirement to convert its US dollar receivables immediately into Canadian dollars. The NHL was allowed to maintain its US dollar bank account until the end of the season. Unfortunately, the distribution of playoff proceeds coincided with the April 1940 order requiring all foreign exchange to be turned in. Since the NHL was considered a Canadian resident, it would be expected to convert more than US$39,000, but Calder had already redistributed all but US$3,203.45 back to the American clubs. In response to the FECB demand for the full amount, Calder tried a novel argument. He said the US funds were for incidental expenses over the summer and "are not used for commercial purposes in the strict sense of the word." He based this reasoning on the special character of the NHL, maintaining that the league "is not an incorporated body and is merely a voluntary association of the participating clubs, formed to look after their mutual interests. The clubs themselves obtain their revenue from the gate receipts of their home games and all clubs pay their own expenses." In addition to arguing that the league was technically a noncommercial entity, Calder also pointed out that the majority of the funds were contributed by American clubs, which were exempt from FECB regulations anyway, and that many of their expenditures were in Canada, which thereby benefited the Canadian foreign exchange position. Persuaded, the FECB agreed to treat the NHL's American dollar account as "the property of non-residents" and exempt it from the Canadian regulations, in effect giving the NHL a special binational status.[14]

In the course of his negotiations with the FECB, Calder also pointed out another way the league could help: 95 percent of professional hockey players were Canadian, and players employed by American clubs brought most of their US dollar salaries back home at the end of the hockey season. Nothing was done about this situation in the 1939–40 hockey season, but in the summer of 1940 Conn Smythe proposed that all professional hockey players playing hockey in the United States sign a form obligating them to bring back to Canada all their American income, less "a reasonable living allowance" determined by the FECB. (Canadian dollars bought in the United States negatively affected Canada's balance of payments, while Canadian dollars bought with US funds brought to Canada had a positive effect.) Smythe emphasized the advantage for the FECB: the procedure would "control the return of foreign exchange to our country, because Mr. Calder could see that all contracts were registered in his office and force the clubs to guarantee the performance of the players signing applications with respect to foreign exchange." As a plan that might bring hundreds of thousands of US dollars into Canada, it seemed attractive, but it was by no means purely altruistic. Smythe's self-interest was made clear: "From our angle, of course, what we want is the authority vested in Mr. Calder so that he would have entire control of professional players going to the States, from our Government. This, of course, would control any outlaw league because they would be unable to operate unless they complied with Mr. Calder's regulations."[15]

The outlaw league Smythe was worried about was the American Hockey League, which had recently dropped *International* from its name and was seen to be conserving resources until it could openly challenge the NHL's major league status. In February 1940 Cleveland Barons owner Al Sutphin announced the formation of a seven-man scouting staff to scour Canada for new talent, especially in the western provinces, a move that threatened to drive up the cost of players for NHL clubs. In Smythe's mind, control over cross-border players was key to thwarting any AHL challenge, and it would also prevent any scenario in which NHL clubs might be blocked from crossing the border to play and the league forced to either suspend or divide in two. The FECB ignored Smythe's anticompetitive reasoning, but did agree to let Calder supervise the system. After all, as D. B. Mansur of the FECB wrote to the board's secretary, James Coyne, there was some half-million dollars per year at stake, and "if a convenient way can be established to see that we secure some $350,000 of this amount, I think that we should make the effort." Coyne agreed.[16]

Under the plan, Calder would act as intermediary for the NHL players and also for players of the American Hockey Association and the Pacific Coast Hockey League (not to be confused with the PCHA). Except for the ones in the PCHL, players from these leagues were already being admitted into the United States under an alien labor bond for temporary workers that had been required since 1930 and was executed by the NHL. Over the months of August and September, a procedure was developed with application forms and appropriate living allowances, initially fixed at twenty-five dollars per week for single men and fifty dollars for married and later changed to reflect the differential (and rising) costs of living in American cities. Efforts were also made through W. G. Hardy, the Canadian president of the International Ice Hockey Association (IIHA), a new governing body of North American amateur hockey, to bring the amateur hockey teams into the plan.[17]

Over the course of the war, clubs occasionally violated it, but overall the deal proved to be a good one for the FECB, which got control over hundreds of thousands of US dollars from hundreds of professional and amateur players administered by the NHL. The board also made good use of the publicity aspects, as did the NHL itself, which cited the plan when professional hockey's contribution to the war effort was discussed later in the war. Much more important, the deal meant the league would actually continue to operate, for without the agreement with the FECB, which controlled how money crossed the border, travel would have been much more difficult. However, the FECB was not the only regulatory agency that could hinder players from crossing the border, and human capital, not just financial, also had to be aligned with the war effort or else the league would not be allowed to function.[18]

Business as Usual

After the fall of Poland in October 1939, a period of military inactivity persisted until the spring of 1940. Over these months, which became known as the "phony war," the 1939–40 hockey season played out with business as usual. Unfortunately for the NHL, weak economic conditions still persisted, and any war stimulus had not yet trickled down to ticket buyers. Chicago's gate receipts showed an upswing (+9 percent), Toronto's remained the same, but all the rest were down: Canadiens (20 percent), Americans (-13 percent), Boston (-11 percent), and Rangers (-5 percent). Detroit was down an incredible 43 percent, perhaps an indication of its dependence on a Canadian audience now cut off by border-travel and currency restrictions. When the phony war became real with the invasion of France in May 1940, however, it was the continued availability of players that became the more pressing issue.[19]

In March Prime Minister Mackenzie King had called a snap election and won a solid majority after a campaign marked by Canadians' ambivalent feelings toward so-called war preparedness. Sentiment quickly changed in June after the collapse of the Anglo-French front, the emergency evacuation at Dunkirk, and the fall of France. The Liberal government quickly passed a National Resources Mobilization Act requiring national registration of all Canadians and giving great powers to the government to allocate manpower. The NRMA allowed conscription only for domestic defense, and overseas service remained strictly voluntary, a recognition that a good proportion of the Canadian populace, particularly in Quebec, still resisted any notion of foreign obligation. The act's immediate effect was to provide a training period (initially thirty days) for those men who were eligible for call-up, with the process to be administered by the newly formed Department of National War Services (DNWS).[20]

Responding to the legislation, NHL managers actively encouraged their players to sign up with Non-Permanent Active Militia (NPAM) units in order to get the required thirty days of training completed before the hockey season began. Conn Smythe outlined his reasoning in a July letter to Maple Leafs players. Once trained, he wrote, if a player were subsequently called up for service, he would be ready, but in the meantime, he "will have complied with the regulations and be free to play hockey until called on." Smythe was working on a plan to have Maple Leafs players join the Toronto Scottish Regiment, and already the club's executive officers were being seconded to government agencies in management capacities (and Smythe himself was trying to enlist). Smythe directed the players to obtain passports for travel to the United States, a new requirement just recently implemented owing to American fear that fifth columnists might gain access to the United States. Lester Patrick, manager of the New York Rangers, wrote a similar missive to seventy-five players in the Rangers' system, advising them to volunteer for the training before the "defense act" went into effect 15 August and to apply for a passport early in the summer, as it was "easy then" but "might become difficult later" because of the increasing American government restrictions on cross-border travel. Patrick added that no one could play who had not completed army service requirements and who did not have a passport.[21]

Planning preseason military training to avoid midseason labor interruption was prudent, but a sudden change in government policy could still bring the season to a sudden stop. To forestall this situation, according to the *Toronto Daily Star*, in September Frank Calder spent "considerable time at Ottawa getting the green light from government agencies for hockey." Calder was looking for assurances that the league "would not be molested by war agencies during our playing season. Failing that," he told the paper, "we would hardly have contemplated operating." Calder got his assurances. At the NHL semiannual meeting held the next week in New York, it was reported that "practically all" NHL players had done military training and joined NPAM units, and after Calder's successful lobbying efforts, the feeling of the meeting was that there was now "little possibility of hockey players being taken into the military in such numbers as to make the operation of professional hockey impossible." It also helped that in December, a tentative deal was reached between the NHL and the CAHA, allowing the NHL to sign amateurs upon payment of $500 for each player called up to the NHL and $250 for players signed to the minor leagues. This agreement smoothed the way for the NHL to use more amateurs should the need arise.[22]

Conflicts of Interest

Wartime did not allow the putting aside of everyday details of league management, and the records of the meetings of the league's board of governors show that spirited discussions over a range of issues remained the norm throughout the war. Attended by owners or their proxies, as had been the prewar practice meetings were held every month or two throughout the season in club cities, most often the Royal York in Toronto, NHL headquarters in the Sun Life building in Montreal, the Roosevelt or the Commodore in New York, and the Copley-Plaza in Boston. In addition to the annual meeting in May and a semiannual meeting in September, other special meetings were called on short notice to deal with unexpected problems, and the war provided several. Each gathering was chaired by Calder and had its conversations transcribed verbatim by the official recorder, R. Holmes Parson, who was also known as "Penciller." Some of these verbatim minutes survive and give readers fascinating insights into the personalities and policies that shaped the management of the league. Recurring debates over pedestrian topics like the fairness of schedules, the character and competence of referees, and the density of pucks were interspersed with compelling exchanges in which governors reveal much about themselves, their relationships to each other, and, in one telling episode, their understanding of the special nature of their business.[23]

The 17 October 1940 conference at New York's Hotel Commodore was one such meeting where a discussion about the right of the NHL to assign and enforce territorial rights vis-à-vis the minor leagues evolved into an argument over the very legality of the league's business model itself. In a letter circulated beforehand, Conn Smythe primed the governors to be prepared to help the Leafs enforce their territorial rights in a novel way. Traditionally, territorial rights gave clubs exclusivity to the playing of professional hockey and were usually restricted to the city of the club. Under interleague agreements, the NHL persuaded the minor leagues to respect these rights and in return let them assume their own. In the late 1930s, the NHL began to extend territorial rights for some of its clubs well outside their cities of operation to include nearby markets: Buffalo for Toronto, Indianapolis for Detroit, and Minneapolis for Chicago. There were several motives. In Toronto's case, Buffalo was seen as a market for Leafs tickets, and it also came up in conversations about future expansion, but the main idea was also to reserve it for a Leafs-owned minor league club. In the case of Indianapolis, where James Norris and his partner, Arthur Wirtz, owned the Indianapolis Arena, the intent was more obviously to reserve the city for a Detroit-owned minor league team.

The direct ownership by NHL clubs of minor league clubs made a great deal of business sense. With minor league partners, the major league club was assured of both a training ground and an overflow mechanism for its player pool. Ownership secured this system and also helped keep leagues like the AHL subordinate, a strategy also reflected in Smythe's proposal to the FECB a few months before. Furthermore, there was a commercial aspect. Unlike most businesses, NHL clubs could not expand their markets beyond the capacities of their home rinks, and so buying a minor league franchise allowed them to leverage expertise in managing professional hockey beyond its home territory. In the case of Norris and Wirtz, this idea went even further, as they pursued the Rickardian dream of filling large urban arenas with hockey teams.

In 1939 both Norris-Wirtz and Smythe applied for franchises in the IAHL, where Madison Square Garden already had a club, the Philadelphia Ramblers. Norris and Wirtz succeeded, but Smythe did not. Buffalo went to another applicant, and though it was later offered to him through the intercession of Norris, Smythe refused the terms (and remained annoyed at Norris for not supporting him in the first place). This setback did not end his desire to control Buffalo and maintain pressure on the minor league. In fact, it amplified it, and to do so he tried to enlist his fellow NHL governors to extend the scope of major league territorial rights, which the minor leagues would be obliged to respect as affiliates under the inter-league agreements.[24]

Smythe could have asked the NHL to tell the AHL to forget about expanding to Buffalo at all, but he knew he would have little support, especially since Norris and J. R. Kilpatrick were AHL owners. Instead, Smythe asked that the NHL governors, and the minor league affiliates they controlled, not make any player deals with Buffalo directly, but allow Smythe to arrange any transactions. Doing so would, as Smythe put it, "establish the fact that the National [Hockey] League was a group that the minor leagues had to pay some attention to and do business with." (Though left unsaid, it would presumably also pressure the Buffalo owners to consider giving Smythe a better deal for the franchise itself.)[25]

While Smythe's gambit may have been seen by the other governors for what it was—simple punishment of a minor league club for thwarting Smythe's ambitions—Fred McLaughlin saw it as a chance to review NHL property rights and the relationships between major and minor league clubs. After all, Paragraph B of the NHL league agreement of 1926 specified that NHL clubs should have no involvement in any club or league except the NHL. In light of the extensive involvements of NHL clubs with minor league teams, of which Indianapolis was simply the latest, the major pointed out the obvious: "We have never lived up to that, we have never given any [NHL] team permission to operate a minor league team. No team in the league has lived up to this agreement." In order to do so, McLaughlin argued, NHL clubs should have no involvement with Buffalo at all, either by owning the franchise or even by loaning players to teams that might play against Buffalo. James Norris called it "a dog in the manger policy" and maintained that NHL territorial rights should not prevent minor league clubs from operating in a city. When he also wondered whether if it was even legal, the conversation took an interesting turn.[26]

The legality of the cartel-league form in the United States was a question ostensibly settled by the *Federal Baseball* decision of 1922, which allowed baseball's major leagues to constrain competition by restricting club entry and participation in their leagues. The judgment came to be understood as an exemption from the restrictions on monopoly and restraint of trade contained in the Sherman and Clayton Antitrust Acts. Leagues organized on the same model, like the NHL and NFL, benefited from the analogy with baseball, although they made no outright claims of exemption. One reason may have been that the NHL owners were not themselves all that clear on the nature of their business.[27]

Major McLaughlin was one who turned out to have a well-informed and pragmatic opinion on the matter, in contrast to others who were surprisingly oblivious to antitrust status and its ramifications. The major responded to Norris's question about whether the NHL had the right to prevent minor league clubs from entering territories with a general statement on the legal nature of sport leagues like baseball and hockey: "If you want to take it legally, neither have any standing at all." When Norris wondered if there would be any possibility of being sued for conspiracy to restrain trade (the antitrust charge), McLaughlin noted that although it had been brought up in baseball several times, it had not been pursued. And it was not relevant anyway, as far as he was concerned. The real issue was whether the NHL clubs felt bound by the May 1926 agreement, "whether it is legal or not."[28]

McLaughlin felt that the NHL should use its market clout. He argued that if the minor leagues wanted to continue to share in the "golden harvest" that the NHL had brought to the United States, they should be encouraged to remember that they were "off-shoots of the prosperity of the National League" and "that the goose that lays the golden egg was the National League team." When Norris stressed that no NHL club was actually operating in Buffalo, McLaughlin pointed out that the territorial rights had been assigned to protect Toronto's drawing power, particularly the "crowd of people" who came from Buffalo to see Leafs games." And now that the decision had been made, it had to be defended on principle. For McLaughlin, like Smythe, it was a case of being pushed around: "We have to decide who is really to be the leaders. I don't see we get much out of the International [IAHL] except they go tell us to jump in the lake and sometime we will have to decide which is the major league." And the legal dimension would not prevent the league from exerting its power: "No minor league has to give us permission for us to make an agreement between ourselves, but that too is conspiracy and legally if you want to prove it the whole thing is illegal, we are in an illegal business, so is baseball, on a much bigger scale."[29]

For Kilpatrick, the idea that the NHL was illegal was "a sort of bombshell." With this new perspective, he decided that Smythe's proposal to act as the agent for the NHL clubs in their dealings with Buffalo was "something that I don't think any group has a right to do or actually can do" and suggested it was against the "public interest" for the NHL to try to prevent another team from operating. McLaughlin admitted that such behavior was selfish, but could be accomplished by having the Garden-controlled Ramblers simply not play Buffalo. Kilpatrick feared this proposal would lead to charges of restraint of trade, but McLaughlin for one did not seem to mind if the issues were brought "out in the open." He seemed to enjoy pointing out to his peers that when they had tried to push leagues like the AHA out of the organized hockey system in the early 1930s, it was not legal: "We did not have any right to outlaw hockey, but we did it." And the league agreement itself was likely not legal, but it was a necessity. In McLaughlin's view, without the agreement, "there is no such thing as a hockey league."[30]

Smythe felt the issue of legality was clouding the issue, and he clarified that he did not expect Indianapolis or Philadelphia to stop playing Buffalo, but simply wanted to let Toronto control the selling and buying of players with Buffalo. But Kilpatrick was spooked and stated that he would not enter into any agreement, even though he actually had no intention of selling or buying players with Buffalo. By this point, McLaughlin was beginning to enjoy needling Kilpatrick, telling him, "You ought to get out of it [the NHL agreement] if you are afraid it is illegal." Kilpatrick decided that the business would work "all right so long as it is secret but if somebody gets wise and cracks a[n antitrust] suit against all of us."[31]

Trying to wrest back the discussion, Smythe took up McLaughlin's arguments about league solidarity. He was worried about the NHL standing firm against outsiders and the threat posed by protecting Buffalo, which he saw as "a potential opponent of the National League." He worried that they might join up with others and form a rival league. According to Smythe, the Maple Leaf Gardens' board of directors was "worried this is the start of the break-up of the National Hockey League; that territorial rights don't mean anything; that the Colonel [Kilpatrick] wants them in New York or [sic] does not want them anywhere else." Smythe was willing to accept a limited informal agreement to enforce his rights in the meantime. He was not overly concerned with the legal niceties, unless it allowed him to claim that it was *the AHL* that was in restraint of trade— a rather dangerous precedent for the NHL to make. Otherwise, Smythe wanted to ignore "this constitutional business" and simply get the right to approve all player trades to Buffalo. Kilpatrick and Norris agreed but wanted Smythe to accept the current offer to buy Buffalo. McLaughlin wanted to keep going and define major league rights in the league agreement and weigh the antitrust implications.[32]

Calder entered the discussion and pointed out that the "agreement was drawn up by a first class lawyer." (What he did not note was that the lawyer had been in Canada, where the law treated restraint of trade quite differently from the United States. North of the border, services like hockey were not subject to competition [antitrust] law, and neither was there a strong antitrust legal tradition.)

In Calder's opinion, the purpose of the league agreement was to protect against defection by the clubs and not competition from other leagues. He did not see any harm in the league agreement, since "it was fundamentally to protect yourselves against the others and not against outsiders." The nature of the cartel-league structure, Calder argued, was benign: "When it comes to cases any group of men gathered together for their own mutual interest and welfare, bound together by any agreement, so long as they stick [together] are all right, but if they assail the interests of anyone else they do lay themselves open as a group to attack." When Norris retorted that assailing others is what the league proposed to do in Buffalo, Calder suggested the same behavior was evident in other cooperative businesses, like "the Stock Exchange and the Produce market and all the rest of them," but Norris observed that in his own primary business interest, grain trading, any cooperation between competitors would be illegal. Calder did not disagree, but countered that Norris was not obliged to sell wheat to his competitors. The implication was that the NHL should not have to sell players to Buffalo.[33]

The analogies were imperfect, but that was the point: there was something special about business in a cartel league. Even Calder's comment about "any group of men gathered together for their own mutual interest and welfare" brings to mind one of the most famous maxims about the effects of monopolies, because it provides a striking contradiction to it. In his famous argument against anticompetitive behavior in *The Wealth of Nations*, Scottish philosopher Adam Smith pointed out how innocently it could come about: "People of the same trade seldom meet together, even for merriment and diversion, but the conversation ends in a conspiracy against the public, or in some contrivance to raise prices."[34]

For Smith and subsequent critics of monopolies and cartels, price-fixing was the most obvious negative outcome of producer communication, but in North American professional sports leagues it was not prices but access to the league that was the primary issue. In hockey, unlike grain, it was availability of games, rinks, players, and markets, not prices, that provided the anticompetitive barriers. And as some governors of the NHL realized, communication and coordination of production were necessary to the management of the league—indeed, they were the rationale for the league's existence. For Calder, this necessity made the cartel form natural and acceptable. McLaughlin agreed that it was necessary, but also saw it as a vulnerable creation that threatened to melt under any legal heat.

Calder and McLaughlin agreed that a full definition of the rights assigned to territories needed to follow, but until that happened Smythe's request needed to be dealt with. After returning from the lunch break, Smythe reiterated his proposal to act as the agent for player transactions with Buffalo for the year, at least until a new interleague agreement could be reached. In practice, Smythe said he intended to offer players to everyone but Buffalo first and then sell to Buffalo if need be—making the point that the major league was standing together. There seemed to be general support for this notion, despite some skepticism from Norris, but the previous discussion over illegal agreements made the form the decision could take unclear. Art Ross, who did not think the league was doing anything illegal, was ready to forge ahead and agree, on the principle that "this is all the bunk, we don't have to deal with anybody if we don't want to." McLaughlin cautioned, "We can't agree to that effect," and Kilpatrick added that boycotting someone was "definitely illegal." Norris continued to justify his disagreement behind the principle that he was unwilling to conspire to prevent minor leagues from playing, but McLaughlin once again sounded his refrain in response to this naïveté: "If you think we must not conspire together to do anything what power do you think we would have as a League. What would be left to us, how could we protect any rights anywhere without conspiring?"[35]

Smythe made sure everyone understood he had no ulterior motive. Responding to Norris's concern that Toronto might stand in the way if a future NHL franchise was granted to Buffalo, Smythe said Toronto would waive its rights, but was keeping watch so that the territory did not "suddenly go against us with the help of members of our own League. That may be far-fetched, but we see that possibility."[36]

As was usual in the course of board meetings, tangents pulled conversations away from their main line before decisions were rendered. Kilpatrick began to muse about expansion, saying that it would be logical to add two more cities, such as Buffalo and Cleveland, to help smooth scheduling difficulties, cut down traveling costs, and increase intercity rivalries. This being the case, perhaps a more generous spirit might be shown to the AHL teams—as he put it, "Is the best way to do that to try and discipline or work with them?" Smythe, irritated, started questioning the value of the minor leagues in general. The NHL had subsidized them for a decade, and what had they gotten out of it? Smythe told Kilpatrick that he (Kilpatrick) had given "$20,000 or $30,000 . . . [and] the best players they ever had—you think you are doing a fine job for the League, I think you are doing a terrible job." Smythe even regretted his own arrangement with AHL Providence, as it had not provided enough players for the Leafs.[37]

Tiring of the discussion and unable to get the board to effectively pressure Smythe into simply buying into the AHL, Norris pushed for a vote, even though he expected it to go against him. Since most issues coming before the board eventually obtained compromise, Norris felt the need to comment that if the others voted against him, "you are not going to hurt my feelings." So with Norris against, the rest voted to support a motion to affirm the right of the Toronto Maple Leafs Hockey Club to be "protected against any National [Hockey] League team trading with Buffalo."[38]

With this item out of the way, the agenda soon moved into another site of conflict of interest. Earlier, Kilpatrick had complained of the frictions that arose for those owners that held both the club and the rink and referred to a recent embarrassing position where he had to take sides against the Boston Garden and James Norris. He thought it was "a source of weakness" that Madison Square Garden was a partner in hockey with NHL clubs but a partner with Norris alone in other arena shows. In league discussions he felt he had "to be on both sides of the fence in certain respects." He warned that "our interests are not always the same," but also stated that the Rangers would not hurt any other team in the league, even if not in the best interests of Madison Square Garden.[39]

The issue seems to have been the Bruins' lease, and Kilpatrick's commitment to support NHL clubs was quickly put to the test when Art Ross brought it up for discussion. Ross wanted to prevent the Boston Garden from entering a team in the minor league Eastern Amateur Hockey League, but in doing so he worried about hurting Madison Square Garden, whose Rovers already played there. Kilpatrick argued the merits of the EAHL and that preventing the Boston Garden from icing a team in the end would backfire because the Boston Garden would be making less money on amateurs and would need to make it up on the Bruins' lease. Ross was prepared to take that risk because the Bruins had won the Stanley Cup and had good attendance the season before but had still lost thirty-seven thousand dollars. Ross asked Kilpatrick to use his influence and tell the Boston Garden that the Rovers would not play unless they "get together" with the Bruins on the lease. Kilpatrick tried to argue that amateur teams had a right to play wherever they wanted, but as a partner in the NHL he agreed to do Ross's bidding, even though he expected to "get hell for that" from his EAHL partners. The meeting adjourned shortly after.[40]

This October meeting in New York served up two instances where conflicts of interest were becoming acute after a decade of direct major league involvement in minor leagues, alongside a greater integration of clubs with arenas. At least for the American clubs, the benefits of major and minor league connection were twofold: first was the development of a sound player-training system to bring skill to the major league team, and the second was the creation of a second- or even third-tier hockey product to fill dark nights in the large American arenas. The discussion at the board of governors meeting and the view of Kilpatrick and Norris show that the benefits were offset by the difficulty in reconciling the competing priorities of major and minor circuits and negotiating with partners who did not have the same relationship between club, arena, and league.

The meeting had uncovered some fundamental disagreements and misunderstandings as to the very nature of the NHL as a business organization. Nevertheless, even with principles often at odds, and the constitution ignored, in the end pragmatism reigned and Smythe got his arrangement. In the short term, the expansion talk was taken seriously, and Washington and Buffalo would be investigated as target cities, with the potential for competition with the AHL always foremost in mind. And over the long term, quite understandably, the meeting set in motion discussions toward a new league constitution clarifying the issues that had come to the table. Wartime would not be the best time to discuss them, but the ideas would percolate and become a priority when the war's end finally came into view.[41]

Passport Crisis

In 1940–41, the second wartime season, the NHL finally saw the effects of the growing war economy at its arena gates. Sell-outs returned, and attendance grew in all NHL cities except New York, where the poor on-ice records of the Americans and Rangers were owing to their growing inability to obtain skilled players. Montreal and Detroit in particular made huge recoveries, with gate receipts up 45 percent and 50 percent, respectively. The only flies in the ointment were a Black Hawks dispute with Chicago

Stadium over the terms of their lease and the struggling Americans who, unlike the Rangers, could not depend on the deep pockets of their arena owners to sustain them through trying times.[42]

The idea that hockey was about more than dollars and cents also began to appear in the press. Many writers noted the cultural importance of hockey, especially its contribution to wartime civilian morale. The author of an article in the *National Home Monthly* waxed that hockey was "a welcome diversion" at which spectators might "rid their minds of the strain of war news and the constant knowledge that the future of democracy and freedom hangs in the balance." Such messages began to contribute to a public perception of the league as an essential morale booster on the home front.[43]

To be effective, however, morale had to be practical, not just rhetorical, and the NHL became active in making the connection, especially if it had economic effects. In May 1941 the financial requirements of the war intruded into its Canadian arenas in the form of a proposed amusement tax. Initially, the Special War Revenue Act had suggested only a 20 percent tax on motion picture tickets, but, after intense lobbying by theater owners, Minister of Finance James Ilsley broadened it to include "all entertainments," including hockey, baseball, and other sports. To fight this proposal, Conn Smythe sought advice from his local member of Parliament, Rodney Adamson, who recommended several lines of argument: the difficulty of collecting tax in small rinks, the damage the tax would do to amateur hockey and "Canada's National Sport," the value of sports to the nation's youth (who should be "getting out and playing games rather than sitting in stuffy movie houses watching frustrated sex dramas"), and, not least, "the value of the Toronto Maple Leafs as an advertising medium for Canada."[44]

Smythe probably never got to Ilsley personally—it would not have helped that Smythe was an ardent Conservative—but he certainly pushed Toronto-area members of Parliament into action, and when the tax came up for debate in the House of Commons, they lined up to denounce its effects on amateur, youth, and public participation in sport. Ilsley was not inclined to exempt hockey, however, and when the act came into force on Dominion Day, 1 July 1941, Maple Leaf Gardens and the Montreal Forum, as well as smaller arenas, movie houses, and theaters, were now obliged to serve as collection points for the coffers of war. This tax scheme did not mean the political loss could not be turned into a public relations advantage. Thereafter, the Gardens would disingenuously claim that the corporation itself was paying the tax when it was actually a surcharge added to the cost of tickets.[45]

Despite a modicum of publicity for this and other contributions like the FECB currency scheme, and even the occasional hockey player enlistment, to this point there was little public comment on the wartime role of NHL hockey. On occasion, letters had appeared in the sports pages complaining about hockey players not being in uniform, but it was only as the NHL was gearing up for its third wartime season in the fall of 1941 that public controversy was stirred up and exposed the NHL's Achilles' heel: permissions given to professional hockey players to travel to the United States for the winter.

According to NRMA regulations, men who were eligible for call-up (ages twenty-one to twenty-four) required a letter of permission from the chairman of their local National War Services Board in order to obtain a passport. In September the Manitoba NWSB chairman, Justice J. E. Adamson, refused to give such permission to six U.S.-bound NHL and NHL farm-team players, on the grounds that "Canada needs men and that they are the type who would make good soldiers." In Ottawa the minister of the National War Services (NWS), J. T. Thorson, seemed to concur with the decision, saying that "since the needs of our army [sic] services come first, any board rulings must override any of the conveniences of sport in time of war." He predicted that the precedent would no doubt "have a tendency to influence decisions in other regions" and also confirmed that there could be no appeal of local board decisions.[46]

The day the Manitoba ruling came down, the NHL was holding its semiannual meeting at the Royal York in Toronto. Frank Calder seemed resigned to the news and responded by reformulating Tennyson: "Ours is not to reason why, but to follow any and all decisions of the national war services." Sportswriters and editorial page writers were more critical, and a regional divide was evident. Western Canadian papers like the *Winnipeg Free Press* lined up behind the decision and editorialized that "young men who are physically fit and not in uniform are shirking the major duty that citizenship imposes on them." Eastern organs were more apt to see hypocrisy and discrimination against hockey players. The *Ottawa Evening Citizen* argued that there was a fine line between moral suasion and coercion and that if "voluntary participation" was the government's policy, then it should let every man decide for himself or else apply universal selective service (that is, conscription) for overseas service.[47]

Press opinion aside, the real question was whether the other regional boards would follow suit. The Saskatchewan board sided with Manitoba, but Toronto's was permitting players to go under certain circumstances. Others had had very few applications on which to base policy, but the chairman of the London, Ontario, board stated that he would also refuse permission to hockey players aged twenty-one to twenty-four to cross the border to play in the United States. He announced that members of the Western Ontario Reserve Army of that age range would thereafter be required to undergo four months of compulsory military training. This ruling affected eight thousand men, including five NHL players and two stars of the Boston Bruins' "Kraut Line," Milt Schmidt and Woody Dumart.[48]

Responding to the national debate, the Manitoba board sent out copies of its decision to the other boards, explaining that "young men of athletic ability should be serving in Canada's army at this time, instead of playing hockey." There was another, more interesting, reason. The board worried that "if Canadian hockey players were allowed to play in the United States it would cause criticism of Canada and would be used as a pretext by men, such as Colonel Lindbergh and Senator Wheeler, who allege that Canada is not making an all-out war effort." Charles Lindbergh and Burton Wheeler were prominent and outspoken members of the isolationist America First Committee, which bitterly opposed US intervention in the European war, and the Manitoba board showed it was politically sensitive to American opinion and not a little fearful that Canadian inaction might help dissuade America from entering the war.[49]

The *Winnipeg Free Press* suggested that, given the differences in board policies, players might simply begin to transfer their residences to obtain more favorable decisions. Major-General Léo Laflèche, the associate deputy minister of the NWS, thought this notion unlikely, since "these hockey men are serious, responsible people, and ought to be regarded as such. . . . I have had no indication that any of them would try to escape their responsibilities to their country. It would be subterfuge to be turned down by one board and go before another. I'm convinced our hockey players wouldn't do that, and also that their league officials would not countenance it either!" He also tried to calm the waters by clarifying that boards could not simply reject all passport requests from hockey players, but only from those players aged twenty-one to twenty-four.[50]

Calder called the situation "considerably confused." It appeared that while he had helped convince the authorities in Ottawa to allow hockey to continue, under the DNWS recruitment system the important decisions were really made at the discretion of the regional boards. And if professional hockey leagues wanted these rules changed, they would require a new strategy and the ability to execute it while treading lightly.[51]

Amid rumors that the NHL was developing a contingency plan whereby its American clubs would be moved to Canada, Frank Calder quietly flew west to lobby the Manitoba board members in person. In Winnipeg he consulted with Kilpatrick and Dutton and arranged a meeting with Justice Adamson. After this meeting, he planned to visit Regina to see the members of the Saskatchewan board. When he was buttonholed by a *Free Press* reporter at the Fort Garry Hotel in Winnipeg, Calder insisted the NHL would comply with the laws of the land, adding only that even war-plagued Britain was continuing to play football (soccer), watched and supported by none other than Churchill himself. The *Free Press* editors disparaged what they perceived to be the Calder message—that "business as usual" helped the war effort or, as they put it, that "in order to smash Hitlerism . . . the front line of the Boston Bruins must be kept intact." Again showing the sensitivity to American opinion, the *Free Press* cited sports columnist Dave Egan of the *Boston Sunday Advertiser*, who complained that "something is phony" when Hank Greenberg of the Detroit Tigers and others had to settle for army pay of twenty-one dollars a month, while "our Canadian cousins continue to ring the cash register." Back in Winnipeg, the editors of the *Free Press* agreed and contended there was absolutely no "business-like argument" for hockey in wartime.[52]

Wanting to highlight the American angle, Calder brought Kilpatrick and Lester Patrick along to his meeting with Adamson, but the chairman would not revise his policy. That same day, the *Winnipeg Tribune* reported that the files of two Winnipeg-native Toronto Maple Leafs players, Wally Stanowski and Pete Langelle, had been transferred to the Ontario (presumably Toronto) NWS Board and that "the board here [Manitoba] was of the opinion the request for the transfer was made only because Ontario restrictions were more lenient." That fall at least six western players crossed the border through Ontario, and at least one NHL player was transferred to a Canadian club to avoid passport permission difficulties. Whether these moves were encouraged by the Maple Leafs or any other professional club is not clear, and Major-General Laflèche's reaction is not known.[53]

"Like Any Other Business"

What became known as the "passport crisis" over NHL hockey player travel contributed to the increasing public disenchantment over the slow pace of Canadian recruitment more generally and led to changes that altered the landscape once again. More voices were raised in support of conscription, and the Liberal government reacted in two ways. First, in March 1942 Mackenzie King announced the creation of the National Selective Service under the Department of Labour. The NSS would take over coordination of both military *and* civilian manpower allocation. Liability for service under the NRMA was extended, with all single men and widowers born between 1912 and 1921 (ages twenty-one to thirty) now liable for call-up. In addition, no physically fit man seventeen to forty-five could be employed in specified nonessential occupations, which included "those employed in entertainment-related industries." The second tactic Mackenzie King used to appease the conscriptionist camp was the calling of a plebiscite for 27 April 1942, which released him from his election promise not to impose conscription for overseas service. For now, however, King did not act on his new authority.[54]

From the NHL perspective, the new NSS structure, though still regional in emphasis (the NWS boards simply changed names to NSS boards and retained the same membership), may have inspired hope of a consistent national policy favoring their business. Also, the recent personal support from President Franklin Roosevelt to professional baseball may have emboldened the league's arguments. In what became known as "the green light letter," Roosevelt cited the moral and economic importance of baseball, concluding that baseball players were "a definite recreational asset to at least 20,000,000 of their fellow citizens—and that in my judgment is thoroughly worthwhile." At the May 1942 NHL annual meeting in Toronto, Jack Adams, manager of the Detroit Red Wings, applied the same logic to hockey. He cited its necessity as an alternative to movies as war-worker recreation, but also belligerently announced he would "buck" any move to cancel hockey for the duration of the war. Less confrontational was the official press statement released at the conclusion of the meetings, which reflected Calder's calm and conciliatory stance: the NHL expected to operate but, "like any other business, will do whatever the governments of Canada and the United States request it to do." Like any other business, however, the NHL would also continue to try to influence those governments.[55]

In 1942 the pressure to get assurance grew as enlistments started to hurt, especially the American clubs. In January the whole Bruins "Kraut Line" of Schmidt, Dumart, and Bobby Bauer joined the Royal Canadian Air Force. That summer they were followed by Alex Shibicky, Bill Juzda, Neil Colville, and Mac Colville of the Rangers; Joe Cooper of the Hawks; Stanowski, Langelle, and Nick Metz of the Leafs; and Eddie Wiseman of the Bruins. Yet even as these young stars joined the armed forces, behind the scenes Calder started lobbying the new NSS director, Elliott Little, for the league's continuation. Calder met Little on 6 August 1942 to make his case, and the meeting went well. Afterward, Little issued a statement that "it may be necessary to give some consideration to maintaining the N.H.L. in some form, or on some basis, or else we would face the problem of replacing what it at present means to hundreds of thousands of Canadians in entertainment and maintenance of morale." Significantly, this announcement was the first official recognition of the league's importance to morale. The assurance of Little's statement reflected the growing influence of the NSS in Ottawa; while the local board chairmen still officially decided the exemptions, Little believed that a uniform national policy was his to formulate.[56]

Calder hoped Little could impose his will on the boards and pressed his case in a follow-up memorandum the day after the meeting, noting that "to one so conversant with the conduct of the winter sport, I need hardly emphasize the place which the National League holds in the public mind in the Dominion." Flattery aside, Calder's themes were the league's contribution to morale and its economic impact. More than five hundred thousand fans personally attended games in Montreal and Toronto, and several million listened to games on the highly popular weekly *Imperial Oil Hockey Broadcast* hosted by Foster Hewitt. For the duration of the war, Imperial Oil had committed to replacing its own advertisements with spots featuring War Savings and Victory Bond Drives and other government appeals. Furthermore, each week Hewitt distilled the show into thirty-minute summary recordings for transmission and rebroadcast by the BBC to Canadian troops overseas on Sunday afternoons. Calder enclosed a public statement by Imperial Oil claiming it had received thousands of letters testifying to the broadcast's popularity, both with overseas servicemen and also on the home front, helping in "the maintenance of public morale by diversion." As to the league's economic value, Calder pointed out that the Maple Leaf Gardens estimated it would pay more than $95,000 in income and excess-profits taxes, in addition to $134,506 in amusement tax. Furthermore, the FECB regulations had brought in approximately $250,000 in 1941–42 alone. Calder ended his letter with a reiteration that the league was "firmly of the opinion that it is to the interest of national morale that our activities should be carried on for this coming winter." A few days later, the AHL, which was even more vulnerable to manpower restrictions, had its own meeting with Little and mustered similar arguments.[57]

The lobbying effort was successful. Little confirmed that the NSS was willing to allow Canadians not subject to military service to cross the border if American authorities "agreed that it was desirable to maintain professional hockey." He asked Hugh Keenleyside, the assistant undersecretary of state for external affairs, to ascertain the views of the US officials on the issue. In due course, Paul V. McNutt, the chairman of the recently established US War Manpower Commission (WMC), agreed to the policy, and Keenleyside provided a draft of a brief joint press release that was issued in both Ottawa and Washington at eleven o'clock on 15 September 1942. It read: "While neither country has any intention of granting exemption from military service to hockey players or other athletes, there is no objection to allowing any men who are not subject to military service to continue their professional athletic activities unless and until they are requested to engage in some non-military war duty." Although this statement did not give any special treatment to players per se, a subsequent NSS press release on 22 October did specify that, in Canada at least, "if a person is engaged in work of low priority and there is no vacancy in work of high labor priority for which he is particularly skilled, he may be given a permit to play professional sport."[58]

Although this policy meant the NHL would have to rely increasingly on married men and players under twenty-one, Calder and the governors appeared pleased. At least the NHL could draft AHL players when the need arose and also had access to amateurs. (The AHL, in contrast, depended on unmarried players in their twenties and would soon find itself in more dire straits.) So it was easier for the NHL governors to affirm and approve "as a matter of general policy, that the N.H.L. was opposed to employment by any club of any person who should properly be in the active service of his country, whether of Canada or the U.S.A." How clubs could get players across the border was the big challenge, and not all the clubs agreed on to what extent they should push the envelope.[59]

A special meeting was convened in November to discuss the "many difficulties that had arisen from war-time restrictions due to Canadian and American regulations." To aggravate matters, Art Ross was breaking unity again. He was quoted in the *Montreal Standard* as claiming that some teams were pulling strings to get war work and deferments for their players. (Ross would have been pleased to learn that as a direct result of his comments, when Gorman of the Canadiens went to the NWS office to get a deferment for a player, the man at the desk "flashed the article and refused to help.") At the meeting, the Bruins suggested that a partial solution to the problem of player availability was to reduce game rosters to thirteen players. Border-crossing teams were often at a disadvantage if they could not bring all their players, and Gorman noted the Canadiens sometimes got only eleven players across the line. At the start of the season, Maurice

Richard, Elmer Lach, Terry Reardon, and Emile Bouchard had passport troubles, and other clubs had similar stories. Gorman even traded two players to the Bruins to help with the desperate need for players.[60]

The governors agreed to set rosters at thirteen plus goalies, but it did not solve the underlying skilled-player drought, which contributed to a growing on-ice performance disparity between clubs. Stanley Cup winners in 1939–40, the Rangers went from first in 1941–42 to last for the next four seasons. They were joined in the bottom half by Chicago and Boston. At the other end were Toronto and Detroit, who both won wartime cups, and the Canadiens, who had been bottom dwellers since the last decade and now moved up from second to last in 1941–42 to first place in 1943–44, remaining there until 1946–47 and winning two Stanley Cups along the way.

Casualties

The worst of the American clubs was the New York Americans. Run by the league and managed by Mervyn Dutton, the club had little going for it other than the support of Frank Calder and some of the other clubs who were eager to keep it viable as a step toward paying off its debts and becoming independent. As it stood, the stock in the club was in escrow under Calder's name, a device likely used to distance the profit-seeking club from the NHL, a technically nonprofit entity, and from the other clubs, its on-ice competitors. In the fall of 1941, the league looked into giving Dutton an option to buy the franchise from the league. J. R. Kilpatrick claimed he was wanting to get the Americans into a strong hand independent of the league and to this end had approached Dan Topping, of the NFL New York Dodgers football club, and Larry MacPhail, president of the NL Brooklyn Dodgers, with the idea that they could "agitate for a Brooklyn hockey team to complete the baseball and football triumvirate in a new facility." Kilpatrick said Topping and MacPhail were interested, and Dutton agreed that he thought it was "a mighty good idea." Kilpatrick was enthusiastic about the promise of "squabbles with Rangers" generating the kind of publicity that Topping and MacPhail had been able to generate for their respective clubs.[61]

However, the league agreement was still seen as standing in the way of admitting new partners. It had been extended to after the war, but sorely needed revision. Calder expected that neither Topping, MacPhail, Dutton, nor any other partner was likely to sign on should it remain in limbo. The ideal was a long-term agreement that tied not only the clubs to each other but also the clubs to their rinks. Norris invited Calder to investigate how baseball arranged itself to create a "definite franchise" and a "better asset," and Calder promised he would conduct "a very exhaustive survey of the whole thing" in time for the next meeting. In the meantime, with the understanding that he could intimate that a new league agreement would be put in place, Kilpatrick was encouraged to pursue Topping and MacPhail.[62]

For the upcoming season, 1941–42, the Americans would truck along and move to Brooklyn in expectation of developing that market. The other clubs agreed to help the Americans with cash, players, and the right to pick up anyone being sent down to the minors. The optimistic picture was clouded somewhat by a discussion of the Americans' balance sheet. Until the season just completed, the club had not posted an operating deficit, and Kilpatrick claimed that this assessment was owing to adjustments the Garden had made to the lease to make sure the club did not lose money. With the club doing well enough financially, he withdrew the aid after concluding that the Americans' "operation in the Garden was to our financial detriment."[63]

Dutton got his option to buy, but with the war still on and no end in sight, serious capital investment was unlikely by Dutton or any partner, so it expired in May 1942 unexercised. And the very existence of the franchise was now at risk after the Americans finished out the 1941–42 season with the atrocious record of only eight wins out of forty-eight games. The owners discussed financial support for the Americans (as well as for the Canadiens) and the day before the May annual meeting talked over the whole situation at length. Every club was in favor of continuation, save Boston and the Rangers, although Norris claimed that Patrick's opposition on behalf of the Garden was "half-hearted" and would not be an impediment to the Americans securing a lease. The two Gardens, however, announced they would refuse to share in any future Americans losses. The owners agreed that Dutton should get a new option on the franchise at the cost of assuming the club's debts, but they declined to formalize it until the outcome of a recent lawsuit from Bill Dwyer was resolved. At the annual meeting Calder was asked to request that Madison Square Garden reserve dates for the upcoming season. Then the governors voted to let the Americans continue for another year, with Boston and the Rangers against.[64]

Lester Patrick's halfhearted opposition to the Americans' continuation became whole by September, when the Garden declined to give the Americans dates at the rink. Dutton was forced to ask to suspend operations, although doing so was probably for the best, as he could name only three players who were definitely available to him for the upcoming season. All the rest were in uniform or essential war work. The Americans were not alone: the AHL dropped Springfield and Philadelphia, and the minor league AHA suspended for good. Andy Lytle of the *Toronto Star* wrote: "Dutton was hockey's Peter Pan and his Americans were the league Cinderellas. . . . His team had no home base and seldom had money. Red had no farm club, and no scouts except friends on the prairies. . . . He was an independent operator in a chain store set-up. It was inevitable that he got the brush-off." Though possibly inevitable that the team would never prosper in New York with the opposition of the Garden, its profitability and market size had always convinced the other owners to keep it going, until war conditions and Garden intransigence made it next to impossible.[65]

Like Boston and Chicago, the Americans were at a disadvantage in not being owned by their arena, which could help them sustain losses and keep them going under adverse conditions. (Unlike Chicago and Boston, the Garden had another team to fill the building.) Yet Dutton did not lose hope that the club could be resuscitated after the conflict was over, and he got the governors to agree to reserve any postwar Brooklyn franchise for him. Unusually, he was able to retain his seat on the board of governors.[66]

Dutton was not the only one changing roles. In June 1941 Conn Smythe had successfully enlisted in active combat duty at age forty-five and was busy training an artillery battery. He left specific instructions for Frank Selke and E. W. Bickle on how to run the hockey team and the Gardens in his absence. Reed Kilpatrick, a First World War veteran like Smythe, joined the American Army the next year and came to command the Hampton Roads Port of Embarkation in Virginia. Fred McLaughlin withdrew from active participation on the board and left his place to his less able lieutenant, Bill Tobin. No one left a more searing mark on departure than Art Ross, who resigned in September 1941 after Calder showed Ross to have lied about signing a player to a contract. (Ross's ire was still in evidence in his January 1943 diatribe, which opened this chapter.) Taking Ross's place was Robert Duncan, who took up Ross's project of getting NHL clubs to play games for war charities and represented Boston's independent stance on many league issues.[67]

It may have been this dilution of rank on the board of governors that led to the creation of a level of governance separate from the formal board of governors. The May 1942 annual meeting was preceded by a meeting of the owners at which the Americans' situation had been discussed. The owners' decisions were subsequently ratified at the annual meeting. Calder does not seem to have attended this meeting, which was notable, and this absence was likely deliberate, since the owners had decided to delegate some of Calder's duties to committees. In addition to new bodies for minor league and amateur relations, finance, and rules, they also created a committee of management to deal with the specific details of appointing referees, scheduling, and disputes over player rights. The members of this latter committee were the active managers of the clubs, which became the forerunner of the general manager meetings in the postwar era.[68]

One might speculate that the committee setup was at least partially a way to reduce Calder's workload, as passport permissions and the FECB deal were adding considerably to his prewar ambit. If so, then it was prudent, but also too late. On 25 January 1943 Calder collapsed at a board of governors meeting in Toronto. Suffering from heart trouble, he was taken to St. Michael's Hospital, where he recovered enough to return to making telephone calls and working on league files from his bed, until his briefcase was taken away. Bickle pleaded with him to take it easy, and on 3 February the league governors arranged to have interim leadership of the league given to Dutton as managing director, assisted by an executive committee composed of Bickle and Lester Patrick. The next day, soon after returning from Montreal, Calder suffered a fatal coronary thrombosis.[69]

After a quarter century at the helm, Calder had had a profound effect on the direction of the league, in particular its early survival and its solidarity in the face of internal and external challenges. He accomplished these tasks through shrewd management of a succession of club owners of very different ambition and temperament. The most accurate tribute to Calder's abilities came from Charles Mayer, who knew him well: "He showed . . . diplomacy by letting the interested parties discuss, by letting them argue, by keeping patient until the often harsh words were out. . . . When they were finished, Calder arrived like the sun after the storm in the sense that he found the good points that could be acceptable to everyone. . . . It is because of his extraordinary qualities that he remained the head of the National league." At the first NHL meeting without Calder, Bickle drafted a motion to acknowledge Calder's role, noting that "from small and precarious beginnings he fostered this organization until it became one of the premier sports enterprises in the world."[70]

It was an accurate assessment. Unlike the owners, who gave their egos free rein (Calder at one point referred to some as "crazy"), Calder's survival owed as much to humility as a strong will. Although he did lose his temper on occasion, he was more likely to acquiesce and accept an undesirable outcome if it seemed best to do so. When his power was challenged and even curtailed, as it had been after his last run-in with Charles Adams in 1933, Calder retreated but did not resign and lived to see a later day when his influence would return. He was also surprisingly candid about his role as mediator and facilitator and remained stoic as his power waxed and waned. Significant power accrued to him as the man at the center of the web of information and relationships that constituted the North American professional hockey industry, but as the full-time executive director of a league composed of mostly part-time owners, he did not abuse his great advantage, but used it invariably to further the league over the interests of individual clubs, or his own.[71]

Calder's skilled diplomacy reached its apogee during the war in the careful cultivation of relations among club owners, amateur leagues, government authorities, the media, and the public in two countries. The loss of his personality at the head of the league would be tested by its absence. In the short term, the death sent the NHL administration into disarray. Since Dutton was a partner in a Calgary construction business and was often away from Montreal, as were Patrick and Bickle, it fell to Calder's secretary, Dorothy Pinard, to keep the day-to-day administration of the league in order. She was aided in the NHL office by Olga Boyer, a stenographer, and from afar by John Chick of the AHL, who helped with obtaining the passport permissions. How much of the league office's knowledge had been lost with Calder's death is unknown, but one telling example was the discovery that the conditions for the Calder trophy for rookie of the year were all in his head and had never been written down.[72]

The peculiar legal framework of the NHL also became evident with Calder's death. The Americans ownership was held by Calder in trust for the clubs, and it turned out he also stood in personally for other league relationships. He was the trustee for several trophies, including the O'Brien and Prince of Wales Trophies, and, according to Dutton, the Stanley Cup as well. P. D. Ross and William Foran were still the official trustees, but with a decade since the last challenge, Dutton seems to have understood that the cup was under Calder's control. At the March 1943 board of governors meeting, no one suggested otherwise when they agreed to change the trustee names for all the trophies to the "Governors of the NHL."[73]

Since it was accepted as necessary, albeit somewhat risky, to have some league business transacted in Calder's own name, from 1932 Calder had also been bonded for $50,000. Although the bond was perhaps to insure Calder's financial probity—the league budget often exceeded $100,000 in a year—Lester Patrick simply understood insurance to be in case Calder died and the league money got wrapped up in his estate. In 1942 James Norris had come out against continuing Calder's bond, showing his high level of trust in the league president, and there was no hint of impropriety after Calder's death or that the insurance had to be claimed.[74]

Dutton and Pinard did yeoman's work to keep the league on course, and the horizon at the end of the 1942–43 season looked promising. At the gate the league was in very good shape. With the Americans gone, the governors had added two games per club, bringing it up to 50 per club but down to 150 overall (from 168). Yet by May Dutton was reporting it was the best season in league history for receipts ($1,862,013) and attendance (1,446,827), despite the fact that attendance had still actually not attained prewar levels. Except Boston, all clubs improved their gate receipts and played to full houses. Chicago led the league at the gate for the first time, topping the $400,000 mark, and Detroit made a remarkable 80 percent improvement. The most telling growth figure was the league's average gate per game, which rose 19 percent to $12,413, the first significant upward movement in five seasons.[75]

Draft Pressure

During the 1942–43 season the constant question of whether hockey would continue for the next was already under consideration in Ottawa. It appeared Calder's last efforts may have been for naught, since Elliott Little had been replaced as NSS head, having lost a power struggle over wartime labor management policy when Mackenzie King and the cabinet rejected his policies as too draconian. Little's successor was Arthur MacNamara, the chief commissioner of the Unemployment Insurance Commission and associate deputy minister of the Department of Labour. Like Mackenzie King, MacNamara proved to be highly sensitive to public opinion, and he aimed to bring NSS policy into line with the government's conservative war manpower objectives.[76]

Representing the league in Ottawa now fell to Dutton. Andy Lytle of the *Toronto Star* suggested that it was "widely suspected that to turn Red Dutton into the hallowed halls of political Ottawa would have the same repercussions . . . as would occur should a range bull be suddenly turned loose, after being well prodded, in the crockery department at Eaton's [department store]." Dutton's motto was, after all, "Keep Punching!" and he had backed it up with fights against at least two hockey associates in league meetings, but in this case he was cool enough to lead the hockey lobby to the capital in August, along with expert help. He took along Maurice Podoloff, the president of the AHL, and hired a local Ottawa lawyer, John P. Ebbs, "to act as liaison man" and handle all the border and passport permit issues. (Ebbs had played briefly for Ottawa in the ECAHA but, more important, was now politically well connected to the governing Liberal Party establishment.) After meeting with MacNamara, the hockey men were assured that the Canadian government still "realizes that hockey is a great morale-builder," and MacNamara confirmed they might expect concessions to keep the league functioning the next season. Recognizing the decision also required American accommodation, the hockey men encouraged MacNamara to consult with the Americans, hoping that the continued green light given to baseball might keep hockey going as well. To help the public relations aspect of cross-border support, in April the Canadiens team made an exhibition tour to Southern California.[77]

Thinking it prudent to confirm with the Americans that the policy of 15 September 1942 would still apply for the 1943–44 season, MacNamara made inquiries through Hugh Keenleyside at External Affairs. Despite an argument from Lester Pearson, the number-two man at the Washington embassy, that Canada itself should prevent hockey players from going to the United States for the winter, most of the External Affairs mandarins were ambivalent, as long as publicity could be kept to a minimum. When Paul McNutt conveyed that "the continuance of hockey along with other recognized sports is desirable," MacNamara took it as a sign to go ahead and directed the NSS Mobilization Boards and their divisional registrars to grant exit permits to any hockey player who was not in the military call-up age group, unless they were employed in essential war labor. Unfortunately, MacNamara had misconstrued McNutt's letter, and in the fall of 1943 his ignorance of the gap between American recruitment policy and practice became evident.[78]

The crux of the problem was the same as it was in Canada, in that central authorities like the NSS and the WMC might express general policy desires, but the actual decisions were made by local authorities, which varied in their interpretations. The Canadian legation in Washington explained to MacNamara that American law stipulated that after the three-month period, all males resident in the United States between the ages of eighteen and thirty-eight—even noncitizens—were subject to the draft. There were two important differences from Canadian law: the age range was much wider (twenty years compared to nine), and exemption from the Canadian draft did not necessarily exempt one from the US draft. In addition, the local draft boards that made the decisions about exemptions could be influenced by public opinion, which was currently being driven by American press containing "invidious and inaccurate statements with regards to the war efforts of other nations." In short, the likelihood that hockey players would be drafted midseason looked very possible.[79]

MacNamara panicked and wired McNutt to ask for five-month exemptions for hockey players, but McNutt would not budge. MacNamara resigned himself to the likelihood that "all professional hockey will stop sometime in January." External Affairs staff were little bothered by the prospect of hockey ending and remained content to let the Americans decide the issue.[80]

Yet professional hockey did continue for the rest of the 1943–44 season for two reasons. The first was the paucity of players still eligible for call-up, and the second was because of the behavior of the American draft boards. Like their Canadian counterparts, American draft boards and recruitment authorities treated hockey players differently, and inconsistently, illustrating the constant interaction and negotiation of local and national interests in both wartime societies. On both sides of the border, hockey players were exempted, accommodated, or even remanded in different contexts.

In Chicago the regional WMC director received a legal opinion that players who worked in essential industries during the off-season were free to play hockey in the winter. While this opinion did not exempt them from National Selective Service obligations, it seems no Black Hawk had any publicized problems on that score. In New York State, problems abounded. Three months and one day after the start of the NHL season, the *New York Daily News* reported that Rangers players Ott Heller and Bryan Hextall, both Canadian citizens, were in danger of induction into the US armed services. Although the Rangers had registered in October 1940 under the US manpower regulations, the *Daily News* reported that they had not applied for Certificates of Non-Residence within the three-month period, which would have canceled their draft liability (something MacNamara did not know about and McNutt did not mention). As the matter now stood, granting such a certificate would be at the discretion of the draft board. The paper called it "a clerical error" and a "misunderstanding" and suggested that given Heller's age (thirty-three), his marital status (married), and his medical fitness (two previous broken shoulders), he was unlikely to be wanted. Hextall, on the other hand, was a more likely draftee, but he said he was expecting to be exempted by the London,

Ontario, NSS Board owing to diabetes. But that was Canada. In the end, both were allowed to play out the season, but Hextall was subsequently refused permission to enter the United States for the following season by the NSS board in Saskatchewan. The board decided Hextall was a military category "A" man and that "the regional board was not going to issue cross-border permits to such men." The only permits issued would be to rejects from the army "of a category so low the army won't take them.[81]

If it seemed odd that Hextall would switch his case to a western board, which had a strict reputation, it may have been because the Saskatchewan board had a new chairman who was considered softer on hockey players. One of the board members had even resigned after another player, Doug Bentley of the Chicago Black Hawks, "a hockey player of 'A1' category," was given permission to play in the winter. The board member claimed Bentley had been usually refused permission. It did look suspicious that another member of the board, C. W. McCool, was a scout for the Chicago Black Hawks. As for Bentley himself, while he owned a farm in Delisle, Saskatchewan, and was on an apparently legitimate agricultural deferment, in the 1942–43 season he had also been the NHL's scoring leader. The Bentley decision was criticized by the Canadian Legion, and after an investigation by the NSS the chairman admitted that he had "made a mistake regarding Bentley" and two other hockey players. The next time Bentley came in front of the board, he was not permitted to leave for the 1944–45 season and wound up staying home to play senior amateur hockey in Canada.[82]

These cases were probably exasperating for players and clubs, but the consequences for contravening the rules, no matter how arbitrary they might seem, could be even higher. In July 1943 Jimmy Orlando of the Detroit Red Wings was convicted of draft evasion after it was determined he had transferred from essential war work to a clerical job without informing his American draft board. With his four-year prison sentence and two-thousand-dollar fine under appeal, in March 1944 Orlando was permitted to return to Canada for his mother's funeral, whereupon he enlisted in the Canadian Army. He never resumed his NHL career, and one observer implied that he had been "very badly advised" by the Red Wings.[83]

The role of the NHL and its clubs behind the scenes of these various draft deferment and exemption activities can only be speculated upon.

After the failed Calder western lobbying trip in 1941, there does not seem to be much evidence of attempts to sway the boards by direct representation, although Gorman had spoken of making personal visits to NSS offices in Montreal. With the negative publicity of the 1941 passport crisis, the league tactic seems to have been to avoid the potentially erratic local boards and concentrate on the national policy makers, leaving clubs to deal with individual cases. After 1941 direct public criticism of the NHL was rare, but did come up occasionally. Jim Coleman of Toronto's *Globe and Mail* reported that "every year, about this time [the start of hockey season], this department is deluged by mail from indignant correspondents who enclose clipped pictures of professional hockey players, with bitter comment pencilled in the margins." He quoted a local judge who said that it was "perfectly disgusting that husky hockey players were able to obtain military deferments," and Coleman saw NHL clubs behind them. It was not the players who were to blame, but rather "the club owners who have countenanced and counselled this 'war job' hanky-panky in the past few years." He argued that deferments could not be obtained by individual hockey players any easier than by "a bank clerk, a bellboy or a newspaperman," but insinuated that the club owners may have "exerted their influence" to obtain medical deferments or rejections.[84]

If owners were exerting their influence, it was not always effective at accounting for the different standards being applied by boards in Canada and the United States. Furthermore, Coleman had to know that within the NHL itself, there was much disagreement about the use of players exempted on occupational and medical grounds. The debate would soon come to a head within the league boardroom itself, putting on display the cartel's internal disagreements over how the NHL should serve both clubs and countries.

War Rules

Wartime required changing rules governing both play and player acquisition, and NHL owners spent a lot of time discussing enforcement. The goal was to keep competition between the clubs in both areas on equal footing as the league adapted to war conditions. To accommodate military enlistments, the governors created a new list, the Contingent Reserve List, which protected club rights over the services of players who had joined the armed forces, in addition to the existing Reserve and Negotiation Lists. The proper use of these lists, along with the tryout provision for amateurs, led to some questionable tactics and no end of disputes over rights to players. The product on the ice was also a concern, especially to keep the game moving and scoring up. The effect on the flow of the game and customer experience provoked passionate action, especially when it came to how individual referees treated the rules and specific clubs.

One prominent feature of NHL hockey, fighting, converged the issues of game style, referee discretion, and the enforcement of appropriate player behavior. In January 1942 several on-ice brawls prompted the board of governors to discuss the possibility of banning fighting. Automatic fines for leaving the bench to join a fight had been imposed after the series of bench-clearing brawls two years before, and Calder believed they had worked so well that, if the fines were extended to all fighters, he now speculated that "we could stop fighting" entirely. However, he also described fighting as a necessary outlet for a physical game: "You are always going to get fights if you have body contact and you cannot stop it. You get hit and the first instinct is to turn around and hit somebody else." Lester Patrick was incredulous that the subject of restricting fighting was even being contemplated and argued that the entertainment benefits outweighed any minor physical costs: "Who has ever been hurt in a fight in a hockey game? You are throwing gold out of the window." Red Dutton mused about the tactical value, wishing that "we had two or three good fighters on our club, [then] we would be better." Given the lack of agreement, a complete ban was a nonstarter, so the governors focused instead on punishments. Bench penalties were considered undesirable, as they would lead to shorthanded play, so instead a fine was added for joining an ongoing fight (but not for the initial combatants). This ruling hardly changed the existing policy and ensured that pugilism would be retained as an accepted feature of the game. Patrick and the other governors were not the only ones who thought this outcome desirable. As a New York sportswriter put it, "Although [the fan] recognizes the intricacies of team play . . . he goes away most thrilled if he has seen wound stripes conferred."[85]

The many disagreements over rules led to the appointment of Frank Boucher, the Rangers' coach and chairman of the league rules committee, to the task of revising the playing rules wholesale. According to Boucher, the unindexed rule book was "close to incomprehensible," with repetitions, contradictions, and different penalties for the same infraction. And the style of play on the ice also needed addressing. For several seasons, defensemen had been stationing themselves in the neutral zone to break up attacking plays, with the result that opposing forwards shot the puck behind them and then chased after it into the attacking zone. Boucher had noticed the new five-man attack tactic as early as January 1940, when he at first credited it with opening up the game and making it more exciting, but as the quality of wartime players slipped he worried that the "endless jamming sessions in front of the net" were leading to a loss of the traditional, exciting end-to-end play. (Conn Smythe later recalled this "'power play,' with five men storming the goal," as "the wartime vogue. The puck was thrown in from mid-ice with everybody chasing it. Men swarmed around the cage, scrubbed in the corners for the puck, played 'grab and hold.' This produced bigger scores, bigger squads, more substitutions, [and] less emphasis on individual play.") To help prevent this strategy (an early version of what would later be called "dump and chase"), in consultation with the CAHA Boucher recommended allowing forward passing across the blue lines, but to limit the length of the pass by establishing a new red line in the middle of the ice, between and parallel to the blue lines. Defenders would be allowed to pass across one line but not across two (no two-line passes).[86]

Boucher's new rule book with the red-line rule was quickly ratified by the NHL and the amateur organizations. In the fall of 1943, the red line led to a rash of breakaways, as attackers adapted more quickly to the fast-break style than defenses did. Goal scoring increased significantly until teams adjusted, and freer play was somewhat reestablished. That season scoring reached a wartime high of 8.17 goals per game, far above scoring of the last prewar season (5.07 in 1938–39). The Canadiens were the quickest to adapt, winning fifteen games, losing only two, and tying three by the new year. In 1944–45 the average fell to 7.35 goals per game, but it was still enough to help Maurice Richard to achieve a 50-goal season, a record that stood for sixteen years.[87]

The biggest arguments came over the question of who would be eligible to play in the league. By midwar player availability was the most significant effect on the low quality of play, and the pressure to allow as many as the selective service regimes would let through was high. Since 1940 the NHL had been in the habit of advertising a list of its players—often numbering sixty to seventy—who were said to be "proudly serving in the Armed Forces of the United States and Canada," but these lists often included many nonregular players, minor leaguers, and prospects. By the fall of 1943, however, they contained more NHL regulars and even a few stars. The American clubs (save Detroit) were especially hard up: Boston begged for players, the Americans folded, and the Rangers used thirty-two different players in 1942–43, including Frank Boucher himself at age forty-two. The Maple Leafs were able to benefit from their deep amateur ranks, and the Canadiens were fortunate enough to have their players employed in Montreal-area essential war industries.[88]

Generally speaking, NHL owners and managers often spoke positively of their fellow member clubs' contributions to the war effort in public, but as the Art Ross diatribe to Frank Selke made clear, there was some profound dissatisfaction. Most was suppressed, but the long tradition of internecine conflict made it inevitable that some would emerge in the press. Ross was very critical of the Canadian teams' lack of charitable contributions in general, and his comments about the Canadiens canceling a charity exhibition game with the Bruins had been reported in the newspapers. As his letter to Selke mentioned, he disapproved of Toronto's policy against allowing military personnel free tickets to NHL games, and he sarcastically referred to the Montreal Canadiens as "The Essential War Workers." He liked to point out that it was the American NHL clubs—Boston and Chicago—that led the way in raising money with bond drives and charity games. (In particular, the Bruins promoted the idea of an all-star game, which had become the rage for wartime leagues, though none ever came about.)[89]

The biggest issue was the legitimacy of exemption from military service for hockey players on either occupational or medical grounds, which came to a head at the May 1944 annual meeting when Ross, who returned to the board after Calder's death, brought a resolution to the table of the NHL board of governors. He wanted it stipulated that, "for the duration of the war, no person will be eligible to play in the National Hockey League whose induction into the Armed Forces of the Dominion of Canada or of the United States of America has been deferred or may hereafter be deferred for other than physical reasons." Donat Raymond clearly saw the motion for what it was—an attack on the Canadiens, whose players were almost to a man exempt for occupational and not physical reasons. He counterattacked with a poison-pill amendment to the motion: "That in view of the object of Mr. Ross' motion, the National Hockey League go further and request the Dominion government that no permit to leave Canada be granted to any professional hockey player who could be used for any purpose in connection with our war effort." If the Canadiens would have no players, Boston and the other American clubs would not either. By suggesting the league essentially end the very foundation of its continuance—player border crossing—Raymond certainly made his point, but with four American teams depending on Canadian players, and with the Leafs seconding the motion, there was no hope his amendment would survive.[90]

The governors passed Ross's resolution unaltered, but held off announcing its contents until the fall for publicity reasons. They recognized the public relations value in having such a strong statement, but had been advised by the NSS to keep the hockey player issue off the political radar while the European invasion was being planned, for fear it would stir up the public and force the government to consider an even stricter policy. So the governors waited until September, although when the time came to make it public, the effect was muted. Charles Mayer noted smugly that, despite predictions of eight or nine, Montreal had lost only two players, Gerry Heffernan and Mike McMahon. Frank Selke reported none of the Maple Leafs would be affected by the ruling. In December Bill Tobin said his Black Hawks "all either have been rejected, discharged, or are over or under the military age limit." The ruling did cause problems for Phil Watson, who had been on loan to the Canadiens from the Rangers owing to passport permission difficulties. The new regulation meant he would not be able to play even for the Canadiens in the upcoming season, but in November he obtained a medical deferment and was then able to rejoin the Rangers.[91]

Work or Fight

The NHL's own rigid policy did not have the feared effect, as so many players were either enlisted or exempt already, but it reflected the more general hardening of American attitudes toward athletes, which spilled over into Canada. In late November 1944, with the Allies fighting in several theaters from Italy to the Pacific, and with rationing tightened up, there emerged charges of favoritism toward athletes, especially baseball players. James F. Byrnes, head of the US Office of War Mobilization and Reconversion, suggested to the Selective Service director, General Lewis B. Hershey, that athletes with medical discharges be recalled and ballplayers designated "4-F" (the lowest) be reexamined. Six days later Hershey directed local draft boards to review athlete cases, while Byrnes ordered horse racetracks closed to address war-plant absenteeism as part of the crackdown. Finally, in his 6 January 1945 State of the Union address, President Roosevelt spoke in support of legislation making better use of the 4-Fs— so-called work or fight legislation. On 20 January the War Department announced it would review any professional ballplayer rejected by draft boards, and the National and American Leagues began making plans to play the 1945 season with draft rejects. The American green light for sport had just changed to amber.[92]

In Canada MacNamara's goal all along had been to bring the NSS boards into line with a national policy, one that was flexible on the subject of exemptions, but he also wanted it to be more consistent with American policy, so the NSS followed the American lead. On 18 January 1945 a circular was issued to all NSS officers and boards, decreeing that "effective immediately and for the balance of the current hockey season a Labour Exit Permit may not be granted to any man to leave Canada to play professional, semi-professional, or amateur hockey, unless the applicant is a veteran entitled to the preference, that is, a veteran who has had overseas service or is in receipt of a pension." The NHL men seemed unsure what this decree would mean. Lester Patrick of the Rangers saw this change as a blow for hockey and, always the pessimist, predicted that "hockey may be stopped next season," but Red Dutton noted that only three or four players would actually be affected.[93]

In addition to the NSS policy change, the Canadian government even became gun-shy about releasing discharged veterans to play hockey. Conn Smythe, recently invalided home after being injured in the Normandy campaign, demanded veterans be demobilized to play hockey. He was already unpopular with the Canadian authorities after returning from Europe in September 1944 and publicly blasting the minister of defense, J. L. Ralston, on the front page of the *Globe and Mail* for sending untrained troops overseas. Smythe's charges had ignited what became known as the second conscription crisis and forced Ralston to visit Europe to investigate. Undeterred by the uproar he had created, Smythe continued his convalescence into the new year and formed his plans.[94]

Smythe was recovered enough to attend the NHL board of governors meeting in February, where he presented six motions that showed that in his absence he had been thinking hard about present and future league issues. Smythe wanted to extend the league agreement, to have Dutton investigate expansion to two American cities, to experiment with eliminating the blue lines, and to bring the waiver price back to five thousand dollars. As a spur to more effective decision making, which was often hindered by the need to consult club superiors, Smythe also recommended dividing the board of governors into two groups—governors (owners) and alternates (managers and coaches)—with duties to be determined by the president. As to the latter office, he wanted Dutton made permanent (his contract was set to expire in June 1945) and agreed to work with James Norris to effect it. In the meantime, he urged his fellow governors to push the Canadian government to relax its policies and allow discharged men, rejected men employed in essential war work, and others to play hockey. He was of the opinion that the league should be unapologetic about asking for this concession: the NHL had "done everything for the war effort, why not say so?"[95]

All Smythe's motions were either passed or put forward to the annual meeting as constitutional amendments. Afterward Smythe went on a public relations offensive on the manpower issue. He interviewed with Baz

O'Meara of the *Montreal Star* and put the point bluntly: the league was going to press for a clear mandate to take back hockey players who had received army discharges. Smythe wanted "the plain facts" to be known and for the government to permit 150 men to play hockey the next season, "to pursue their business the same as everybody else." He pointed out that no border restrictions existed for other demobilized soldiers and then disingenuously suggested that the league needed only 150 players "out of a manpower pool of 142,000,000 people" (the entire population of the United States and Canada!). However, just as Smythe was gearing up for another fight, the war was turning, and the surrender of Germany and Japan over the spring and summer of 1945 eased the labor pressures, as many veterans were freed up to join their clubs in the fall.[96]

A Patriotic Stance

Like other major league sports, the NHL survived the war. At the box office, it had even thrived. Just as it had done for the general American and Canadian economies, the war brought the league out of the Depression to new highs. Attendance was pushing two million customers (and gate receipts over two million dollars), finally reaching pre-Depression levels, and with only six clubs, not seven. There was even talk of league expansion, perhaps even to the US West Coast.

Despite the inroads on player personnel for military and industrial requirements, the league had been able to stay in business at least in part by assuming a patriotic stance and defining itself as a morale industry that provided both economic and cultural service. From the outset of the war, the league narrated its role in home-front morale, providing regular, cheap, easily accessible, and "moral" entertainment to war workers and other civilians, while also arguing it sustained military morale through its overseas broadcasts. By also making and publicizing economic and labor contributions—the FECB plan, taxpaying, war-bond buying, player and executive enlistment—the NHL could argue it was making concrete contributions to the war effort. However, the continuation of the sport was owed most to American and Canadian policy decisions about labor requirements and their differential enforcement. Canadian bureaucrats factored in the high cultural profile of the sport in comparison to the physical and labor resources it diverted, but in the end would have let the league be sundered if the Americans had wished it. In the United States, the labor issue was less relevant, and there hockey benefited from the exemption accorded to baseball, as well as from American draft-board indulgence. Until late in the war, both Canadian and American bureaucrats deemed the benefit from diverting resources and manpower into more obviously essential industry not worth the price of losing a relatively cheap publicity tool and social diversion.[97]

Like North American society in general, the NHL was also changed during the war. First, there were the personal trials and tragedies of players, managers, and owners who served personally or had children in armed service (Ross, Smythe, Dutton, Calder, Patrick, Norris, Adams, and Gorman). For the league itself, there were losses that were profound for its later development. It lost a club, the Americans, and a strong-willed owner, Frederic McLaughlin, who succumbed after a long illness in December 1944, leaving the Black Hawks to his fifteen-year-old son. It also lost its founding president and expert conciliator, Frank Calder, whose death might have been attributable to the heavy workload and stress brought by war on a man who with his small staff ran the league nearly single-handedly. For the league to move forward, his successor, Mervyn Dutton, needed to be convinced he was the man to take up Calder's mantle or else be encouraged to cede the place to someone else.[98]

Within the cartel, maintaining player movement had been the most crucial issue, and, though overcome, there would be long-term effects. Despite the many passports issued, enlistments and restrictions had eaten away at NHL club rosters, especially of the American clubs. The Canadian clubs actually benefited from the restrictions on US-bound players (indirectly and directly through loan arrangements), and it portended a shift in on-ice (and off-ice) success. The wartime withering of American club rosters and farm systems would have a legacy effect on the postwar fortunes of these clubs, and, excepting Detroit, for two decades after 1941 no other American team would win the Stanley Cup.

During the war the league had also been forced to redefine its role in Canadian and American society—socially, economically, and also vis-à-vis the state. It is not surprising that the NHL and clubs acted to defend their business, but they did so with a sincere appreciation of the various roles the league could and should play, though not without internal disagreement or some cognitive dissonance. Conn Smythe personally exemplified the contradictions of sport and business in time of war through his ardent defense of the Maple Leaf Gardens business and his own choice to participate in combat. The FECB plan was a model conjunction of interests between the state and the league, and negotiations over the currency restrictions questioned the national definitions of the league itself. (When useful, Calder redefined the NHL's nationality as nonresident Canadian, if not American, and continued to emphasize its noncommercial nature.) This attention to the state, and by the state, was also new. Until the war, governments at any level had had little influence over or interest in hockey. During the war federal bureaucrats, politicians, and diplomats mediated the league's place in North American society. As in other sectors, once states became involved, their influence could be expected to deepen and would do so in the postwar era. The governors would have to negotiate this new state attitude with their new awareness of the legal nature of the league and future attempts to enforce policies such as club territorial rights that flew in the face of the spirit of free competition.

The league's bifurcated binational nature was on display in how the clubs reacted to wartime exigencies. Ross felt the American clubs were doing more for the war effort than the Canadian. His Bruins supported many charity events, Madison Square Garden opened its turnstiles to servicemen, and Chicago reportedly offered all its profits to a war charity—all contributions that seemed more substantial than the investment of windfall profits in war bonds by the Canadian clubs. If American clubs were more likely to make public gestures of war support, one might speculate that at least part of the answer lay in the weaker cultural position of the American clubs. The Leafs and Canadiens were more confident their operations would continue, but the Americans less so, and so perhaps felt obliged to act in a more obviously patriotic manner. The governors debated these issues in the boardroom, and, while there were many disputes, the cartel was equal to the task of managing them. Even without Calder, the league had a long tradition of resolving conflicts and adapting to new realities with new rules and a pragmatic attitude.[99]

NHL players also saw beyond the day-to-day demands of the war and, at least before recruitment decimated rosters, were able to look to their own interests. In 1941 a former player, George P. Geran, wrote to Frank Calder, proposing to establish a hockey version of the Association of Professional Ball Players of America, a benevolent society for retired players. Geran got some publicity and support from Rangers players, but by fall the plan dissipated for apparent lack of interest, and player issues continued to be addressed within the councils of the league by the owners, without player consultation. Informed by the owners' paternalism, the clubs made business decisions on issues such as taking out life and disability insurance on the players, compensating players for serious injuries through the Injured Players' Fund, and prorating seasonal salaries to account for the playoffs. With peace, player interest in collective negotiation would be renewed, and the clubs would be asked for even more.[100]

At the end of the war, the NHL owners knew they still had a viable business, and one poised to grow further, and so they were eager to extend the league agreement between the clubs. No doubt they also recognized the important repercussions of war for the NHL's competitive landscape: economic and cultural demands had helped extend the major league's structural control over the hockey business. The player bond requirements and the FECB plan helped consolidate NHL control over hockey laborers, both major and minor league, and the league would keep up the centralized registration of amateur and professional players into the postwar era. Fortuitously, wartime restrictions had checked the growth of the AHL, its latent competitor, which had been itching to challenge the hegemony of the NHL. By 1945 the AHL was decimated by player shortages and pared down to six clubs. For now, the NHL remained firmly on top of the commercial hockey industry.

Conclusion

Culture and Structure

The end of the Second World War signaled the arrival of a new era for Canadian and American society, and it was hoped the National Hockey League would benefit from the peace and get back to regular business. The league would soon have a new president, former league referee and amateur hockey administrator Clarence Campbell who, after seventeen years on the job, would tell an audience that he headed "a rather unique sort of organization." By that time Campbell had spent years helping mold its features, but even by 1945 most were already on full display. What was also clear is that, contra Campbell, "the nature of things" that helped form the league and give it influence was not a passive process, but one that saw considerable agency on the part of the men who governed the league and its clubs. The NHL men made choices and decisions to shape the league and also the wider institution of hockey.

The historical process that led to the NHL and its "extraordinary influence" was one that originated in the traditional arrangements of bourgeois club culture and culminated in a full-blown modern industrial mode geared to North American consumers. For Montreal's professional and commercial classes, hockey was at first a novel cultural diversion that delineated their class identity in the new industrial world, but amateur ideology did not isolate it from the pressures to commercialize. The sport was popular, and although early noncommercial hockey clubs had no desire or means to expand into neighboring cities, they were interested in searching out, negotiating, and scheduling matches with other clubs. Rather than repeatedly contract with each other as would autonomous firms in the market, they created rather weak leagues as coordinating mechanisms. Gradually, as capital investment grew and the contracting commitments with rinks and players became more serious, the strength of the league mechanism grew to become more influential in enforcing those contracts. It began to police labor, coordinate revenue sharing, and bridge the space between the local markets of the clubs and the "national" scope of the league. It also attracted entrepreneurs, sometimes the club members themselves but often a new class of man, who stepped in to brand and standardize the sport as a consumer product.

The degree of coordination of competition and cooperation the hockey men used to reduce the costs of organizing games oscillated in response to the economic and cultural context over the league's history. Culture continued to influence structure, even after the formation of the NHL in 1917. The major league continually strove to balance individual with collective interests and local entrepreneurial effort with collective support. The thresholds continued to change according to market realities, as the league expanded, grew, and then contracted. What made the NHL "a rather unique sort of organization" was that it did not follow the path of many contemporary businesses and create a hierarchical corporation (for example, a syndicate league), nor did it ever consider returning to the earlier era of independent clubs that organized games in the market on a one-off basis. The NHL actually rejected the corporate nature of its NHA predecessor in favor of a nonprofit association model (and calling into question any assumption that the limited liability corporation was an organizational prerequisite for successful twentieth-century industries). Instead, the NHL was an intermediate entity, positioned halfway between hierarchies and markets, and maintaining this position required that culture play a pivotal role in determining the degree of mutual confidence that existed among economic actors. Though at various times clubs and administrators tried to tighten the league into a more hierarchical form through a series of enforceable contracts, like quasi-legal partnership agreements and constitutions, the real recipe for successfully joining the clubs was based on codependent relationships for which the binding agent was social cooperation (trust between clubs).[1]

Though the NHL was often referred to as "big business," its size paled in comparison to the mass manufactures to which the term was usually applied, and it was structured very differently. Typical twentieth-century big businesses emphasized managerial hierarchies, a centralizing tendency, and the creation of national markets, but North American sports industry organizations like the NHL had to be wary of these goals. Tex Rickard's scheme to create a chain of Gardens was fully in keeping with contemporary American business trends, but was considered anathema to American sports observers. W. O. McGeehan of the *New York Herald Tribune* echoed the criticisms made of Gilded Age robber barons by facetiously applauding Rickard's desire to corner the market in athletics and "standardize" it. Yet while Rickard was unsuccessful in creating his chain, hockey was not completely immune from the trends of growth and rationalization for efficiency that had characterized American big business since the nineteenth century. The NHL was itself an integrated symbiotic network of rinks, sports, media, and markets, an example of the sports industrial mode of big business. And national leagues based in urban arenas would become one of the dominant patterns of North American sport production in the century.[2]

The NHL balanced efficiency and integration with a continuing validation of urban markets under local control. No one could accuse Tex Rickard of being out of touch with the average sport consumer, and by acting through proxies like Tack Hardwick, Rickard himself appears to have recognized the cultural imperative, namely, that overt multiple ownership was undesirable. Even as he tried to plant more Gardens, he realized the hockey clubs housed therein had to be perceived to be owned separately. Hockey consumers, like other big-league fans, were used to identifying with a local version of a national product, at the same time as they demanded an elite brand of skilled hockey that could be provided only by a league of "national" scope and status. This dual requirement in itself was symbolic of the tension created by the modern shift from local community and more personal markets to national impersonal markets; consumers wanted products that let them identify with both. Since the days were quickly passing when the local team was made up of local players, local representation was made through the owners who ran the club and also the name, which often combined the civic with the national (for example, the Toronto Maple Leafs and the New York Americans). For competition to be seen as legitimate, then, the business had to be local and separate, and the form of the league (as competing businesses) had to express the on-ice competition even as the league's name proclaimed its national import. Arguably, customers wanted to participate vicariously in the economic competition as well. Thus, a single-entity syndicate league was unsatisfying, as was ownership of multiple clubs by one person. When it happened, as with the Canadiens and Maroons, or Quakers and Americans, it was kept hidden.[3]

So a compromise was maintained—a form that could accommodate this duality of a "competitive league in sport, [and] a partnership in business," as Campbell would have it. As a coordination mechanism for a group of for-profit producers of hockey games that itself did not seek profits, it had elements of a simple trade association, but was more than that because it limited membership, controlled production, and determined the rules for capital allocation, especially of labor. In fact, the compromise was a cartel, and it was able to emerge and exist despite the American legal environment in which it should not have been tolerated, but where exceptions were made for major league team sports as an extension of the latitude given to baseball.

Even as a cartel, the NHL had some odd characteristics. Unlike nonsport cartels, the NHL was not concerned with setting prices but worried only about controlling the sale of elite hockey. (Unlike a standard cartel, because of their exclusive rights over local markets, the hockey clubs were free to set their own consumer prices.) And whereas most cartels are associations of firms that can survive independently, the components of the sports cartel—clubs—did not exist outside a league formation (although in theory they could). After initially unstable origins, it was because of this dependence that cartel leagues were so durable. When able to subordinate competitors, they could last for decades, and the NHL had succeeded in doing so. Through the hierarchical major-minor system, the NHL exercised direct and indirect powers of monopoly (the control over production of major league–brand hockey) and monopsony (the control over purchase of elite hockey labor). Also, the league's monopoly was restricted to its own professional commercial version, and it could not completely eliminate competition from other versions of hockey, minor or amateur, and neither could it prevent other competing sports and entertainment products. Even the monopsony was not total, as clubs maintained a degree of competition among themselves for the purchase of labor and still had to compete with minor and amateur clubs to some degree.

In the same way as the NHL provides a unique alternative path to horizontal integration in industry (through cartelization as opposed to single-firm consolidation), it also illustrates a variation of vertical integration. Instead of a clear-cut strategy of purchasing firms down the chain (minor professionals, junior, and so forth), major league clubs used full and partial purchase of clubs, sponsorship, affiliation, and one-off transactions. As with its own league-club relationship, this arrangement both kept entrepreneurial risk and initiative at the local level and also maintained a competitive aspect for the consumer. It also accommodated the nominally noncommercial character of amateur clubs. In the postwar era, the integration process would continue, as would the tightening of relations between the clubs and their rinks. The Depression had shown that ownership of club by rink created stability, as did the concurrent process of eliminating the two-club markets in Montreal and New York. Absent multiple ownership of rinks, it appeared to be the model for the future, and "independent" clubs like Chicago and Boston would experience pressure to join forces with their landlords in trying times ahead.

Overall, the cartel form supported the creation of an attractive national branded product and also gave incentives to individual clubs to sell it in their local markets. As long as a market was deemed viable, the league would support local entrepreneurial efforts to exploit it and make the product successful and let the clubs keep the rewards. The price for local autonomy was weak central control, which meant that the standard goals of business organizations—profit maximization and growth—were often made secondary to maintaining league stability. Yet the league's chosen form proved adaptable enough to subordinate individual interests and proved flexible enough to allow the NHL to survive competitive imbalance and club failure. It also allowed the NHL to expand to create a regional and international entity, although it helps explain why expansion (and contraction) was not well planned and deliberate, as it could have been, but was mostly defensive and often disputed.

But the NHL was not just a cartel; it had transcended the functional commercial aspects of its business form and become an institution, one that guided (or mandated) the rules, beliefs, and norms of hockey, and not just its business aspects. As Clarence Campbell suggested, the NHL was "a name," a metonym for a set of institutional values whose aim was to keep professional, commercial, urban arena hockey at the top of the sport-entertainment pyramid. The league's "extraordinary amount of influence" not only had determined the direction of the business, but through radio broadcasts, amateur agreements, and wartime service was also guiding noncommercial organizations to generate a regularity of behavior in line with its own priorities. Increasingly, the NHL was being identified with the very game of hockey itself.

The motives of the men who encouraged this conflation of hockey and the NHL are also evident in the history of the league. In 1969 economist J. C. H. Jones argued that "the conduct of the NHL can be explained without any behavioral assumption of 'love' [of the game but] by the application of basic microtheory based on a profit-maximizing hypothesis." At least before 1945, however, there was clearly more to the game than money alone. Admittedly, economic considerations drove much of league and club behavior, but it is also clear from the history of the NHL that ascribing purely economic motives to owners and economic efficiency models to industrial organizations and labor relations leads one to miss out on some of the central characteristics of the business. Economic incentive does not entirely explain personality conflicts, civic and nationalist motives, or the willingness of owners to sustain large financial losses in pursuit of having their names associated with the local NHL club, let alone be engraved on a sterling silver bowl.[4]

Hockey club owners embodied the dual and often conflicting roles of "sound sportsmen" and entertainment businessmen, but the balance changed over time and from owner to owner. In the pre-NHL phase, the weight was toward sportsmanship, but as the sport began attracting broader commercial attention, dedicated sports promoters from other socioeconomic strata and ethnic groups got into the game. In the twentieth century the entertainment business principles of the men who ran the league and its clubs were more obvious than the high motives of the "sportsman." Men like Sam Lichtenhein, George Kennedy, Leo Dandurand, Tommy Gorman, and Eddie Livingstone (as well as Tom Duggan and Tex Rickard) were impelled by commercial motivation, and it is sometimes difficult to tease out any elements of sportsmanship that did not conform tightly to commercial expediency. To some observers, the nineteenth-century amateur seemed long gone from the ice and the boardroom by the mid-1920s.

Yet the profit motive was not the only driving motivation for hockey entrepreneurs. National, civic, and ethnic pride, as well as social prestige, family, and other motivations, could be just as important. In George Kennedy and Tom Duggan, we also see the last phase of the nineteenth-century class struggle to force the Anglophone Westmount elites to share elite hockey with the French and Irish of working-class Montreal. Along with Donat Raymond, they applied an ethnic frame, seeing their participation as part of a mission to establish and maintain a distinct sporting identity for French Montreal, but it was not possible without a successful commercial proposition. Cattarinich and Dandurand expressed civic and nationalistic sentiments, and Frank Ahearn of the Senators was to a great extent motivated by a desire to keep his money-losing club in Ottawa—and the NHL in Canada. Even Conn Smythe, whose behavior seemed more selfish, used similar language to describe his own motivations for forming the Maple Leafs, building the Gardens, and personally participating in the war. The nationalism was not just Canadian. While "Tex Rickard's Americans" were more marketing ploy, Frederic McLaughlin in Chicago was intent on producing an American-born team that could compete with Canadians, and Jack Adams and Art Ross, both Canadians who became naturalized Americans, would also let their red, white, and blue colors show through on occasion.[5]

Social prestige was no doubt a factor, although direct evidence is slim. The public attention that owners of major league teams experienced no doubt fed their status appetites in a way that their main businesses often did not. For rich businessmen like Fred McLaughlin, sports leadership was a more natural extension of social class; for criminals like Bill Dwyer, it was social legitimization of his illicit activities. The degree to which prestige mattered was tightly linked to wealth. Smythe was only a half-time hockey operator (he also owned a quarry) who needed to run the Gardens as a profit-making venture, so for him social standing was secondary. Others, like James Norris or Charles Adams, were wealthy men who could sustain losses and treat the activity more as an indulgence in personal passion. Over the course of the early history of the league, the boardroom of the NHL saw sound sportsmanship and entertainment business mix, and both civic-minded community interest and ambitious industrial monopolizing appeared, as well as many variations in between.

It is also noteworthy that the pattern of ownership shifted toward individual ownership or partnerships (albeit often through a corporate instrument). In the pre-NHA years, the fraternal associative nonprofit community nature of clubs meant that group ownership or partnership was initially preferred, but in the first decade of the century the clubs shed their members and evolved into commercial corporations with sole owners or a few partners. With exceptions, the club was becoming the personal commercial expression of a single capitalist.

Managing the sportsmen-businessmen fell to Frank Calder, and his role in the direction of the league was central to its success. His survival of the turbulent last days of the NHA and the uncertain beginning of the NHL is testament to his instincts, as was his ability to retain the post of president after run-ins with powerful American owners like Charles Adams. He was not immune from charges of bias and partiality, but he steered his way through trouble with the strong backing of the Montreal clubs and his support for the expansion program. In the end, he was usually able to argue that compromise was a good substitute for unanimity, but his greatest lasting contribution may have been behind the scenes in the creation of an administrative system that centralized information from all professional leagues in his office in Montreal.

Calder was also prominently involved in elaborating the league's curious legal ambiguity, which, among other things, allowed the NHL to skirt formal American antitrust law and exert control over potential competitors and its own laborers. Aided in some cases by its transnational aspect, the NHL also had several legal identities, under several different systems of law, and was able to elaborate the institution of "hockey law" according to its own definition.

The peculiar legal nature of the industry was most evident in its labor relations. In the nineteenth century, many hockey players resisted pay for play, preferring to adhere to an amateur ethos that saw sport as a moral, physical, and spiritual pursuit—a cultural activity, not a commercial one. This resistance to the conflation of work with play persisted in athletes and sports organizations into the twentieth century and set the athlete up as a unique sort of industrial laborer, one whose place in the industrial and social hierarchy was contested and ill defined, and thus open to manipulation by employers. Initially, players were contractors free to sell their labor to the highest bidder, but they became vulnerable once the NHL succeeded in attaining a monopoly and then monopsony over the player market. This truth is especially evident in the establishment of the option clause, which, like baseball's reserve clause, hindered player mobility and any collective bargaining, but was unchallenged despite its legal dubiousness.

By its domination of other leagues of "organized" (professional) hockey, the NHL also sat at the top of a "cartel of cartels," a major league among minors, a primus inter pares of organized hockey. The NHL also arrogated to itself the legitimacy of conveying hockey "law" and could declare those individuals and clubs outside the NHL affiliation system to be "outlaws." Frank Calder was not afraid of wielding this weapon, but he preferred to diplomatically manage minor league expectations and convince them—and the NHL owners themselves—that it was best for the minors to submit to a hierarchy of leagues with the NHL as the major partner. Being the arbiter of hockey law also made the NHL a legitimizer of industrial participation, giving it a powerful role in the marketplace and extending its influence into the ostensibly nonmarket amateur aspects of the hockey institution. Commercial pressures emanating from professional hockey pushed organizations such as the CAHA to sign a series of agreements that helped the NHL fortify its hegemony. During the Second World War, the state even abetted a further official legal status, giving the league a significant role as a self-regulatory organization over the entire hockey industry in respect to immigration and currency issues. Furthermore, the NHL could act as a standards organization, an institution that set rules and regulations for "the game" writ large and lobbied for universal application across all leagues. Standard rules served the NHL clubs by training its labor force and smoothing the transition from amateur athlete and minor professional to the major league. All told, informal law helped establish NHL hegemony over commercial hockey production.

Widening the distinction between amateur and professional, and minor and major league, helped the NHL define itself as a brand, one that embodied not only a commercial product, but also a set of modern consumer aspirations and cultural identifications. This self-definition was especially true for Canadians, who in the 1930s with the help of national radio started tracing a linear path from their local frozen ponds to amateur hockey and then to the big league. Conn Smythe later wrote that he had not realized in 1927 that some fans "in later years would travel clear across the country to buy tickets for a team they'd never seen but felt they knew through Foster's broadcasts." The NHL's major league and international status amplified the sense of cultural importance.[6]

Of course, the growth in popularity of the NHL brand of hockey was not inevitable, but depended on a convergence of interests, particularly between the consumer interest in novel sports and investor interest in arena building. Indoor artificial-ice technology freed the sport from geographic limitations and promised even wider appeal across the United States, where it fitted nicely as a winter component of the golden age of American sports, providing the style, stars, and symbolism of modernity that consumers desired.

Although a deep examination of the consumption side of NHL hockey is outside the scope of this book, we can see that the NHL's product was consciously redesigned and modified by its producers for North American consumers. We also see that part of the appeal of hockey for spectators was the modern attraction of high speed, the novelty of technology-mediated ice, and sophisticated team play—but also to the primal and *premodern* in its show of physical violence and the elevation of stars like Howie Morenz as cultural heroes. In the 1930s hockey violence was even seen to be superior to boxing: a writer for *Collier's* wrote that the hockey spectator was "frequently treated to a slam fest that makes the average boxing match look like a pink tea." Much was also made of the attraction of women to

the sport, in an era that was seeing their emergence as important spectators, ones who were seen to appreciate even the more rigorous aspects of
the game. Lester Patrick was quoted as saying, "Women like it best when
its [*sic*] rough, but rough or tame they like it. If you take ten women to a
hockey game for the first time, nine of them will become fans, because
they have no prior loves in the world of sport." (In comparison, Patrick
said, if you "take ten men to their first hockey game only three or four of
them will become fans.") Whichever the attraction, what is obvious is that
the league gave customers an experience with meaning and contributed to
an elaboration of an identity that was often looking to harmonize the tension between affiliation with a traditional local area and a wider modern
"national" world.[7]

Despite the general appeal to the industrial-era consumer, it must also
be kept in mind that consumer demand for NHL hockey was not homo-
geneous. There were several "markets" with political, geographic, cultural,
and economic boundaries, of which the national boundary between Canada and the United States was foremost, and the league's negotiation of
this threshold was the most important part of the league's survival as an
international entity. Yet also significant were regional differences, particularly between central Canada (Ontario and Quebec) and western Canada
and between American northeastern and midwestern regions. The diffusion of technologies such as train travel, artificial ice, and radio was a key
solvent needed to make these areas accessible to the NHL product.

Diffusion of the sport also depended on the success of entrepreneurial efforts to commercialize it and to broaden its market grasp to reach a
"national" dimension. Without effective marketing, hockey threatened to
follow the path of lacrosse or soccer, which never transcended the regional
to get national exposure. (Even the NHL brand had to be distinguished
from the OHA's in Toronto and Hamilton.) And the price for the failure to
"go national" would have been steep. Canadian hockey would have been
marginalized and would likely have lost much of its appeal. In rendering
the sport fungible through monetization, entrepreneurs made it accessible to a wider stratum of society, and the ensuing capital investment in
technology and infrastructure, and promotion through media, drew the

Montreal game out of the Laurentian Valley and across the country and the continent in front of new audiences with new entrepreneurs to serve them.[8]

To attract first southern Ontario and then American capital, the game had to be fully commercialized at the elite level, and with the latter came a new nationalist narrative. In the 1920s "Americanization" of the game came to be shorthand for the commercialization process (professionalization), which represented for many the deplorable aspects of the game—club and player movement to bigger urban areas, salary escalation, a win-at-all-costs attitude, an increase in speed, and an apparent increase in violence. Rather than retreat back home, the Laurentian NHL club owners chose to make the required adaptations to the game to share it with southern Ontarians and Americans (and also to accept the contradictions of becoming an *international* National Hockey League). Of course, the decision was not made without pressure, for the external threat of a Livingstone league or a professionalized USAHA was easily apparent. And the decision was also not easily maintained, for the national boundary highlighted large differences in economic performance. Though this problem was partially solved through contraction, the imbalance would bedevil the league into the future as well, as would the differential popularity of the NHL in Canada and the United States.

The transnational perspective of the story illuminates the uneven pace of the commercialization of leisure in Canada and the United States and of cultural transfer more generally. Canadians and Americans consumed hockey differently, and the NHL as a producer reacted to these differences by changing and modifying the game's rules and pace. Yet the extensive commonality between the Canadian and American markets also allowed the hockey men to borrow American sport developments, especially baseball rules and institutions, which were then reexported back to the United States as the NHL went south. This dynamic interaction showed the back-and-forth movement of institutional development and also indicated the convergence of a major league model to which football and basketball would also subscribe. As such, the NHL is a wonderful example of "reverse diffusion" of sport business practices, wherein the less dominant cultural and economic environment, in this case Canada, received, reformulated, and returned a unique sport business model in partnership with a dominant partner, the United States.[9]

Ironically, it was the very success of the league as a Canadian export that made it vulnerable to criticism of its patriotism. By moving south, the NHL had guaranteed its own survival as the elite league of hockey, but at the cost of several of its Canadian clubs and with them a singular national identity. Only Montreal and Toronto could compete with the capital and population of the large American centers. Herein lay a paradox: to compete in the marketplace and become successful, a Canadian business had to become at least partially non-Canadian, which threatened its national identity. Therefore, commercial success could be seen as inconsistent with Canadian cultural success, which was increasingly viewed in opposition to the culture and economic example provided by the United States. This resistance would grow in the postwar era.[10]

For better or worse, by 1945 the league had taken on the form that was to be more or less unchanged for the next two decades. With the loss of the Wanderers, Quebec, Hamilton, Ottawa–St. Louis, Pittsburgh-Philadelphia, the Maroons, and the Americans, the league was distilled down to only six clubs. Canadiens, Maple Leafs, Bruins, Rangers, Red Wings, and Black Hawks were all situated in large markets closely clustered around the Great Lakes watershed and northeastern United States and had proven they had the customer bases and arena spaces to sustain NHL hockey. They had also shown that even such a small circuit could come to dominate a sport and have a profound cultural influence. With the many changes to come after the war—including the arrival of television, antitrust investigation, player revolt, and a growing divergence between Canadian and American club performance—the NHL's unique model would continue to be tested.

Appendix

Notes

Bibliography

Index

Appendix

Table 1. NHA and NHL Club Gate Receipts, 1912–13 to 1944–45 (in Canadian or US Dollars, as Appropriate)

	1912–13	1913–14	1914–15	1915–16	1916–17	1917–18	1918–19	1919–20	1920–21
Ottawa	16,344	28,870	33,244		22,905	18,500			
Canadiens									
Toronto						29,184			
Hamilton									35,448
Boston									
Maroons									
Detroit									
Rangers									
Chicago									
Pittsburgh/Philadelphia									
NHL Total									

Table 1 (*continued*)

	1924–25[a]	1925–26	1926–27	1927–28	1928–29	1929–30	1930–31	1931–32
Ottawa		92,105	75,777	97,046	78,892			
Canadiens			232,182	226,143	229,386	235,528	254,006	
Toronto			123,469	180,087	186,251	201,881	355,931	
Hamilton/Americans		235,466	294,448	285,516	292,096	234,352		
Boston			220,720	224,848	476,590	502,136	498,254	487,869
Maroons	91,370	123,360		223,682	225,944	224,331	225,988	220,175
Detroit		81,494	211,026	249,673	163,461	183,426	147,912	
Rangers		317,244	336,637	380,013	397,290	364,850	350,880	
Chicago		115,307	101,670	97,848	282,350	303,607	245,003	
Pittsburgh/Philadelphia	50,472	67,376[b]	54,997[c]	40,637				
NHL Total				2,266,944	2,375,464	2,413,424	2,387,951	

Table 1 (*continued*)

	1932–33	1933–34	1934–35	1935–36	1936–37	1937–38	1938–39
Ottawa/St. Louis	91,824	58,798	61,259				
Canadiens	210,138	158,480	114,689	81,462	117,228	126,302	144,009
Toronto	258,510	253,585	281,233	263,452	322,804	375,949	354,838
Americans	178,224	174,192	217,232	221,088	240,139	263,016	247,161
Boston	275,376	180,679	218,465	265,331	306,331	326,783	333,263
Maroons	168,049	124,219	134,993	124,833	115,711	95,526	
Detroit	132,225	165,372	139,755	183,786	230,531	188,670	206,243
Rangers	265,811	289,696	290,417	315,149	306,126	341,157	292,982
Chicago	135,767	231,052	245,196	290,715	242,344	264,488	308,401
Pittsburgh/Philadelphia							
NHL Total	1,627,265	1,636,073	1,703,285	1,745,820	1,881,214	1,981,893	1,886,887

Table 1 (*continued*)

	1939–40	1940–41	1941–42	1942–43	1943–44	1944–45
Ottawa/St. Louis						
Canadiens	114,476	166,285	175,898	180,743	238,431	306,947
Toronto	352,264	384,713	371,852	389,420	363,305	416,968
Americans	215,948	185,284	197,269			
Boston	296,077	305,458	293,095	284,693	329,536	364,246
Maroons						
Detroit	118,386	177,854	182,681	328,741	326,748	349,580
Rangers	278,988	265,527	308,685	320,445	384,798	438,562
Chicago	336,454	356,377	382,930	405,834	414,173	405,834
Pittsburgh/Philadelphia						
NHL Total	*1,712,773*	*1,841,497*	*1,757,428*	*1,862,013*	*2,056,992*	*2,315,814*

[a] No data available for 1921–22 to 1923–24.

[b] Only twenty-one games (of twenty-two).

[c] Only twenty games (of twenty-two).

Italicized figures indicate the receipts that have been calculated or derived from other sources or are clearly estimates. While efforts have been made to use the strongest source where possible, even they sometimes conflicted, often only by tens or hundreds, but sometimes by tens of thousands. Generally speaking, the figures indicate net revenues to the clubs after paying taxes and rink rentals, but this element is not always specified and there are likely discrepancies. Currencies are US and Canadian dollars for clubs as appropriate, and league figures are combined US and Canadian figures without conversion. My thanks to John Wong for providing his database of NHL game gate receipts. The other major sources are the NHL compilations contained in AO, Conn Smythe fonds, F223-3-1-48, -53, -61, -120, -121, -122, and -123 and F223-3-3-36 and -43; LAC, Gorman fonds: Journal, Ledger, and vol. 1, file 6, Annual Report; Vearncombe examination, 7 Oct. 1918, *THC Ltd. v. AG Ltd.*; Stanley Woodward, "Hockey—Here and There," *NYHT*, n.d.; and LAC, HOF fonds, vol. 7, New York Americans—Scrap-book, season 1931–32, 93.

Table 2. NHL Club Attendance, 1924–25 to 1944–45

	Ottawa	Canadiens	Toronto	Americans	Boston	Maroons	Detroit	Chicago	Pitt./Phila.	NHL Total
1924–25		_91,854_[a]				91,854				
1925–26		_117,588_[b]		237,500		117,588				
1926–27	81,872	_198,000_	_99,000_	123,000	133,000	175,000	_48,000_[c]	73,000	_45,000_	1,221,305[d]
1927–28	99,872[e]	_219,000_	_101,000_	125,000	149,000	192,000	_142,000_	73,000	_40,000_	1,350,000[f]
1928–29					294,000		_167,966_			1,603,526
1929–30							_176,500_	186,920		1,682,915
1930–31							_201,066_			1,733,317
1931–32			_249,900_		295,548		_164,232_	230,000		1,627,702
1932–33			_204,377_				_209,481_			1,556,180
1933–34			_228,181_				_239,963_			1,750,000
1934–35			_249,315_	178,813			_158,896_			
1935–36			_227,708_				_210,272_			1,504,000
1936–37			_262,811_				_271,559_			1,628,785
1937–38			_282,211_				_224,057_			
1938–39			_267,147_				_203,302_		Rangers	>1,500,000
1939–40		121,792	_271,031/_ _268,960_	170,903	245,795		_107,512/_ _159,916_	275,032	239,928	1,431,995

Table 2 (*continued*)

	Ottawa	Canadiens	Toronto	Americans	Boston	Maroons	Detroit	Chicago	Pitt./Phila.	NHL Total
1940–41		169,229	293,749/ 290,970	145,507	247,819		173,699/ 219,913	288,315	203,958	1,522,276
1941–42		190,000	278,138				183,880			
1942–43			292,644				271,337			1,446,827
1943–44			278,511				285,644			
1944–45			305,597				275,821			

[a] Estimate (NB: same as Maroons figure).

[b] Estimate (NB: same as Maroons figure).

[c] All the Detroit figures are based on a complete range of Detroit attendance from 1926–27 to 1970–71, but other available sources suggest this range might be inflated in the range 9–20 percent.

[d] As the only missing club, 1926–27 Rangers attendance can be estimated at 245,433 from the total.

[e] Only twenty games of twenty-two included.

[f] As the only missing club, 1926–27 Rangers attendance can be estimated at 209,128 from the total.

Italicized figures indicate numbers that have been calculated or derived from other sources or are clearly estimates. While efforts have been made to use the strongest source where possible, even they sometimes conflicted, often only by tens or hundreds, but sometimes by tens of thousands. Particularly notable divergences have been noted, but not all. My thanks to Professor Rodney Fort for the use of his database. The other major sources are the NHL compilations contained in AO, Conn Smythe fonds, F223-3-1-1, -61, -120, -121, -122, and F223-3-3-36. References include: *NYT*, 28 Mar. 1926; 10 Apr. 1927, 5; 31 Mar. 1928, 16; 3 May 1930, 20; 11 May 1932, 24; 14 May 1933, S6; 7 Apr. 1934, 10; *CDT*, 10 Sept. 1932; *Time*, 11 Feb. 1935; *New York Sun*, 20 Apr. 1935; *CSM*, 10 May 1937, 10; *NYDM*, 13 Apr. 1941; *NYHT*, 13 Apr. 1941; and *Leader-Post* (Regina, SK), 4 Dec. 1943. 18.

Note: Rangers data are unavailable except for 1939–40 and 1940–41.

Notes

Introduction

1. Clarence Campbell, "Hockey as a Business and as a Career." Portions of this introduction appear in J. Andrew Ross, "Hockey Capital: Approaches to the Study of Sports Industry."

2. Campbell, "Hockey as a Business and as a Career."

3. *Oxford English Dictionary*, s.v. "sport." On play and work, see Richard Butsch, "Introduction: Leisure and Hegemony in America," in *For Fun and Profit: The Transformation of Leisure into Consumption.*

4. Rodney Fort, "Market Power in Pro Sports: Problems and Solutions," 7.

5. Harold Seymour, *Baseball: The Early Years*; David Quentin Voigt, *American Baseball*; Stephen H. Hardy, "Entrepreneurs, Organizations, and the Sports Marketplace." League studies include Matthew Taylor, *The Leaguers: The Making of Professional Football in England, 1900–1939*; Craig Coenen, *From Sandlots to the Super Bowl: The National Football League, 1920–67*; David G. Surdam, *The Rise of the National Basketball Association*; and Murry R. Nelson, *The Originals: The New York Celtics Invent Modern Basketball* and *The National Basketball League: A History, 1935–1949*. For a review of the historiography of sports business history, see J. Andrew Ross, "Explaining Exceptionalism: Approaches to the Study of American Sport Business History."

6. Franco Amatori and Geoffrey Jones, introduction to *Business History around the World at the Turn of the Twenty-First Century*, 7; Kenneth Lipartito, "Culture and the Practice of Business History," 2, 33.

7. On major league strategies, see Eric Leifer, *Making the Majors: The Transformation of Team Sports in America.*

8. Though varieties and definitions of culture abound, for the purposes of this study culture is defined as "the distinctive ideas, customs, social behavior, products, or way of life of a particular society, people, or period," as well as the symbolic manifestations thereof (*Oxford English Dictionary* [*OED Online*], s.v. "culture"). For a discussion of 164 definitions of culture, see A. L. Kroeber and Charles Kluckhohn, *Culture: A Critical Review of Concepts and Definitions.*

9. Bruce Kidd, *The Struggle for Canadian Sport*, chap. 5; John Chi-Kit Wong, *Lords of the Rinks: The Emergence of the National Hockey League, 1875–1936*. Most early histories of hockey and the NHL depend on the urtext of hockey history, the three volumes of Charles Coleman's *The Trail of*

the Stanley Cup (1964–69), which compiled player statistics and information on the elite leagues from newspaper clippings. Generally derivative histories of the league include Brian McFarlane, *One Hundred Years of Hockey* (and earlier variations); and Neil D. Isaacs, *Checking Back: A History of the National Hockey League.*

10. Avner Greif, *Institutions and the Path to the Modern Economy: Lessons from Medieval Trade*, 30.

11. Hardy, "Entrepreneurs, Organizations, and the Sports Marketplace," 16. Scholars often focus on the propagation of American economic power and culture abroad and can miss the reciprocal influences that other nations have on the United States. On Canada's influence, see David Flaherty and William McKercher, eds., *Southern Exposure: Canadian Perspectives on the United States*; and Frank Manning, "Reversible Resistance." The reciprocity of sport development specifically is examined in Allen Guttmann, *Games and Empires: Modern Sports and Cultural Imperialism*; and most recently Maarten Van Bottenburg, "Beyond Diffusion: Sport and Its Remaking in Cross-cultural Contexts."

1. Industrializing a Game

1. "Victoria Rink," *MG*, 3 Mar. 1875, 3.

2. "Hockey," *MG*, 4 Mar. 1875, 4; "Round Town" and "The Victoria Rink," *MDS*, 4 Mar. 1875, 2, 4. For another report, see "Hockey in the Victoria Skating Rink," *Montreal Daily Witness*, 4 Mar. 1875, 2. For details on the 1875 game players, see Patrick Houda and Carl Giden, "Stick and Ball Game Timeline," 490–99.

3. Another game was played two weeks later and others in ensuing years. "Victoria Skating Rink," *MG*, 17 Mar. 1875, 2; "Hockey on the Ice," *MG*, 6 Feb. 1876, 4; J. W. Fitsell, *Hockey's Captains, Colonels and Kings*, 38. See also Donald Guay, *L'histoire du hockey au Québec: Origine et développement d'un phénomène culturel*; and Michel Vigneault, "La naissance d'un sport organisé au Canada: Le hockey à Montréal, 1875–1917."

4. There are many fine works discussing the emergence of industrial sport in the modern American context, including but not limited to John R. Betts, "The Technological Revolution and the Rise of Sport, 1850–1900"; Seymour, *Baseball: The Early Years*; Melvin L. Adelman, *A Sporting Time: New York City and the Rise of Modern Athletics, 1820–70*; Stephen Hardy, *How Boston Played: Sport, Recreation, and Community, 1865–1915*; Benjamin Rader, *American Sports: From the Age of Folk Games to the Age of Televised Sports*; Steven A. Riess, *City Games: The Evolution of American Urban Society and the Rise of Sports*; and Michael Oriard, *King Football: Sport and Spectacle in the Golden Age of Radio and Newsreels, Movies and Magazines, the Weekly and the Daily Press* and *Reading Football: How the Popular Press Created an American Spectacle.*

5. In lacrosse, which is a close analogy to hockey, Don Morrow identified four temporal stages of institutional development: adoption to codification of rules, development of league structure, stabilization and refinement, and professional and commercial entrenchment ("The Institutionalization of Sport: A Case Study of Canadian Lacrosse, 1844–1914").

6. For the location of the Victoria Rink and other Montreal athletics landmarks, see the map after page xi in Gillian Poulter, *Becoming Native in a Foreign Land: Sport, Visual Culture, and Identity in Montreal, 1840–1885.*

7. Ibid., 5; Alan Metcalfe, "The Evolution of Organized Physical Recreation in Montreal, 1840–1895," 148, fig. 2; Benjamin G. Rader, "The Quest for Subcommunities and the Rise of American Sport"; Robert Wiebe, *The Search for Order, 1877–1920,* xiv. On American bourgeois culture (albeit absent a discussion of sport), see Sven Beckert, *The Monied Metropolis: New York City and the Consolidation of the American Bourgeoisie, 1850–1896*; and Sven Beckert and Julia Rosenbaum, eds., *The American Bourgeoisie: Distinction and Identity in the Nineteenth Century.*

8. Poulter, *Becoming Native,* 7–8, 11. The middle-class aspiration was not limited to Montreal, but also took hold in Ontario. See Nancy Bouchier, *For the Love of the Game: Amateur Sport in Small-Town Ontario, 1838–1895*; Andrew C. Holman, *A Sense of Their Duty: Middle-Class Formation in Victorian Ontario Towns*; and Lynne Marks, *Revivals and Roller Rinks: Religion, Leisure and Identity in Late-Nineteenth-Century Small-Town Ontario.*

9. Donald M. Fisher, *Lacrosse: A History of the Game,* 24–34; Poulter, *Becoming Native,* 120; Alan Metcalfe, *Canada Learns to Play: The Emergence of Organized Sport, 1807–1914,* 135; D. A. L. MacDonald, "A Winter Stadium," 21.

10. For a contemporary version of the idea of convergent evolution applied to football, see E. Tylor, "The History of Games," 747, cited in Adrian Harvey, *Football: The First Hundred Years, the Untold Story,* 51–52. For a description of the variety of stick and ball games antecedent to the Montreal game, see Houda and Giden, "Stick and Ball Game Timeline."

11. Fitsell, *Hockey's Captains, Colonels and Kings,* 25; "Skating Scriblings," *Halifax (NS) Reporter,* 19 Feb. 1867, 2; Montreal Football Club Minute Book, 1872–1884, in LAC, Montreal Amateur Athletic Association fonds (MG28 I351) (hereafter MAAA fonds), vol. 6, file 9. The best source on early hockey rules is Fitsell, who suggests that the first recorded game to be called "hockey" was played in Dartmouth, Nova Scotia, in 1867. For indications of early influences, see Fitsell, *Hockey's Captains, Colonels and Kings,* 33, 34, 36, 38–39.

12. Metcalfe, "Evolution of Organized Physical Recreation," 150–51; Metcalfe, *Canada Learns to Play,* 135–36, 145; Guay, *L'histoire du hockey,* 39. For a brief discussion of the origins of hockey rinks, see Howard Shubert, "The Evolution of the Hockey Arena: Building Better Hockey Barns, 1860 to 2000."

13. Vigneault, "La naissance," 98; Metcalfe, "Evolution of Organized Physical Recreation," table 1. See also Sylvie Dufresne, "Le Carnaval d'hiver de Montréal," 25–45.

14. Don Morrow, *A Sporting Evolution: Montreal Amateur Athletic Association, 1881–1981,* 14, 29–30, 52, 58, 63.

15. Adrian Harvey, *The Beginnings of a Commercial Sporting Culture in Britain, 1793–1850,* 189–90, 204–8. The MAAA amateur definition is from Article III of the Constitution and By-Laws of the Montreal Amateur Athletic Association, reprinted in Morrow, *Sporting Evolution,* 183–84.

16. "The Dominion Association," *MG*, 23 Dec. 1886, 8; Michel Vigneault, "Out of the Mists of Memory: Montreal's Hockey History, 1875–1910," 12; "New Rules for the Regulation of the Game," *MG*, 8 Jan. 1886, 8.

17. On the importance of transaction costs to business forms, see Naomi R. Lamoreaux, Daniel M. G. Raff, and Peter Temin, "Beyond Markets and Hierarchies: Toward a New Synthesis of American Business History," 405, 407–8.

18. Paul Kitchen, "Before *The Trail of the Stanley Cup*."

19. Paul Kitchen, *Win, Tie, or Wrangle: The Inside Story of the Old Ottawa Senators, 1883–1935*, 13–14, 35. The author provides a detailed background on the members of the club on pages 14–20.

20. The best description of the early Ottawa hockey scene, on which the foregoing depends, is ibid., chaps. 1–4. The Ottawa city league used the AHAC playing code (ibid., 48).

21. E. M. Orlick, "McGill's Contribution to the Origins of Ice Hockey"; Fitsell, *Hockey's Captains, Colonels and Kings*, 53–60, 75; A. E. Cox, "A History of Sports in Canada, 1868–1900," 236; Charles Anthony Joyce, "'From Left Field': Sport and Class in Toronto, 1845–1886," 232–39, 246–47, 257. For reports of early Toronto games, see *TG*, 16 Jan. 1888, 2; 19 Jan. 1888, 2; and 17 Feb. 1888, 2. By 1885 there were 186 Toronto clubs with more than four thousand members playing thirty-three sports (Joyce, "'From Left Field,'" 32–33).

22. Scott Young, *100 Years of Dropping the Puck: A History of the OHA*, 11–16; Alan Metcalfe, "Power: A Case Study of the Ontario Hockey Association, 1890–1936," 6.

23. "The Champions Dined," *OC*, 19 Mar. 1892, 1; P. D. Ross Journal, 22 and 23 Apr. and 1 and 2 May 1893, LAC, Philip Dansken Ross fonds (MG30 D98), vol. 3; "'The Stanley Cup,'" *Ottawa Journal*, 1 May 1893, 5; Frank Cosentino, "A History of the Concept of Professionalism in Canadian Sport," 161–62. On Ross and his role in creating the cup rules, see Kitchen, *Win, Tie, or Wrangle*, 37–45, 90–92; and Paul Kitchen, "P. D. Ross: How He Came to Be a Stanley Cup Trustee," 4–6.

24. Kenneth Norrie, Douglas Owram, and J. C. Herbert Emery, *A History of the Canadian Economy*, 185–92; Cox, "History of Sports," 232–43; Morris Mott, "Flawed Games, Splendid Ceremonies: The Hockey Matches of the Winnipeg Vics, 1890–1903," 180–81.

25. Stephen Hardy, "Memory, Performance, and History: The Making of American Ice Hockey at St. Paul's School, 1860–1915," 99–100; Charles J. Foster, "The Winter Sports: Skating," 163; Charles J. Foster, "Other Winter Games," 245–46; *Harvard Crimson*, 11, 25, 28 Nov, 12 Dec. 1884, 21 Dec. 1885, 18 Jan. 1888, and others; J. W. Fitsell, "The Rise and Fall of Ice Polo and Its Influence of Maritime Hockey"; "Hockey Games Arranged," *NYT*, 29 Nov. 1897, 5. Other sources on early American hockey include Stephen Hardy, "Long before Orr: Placing Hockey in Boston, 1897–1929," 247–48; and Donald M. Clark, "Early Artificial Ice: The Development of Refrigeration Allowed the Game to Spread." On ice polo, see Stephen Hardy, "Polo at the Rinks: Shaping Markets for Ice Hockey in America, 1880–1900."

26. Vigneault, "La naissance," 34–35; Stacy Lorenz, "'In the Field of Sport at Home and Abroad': Sports Coverage in Canadian Newspapers, 1850–1914," 137–38, 144–45; Paul Rutherford, *A Victorian Authority: The Daily Press in Late Nineteenth-Century Canada*, 139; Minko Sotiron, *From Politics to Profit: The Commercialization of Canadian Daily Newspapers, 1890–1920*, 4, 6;

Joyce "'From Left Field,'" 238, 258–59, 272–73; Charles L. Coleman, *The Trail of the Stanley Cup*, 1:30; Don Morrow, "The Little Men of Iron: The 1902 Montreal Hockey Club," 60–61. The first Spalding guide on hockey appeared in the United States in 1898, J. A. Tuthill's *Ice Hockey and Ice Polo Guide*.

27. Fisher, *Lacrosse*, 35; Metcalfe, *Canada Learns to Play*, 133.

28. On the business activities of the MAAA, see Morrow, *Sporting Evolution*, 23, 30–32, 36, 58, 59, 62.

29. Minutes of MHC Committee Meetings of 15 Nov. 1894, 10 Jan. 1901, LAC, MAAA fonds, vol. 6, file 1; Minutes of Meetings of 30 Dec. 1899 and 15 Oct. 1904, LAC, MAAA fonds, file 6.

30. Metcalfe, *Canada Learns to Play*, 134–35; Metcalfe, "Evolution of Organized Physical Recreation," 158.

31. Shubert, "Evolution of the Hockey Arena," 554; Howard Shubert, "The Changing Experience of Hockey Spectatorship: Architecture, Design, Technology and Economics"; William M. Northey to Gault, 12 Mar. 1959, LAC, W. Lea Gault Papers (MG30 E419), "William Northey to Lea Gault, 1959" file; "Government Notice," *Gazette de Québec* (Dec. 1898): 2326–28; Guay, *L'histoire du hockey*, 92. A contemporary source specified the arena's capacity at ten thousand, but this figure likely was for nonhockey events (Arthur Farrell, *Hockey: Canada's Royal Winter Game*, 16).

32. Alan Metcalfe, "Organized Sport and Social Stratification in Montreal, 1840–1901"; Metcalfe, "Evolution of Organized Physical Recreation," 149, 151, 159; Metcalfe, *Canada Learns to Play*, 135, 137; John Matthew Barlow, "'Scientific Aggression': Irishness, Manliness, Class, and Commercialization in the Shamrock Hockey Club of Montreal, 1894–1901," 38, 47; Vigneault, "La naissance," 141, 146; Cox, "History of Sports," 244.

33. "The Dominion Association," *MG*, 23 Dec. 1886, 8; Kitchen, *Win, Tie, or Wrangle*, 32. The 1878 version of the NLA constitution is contained in W. G. Beers, *Lacrosse: The National Game of Canada*, 269–76. On lacrosse professionalism, see Fisher, *Lacrosse*, 36–37; and Cosentino, "Concept of Professionalism," 204. On toleration of gambling, see Joyce, "'From Left Field,'" 270–71; and Fitsell, *Hockey's Captains, Colonels and Kings*, 84.

34. Cosentino, "Concept of Professionalism," 9–10.

35. On lacrosse, see Fisher, *Lacrosse*, 37.

36. Minutes of CAHL Meeting, 14 Dec. 1898, LAC, MAAA fonds, vol. 6, file 6; Kitchen, *Win, Tie, or Wrangle*, 76–77.

37. Two years later, the president of the Capitals club, which had still not been admitted to the CAHL, suggested a three-division structure with a relegation playoff (Kitchen, *Win, Tie, or Wrangle*, 80). On the reasons for the formation of the English Football league and addition of its Second Division, see Taylor, *Leaguers*, 6–8. Cain and Haddock analyze the difference between English football and American baseball and argue that geographic compactness, the entertainment level of games, and territorial monopolies determined their structure. In fact, the CAHL seems to have closed itself off well before these factors came into play. Louis P. Cain and David D. Haddock, "Similar Economic Histories, Different Industrial Structures: Transatlantic Contrasts in the Evolution of Professional Sports Leagues," 1116–47.

38. CAHL Minutes of Annual Meetings, 9 Dec. 1899, Dec. 1900, 14 Dec. 1901, 12 Dec. 1902, in LAC, MAAA fonds, vol. 6, file 6; and Article X, Section 3, *Constitution of the Canadian Amateur Hockey League* [with amendments adopted to 1901], LAC, MAAA fonds, vol. 6, file 1; *MG*, 3 Dec. 1903, 2.

39. Minutes of MHC Annual Meeting, 15 Nov. 1901, and Committee Meeting of 22 Nov. 1901, LAC, MAAA fonds, vol. 6, file 2.

40. Minutes of MHC Committee Meetings of 22 Mar., 25 Apr., 18 Nov. 1902, 24 Mar., 7 May 1903, all in LAC, MAAA fonds, vol. 6, file 2. In 1899 Ottawa players received $100 for the season and in 1903 $250 for winning the Stanley Cup (Kitchen, *Win, Tie, or Wrangle*, 151). For other figures, see Coleman, *Trail of the Stanley Cup*, 1:181.

41. Kitchen, *Win, Tie, or Wrangle*, 87, 103–5; Metcalfe, *Canada Learns to Play*, 70; Young, *100 Years of Dropping the Puck*, 39–40; Fitsell, *Hockey's Captains, Colonels and Kings*, 117; MHC Committee Meeting Minutes, 9 Feb. 1903, LAC, MAAA fonds, vol. 6, file 2; "Berlin Is Reinstated," *TG*, 8 Mar. 1898. For an example of an ad for hockey players, see the classified ad "Two Good Hockey Players Wanted," *TG*, 30 Sept. 1902, 3.

42. Cosentino, "Concept of Professionalism," 224. Another constitutional difference was a clause calling for expulsion of any player who defected to another club, a policy the CAHL then emulated. "New League Ready," *MG*, 7 Dec. 1903, 2; Minutes of CAHL Annual Meeting, 12 Dec. 1903, LAC, MAAA fonds, vol. 6, file 6. Foran's civil service career culminated in his appointment in 1908 as head of the Civil Service Commission, one of the most powerful positions in the Canadian bureaucracy. See "One Man's View," *MG*, 7 Dec. 1903, 2; and "The Retirement of William Foran," *Civil Service Review* (Mar. 1939): 28.

43. "Form New League; Also a New Club," *MG*, 2 Dec. 1903, 2; "New League Ready," *MG*, 7 Dec. 1903, 2; Minutes of CAHL Meetings, 6 and 12 Feb. 1904, LAC, MAAA fonds, vol. 6, file 6; Wong, *Lords of the Rinks*, 34–37. Kitchen shows that Ottawa resigned only after getting assurance that they would retain the Stanley Cup and be admitted to the FAHL the next season (*Win, Tie, or Wrangle*, 126–27).

44. "League Is Formed," *MG*, 12 Dec. 1905, 2; Wong, *Lords of the Rinks*, 37, 39; Kitchen, *Win, Tie, or Wrangle*, 127–30.

45. Kitchen, *Win, Tie, or Wrangle*, 129–30; Coleman, *Trail of the Stanley Cup*, 1:118; Wong, *Lords of the Rinks*, 39–40. By 1904–5, the arena could also cancel a game if a team was not good enough to play (1904/05 Senior Hockey Club Agreement, LAC, MAAA fonds, vol. 6, file 4). For the ECHA Constitution, see *MG*, 12 Dec. 1905, 2.

46. Daniel S. Mason, "The Origins and Development of the International Hockey League and Its Effects on the Sport of Professional Ice Hockey in North America," 101, 220. Liffiton was fired from his job in Montreal after his boss, an MAAA member, found out he was playing for the Wanderers (Kitchen, *Win, Tie, or Wrangle*, 132). On the IHL, see also Daniel S. Mason, "The International Hockey League and the Professionalization of Ice Hockey, 1904–1907"; and Daniel S. Mason and Barbara Schrodt, "Hockey's First Professional Team: The Portage Lakes Hockey Club of Houghton, Michigan."

47. Metcalfe, "Power," 7–9, 18; Mason, "Origins and Development," 240–41, 274–75.

48. On reasons for the demise of the IHL, see Mason, "Origins and Development," 90, 213, 214, 219, 220–23, 246. On expansion ambition, see ibid., 106–8, 110; and "A Pro Team for Toronto," *G&M*, 13 Nov. 1906, 11. On the impact on the ECAHA, see Mason, "Origins and Development," 246, 255, 274, 281. On American values, see ibid., 267–72. On the Pittsburgh strike, see "Calumet and Pittsburgh Won Professional Games," *TDS*, 28 Feb. 1906, 12.

49. "Caught in the Net," *Ottawa Journal*, 15 Dec. 1905, 2. Salary limits had been used in baseball's National League since 1894 and in the IHL since 1903 (Mason, "Origins and Development," 68).

50. Don Morrow, "A Case Study in Amateur Conflict: The Athletic War in Canada, 1906–08," 179. Morrow notes that the Athletic War also had earlier analogues in the United States (1886–89) and England (1895). The CAAU was the successor of the Amateur Athletic Association of Canada.

51. Kitchen, *Win, Tie, or Wrangle*, 152–53; "Stanley Cup Games before the Fifth of January Next," *TDS*, 13 Nov. 1906, 10; Cosentino, "Concept of Professionalism," 202–6, 233; Wong, *Lords of the Rinks*, 44–45.

52. Coleman, *Trail of the Stanley Cup*, 1:166; Morrow, "Case Study in Amateur Conflict," 184–85; "No Limit for the Cup," *G&M*, 16 Dec. 1908, 9.

53. "Tom Phillips Heard From," *Ottawa Journal*, 18 Dec. 1907, 2; Coleman, *Trail of the Stanley Cup*, 1:166, 178; Cosentino, "Concept of Professionalism," 227–30; Wong, *Lords of the Rinks*, 48; Frank Cosentino, *The Renfrew Millionaires: The Valley Boys of Winter 1910*, 36.

54. Coleman, *Trail of the Stanley Cup*, 1:178. The new Wanderers ownership group included Fred and James Strachan, P. J. Doran, R. R. (Dickie) Boon, and Jimmy Gardner (Cosentino, *Renfrew Millionaires*, 36–38). See also Kitchen, *Win, Tie, or Wrangle*, 162–63; and Wong, *Lords of the Rinks*, 49. On the O'Briens, see Scott Young and Astrid Young, *O'Brien*.

55. Young and Young, *O'Brien*, 62.

56. Cosentino, *Renfrew Millionaires*, 72–73; Young and Young, *O'Brien*, 66; "Too Much Hockey?," *MG*, 4 Dec. 1901, 2.

57. On the Quebec City club, see John Chi-Kit Wong and Michel Vigneault, "An English Team in a French Environment: The Rise and Fall of Professional Hockey in Quebec City, 1911–1920," 19.

58. Gilles Janson, "George Washington Kendall, dit George Kennedy"; "Humorous Yarns Are Told of Geo. Kennedy," [n.p.], 2 Nov. 1921, LAC, MG28 I99 (Hockey Hall of Fame fonds) (hereafter HHOF fonds), vol. 21, Lester Patrick Scrapbook, 1902–34.

59. Population figures are from 1911.

60. Coleman, *Trail of the Stanley Cup*, 1:151; "To Place Hockey on Better Basis," *MG*, 9 Nov. 1910, 10; Wong, *Lords of the Rinks*, 61–62. On Quinn's career, see "Famous Sportsman Passes in Montreal," *OC*, 11 Feb. 1930, 10.

61. "Clubs Unite to Form New League," *MG*, 3 Dec. 1909, 2; "Wanderers a Company," *MG*, 9 Nov. 1910, 10; "Hockey Impressario [*sic*], Too," *MG*, 31 Dec. 1910, 13; "Sam Lichtenhein, Sportsman, Dead," *MG*, 22 June 1936, 7; Morey Holzman and Joseph Nieforth, *Deceptions and Doublecross: How the NHL Conquered Hockey*, 40; Bernard Postal, Jesse Silver, and Roy Silver, eds., *Encyclopedia*

of Jews in Sports, 334. On McCafferty and Lichtenhein's baseball connections, see William Brown, *Baseball's Fabulous Montreal Royals*, 18, 21.

62. "To Place Hockey on Better Basis," *MG*, 9 Nov. 1910, 10. The reservation clause should not be confused with the option clause that was later written into the player contract, although they served the same purpose—binding a player to a team whether currently under contract or not. This reservation clause can also be seen as a precursor to the negotiation or protected list. Wong notes that there was an attempt to "reserve" players in the ECAHA, but the motion did not pass (*Lords of the Rinks*, 43).

63. "Clubs Unite to Form New League," *MG*, 3 Dec. 1909, 2; *National Agreement for the Government of Professional Base Ball Clubs* [1903].

64. Letters Patent for "The National Hockey Association of Canada, Limited," 20 May 1912, LAC, RG95, vol. 2612, National Hockey Association of Canada, Ltd., file; Public Notice of Letters Patent, "The Ottawa Hockey Association, Limited," 29 Nov. 1911, LAC, RG95 (Department of Consumer and Corporate Affairs Corporations Branch), vol. 1765, Ottawa Hockey Association, Ltd., file; Pierre Bruneau and Léandre Normand, *La glorieuse histoire des Canadiens*, 68. The NHA letters patent were issued in May 1912, and the full-share position of an NHA member club was later fifty shares. The Canadiens corporation had two thousand shares at ten dollars apiece.

65. The distance from Toronto and Quebec City, the league outliers, was about five hundred miles (eight hundred kilometers).

66. "Hockey Gossip in Ottawa," *MG*, 9 Nov. 1910, 10; "Tries to Make It Clear That Wanderers and Ottawa Men Have Just Grievance," *Montreal Daily Herald*, 25 Nov. 1910, 12. For details on the contract, see "How the National Hockey Association Proposes to Tie Down Its Puckchasers," *OC*, 29 Dec. 1910, 8; or Cosentino, *Renfrew Millionaires*, appx. B. For a pre-NHL contract, see Agreement between Arthur Ross and Haileybury Hockey Club, 15 Jan. 1910, HHFM, Art Ross file.

67. Coleman, *Trail of the Stanley Cup*, 1:203–5; "How the National Hockey Association Proposes to Tie Down Its Puckchasers"; Wong, *Lords of the Rinks*, 60–61; "Three Games More in N.H.A.," *MG*, 7 Mar. 1911, 10; Kitchen, *Win, Tie, or Wrangle*, 168.

68. Jos. Gorman, "Professional Hockey Is but Commercial Enterprise," *TDS*, 21 Oct. 1911, 24; Coleman, *Trail of the Stanley Cup*, 1:219; "To Place Hockey on Better Basis," *MG*, 9 Nov. 1910, 10; Cosentino, "Concept of Professionalism," 242–43, 245–46. It is also noteworthy that the league designated the O'Brien Cup as the league trophy, "replacing" the Stanley Cup, even though (and perhaps because) the latter was not under their control (Coleman, *Trail of the Stanley Cup*, 1:220–21). The NHA briefly reverted to seven-man hockey for two weeks in 1913 (ibid., 236, 237).

69. On Toronto's amateur hockey culture and its resistance to professionalism, see Stephen J. Harper, *A Great Game: The Forgotten Leafs and the Rise of Professional Hockey*.

70. Kevin Slater, *Trolley League: The Complete History of the Ontario Professional Hockey League, 1908–1911*, 75, 91, 127, 164–66; *Brantford (ON) Expositor*, 20 Nov. 20, 1909, cited in Slater, *Trolley League*, 164–65.

71. On the Arena Gardens, see *Official Souvenir Programme of the Toronto Musical Festival*, 6–8; "New Arena Directors with Sir Henry Pellatt President" and "Two Pro. Hockey Teams for

Arena," *TDS*, 19 Sept. 1911, 17. The *Star* and *Souvenir* mention Joseph Kilgour, Aemilius Jarvis, R. A. Smith, T. W. Horn, A. G. Brooke Claxton, and Edward Sheppard as directors, with W. J. Bellingham as manager, Ernest S. Ball as secretary, and Solman as managing director. Claxton was a shareholder in the Montreal Arena, and "Edward" Sheppard was likely Edmond Sheppard, also of the Montreal Arena. On the aborted 1911–12 start by the Toronto clubs, see S. Harper, *Great Game*, chap. 12.

72. L. Patrick to R. W. Hewitson, 28 Feb. 1958, HHFM, Lester Patrick (2) file; "Challenge from Coast," *MG*, 23 Feb. 1912, 10; John Chi-Kit Wong, "Boomtown Hockey: The Vancouver Millionaires," 234–40; Eric Whitehead, *The Patricks, Hockey's Royal Family*, chap. 4. Frank Patrick became PCHA president in 1913 and maintained the position thereafter. Coleman, *Trail of the Stanley Cup*, 1:227, 241. Much of the criticism of the syndicate form derived from baseball's experiment with multiple ownership in the 1890s. See Seymour, *Baseball: The Early Years*, chap. 24.

73. "Note to Andy Lytle," HHFM, Lester Patrick file; Kitchen, *Win, Tie, or Wrangle*, 171. On Taylor and his salaries, see ibid., 154–56.

74. "Sporting Comment," *Ottawa Journal*, 16 Jan. 1912, 4.

75. "Hockey Agreement Has Been Reached," *MG*, 5 Sept. 1913, 11; "T. Emmett Quinn Elected President"; Coleman, *Trail of the Stanley Cup*, 1:262; Archie Wills, "Patrick of the Puck," *Maclean's*, 7 Apr. 1928, 62, 64, 66; "Trustees Dodging Stanley Cup Trouble," *TG*, 25 Mar. 1914, 14.

76. "Lol Solman and McCaffrey Buy Shamrocks of Toronto," n.p., 8 Nov. [1915], LAC, HHOF fonds, vol. 21, Lester Patrick Scrapbook, 1902–34. On the player revolt, see Coleman, *Trail of the Stanley Cup*, 1:267. The option clause was created in response to the Federal League challenge to the supremacy of the NL-AL combine.

77. "Endorse Action of President Quinn," *MG*, 26 Jan. 1915, 10; "Players Going West," *MG*, 15 Nov. 1915, 15; Coleman, *Trail of the Stanley Cup*, 1:286–87, 295, 297; Holzman and Nieforth, *Deceptions and Doublecross*, 61–72. Holzman and Nieforth suspect that the "raid" involved collusion from the Toronto NHA owners, Frank Robinson and Eddie Livingstone (ibid., 86–91, 98).

78. Holzman and Nieforth, *Deceptions and Doublecross*, 100, 102–4; Andy Lytle, "He Smokes the Pipe of Peace," *Toronto Star Weekly*, 1 Feb. 1941, LAC, Mayer fonds, vol. 42, Hockey Clippings, General [II] file.

79. Verbatim Minutes of NHL Annual Meeting [and Board of Governors Meeting], 11 May 1935, 19, HHFM.

80. "N.H.A. Decide to Continue," *MG*, 27 Sept. 1915, 15. Coleman lists thirteen players enlisted, in addition to five already overseas, two of which, Frank McGee and Alan (Scotty) Davidson, had been killed (*Trail of the Stanley Cup*, 1:305). On the effect of war on Canadian hockey and sport, see Kitchen, *Win, Tie, or Wrangle*, 184–89; Cosentino, "Concept of Professionalism," 251–54; and J. J. Wilson, "Skating to Armageddon: Canada, Hockey and the First World War."

81. Kitchen, *Win, Tie, or Wrangle*, 190. On Quebec's struggles, see Wong and Vigneault, "English Team." On the lagging participation of French Canadians in Montreal hockey, see Vigneault, "La naissance," 354.

82. The Tecumsehs of 1912–13 were renamed the Toronto Ontarios in 1913–14, then the Toronto Shamrocks in 1914–15, and then went defunct. The Toronto Blueshirts played from 1912–13

to 1916–17. On the importance of winning to Toronto crowds, see S. Harper, *Great Game*, 246, and for a narrative of the early NHA clubs, see also chap. 12 as well as Holzman and Nieforth, *Deceptions and Doublecross*, 57–58.

83. Livingstone's corporate vehicle was the Toronto Hockey Club, Ltd., which from 1916 was majority owned by the Toronto Hockey and Amusement Club, Ltd. For more on Livingstone's background and involvement in the Toronto sports scene, see Holzman and Nieforth, *Deceptions and Doublecross*, chap. 5.

84. For an argument on the importance of a multipolar approach to the development of hockey, and for a perspective on the periodization of hockey and the global diffusion of the Montreal game, see Stephen Hardy and Andrew Holman, "Periodizing Hockey History: One Approach"; and Stephen Hardy, "Two-Way Hockey: Selling Canada's Game in America, 1885–1935." Poulter discusses the historiography of the metropole-hinterland dynamic in *Becoming Native*, 275.

85. Mary-Anne Clawson, *Constructing Brotherhood: Class, Gender, and Fraternalism*, 17; T. J. Jackson Lears, *No Place of Grace: Antimodernism and the Transformation of American Culture, 1880–1920*, xii, xiii–xiv.

86. Wray Vamplew, *Pay Up and Play the Game: Professional Sports in Britain, 1875–1914*, 15.

87. On the shinny game, which featured former Victorias players, as well as a member of the Molson family and the president of the MAAA, see "Shinny," *MG*, 24 Oct. 1901, 2. For a discussion about regional development and the importance of geographic boundaries, see Andrew C. Holman, "Playing in the Neutral Zone: Meanings and Uses of Ice Hockey in the Canada-US Borderlands, 1895–1915." The CAHA was responsible for coordinating the senior Allan Cup and the junior Memorial Cup playoffs and representing hockey at the Amateur Athletic Union of Canada.

88. The Maritime Professional Hockey League did not outlast the decade (Kevin Jones, "Sport and Games from 1900–1920," 203).

89. Having two Toronto clubs was supposed to have offered travel savings, but in 1913 the NHA decided that they were offset by the cost of hotel rooms and that losing road trips hurt subsequent home rink attendance, so the schedule reverted to single games on the road ("T. Emmett Quinn Elected President").

90. On social criticism of professionalism in the 1910s, as well as the effects of hockey developments on other sports, see Cosentino, "Concept of Professionalism," 247–58.

2. A Reorganization

1. Minutes, 22 Nov. 1917, Hockey Hall of Fame and Museum (hereafter HHFM), Minute Book of National Hockey League, 22 Nov. 1917 to 7 Nov. 1925 (hereafter Minute Book). The traditional date of birth of the National Hockey League is Monday, 26 Nov. 1917 (Coleman, *Trail of the Stanley Cup*, 1:329).

2. Verbatim Minutes, NHL Annual Meeting [and Board of Governors Meeting], 11 May 1935, 19; "Here to Talk Preliminary to Pro. Hockey Meet," *MDS*, 22 Nov. 1917, 6; "Quebec Hockey Crisis; Dr. Quinn Still Has Hopes," *MDS*, 23 Nov. 1917, 6. Calder's motives for adjusting the minutes are unclear (the next meeting recorded after 22 Nov. 1917 is 3 Jan. 1918).

3. "Quebec Players Distributed to Other NHA Clubs," *MDS*, 27 Nov. 1917, 6; Minutes of Meeting, 22 Nov. 1917, HHFM, Minute Book. See also "N.H.L. to Be Formed Today; Toronto In; Quebec Drops Out," *MDS*, 26 Nov. 1917, 6; "'Jimmy' Murphy Is Already Picking Up New Players," *MDS*, 29 Nov. 1917, 6; Affidavit of Edward J. Livingstone, 26 Apr. 1917, in *The Toronto Hockey Club Limited v. Ottawa Hockey Association Limited, The National Hockey Association of Canada Limited, Wanderer's Hockey Club Limited, The Canadian Hockey Club Incorporated, and Quebec Hockey Club Incorporated*, Supreme Court of Ontario, AO, RG22-5800 Supreme Court of Ontario Central Office action files, #434 (1917) (hereafter *THC v. Ottawa et al.*) See also Examinations of Hubert Vearncombe, E. J. Livingstone, and the Players, *The Toronto Hockey Club Limited v. The Arena Gardens of Toronto Limited, Charles Querrie, Hubert Vearncombe, Corbett Dennennay, E. Reginald Noble, Harry Cameron, Harry Meeking, Kenneth Randall, Alfred Skinner, and Jack Adams*, Supreme Court of Ontario, AO, RG22-5800 Supreme Court of Ontario Central Office action files, #849 (1918) (hereafter *THC v. AG et al.*). Denneny's name was also spelled as Denneney and Dennenay.

4. Holzman and Nieforth, *Deceptions and Doublecross*, 92–94; "Coach Smith Starts Roundup of Local Men for Ottawas; Indoor Work Begins Monday," *OC*, 16 Nov. 1915, 8. As noted in chapter 1, the PCHA raid, which emptied Robinson's club of players and allowed Livingstone to stock it with his Shamrocks, may have been part of this strategy.

5. Examination of Frank Calder, *The National Hockey Association of Canada Limited v. Ocean Accident and Guarantee Corporation*, Supreme Court of Ontario, AO, RG22-5800 Supreme Court of Ontario Central Office action files, #752 (1917). See also "Will Appeal $3,000 Bond Case at Once," *MDS*, 10 Oct. 1918, 6; and Holzman and Nieforth, *Deceptions and Doublecross*, 103.

6. Lichtenhein threatened Livingstone frequently during league meetings that he would be deprived of his franchise. Affidavit of Leon Wilson Reade, 26 Apr. 1917, *THC v. Ottawa et al.*; Affidavit of Edward J. Livingstone, 9 Mar. 1917, ibid. On the 228th, see C. H. Good, "Sport Editorials," *Toronto Daily News*, 8 Feb. 1917, 10; and Holzman and Nieforth, *Deceptions and Doublecross*, 127–30.

7. Affidavit of Edward J. Livingstone, 9 Mar. 1917, *THC v. Ottawa et al.*; Examination of Edward J. Livingstone, 20 Apr. 1917, ibid.; *THC v. Ottawa et al.*, in *The Ontario Weekly Notes: Notes of Judgments of the Supreme Court of Ontario and Other Ontario Courts*, 145; Statement of Claim, 9 Mar. 1917, *THC v. Ottawa et al.*

8. Statement of Claim, 9 Mar. 1917, *THC v. Ottawa et al.*; Affidavit of Edward J. Livingstone, 13 Mar. 1917, ibid.; Statement of Defence, 26 Apr. 1917, ibid.

9. "Ottawa Says Sp'l Meeting N.H.A. to Discuss Toronto," *MDS*, 26 Oct. 1917, 6; "Hockey Hari Kari May Follow Legal Action by Toronto," *MDS*, 23 Oct. 1917, 6; "Cannot Afford to Drop Blue Shirts," *Toronto Daily News*, 26 Oct. 1917, 4; "With Coast League Agreeable N.H.A. Can Do as It Likes," *MDS*, 31 Oct. 1917, 6; "Toronto's Lawyer Demands That N.H.A. Protects Rights," *MDS*, 24 Oct. 1917, 6.

10. "Toronto's Case Is to Be Settled Once and for All Sat'y" and "Ottawa's Toll, 3," *MDS*, 30 Oct. 1917, 6; "Four-Club N.H.A. with Toronto In—Who Will Drop Out?," *MDS*, 7 Nov. 1917, 6. The subsequent agreement signed 9 November agreement is referred to in *THC v. AG*, in *Ontario Law Reports* 55:515; Statement of Claim, 20 July 1918, *THC v. AG*.

11. *MG*, 2 Nov. 1917, 14.

12. "More Camouflage about Senior Pro Hockey Schedule," *MDS*, 12 Nov. 1917, 6; Minutes of NHA Meeting, 10 Nov. 1917, cited in Statement of Claim, 20 July 1918, *THC v. AG*; E. W. Ferguson, "New League Line-Up Is Not yet Certain: Toronto May Be In," *Montreal Herald*, 12 Nov. 1917, 8.

13. "Local Pro Hockey Not to Start Now till Christmas," *MDS*, 28 Nov. 1917, 6; "NHL Games Likely at the Jubilee Rink," *TDS*, 3 Jan. 1918, 19.

14. Minutes of Special Meeting of the League, 3 Jan. 1918, and Minutes of Meeting [of the NHL], [n.d.] Feb. 1918, HHFM, Minute Book.

15. *THC v. AG*, in *Ontario Law Reports*, 57:613; and *Ontario Law Reports*, 55:522; Statement of Claim, 20 July 1918, *THC v. AG*; Examination of Hubert Vearncombe, *THC v. AG*, 18 Sept., 7 Oct. 1918; Counterclaim, 13 Nov. 1918, *THC v. AG*.

16. Holzman and Nieforth, *Deceptions and Doublecross*, 174. Examination of Percy J. Quinn, 14 Jan. 1919, *Percy J. Quinn v. E. P. Dey*, Supreme Court of Ontario, AO, RG22-5800 Supreme Court of Ontario Central Office action files, #1364 (1918).

17. *The National Hockey Association of Canada Limited v. The Ocean Accident and Guarantee Corporation Limited* (hereafter *NHA Ltd. v. Ocean Accident*) AO, RG22-5800, File 752 (#492). On the suit, see "Will Appeal $3,000 Bond Case at Once," *MDS*, 10 Oct. 1918, 6.

18. H. Vearncombe to Frank Calder, 19 Oct. 1918; Minutes of Annual Meeting, 19 Oct. 1918, HHFM, Minute Book. In later litigation, Vearncombe claimed the club was his own personal property and not that of Arena Gardens. Examination of Hubert Vearncombe, *THC v. AG et al.*, 30 Jan. 1919.

19. Minutes of Ottawa Hockey Club Annual Meeting, 4 Nov. 1918, and Ottawa Arena Club [First] Annual Meeting, 14 Nov. 1918, LAC, Thomas Patrick Gorman fonds, vol. 1, file 8; "Frank Foyston to Lead Arena Team," *TDS*, 21 Oct. 1918, 18.

20. Jim Coleman, "Gorman's Fields Are Always Green," *Montreal Standard*, Mar. 1951, 5, 24, in LAC, MG30 C76 (Charles Mayer fonds), vol. 18, T. P. Gorman 1936–61 file. Gorman later claimed George Kennedy had loaned him twenty-five hundred dollars to buy into the club (Tommy Gorman, "Sport's Most Spangled Era," *Montreal Weekend Magazine*, [(7 May) 1957]: 4, 51). Dey explained that the Ottawa Hockey Club was owned equally by himself, Gorman, and Rosenthal, but only the latter two were shareholders in the Ottawa Hockey Association, which was itself owned in equal parts by L. N. Bate, C. A. Irwin, P. J. Baskerville, P. M. Buttler, T. D'Arcy McGee, Rosenthal, and Gorman. The purchase price was said to be seven thousand dollars. "Pro Hockey Operations Were Resumed Here Yesterday with Big Offer for Local Control," *OC*, 4 Oct. 1918, 9.

21. First Annual Report of the Ottawa Hockey Club, 23 Oct. 1918, LAC, MG30 C129, Gorman fonds, vol. 1, file 8; "Pro Hockey Operations Were Resumed Here Yesterday"; "Riopel and Allard May Join Hands," *TDS*, 17 Dec., 26; "Ottawas Will Rent Nighbor to Arenas," *TDS*, 5 Nov. 1918, 22. See also Kitchen, *Win, Tie, or Wrangle*, 189–93; and Holzman and Nieforth, *Deceptions and Doublecross*, 177–83, 185.

22. Minutes of a Meeting of Delegates, 9 Nov. 1918, HHFM, Minute Book. It does not seem that the agreement was actually signed this day. It was supposed to be affixed to page 22 of the Minute Book but does not appear there.

23. "The C.H.A. Is Going after Players Strong," *TDS*, 18 Nov. 1918, 18. Quinn's case against Dey was dismissed in January 1919 (*Percy J. Quinn v. E. P. Dey*, AO, RG22-5800, Supreme Court of Ontario Central Office action files, #1364 [1918]).

24. See Examination of Alfred Skinner, *THC v. AG et al.*, 20 Mar. 1919; Statement of Claim, 3 Feb. 1919, ibid.; Writ of Summons, 21 Dec. 1918, ibid.; and *The Toronto Hockey Club Limited v. Charles Laurens Querrie, Ida Lucy Querrie, and the St. Patrick's Professional Hockey Club Limited* (hereafter *THC Ltd. v. Querrie et al.*), 15 Mar. 1924. According to Holzman and Nieforth, Querrie was a nominal owner of the club along with Hubert Vearncombe in order to maintain a fictional separation from the Arena Gardens (*Deceptions and Doublecross*, 195–98).

25. "Dave Ritchie Turns Down Ottawa Offer," *TDS*, 21 Nov. 1918, 26. The appeals court supported the trial judge in its judgment of 20 November 1919 (*THC v. Ottawa et al.*, in *Ontario Weekly Notes*, 146). Livingstone took it to the Supreme Court of Canada and lost again.

26. "C.H.A. Interests Make Unique Move," *TDS*, 6 Dec. 1918, 26.

27. "N.H.A. Emergency Meeting Split Up," *TDS*, 12 Dec. 1918, 28. It is unclear how Brunswick became involved with Kennedy or why he sold the shares.

28. Ibid. An added benefit, now that Lichtenhein purported to control the NHA, was that the litigation against it by his Toronto Hockey Club could now be "resolved amicably."

29. "N.H.L. Will Draw Up Schedule To-Day," *TDS*, 14 Dec. 1918, 32; Minutes of a Meeting, 14 Dec. 1918, HHFM, Minute Book. The small number of players involved is clear from the roster limits—no fewer than eight and no more than nine players. This limitation meant twenty-four to twenty-seven players for the entire league. Added to the PCHA, there were fewer than sixty professional hockey players in both.

30. Putting another set of nails in the NHA coffin that evening, Ottawa, the Canadiens, and the Wanderers met to pay their two-hundred-dollar assessments to the NHA and decided on fines of two hundred dollars for the remaining clubs that did not do the same within fifteen days ("Claims Quinn Wants to Get into the N.H.A.," *TDS*, 17 Dec. 1918, 26). The NHA relinquished its corporate charter in 1924 for failure to file documents with the government (LAC, RG95, vol. 2612, National Hockey Association of Canada, Ltd., file).

31. "Ottawa Admits Exceeding Limit," *TDS*, 31 Dec. 1918, 20.

32. C. H. Good, "Looking 'Em Over," *Toronto Daily News*, 13 Feb. 1919, 10; "Steve Vair Will Act Again as Referee in Toronto Game," *MDS*, 3 Feb. 1919, 6; "Arrest for Tor. Hockey Accuser," *MDS*, 3 Feb. 1919, 6; "Arena Club Has Dropped Out of N.H.L.," *TDS*, 21 Feb. 1919, 22. Frank Patrick agreed to six-man hockey for all future Stanley Cup matches and to use the eastern penalty system ("Six-Man Hockey for Stanley Cup," *TDS*, 6 Feb. 1919, 29).

33. Minutes of a Special Meeting, 22 [Nov.] 1919, HHFM, Minute Book. The Mount Royal arena was operated by Arena Amusements, Ltd. Oscar Benoit ran the day-to-day operations, while Duggan was to promote boxing and Kennedy wrestling (Lloyd McGowan, "Benoit Recalls Mount Royal Arena," *MDS*, 27 Feb. 1965, 22). Artificial ice was installed in 1924. See also Charles Mayer, "Souvenirs de L'Aréna Mont-Royal," *PJ*, 7 Nov. 1937, 52. On Duggan's background, see Ross, "Hockey Capital," 55n191.

34. Mike Quinn was not present, but Calder had the Quebec proxy in his pocket and had come ready to make a deal (Minutes of a Special Meeting of the Governors, 13 Dec. 1919, HHFM, Minute Book). On the Toronto arrangements, see Charlie Querrie, "Querrie-isms," *Maple Leaf Gardens Programme*, 27 Nov. 1943, 56, AO, F223-7-0-12. In the beginning, the new ownership group included Fred Hambly, Harvey Sproule, Frank Heffernan, Charlie Querrie, and Paul Ciceri, but by December 1920 Sproule and Heffernan were out and Hambly's brother Percy had joined the group. [St. Patricks Hockey Club of Toronto] to [NHL], 13 Dec. 1919, HHFM, Minute Book; Statement of Claim, *THC Ltd. v. Querrie et al.*, 15 Mar. 1924.

35. Quinn wrote that one player's family threatened to disown him if he played professionally (Quinn to Calder, 31 Dec. 1919, National Hockey League Archives, 1918 Miscellaneous file, cited in Wong and Vigneault, "English Team," 21; see also page 20).

36. Minutes of a Special Meeting, 22 [Nov.] 1919, HHFM, Minute Book. The four-club schedule had games on Wednesdays and Saturdays. Ottawa and Quebec had eight Wednesday and four Saturday home games, and the Canadiens and Toronto had eight Saturdays and four Wednesdays. Minutes of a Special Meeting, 22 [Nov.] 1919, HHFM, Minute Book.

37. Judgment, 7 Jan. 1920, *THC v. AG*; "P. J. Quinn Elected Managing Director," *TDS*, 18 June 1920, 26.

38. "Toronto Hockey Club Loses Application," *TDS*, 10 Dec. 1920, 26. See also "Canadian Hockey Ass'n to Operate," *TDS*, 26 June 1920, 24; "Pro Hockey War Is on in Earnest," *TDS*, 9 Sept. 1920, 24; and "In City to Organize International League," *TDS*, 22 Oct. 1920, 26. After several appeals were exhausted, in the end Livingstone got ten thousand dollars.

39. "Hamilton Arena Company Is Offering $200,000 Stock to Public at $100 a Share," *HH*, 2 Aug. 1919, 10; "Hamilton's New Arena Is More Pretentious than Folks Know Of," *HH*, 3 Nov. 1920, 14. The arena ice surface was anticipated to be two hundred by eighty feet, ten feet longer than Arena Gardens.

40. "Talking Things Over," *HH*, 21 Sept. 1920, 10; "NHL Will Operate Whether Hamilton Is in or Out This Year," *HH*, 23 Sept. 1920, 10; "Hamilton for NHL," *HH*, 22 Sept. 1920, 14; "Hamilton Gets Quebec Club," *HH*, 1 Nov. 1920, 10.

41. "Random Notes on Current Sports," *TDS*, 3 Nov. 1920, 26; "Control of Arena Gardens," *TDS*, 24 Nov. 1920, 26; "Toronto Hockey Club Loses Application," *TDS*, 10 Dec. 1920, 26; "St. Patrick's to Play at Arena This Winter," *TDS*, 10 Dec. 1920, 26; "'Livvy' Claims Pro. Arena Privileges," *TDS*, 29 Nov. 1920, 22. Livingstone's letter was also printed in the *Hamilton Herald* on 30 November. He also talked about signing twenty-two players ("Arbour Accepts Terms with C.H.A.," *TDS*, 16 Nov. 1920, 24).

42. Minutes of Special Meeting of Governors, 20 Nov. 1920, HHFM; "Looks Like Hamilton," *HH*, 22 Nov. 1920, 10.

43. *City of Hamilton Directory*; Holzman and Nieforth, *Deceptions and Doublecross*, 243.

44. "Joe Malone Notifies Hamilton Club That He Will Not Play Here," *HH*, 10 Dec. 1920, 18; "Prodgers Doesn't Like Local Team," *HH*, 30 Nov. 1920, 10; "Mummery Didn't Like Lalonde's Attack on Malone Last Season," [*HH*], 21 Nov. 1921, Hamilton Public Library, *Herald* Scrapbooks, vol.

S4.05; "Toronto's St. Pats Will Get Ice for Their NHL Games, Is Report Today," *HH*, 3 Dec. 1920, 20; "Hamilton NHL Club Out after Amateurs—Matte Here to Sign," *HH*, 8 Dec. 1920, 14; "Joe Matte Signs—Reports Monday—Prodgers Too," *HH*, 9 Dec. 1920, 14; "Malone Not Coming, Says Latest Report; Thompson Says 'Yes,'" *HH*, 20 Dec. 1920, 12.

45. "Tigers Get Loan of Babe Dye for Opening Game with Canadiens," *HH*, 22 Dec. 1920, 15; "Carey and Matte Stars of Opening 'Pro' Game Won by Hamilton, 5–0," *HH*, 23 Dec. 1920, 14.

46. "Carey and Matte Stars of Opening 'Pro' Game Won by Hamilton, 5–0," *HH*, 23 Dec. 1920, 14; "Hamilton Fans Would Do Well to Read Up Rules Governing N.H.L. Games," *HH*, 14 Jan. 1921, 14.

47. [Agreement between Gorman and Thompson], 30 Dec. [1920], NHL Minute Book, 46; "St. Pats Here Tonight to Meet Hamilton 'Pros'—Big Crowd Assured," *HH*, 3 Jan. 1921; "Ottawa Might Be Dropped from N.H.L.," *TDS*, 10 Jan. 1921, 16; Minutes of a Special Meeting, 20 Jan. 1921, HHFM, Minute Book.

48. "Joe Malone Suffering from Injured Knee but Will Play against Irish," *HH*, 11 Jan. 1921, 8; "Record-Smashing Crowd Will Watch Ottawa and Hamilton Fight It Out," *HH*, 6 Jan. 1921, 14; "Hamilton Welcome Addition to NHL," *HH*, 8 Jan. 1921, 14; "Joe Malone Notifies Hamilton Club That He Will Not Play Here," *HH*, 10 Dec. 1920, 18; "Malone Arrived This Morning and Took Part in Two-Hour Workout," *HH*, 5 Jan. 1921, 12.

49. "Sporting Comment," *HH*, 14 Jan. 1921, 14; "They'll be Arrested If NHL Doesn't Act," *HH*, 24 Jan. 1921, 8. The *Expositor* article was reprinted in "Sporting Comment," *HH*, 26 Jan. 1921, 14. To mollify Hamilton, Calder fined Lalonde ("Newsy Lalonde Fined $25 for Attacking Joe Malone," *HH*, 29 Jan. 1921, 14).

50. "Newsy Lalonde Fined $25 for Attacking Joe Malone," *HH*, 29 Jan. 1921, 14; Minutes of a Special Meeting, 20 Jan. 1921, HHFM, Minute Book; "Sporting Comment," *HH*, 14 Feb. 1921, 8; [Minutes of the] Annual Meeting of the National Hockey League, 26 Nov. 1921, HHFM, Minute Book; "Hamilton 'Pro' Players Report Here on Dec 5—a New Penalty System," *HH*, 15 Nov. 1921, 10; [Minutes of the] Annual Meeting of the National Hockey League, 26 Nov. 1921, HHFM, Minute Book.

51. Minutes of a Special Meeting, 24 Sept. 1921, HHFM, Minute Book; Wills, "Patrick of the Puck," 62; "Pacific Coast Hockey League Charges the Alberta 'Big Four' with Professionalism," [n.p.] [n.d.], and "Patrick's Evidence Satisfies Amateur Executive Hockey Probe in Big Four Justified," [n p.], 30 Nov. 1920, and "Alberta and Pacific Coast Hockey Leagues Sign One Year Agreement" [n.p.] [Calgary dateline], 22 Aug. 1921, LAC, HHOF fonds, vol. 21, Lester Patrick Scrapbook, 1902–34; "Frank Patrick Makes His Move," *HH*, 20 Nov. 1920, 14; "All Set for Pro Hockey Next Winter," *Calgary Daily Herald*, 22 Aug. 1921, 14; Minutes of a Special Meeting, 24 Sept. 1921, HHFM, Minute Book. Presumably, the WCHL had agreed to recognize the territorial rights of the NHL.

52. Janson, "George Washington Kendall"; Rosaire Barrette, *Léo Dandurand, Sportsman*, 110. In addition to his earlier applications, Duggan had also tried to buy the Quebec franchise for five thousand dollars, but Calder demanded seventy-five hundred, a sum greater than Duggan thought it was worth. Wong, *Lords of the Rinks*, 84; "Who'll Get Canadiens? Tom Duggan or Leo Dandurand?," *MG*, 2 Nov. 1921, 22. Dandurand noted Calder acted as agent in Wilfrid Victor (Bill) Roche, ed., *The Hockey Book*, 107–9.

53. Minutes of Special Meeting of Governors, 14 Nov. 1921, HHFM, Minute Book. Létourneau was a local sportsman and hotel operator and seems to have little direct management in the club, though he remained a company director. For more background on Cattarinich, Dandurand, and Létourneau, see Leslie Roberts, "Louis, Leo and Joe," *Maclean's*, 1 Dec. 1928, 13, 42, 44, 49; Canadian Parliament, *Royal Commission on Racing Inquiry*, 24; and "Dorval Race Track Sold," *NYT*, 23 Nov. 1924, S5.

54. [Minutes of the] Annual Meeting of the National Hockey League, 26 Nov. 1921, HHFM, Minute Book; "Sprague Cleghorn Goes to Canadiens—Mummery and Arbour Come Here," *HH*, 28 Nov. 1921; "Hockey League Changes Rules," *CSM*, 16 Nov. 1921, 10. The minutes of 13 May 1923 note the five-year agreement was signed 26 November 1921, although the minutes of that date do not record it. Minutes of a Meeting of the National Hockey League, 13 May 1923, HHFM, Minute Book. The expiration of this agreement in 1926 is mentioned in January 1923, when Calder's term as president was extended to the same duration (Minutes of a Meeting of the National Hockey League, 27 Jan. 1923, HHFM, Minute Book).

55. The 1921–22 season opened with strong demand for tickets in Hamilton, but crowds dwindled in response to the club's "listless" play. "Hamilton 'Pro' Players Refuse to Believe That Ottawas Lack Condition," *HH*, 14 Dec. 1921; "Ham Guilty of Listless Play," *HH*, 16 Feb. 1922.

56. Kitchen, *Win, Tie, or Wrangle*, 234–35ff. The French Canadian situation coalesced around a dispute over Ottawa rookie Frank Boucher. See Minutes of a Meeting of the League, 14 May 1922, HHFM, Minute Book; "President P.C.H.L. Claims F. Boucher," *OC*, 4 Jan. 1922, 11; and Tommy Gorman, "Gorman Appeals to Trustee Wm Foran for Boucher Ruling," *OC*, [n.d.], LAC, Gorman fonds, vol. 5, Scrapbook.

57. Minutes of a Meeting, 20 Aug. 1922, HHFM, Minute Book; M. J. Rodden, "On the Highways of Sport," *G&M*, 8 Mar. 1930, 12; Minutes of a Meeting, 20 Aug. 1922, HHFM, Minute Book. In the event of more than one club refusing to waive, Calder would allot the player (Minutes of the Annual Meeting, 4 Nov. 1922, HHFM, Minute Book).

58. *THC v. AG*, in *Ontario Law Reports*, 55:522. The baseball clause had been challenged in *Federal Base Ball Club of Baltimore, Inc. v. National League of Professional Base Ball Clubs et al.*, 259 U.S. 200 (1922). Though some dismiss the notion of baseball's not being interstate commerce, the *Federal Baseball* decision was actually consistent with contemporary American antitrust jurisprudence. See Kevin McDonald, "Antitrust and Baseball: Stealing Holmes"; Samuel A. Alito Jr., "The Origin of the Baseball Antitrust Exemption: *Federal Baseball Club of Baltimore, Inc. v. National League of Professional Baseball Clubs*"; and Stuart Banner, *The Baseball Trust: A History of Baseball's Antitrust Exemption*. On Canadian law, see K. A. Hinnegan, "The 'Services Exemption' under the Combines Investigation Act."

59. Articles of Agreement between the Ottawa Hockey Association, Limited, and . . . Frank Clancy, 29 Oct. 1923, LAC, Gorman fonds, vol. 1, file 12; Minutes of a Meeting of the League, 14 May 1922, HHFM, Minute Book; "Record-Smashing Crowd Will Watch Ottawa and Hamilton Fight It Out," *HH*, 6 Jan. 1921, 14; "Hamilton N.H.L. Club Signs Vernon Forbes," *HH*, 27 May 1922, 14. The handwritten clause in Clancy's contract reads, "It is agreed that the Ottawa Hockey Assn. shall not sell, exchange or otherwise dispose of the said Frank Clancy."

60. Peter Handley, *Anent Michael J.: The Life & Times of Michael J. Rodden in Northern Ontario in His Own Words*, 200; Series E41–48, *Historical Statistics of Canada*, last accessed at http://www.statcan.gc.ca/. See also William Abraham Hewitt, *Down the Stretch: Recollections of a Pioneer Sportsman and Journalist*, 54.

61. NHL Playing Contract (Howard Wm. Morenz), 6 July 1923, http://www.ebay.com/itm/World-Rarity-NHL-Howie-Morenz-Players-Contract-Circa-1920s-Value-100K-/190808293525; Barrette, *Léo Dandurand, Sportsman*, 123–25, and Howard Morenz to Dandurand, 10 Aug. 1923, reproduced between pages 144 and 145. The letter was written on Stratford Amateur Athletic Association stationery, suggesting the hockey club was involved, but Morenz's motives may not have been entirely supplied by the Stratford club, as evidenced when Morenz refused to return in the fall to Canadiens training camp, which he had left ostensibly to visit his girlfriend (ibid., 126). On Dandurand's visit to Hewitt, see "Hockey Forces Clash," *MDS*, 27 Sept. 1923, 26; and "Dandurand Returns after Placing Facts in Front of O.H.A. Sec'y," *MDS*, 28 Sept. 1923, 22. For other accounts, see Roche, *The Hockey Book*, 98; Andy O'Brien, "Dandurand Finally Tells All on Signing of Morenz," *Weekend Picture Magazine*, 15 Nov. 1952, 32, LAC, Mayer fonds, vol. 18, Howie Morenz file; Hewitt, *Down the Stretch*, 213; and Dean Robinson, *Howie Morenz: Hockey's First Superstar*, 43–50.

62. Examination of Frank Calder, 2 Feb. 1918, *NHA Ltd. v. Ocean Accident*.

63. Under the 1921 proposal by Toronto, the Canadiens were to have "practically the whole province of Quebec," Ottawa its city and the Ottawa Valley, Hamilton all of western Ontario, and Toronto its own city. Although the newspaper that reported it was favorable to the division of territories for the procurement of players—"In this way the teams will gradually become home brew outfits"—the motion did not make it forward to the annual meeting. In February 1924 the player territorial rights were said to be "open," except for Quebec, possibly suggesting that some other territorial restriction had been in place. See "Sprague Cleghorn Goes to Hamilton . . . ," *Ottawa Journal*, 16 Nov. 1921, 14; Kitchen, *Win, Tie, or Wrangle*, 234–35; and Minutes of Meeting of Governors, 10 Feb. 1924, HHFM, Minute Book.

64. *THC v. AG*, in *Ontario Law Reports*, 57:619.

3. Transplanting the Clubs

1. W. J. Macbeth, "N Y Team Will Make Local Bow Tuesday Night in Benefit Game with Canadiens," *NYHT*, 13 Dec. 1925, X5; Westbrook Pegler, "Rickard Scores a Real Hit with Ice Hockey Matches," *CDT*, 25 Dec. 1925, 25. The hockey game was the official opening event, but a six-day bicycle race event and a Celtics basketball game preceded it.

2. "N.Y. Team Will Make Local Bow Tuesday Night in Benefit Game with Canadiens," X5; "Society to Attend," *NYDM*, 15 Dec. 1925, 34; "Hockey Match at the Garden," *NYT*, 6 Dec. 1925, X16; Riess, *City Games*, 176; "Madison Square Garden," *Fortune*, Nov. 1935, 106. On Rickard's tax strategies, see Westbrook Pegler, "Tex Rickard: A Study of the World's Greatest Sports Promoter," *CDT*, 27 Jan. 1929, A3.

3. "Garden Is Opened in Blaze of Color," *NYT*, 16 Dec. 1925, 29; Russell David Field, "A Night at the Garden(s): A History of Professional Hockey Spectatorship in the 1920s and 1930s," 51–55;

W. J. Macbeth, "Canadiens Conquer New York, 3 to 1, in Opening . . . ," *NYHT*, 16 Dec. 1925, 22; Frederick B. Edwards, "Hockey Debut at Garden Draws Huge and Diversified Gathering," *NYHT*, 16 Dec. 1925, 1, 22; "Notable in Force at Garden Opening," *NYT*, 16 Dec. 1925, 29; "Hockey Games Booked for Broadcasting," *NYT*, 13 Dec. 1925, XX14.

4. "Prince of Wales Donates Trophy for Hockey Title," *NYHT*, 7 Dec. 1925, 19. Despite the newspaper's title, there is no evidence the prince actually donated the trophy or even agreed to have his name used, although he had visited with arena director Bayard Tuckerman a few weeks before the idea was discussed ("Prince of Wales Unlikely to Attend Football Game," *Harvard Crimson*, 6 Oct. 1924, available at http://www.thecrimson.com/article/1924/10/6/prince-of-wales-unlikely-to-attend/). On the origins of the trophy, which cost twenty-five hundred dollars, see G. V. Brown to Duggan, 31 Oct. 1924; and Tuckerman to Bernard J. Woods, Boston, 29 Oct. 1924, both in Thomas J. Duggan Collection, file 1.

5. Gene Smiley, "US Economy in the 1920s"; Jules Tygiel, *Past Time: Baseball as History*, chap. 4; Rader, *American Sports*, 143; *Rodney Fort's Sports Business Data Pages*; Coenen, *From Sandlots to the Super Bowl*, 80–81; Riess, *City Games*, 187–88.

6. Wong discusses Duggan's role in *Lords of the Rinks*, chap. 7.

7. Ibid., 84; Barrette, *Léo Dandurand, Sportsman*, 133; Minutes of a Meeting of Governors, 27 Jan. 1923, HHFM, NHL Minute Book; "Canadians May Enlarge League," *CSM*, 29 Jan. 1923, 12.

8. Duggan to Thomas C. O'Brien, District Attorney, Boston, Mass., 10 Dec. 1924, Duggan Collection, file 1; Minutes of a Meeting of the League, 5 Mar., 13 May 1923, HHFM, NHL Minute Book; "Duggan Pays $2,000 for Year's Option," *TDS*, 14 Feb. 1923, 10; Hardy, "Long before Orr," 259, 261, 263–64; "Canadians May Enlarge League," *CSM*, 29 Jan. 1923, 12; Stan Saplin, untitled ms., 14 July 1949, NYRC.

9. "Charles F. Adams, Boston Sportsman," *NYT*, 3 Oct. 1947, 25; "1,675 Stores in Merger," *NYT*, 26 Nov. 1925, 35; "First National Stores," *NYT*, 8 Apr. 1926, 38; Hardy, "Long before Orr," 256; Fred Hoey, "Hockey through the Years," [pt. 2], *Boston Garden Sport News* 18, no. 7 [1945–46 season]: 6; Duggan to O'Brien, 10 Dec. 1924, Duggan Collection, file 1; Bob Dunbar's columns of 8 and 29 Apr. 1924 in the *Boston Herald*, 15, 21, respectively; Duggan to O'Brien, 10 Dec. 1924, Duggan Collection, file 1.

10. On early New York hockey, see Tuthill, *Ice Hockey and Ice Polo Guide*, 21–33; and Stan Fischler with Tom Sarro, *Metro Ice*, 12–20.

11. Joseph Durso, *Madison Square Garden: 100 Years of History*, 18; Joe Durso, "The Four Gardens and How They Grew," 6; George W. Goman to John Halligan, 23 Aug. 1975. For a short history of the various Gardens, see Riess, *City Games*, 204–8; and Durso, "Four Gardens." On Rickard, see Colleen Aycock and Mark Scott, *Tex Rickard: Boxing's Greatest Promoter*; Roger Kahn, *A Flame of Pure Fire: Jack Dempsey and the Roaring 20s*, 38–50ff; "Madison Square Garden," *Fortune*, Nov. 1935; and a contemporary five-part series by Westbrook Pegler: "Tex Rickard: A Study of the World's Greatest Sports Promoter," *CDT*, 20, 27 Jan., 3, 10, 17 Feb. 1929.

12. Duggan to O'Brien, 10 Dec. 1924, Duggan Collection, file 1; "Col. Hammond Named Chapman's Successor as Aide to Rickard in Managing Garden," *NYT*, 14 Dec. 1928, 35; "Garden

to Hammond," *Time*, 14 May 1934; "Col. J. S. Hammond, Promoter, 59, Dies," *NYT*, 10 Dec. 1939, 71; Stanley Woodward, "Frozen Ears Convinced Hammond Answer to Tex Rickard's Dream Lay in Hockey for the New Garden," *NYHT*, ca. Feb. 1933, LAC, HHOF fonds, vol. 7, New York Americans—Scrap-book, season 1931–32, 101. A detailed account of Hammond's activities is contained in his *Times* obituary.

13. Duggan to O'Brien, 10 Dec. 1924, Duggan Collection, file 1.

14. Ibid. On Pittsburgh, see Frank C. Harper, *Pittsburgh of Today, Its Resources and People*, 4:382–83; George Thornton Fleming, *History of Pittsburgh and Environs, from Prehistoric Days to the Beginning of the American Revolution*, 3:637, 5:15–16; "Oakland: Duquesne Garden"; "Oakland: The World's Most Perfect Ice Palace"; and Lewis Clark Walkinshaw, *Annals of Southwestern Pennsylvania*, 321, 375. On Schooley, see Mike Rodden's column in the *Kingston (ON) Whig-Standard* of 24 Feb. 1962.

15. Duggan to O'Brien, 10 Dec. 1924, Duggan Collection, file 1. One of the Schooley-Brown allies was Charles Stoneham, the president of the National League's New York Giants.

16. Minutes of a Meeting of the [NHL], 13 May 1923, HHFM, NHL Minute Book; George C. Funk, President, Funk and Wilcox Co., Architect and Engineers, to Thomas J. Duggan, 5 July 1923, Duggan Collection, file 1; telegram from George V. Brown to O. Benoit, Mount Royal Arena, 3 Aug. 1923, Duggan Collection, file 1.

17. Minutes of a Meeting of Governors [of the NHL], 27 Jan. 1923, HHFM, NHL Minute Book.

18. Tommy Gorman, "One for Hockey Archives," LAC, Gorman fonds, vol. 1, file 11; Minutes of a Meeting of the [NHL], 13 May 1923, HHFM, NHL Minute Book.

19. On the auditorium and Ahearn, see Kitchen, *Win, Tie, or Wrangle*, 225–31ff; and Minutes of a Meeting [of NHL], 30 Sept. 1923, HHFM, NHL Minute Book.

20. Minutes of a Meeting [of NHL], 2 and 30 Sept. 1923, HHFM, NHL Minute Book; "Plans Hockey Arena Here," *NYT*, 18 Dec. 1923, 24; "Duggan Looking for Site," *CSM*, 19 Dec. 1923, 12; Tex Rickard, President of MSG Sporting Club, Inc., to Duggan, 20 Dec. 1923, Duggan Collection, file 1; Frank B. Flournoy to Duggan, 6 Feb. 1924, Duggan Collection, file 1; "Professional Ice Hockey in Prospect in United States," *CSM*, 5 Feb. 1924, 14.

21. "New York to Have Six," *NYT*, 11 Feb. 1924, 13; Minutes of a Special Meeting, 10 Feb. 1924, HHFM, NHL Minute Book. Livingstone was also included in a group picture after the meeting.

22. Adams to Duggan, 13 Feb. 1924, Duggan Collection, file 1; Funk to Duggan, 28 Feb. 1924, Duggan Collection, file 1.

23. Hammond to Duggan, 6 Mar. 1924, Duggan Collection, file 1.

24. "Rickard to Confer on Rink for Garden," *NYT*, 11 Mar. 1924, 14. Lionel Conacher later related that he was sent by Schooley to sound out Rickard on behalf of the USAHA but that the league had little to offer (Roche, *The Hockey Book*, 134–39).

25. "Rickard Bares Dealings," *NYT*, 21 Mar. 1924, 1; "Rickard and Others Reported Indicted for Marketing Dempsey Fight Pictures," *NYT*, 21 May 1924, 21.

26. Minutes of a Special Meeting [of NHL], 29 Mar. 1924, HHFM, NHL Minute Book; Adams to Duggan, 10 Apr. 1924, Duggan Collection, file 1; "New Pro League Plans," *MG*, 5 Apr. 1924, 22.

Livingstone promised clubs in Toronto, Ottawa, Buffalo, New York, and Brooklyn, with Pittsburgh and Boston also likely.

27. Adams to Calder, 2 Apr. 1924; Adams to Duggan, 2 Apr. 1924; and Adams to Calder, 10 Apr. 1924, Duggan Collection, file 1.

28. Adams to Duggan, 2 Apr. 1924, Duggan Collection, file 1; Hardy, "Long before Orr," 262.

29. "Denies Agreement to Pay Amateurs," NYT, 19 May 1925, 18; "Down the Line," NYHT, 19 May 1925, 20; 26 July 1925, 2.

30. Adams to Calder, 2 Apr. 1924, Duggan Collection, file 1; "Arrest for Tor. Hockey Accuser," MDS, 3 Feb. 1919, 6; "Conacher Emphatically Denies He Is Going to Join Pro Ranks," n.p., 14 Feb. 1924, LAC, HHOF fonds, vol. 20, Lionel Conacher Scrapbook, 1922–44; "Conacher Signs Up with Local Pros at Record Salary," n.p., n.d., LAC, HHOF fonds, vol. 20, Lionel Conacher Scrapbook, 1922–44.

31. "Brooklyn, Not Boston, to Be in Hockey League," NYHT, 8 Apr. 1924, 17; Adams to Duggan, 10 Apr. 1924, Duggan Collection, file 1.

32. Adams to Duggan, 10 Apr. 1924, and telegram from Hammond to Duggan, 17 Apr. 1924, both in Duggan Collection, file 1.

33. Adams to Duggan, 29 May 1924, Duggan Collection, file 1. On prospects in Providence, see the Funk to Duggan, 30 Apr. 1924, Duggan Collection, file 1.

34. "Rickard to Build Garden on 8th Av.," NYT, 18 June 1924, 1; "Plan 2 Big Arenas for Sport Uptown," NYT, 7 Aug. 1924, 8; Rickard to Rush Work on His Arena," NYT, 8 Aug. 1924, 16; "Rickard to Stage Big Hockey Games," NYT, 19 June 1924, 18. See also "Rickard Enlarges New Garden Site," NYT, 20 June 1924, 13.

35. "Rickard to Stage Big Hockey Games"; "Rickard Will Pay $900,000 for Club," NYT, 8 May 1924, 15; Duggan to NHL, 5 July 1924, Duggan Collection, file 1; Funk to Duggan, 25 Aug. 1924, Duggan Collection, file 1; "Garden Manager Resigns," NYT, 16 Oct. 1925, 16; "Jersey City to Have Arena Seating 14,000; Parking Space for 4,000," NYT, 11 Jan. 1926, 24. On movie theater chains, see Douglas Gomery, Shared Pleasures: A History of Movie Presentation in the United States, 34–35.

36. Minutes of a Special Meeting, 6 July 1924, HHFM, NHL Minute Book; Calder to Duggan, 10 July 1924, Duggan Collection, file 1; Funk to Duggan, 11 and 25 July 1924, Duggan Collection, file 1; Funk to L. B. Tansey, 15 July 1924, Duggan Collection, file 1; Funk to Duggan, 25 Aug. 1924, Duggan Collection, file 1; Minutes of a Special Meeting, 31 Aug. 1924, HHFM, NHL Minute Book.

37. Telegram from Funk to Duggan, 28 Aug., Duggan Collection, file 1; telegram from Funk to Duggan, 10 Sept. 1924, Duggan Collection, file 1; Duggan to Calder, 24 Sept. 1924, Duggan Collection, file 1; "Boston to Be the Sixth Club in Ntl. Hockey League Shortly," MDS, 26 Sept. 1924, 22; A. Linde Fowler, "Building Processes of a Championship Hockey Team," [Boston Transcript], [n.d.], LAC MG30 C89 (Fred Lionel Hitchman fonds), vol. 3, Boston Hockey Club (the Bruins) Season 1929–30 scrapbook; copy of Duggan to Calder, 24 Sept. 1924, Duggan Collection, file 1.

38. Minutes of a Special Meeting, 12 Oct. 1924, HHFM, NHL Minute Book; copy of Calder to Duggan, 13 Oct. 1924, Duggan Collection, file 1; Calder to Duggan, 1 Nov. 1924; Judgment, 28 Oct. 1938, William V. Dwyer v. Nathan Fraid et al.; undated memorandum, [page 2 of "Answer to Interrogatories"], Duggan Collection, file 2.

39. Duggan to O'Brien, 10 Dec. 1924, Duggan Collection, file 1. It is unclear when the right to veto new clubs based on territorial exclusivity came into existence, but it was a long-standing practice in baseball.

40. Minutes of Montreal HC Committee Meeting, 18 Nov. 1902, LAC, MAAA fonds, vol. 6, file 2; Cosentino, *Renfrew Millionaires*, 44; "New Windsor Hotel Board," *TDS*, 4 Jan. 1922, 19. On Raymond, see T. D. Regehr, *The Beauharnois Scandal: A Story of Canadian Entrepreneurship and Politics*, 19. On the rarity of French Canadians as financiers, see Marc Egnal, *Divergent Paths: How Culture and Institutions Have Shaped North American Growth*, 156–57. On Raymond's background, see Reginald Whitaker, *The Government Party: Organizing and Financing the Liberal Party of Canada, 1930–58*, 57–58.

41. Chrystian Goyens with Allan Turowetz and Jean-Luc Duguay, *Montreal Forum: Forever Proud*, 14; William Brown, *The Montreal Maroons: The Forgotten Stanley Cup Champions*, 37, 59; Canadian Arena Company Prospectus, 8 Nov. 1924, LAC, MG28 III 57 (Molson fonds), vol. 555, file 11.

42. Brown, *Montreal Maroons*, 12, 17–21, 24; Frank J. Selke with H. Gordon Green, *Behind the Cheering*, 60; Minutes of a Special Meeting, 12 Oct. 1924, HHFM, NHL Minute Book; "Franchises Given to Montreal and Boston by N.H.L.," *MG*, 13 Oct. 1924, 17; Minutes of a Special Meeting, 1 Nov. 1924, HHFM, NHL Minute Book. The Boston Professional Hockey Association, Inc., was formed 23 October 1924 (Articles of Organization, Boston Professional Hockey Association, Inc., 24 Oct. 1924). The Montreal Professional Hockey Club, Ltd., was incorporated on 19 November 1924 (Letters Patent "Montreal Professional Hockey Club, Limited," LAC, RG95, vol. 2231, file 301-1, "Montreal Professional Hockey Club, Limited"). *Maclean's* reported in 1932 that James Strachan took no salary and got no profits and spent five thousand dollars a year of his own money to promote the Maroons (Frederick Edwards, "Magnates under the Microscope," *Maclean's*, 1 Jan. 1932, 28).

43. Memorandum of Agreement, 6 July 1924, HHFM, NHL Minute Book; Minutes of a Special Meeting, 31 Aug. 1924, HHFM, NHL Minute Book; Minutes of NHL Annual Meeting, 1 Nov. 1924, HHFM, NHL Minute Book. Kidd misinterprets this agreement as obliging owners to stay with their clubs and not to sell (*Struggle for Canadian Sport*, 203–4). On Townsend, see Charles Alexander Rook et al., eds., *Western Pennsylvanians: A Work for Newspaper and Library References*, 357. On Callahan, see F. Harper, *Pittsburgh of Today*, 3:263–64.

44. The agreement was signed just after the November 1924 NHL annual meeting, but agreed upon beforehand. Agreement between Thomas H. Duggan and New Madison Square Garden Corporation, exhibit from *NYHC v. Rickard et al.*

45. Ibid.

46. Ibid.; Duggan to Hammond, 22 Jan. 1925, Duggan Collection, file 2; W. J. Macbeth, "'Pro' Hockey Will Be Played Next Winter in New Garden," *NYHT*, 6 Feb. 1925, 16; [copy of new MSG plan], 18 Feb. 1925, Duggan Collection, file 2; Charles Samuels, *The Magnificent Rube: The Life and Gaudy Times of Tex Rickard*, 270; Pat Robinson, "Garden Control Fight On," [ca. 1929], LAC, HHOF fonds, vol. 4, New York Americans—Scrap-book, season 1928–29, 95; Pat Robinson, "Bush Admits Dwyer Contract One-Sided," n.d., n.p., LAC, HHOF fonds, vol. 4, New York Americans—Scrap-book,

season 1928–29, 95. Though not publicized, several of Rickard's financiers also had connections to the brokerage house of W. A. Harriman & Co.

47. Agreement between Boston Arena Company, first part, and Thomas J. Duggan and Boston Professional Hockey Association, second part, 27 Nov. 1924, Duggan Collection, file 1.

48. Decision, *Thomas J. Duggan v. Charles F. Adams & another*, Supreme Judicial Court of Massachusetts, 272 Mass. 311, 172 N. E. 81, 1930 Mass. LEXIS 1185, 3 July 1930; Duffey to Duggan, 10 Mar. 1925, Duggan Collection, file 2; "Pro Hockey Will Rival Baseball in Bruin-Town," *HH*, 14 Mar. 1925, 12.

49. Arthur Siegel, "But Few Will Remember His Aides, Joe LaPorte and Jules Levesque," *Boston Traveler*, 3 Dec. 1949.

50. Hoey, "Hockey through the Years," [pt. 3], 5, 8–9; Hardy, "Long before Orr," 265–66; *NYT*, 20 Nov. 1924, XX19; *NYT*, 7 Dec. 1924, XX16; Hardy, "Long before Orr," 266; "It Is Hard to Say Just How Well Professional Hockey Will Go in This City; It Had a Good Start Anyway," *Boston Globe*, 2 Dec. 1924, 12.

51. "Franchises Given to Montreal and Boston by N.H.L.," *MG*, 13 Oct. 1924, 17; Barrette, *Léo Dandurand, Sportsman*, 134; Brown, *Montreal Maroons*, 29; Selke with Green, *Behind the Cheering*, 60; "Former Maroons 'Great' Dunc Munro Dies at 56," *MDS*, 4 Jan. 1958, 42; LAC, HHOF fonds, vol. 32, Harry Watson Scrap-book.

52. Minutes of a Special Meeting, 28 Dec. [1924], HHFM, NHL Minute Book.

53. Ibid.; Minutes of a Special Meeting, 25 Jan. 1925, HHFM, NHL Minute Book; Canada, Department of Labour, *Investigation into an Alleged Combine in the Motion Picture Industry in Canada*, 21; Charlie Querrie, "What Price Pro Hockey?," *Toronto Star Weekly*, 26 Jan. 1929, 23; Andy Lytle, "Hap Day: He Generates Hustle," *Toronto Star Weekly*, 19 Mar. 1949, LAC, Mayer fonds, vol. 42, Hockey Clippings, General II file. Paul Ciceri also seems to have retained his interest.

54. Ahearn to Gorman, 16 Dec. 1924, LAC, Gorman fonds, vol. 1, file 12A; Kitchen, *Win, Tie, or Wrangle*, 230–32; Minutes of a Special Meeting, 28 Dec. [1924], HHFM, NHL Minute Book; Minutes of a Special Meeting, 25 Jan. 1925, HHFM, NHL Minute Book; "Pro. Hockey Team Sold," *NYT*, 26 Jan. 1925, 11; Tommy Gorman, "Sport's Most Spangled Era," *Montreal Weekend Magazine*, [7 May] 1957, 51, LAC, Gorman fonds, vol. 5, Scrapbook; "The New Maroon Manager," *Montreal Forum Hockey Bulletin and Sports Magazine, Season 1934–35*, LAC, Gorman fonds, vol. 1, file 13.

55. Goyens with Turowetz and Duguay, *Montreal Forum: Forever Proud*, 22; Brown, *Montreal Maroons*, 31, 82; Lloyd McGowan, "Benoit Recalls Mount Royal Arena," *MDS*, 27 Feb. 1965, 22; "L'Aréna Mont-Royal Sera Reconstruite, de Façon à Loger Douze Mille Personnes," *LP*, 14 July 1925, 14. On the lawsuit, which went all the way to the Judicial Committee of the Privy Council in the United Kingdom, see Barrette, *Léo Dandurand, Sportsman*, 151–52; Brown, *Montreal Maroons*, 42–43, 82; and Gerald O'Carroll, "Super-salesman of Sport," n.d., *Montreal Standard*, 16–17, LAC, Mayer fonds, vol. 18, Leo Dandurand 1958–64 file.

56. "Ottawa's Machine Won Opener from Hamilton," *HH*, 17 Dec. 1923, II:2; "'Pro' Hockey Rules," *HH*, 21 Dec. 1923, II:3; "Must Improve Local Pros," *HH*, 7 Mar. 1923, 12; "P. J. Jones Says,"

HH, 28 Dec. 1923, 2:2; "P. J. Jones Says," *HH*, 12 Mar. 1925, 12. Folding seats would increase the arena seating from fifty-two hundred to sixty-seven hundred.

57. "No Change in Local 'Pro' Hockey Situation," *HH*, 13 Mar. 1925, 2:2; Milt Dunnell, "Speaking on Sport," *TDS*, 4 Apr. 1950, 14; Holzman and Nieforth, *Deceptions and Doublecross*, 165.

58. "P. J. Jones Says," *HH*, 13 Mar. 1925, 2:2; " . . . French . . . Trip West," *HH*, 14 Mar. 1925, 10. As Green later recalled, the players "realized that hockey was becoming big. All we asked was the players be given some share of the revenue" (Milt Dunnell, "Speaking on Sport," *TDS*, n.d., reprinted in *HN*, 20 Oct. 1956, 6).

59. "Owners in No Way Blamed, Calder Says," *HH*, 16 Mar. 1925, 1; Coleman, *Trail of the Stanley Cup*, 1:469.

60. "Owners Deny Sale of Franchise to New York—Say They'll Sell Players and Build New Team Next Year" ["P. J. Jones Says"], *HH*, 16 Mar. 1925, 10; "U.S. Clubs May Organize League—Held Meeting at New York Saturday—Tommy Gorman to Manage Duggan's Club for Five Years," *HH*, 16 Mar. 1925, 10. See also "Shorty Green to Lead New York; $10,000 Pay?," *HH*, 18 Mar. 1925, 14.

61. Minutes of a Special Meeting, 11 Apr. 1925, HHFM, NHL Minute Book; "Another New League Bubble Bursts," [*Montreal Herald*], n.d. [ca. 13–17 Apr. 1925]; "E. J. Livingstone Talks on New League," *TDS*, 17 Apr. 1926, 12. The preexpansion clubs (Ottawa, Canadiens, Hamilton, and St. Patrick's) also arranged to divide the franchise money surplus of forty-one thousand dollars among themselves.

62. Minutes of a Special Meeting, 11 Apr. 1925, HHFM, NHL Minute Book. Kidd notes the Canadiens' rights over French Canadian players limited the Maroons' appeal, but dividing the market by language was the intention (*Struggle for Canadian Sport*, 215).

63. Application for Incorporation and Draft Form of Letters Patent, 10 Dec. 1924, LAC, RG95, vol. 1723, National Hockey League, Ltd., file.

64. Minutes of a Special Meeting, 11 Apr. 1925, HHFM, NHL Minute Book. It may not have been the first move to incorporate. See LAC, RG95, vol. 1553, International Hockey League, Ltd., file.

65. "Deal to Buy Hockey Franchise for N.Y. Fails," *NYHT*, 16 Sept. 1925, 25; W. A. Hewitt, "Sporting Views and Reviews," *TDS*, 16 Sept. 1925, 10; Minutes of a Special Meeting, 26 Sept. 1925, HHFM, NHL Minute Book; Milt Dunnell, "Speaking on Sport," *TDS*, 4 Apr. 1950, 14; "Hockey Body Accepts Pittsburgh," *NYT*, 7 Nov. 1925, S5.

66. George W. Goman to John Halligan, 23 Aug. 1975; New York Hockey Club, Inc., [Balance Sheet] and Estimate of Expenses, Season of 1925–26, Duggan Collection, file 2; "Pro Hocky [*sic*] Body Completes League," *NYT*, 27 Sept. 1925, S8; Stanley Woodward, "Frozen Ears Convinced Hammond Answer to Tex Rickard's Dream Lay in Hockey for the New Garden," *NYHT*, n.d. [ca. Feb. 1933], LAC, HHOF fonds, vol. 7, New York Americans: Scrap-book, season 1931–32, 101. Dwyer's income in 1924 can be estimated at about $2.4 million and in 1925 (the year he was arrested) at just under $1 million (Ross, "Hockey Capital," 223n199). For a discussion of the close links between politics, crime, and sports, see Riess, *City Games*, chap. 6. On Dwyer's bootlegging operation, see "Seeks to Extradite Dwyer Defendants," *NYT*, 23 Mar. 1926, 4.

67. Minutes of the Annual Meeting, 7 Nov. 1925, HHFM, NHL Minute Book.

68. Rader, *American Sports*, 136, 156; G. E. White, *Creating the National Pastime: Baseball Transforms Itself, 1903–1953*, 118. Frank Selke later wrote that the rule changes had been pushed by the American owners, who wanted to appeal to American desire for "rugged competition and sustained speed" and not "the finer points of the game." The American owners wanted "something more spectacular," but the Canadians "thought the game was perfect as it was" (Selke with Green, *Behind the Cheering*, 77).

69. Minutes of the Annual Meeting, 7 Nov. 1925, HHFM, NHL Minute Book.

70. National Hockey League Constitution [adopted 25 Sept. 1926], AO, F223-7-0-16.

71. Minutes of the Annual Meeting, 7 Nov. 1925, HHFM, NHL Minute Book.

72. "Heroes of the Week," *New Yorker*, 9 Jan. 1926, 8. For a contemporary perspective on Rickard's techniques, see Paul Gallico, *Farewell to Sport*, chap. 8.

73. William Abbott, "Billy Burch, the 'Red' Grange of Hockey," n.p., 15 Dec. 1925, LAC, HHOF fonds, vol. 1, New York Americans—Scrap-book, season 1925–26. At different times, Burch, Joe Simpson, and Howie Morenz were each referred to as "the Babe Ruth of hockey," Rangers player Murray Murdoch was the "Lou Gehrig of hockey," and Lester Patrick was referred to as "the John McGraw of hockey." See Barrette, *Léo Dandurand, Sportsman*, 153; "Late Billy Burch Termed Hockey's Babe Ruth Once," *HN*, 23 Dec. 1950; and 5. John Kieran, "Sports of the Times," *NYT*, 13 Mar. 1927, S2.

74. Frank Wallace, "Rickard Dons Gloves on Ice with Hockey Players of N.Y. Club," [*New York Daily News*], [19 Nov. 1925 dateline]; W. J. Macbeth, "Rickard Sees N.Y. Hockey Team at Work," *NYHT*, 19 Nov. 1925, 27; *NYHT*, n.d., Nov. 1925, LAC, HHOF fonds, vol. 1, New York Americans—Scrap-book, season 1925–26. On the coincidence of hockey and photographic technology, see Stephen Hardy, Brian Norman, and Sarah Sceery, "Toward a History of Sport Branding."

75. Al Wilson, "Highest Paid Hockey Stars Again Meet as New York Six Face Pirates To-Night," [*New York Evening World*], 19 Jan. [1926], LAC, HHOF fonds, vol. 1, New York Americans—Scrap-book, season 1925–26; "Harold Cotton Signs Pro Contract," *TDS*, 22 Oct. 1925, 16; "Pro Hockey Season Opens Here; Men in High Realms of Sports and Politics to Be Part of Capacity Crowd," *Pittsburgh Gazette-Times*, 2 Dec. 1925, 13; W. J. Macbeth, "New York Shows Star Team in Hockey Debut," *NYHT*, 4 Dec. 1925, 27.

76. "U.S. Smashes Bootleg Trust, Seizing 19 in Opening Raid," *NYHT*, 4 Dec. 1925, 1; "Confession Proves Liquor Ring Bribery, Buckner Declares," *NYT*, 5 Dec. 1925, 1; "Dwyer Is Indicted with 60 Others in Wide Liquor Plot," *NYT*, 27 Jan. 1926; "Dwyer and 16 Named in New Liquor Case," *NYT*, 8 June 1926, 2. The sweep also gathered up many of Dwyer's associates, including Frank Costello, who was soon released and ran the operation in Dwyer's absence. He later became the head of the infamous Luciano organized crime family.

77. "The Garden," *New Yorker*, 25 Dec. 1925, 7; Harry Cross, "Hockey," *NYT*, 18 Jan. 1926, 19; transcript of interview, LAC, MG31 D171 (Trent Frayne fonds), vol. 1, file 7. On the *New Yorker*'s hockey coverage, which included a regular column from 1927 to 1928, see Craig Monk, "When Eustace Tilley Came to Madison Square Garden: Professional Hockey and the Editorial Policy of the *New Yorker* in the 1920s and 1930s."

78. "An Interview in 99 Words," *New York World-Telegram*, ca. Dec. 1934; Richard C. Crepeau, "The Sports Song of Patriotism"; W. J. Macbeth, "New York Adds Indian to Its Hockey Forces," *NYHT*, 23 Jan. 1926, 15; "Canadian Star Joins N.Y. Americans," *NYDM*, 28 Jan. 1926, 37; "Rene Boileau"; New York Draws with Montreal, 1–1," *NYT*, 26 Jan. 1926, 21; W. J. Macbeth, "Canadiens Defeat New York, 2 to 1 . . . ," *NYHT*, 14 Jan. 1926, 26. See also Ag Boucher to Trent Frayne, n.d., LAC, Frayne fonds, vol. 1, file 9.

79. "The Garden"; "Paint," *New Yorker*, 6 Feb. 1926, 12. The practice of painting the ice, although taken up by at least one other rink (Maple Leaf Gardens in 1931), seems to have fallen out of favor in New York by the end of the Second World War, when a spectator remarked on the "reddish" tinge to the ice (John Halligan, "Confessions of Some More New York Rink Rats"). See also Westbrook Pegler, "Rickard Scores a Real Hit with Ice Hockey Matches," *CDT*, 25 Dec. 1925, 25.

80. W. J. Macbeth, "Canadiens Conquer New York, 3 to 1, in Opening . . . ," *NYHT*, 16 Dec. 1925, 22; Macbeth, "Hockey Players Complain about Midsummer Heat in the Garden," *NYHT*, 17 Dec. 1925, 26; Macbeth, "Less Heat at Next Hockey Match Here," *NYHT*, 18 Dec. 1925, 27; "N.Y. Pros to Play Pirate Six Tonight," *NYT*, 6 Feb. 1926, 10.

81. "Asks Court to Cool Garden for Hockey," *NYT*, 24 Dec. 1926; Affidavit of T. P. Gorman, 22 Dec. 1926, *New York Hockey Club, Inc., v. George L. ("Tex") Rickard and Madison Square Garden Corporation* (hereafter *NYHC v. Rickard et al.*); Affidavit of Wilfred T. Green, 22 Dec. 1926, *NYHC v. Rickard et al.* The complaint noted that in Canadian rinks, "no heat is employed in connection with the hockey games." Complaint, *NYHC v. Rickard et al.* The modern NHL standard is 60°F (15.5°C) at 35 percent relative humidity before the game and 65°F (18.3°C) at 45 percent RH after.

82. "Teams in U.S. and Canada Form a New Hockey League," *NYT*, 16 Oct. 1925, 16; "U.S. Association May Seek Peace," *TG*, 21 Oct. 1925, 8; "Soo Stars Consider Offer by New York," *TG*, 21 Oct. 1925, 8; "Metropolitan Hockey League Is Organized," *NYHT*, 8 Dec. 1925, 28; "Amateur Hockey Revived Here with Eastern League Formation," *NYHT*, 9 Dec. 1925, 25.

83. "Hockey War Is On; Men May Unionize," *NYT*, 31 Jan. 1926, S1; "N.Y. Hockey Players Reject Idea of Union," [n.p.], 26 Feb. 1926, LAC, HHOF fonds, vol. 1, New York Americans–Scrapbook, season 1925–26; W. J. Macbeth, "New York Hockey Team to Play Boston in Hub To-Night," *NYHT*, 22 Dec. 1925, 23.

84. Brown, *Montreal Maroons*, 82. Baseball arrangements were either a percentage of the gate or a fixed amount per ticket (John Helyar, *Lords of the Realm: The Real History of Baseball*, 523).

85. "Pro Hockey Officials Withhold Franchises," *NYT*, 11 Jan. 1926, 36; "Brooklyn Seeks Franchise in National Hockey League," *NYT*, 29 Dec. 1925, 29.

86. "Canadians Oppose Syndicate Hockey," *NYT*, 17 Jan. 1926, S2; Archie Wills, "Patrick of the Puck," *Maclean's*, 7 Apr. 1928, 62. In the PCHA, the Patricks rebalanced their team rosters at the start of every season and vehemently denied charges—suspected to be from disaffected gamblers—that the outcomes of the games themselves were in any way controlled.

87. "New Incorporations," *NYT*, 6 Feb. 1926, 24; "New York to Have 2 Pro Sixes Next Year; Hammond Resigns to Organize New Club," *NYT*, 11 Feb. 1926, 15; "Deputy Fire Commissioner Hannon Named President of New York Pro Hockey Club," *NYT*, 14 Mar. 1926, S8; Alfred Dayton,

"Syndicate Hockey a Myth," *New York Sun*, 12 Feb. 1926; "Hockey Officials Will Meet Today," *NYT*, 14 Feb. 1926, S3; W. J. Macbeth, "Hockey Moguls Will Consider Problem To-Day," *NYHT*, 14 Feb. 1926, X2; Wong, *Lords of the Rinks*, 94; "Pro Hockey League Fails to Take New Clubs into Circuit," *NYHT*, 15 Feb. 1926, 18.

88. "League Launched in Secret Session," *NYHT*, 24 Feb. 1926, 21; "Hockey Franchises Raised to $50,000," *NYT*, 15 Feb. 1926, 25; Alfred Dayton, "Plan Changes in Hockey," *New York Sun*, 2 Feb. 1926.

89. "Chicago Plans Arena Like Garden of Its Own," *NYHT*, 10 Jan. 1926, 4; "$8,000,000 'Garden' Planned for Chicago," *Washington Post*, 3 Feb. 1926, 15; Westbrook Pegler, "Rickard to Scatter Gardens Like One-Arm Lunch Rooms," *Washington Post*, 28 Jan. 1926, 19; "Rickard to Build Arena, Similar to Garden, in Chicago," *NYHT*, 18 Apr. 1926, 6; "I'll Build Garden Near Loop—Rickard," *CDT*, 18 Apr. 1926, A1. The back-and-forth between Harmon and Rickard is summarized nicely in the article titles that reported it: Westbrook Pegler, "Rickard Says He'll Build Arena Here; 'Applesauce'—Harmon," *CDT*, 26 Jan. 1926, 23; Westbrook Pegler, "Tex Coming to Chicago, in Disguise, If Harmon Insists," *CDT*, 27 Jan. 1926, 25; "Paddy Forgot to Order Bricks for Stadium, Rickard Asserts," *CDT*, 26 Mar. 1926, 25. On Harmon, see William Howland, *Chicago Jazz: A Cultural History, 1904–1930*, 72–73; "Chicago Stadium"; and Don Maxwell, "Paddy, Born Near Gas House, Builds a $6,000,000 Stadium," *CDT*, 24 Mar. 1929, A3.

90. "Percentage for Visiting Clubs," *CSM*, 19 Apr. 1926, 6; Draft Articles of Agreement between Thomas J. Duggan and New York Hockey Club, Inc., 1927, Duggan Collection, file 2; Wong, *Lords of the Rinks*, 94–95; "New York Rangers Assured of Place in Hockey League," *NYHT*, 18 Apr. 1926, 8; "New Incorporations," *NYT*, 8 May 1926, 29.

91. "Percentage for Visiting Clubs," *CSM*, 19 Apr. 1926, 6; "New York Rangers Assured of Place in Hockey League," *NYHT*, 18 Apr. 1926, 8; Hockey League Split on Chicago Club," *CDT*, 2 May 1926, A1.

92. Selke with Green, *Behind the Cheering*, 183; "Hockey League Split on Chicago Club," *CDT*, 2 May 1926, A1; "2 Hockey Leagues May Follow Split," *NYT*, 2 May 1926, S8; "Hardwick Likely to Get Chicago N.H.L. Franchise," *CDT*, 3 May 1926, 19; "Hockey Club Decision Put Off till May 15," *NYT*, 3 May 1926, 18; "Hardwick Buys Portland, Ore., Hockey Team," *CDT*, 4 May 1926, 23. On Hardwick, see "Chicago to Get Hockey Club but It'll Take Time," *CDT*, 19 Apr. 1926, 21; "Hardwick Denies Rickard Backs Him in Hockey," *CDT*, 23 Apr. 1926, 21; "Hockey League Split on Chicago Club," *CDT*, 2 May 1926, A1; "How Hockey Came to Chicago," *CDT*, 15 Nov. 1953, 134. John Chi-Kit Wong ascribes more independence to Hardwick ("Entrepreneurship and the Rise of the Chicago Blackhawks," 254–80). On Bierer and Friedberg, see Frederick Wilson, "Scanning the Sport Field," *TG*, 4 May 1926, 8; and C. M. Burton, William Stocking, and Gordon K. Miller, *The City of Detroit, Michigan, 1701–1922*, 340. Adding to the confusion, E. L. Garey, the Garden's lawyer, was now reported to be acting on behalf of the *Americans* to obtain an option on the WHL Saskatoon Sheiks in order to stock *Harmon's* club ("Hardwick Likely to Get Chicago N.H.L. Franchise," *CDT*, 3 May 1926, 19).

93. "Lester Says Other Five Clubs in Western League Have Been Sold as Well," n.p., 5 May 1926, LAC, HHOF fonds, vol. 21, Lester Patrick Scrapbook, 1902–34; Kidd, *Struggle for Canadian Sport*,

207; Wong, *Lords of the Rinks*, 99. For Frank Patrick's recollection, see Frank A. Patrick, "Patrick Feels Ross Swung Final Sale," *Boston Globe*, 10 Mar. 1935, A23.

94. Patrick, "Patrick Feels Ross Swung Final Sale"; "Detroit Interests Acquire Cougar Six," *NYT*, 4 May 1926, 34; Wong, "Rise of the Chicago Blackhawks," 258.

95. "Detroit Gets Hockey Birth; But Franchise Goes to Winter Palace, Inc., and Not to Friedberg; John C. Townsend Here after Making Successful Bid in Montreal," *Detroit Free Press*, 17 May 1926, 15; "Hockey League Paves Way to Admit Other Clubs," *NYT*, 16 May 1926, S5; Wong, *Lords of the Rinks*, 97.

96. National Hockey League Constitution [adopted 25 Sept. 1926], 3–5, AO, F223-7-0-16.

97. Coenen, *From Sandlots to Super Bowl*, chaps. 1–2; John Kieran, "Sports of the Times," *NYT*, 15 Nov. 1927, 35.

98. Rader, *American Sports*, 142. On modernity and the building of a national culture, see Mark Dyreson, "The Emergence of Consumer Culture and the Transformation of Physical Culture: American Sport in the 1920s." See also Warren I. Susman, *Culture as History: The Transformation of American Society in the Twentieth Century*, chaps. 7–8; and Tygiel, *Past Time*, 73–86.

99. Hugh Fullerton, "The Fastest Game of All," *Liberty*, 27 Mar. 1926, 53; Damon Runyon, "Runyon Says—Hockey Sweeps Country," [*New York American*], ca. Mar. 1926; Burris Jenkins Jr., "The Week in Sport," *New York Evening World*, 22 Nov. 1926, 21; "The Garden," *New Yorker*, 20 Oct. 1926, 19; "One Year Old," *New Yorker*, 5 Feb. 1927, 19; Al Wilson, "How 'Puck-chasing' Has Become Our National Winter Sport," *Literary Digest*, 15 Jan. 1927, 78–79.

100. "One Year Old."

101. Milt Dunnell, "Speaking on Sport," *TDS*, 4 Apr. 1950, 14.

102. Charles H. Good, "Will U.S. Cash Cripple Our Hockey?," *Maclean's*, 1 Mar. 1926, 18, 55, 56. The *Star* report of Adams's letter is in "Poor Outlook for Canadian Hockey," *TG*, 14 May 1926, 10.

103. "Adams Owner Boston Pro. Club Explains Stand as to Canada," *MDS*, 12 May 1926, 30; "Rickard Heard From," n.p., [2 May 1926 Montreal dateline], LAC, HHOF fonds, vol. 21, Lester Patrick Scrapbook, 1902–34; "Stormy Session National Hockey League Favors Expansion," *OC*, 3 May 1926, 11.

104. Al Wilson, "Professional Hockey Rapidly Assuming Proportion of Organized Baseball," *New York Evening World*, 6 Dec. 1926, 21; "How 'Puck-chasing' Has Become Our National Winter Sport." The connections between rinks are not dealt with by Wong, and the importance of boxing is overemphasized by Kidd (Wong, *Lords of the Rinks*; Kidd, *Struggle for Canadian Sport*, chap. 5).

105. The idea of splitting the league, with Frank Patrick as head of one, comes from Wilson, "How 'Puck-chasing' Has Become Our National Winter Sport." On the importance of attaching teams to cities, see Leifer, *Making the Majors*, 283–84.

4. Creating a Major League

1. See Kitchen, *Win, Tie, or Wrangle*, 239–42; Wong, *Lords of the Rinks*, 99, 100–101; "Threatens Suit," *CDT*, 15 Oct. 1926, 31; "Rangers Get Two Stars," *NYT*, 4 Nov. 1926, 31; and "Awarded N.Y. Rangers Cook Brothers' Services," *NYHT*, 4 Nov. 1926, 31. Frank Selke relates two versions of the

certified check story, which he heard from Smythe. Frank Selke Submission [nominating Joe Cattarinich to the Hockey Hall of Fame], HHFM, Joseph Cattarinich file; and Selke with Green, *Behind the Cheering*, 183. Waivers gave the right of clubs in the same league to either waive or claim players moving out of the league at a particular price.

2. See "Hockey Body Admits Chicago and Detroit," *NYT*, 26 Sept. 1926, S4; and "Enlarged Rink," *New York Evening World*, 19 Nov. 1926, 24.

3. Charles Adams had been emerging as a critic of many Calder decisions, especially about officiating, and threatened to withdraw his support for the president entirely. Wong, *Lords of the Rinks*, 100. For Calder's retrospective view of his changing role in this period, see NHL Verbatim Minutes of Annual Meeting, HHFM, 11 May 1935, 19.

4. "Reorganize Puck Teams for Hawks," *Los Angeles Times*, 9 Apr. 1927, B2; "Black Hawks Puck Stars Here Today," *Los Angeles Times*, 10 Apr. 1927, A7; Tommy Gorman, "Sport's Most Spangled Era," *Montreal Weekend Magazine* [7 May] 1957, 51; "Track, Tennis, Swimming and Baseball at Top," *NYHT*, 26 Dec. 1926, 2:3. See also Hardy, "Two-Way Hockey," 16–17; and Seamus O'Coughlin, *Squaw Valley Gold: American Hockey's Olympic Odyssey*, 100–116.

5. "Still Another Who Wants Hockey Club; E. P. Strong of Cleveland Even Has Faith in Drawing Power of Coliseum," *Detroit Free Press*, 15 May 1926, 15, 17. The *Free Press* was dismissive of the prospect of a Livingstone league: "'Livvy' has been organizing new leagues for the last five or six years and has yet to get one beyond the formative stage."

6. Reinstatement was possible "only in unusual cases where an athlete . . . has been ill-advised and has, without mature consideration, turned to the professional ranks." CAHA Official Hockey Rules, 1929, amended to Mar. 1928, LAC, CAHA fonds, vol. 80.

7. On baseball developments, see White, *Creating the National Pastime*, 278–82, 286–92; and Benjamin G. Rader, *Baseball: A History of America's Game*, 131–32.

8. Patrick's comments are in "Organized Professional Hockey with Graded Leagues Will Cover Whole of Canada in Five Years Says Promoter," n.p., 13 Dec. 1925, LAC, HHOF fonds, vol. 21, Lester Patrick Scrap-book, 1902–1934.

9. "'Farm' for Pro. Players Is Again Considered," *TG*, 14 Jan. 1926, 8; Funk to Duggan, 30 Mar. 1926, Duggan Collection, file 2; "Dandurand Explains the New League," *MDS*, 27 Mar. 1926, 15; Fred Hoey, "Hockey through the Years," [pt. 3], *Boston Garden Sport News* 18, no. 7 [1945–46 season]: 8–9.

10. "N.Y. Helps Launch New Hockey League," *NYT*, 24 Mar. 1926, 17; "Hockey Promoters Vote to Start New League Next Winter," *NYHT*, 24 Mar. 1926, 20; "Offer $100,000 for Ottawa Franchise and Team," *OC*, 22 Feb. 1926, 1; Funk to Duggan, 30 Mar. 1926, Duggan Collection, file 2; "Dandurand Explains the New League," *MDS*, 27 Mar. 1926, 15.

11. Funk to Duggan, 30 Mar. 1926, Duggan Collection, file 2. Funk continued to entice Duggan in a letter of 10 Apr. 1926 (Duggan Collection, file 2).

12. Wong, *Lords of the Rinks*, 100, 212n9, 109.

13. Ibid., 110–11; "Many Certificates Refused by O.H.A.," *TG*, 16 June 1926, 9; "Seven Ontario Teams in Pro Hockey Loop," *TG*, 28 June 1926, 9; telegram from King to Calder, 5 Aug. 1926, cited in Wong, *Lords of the Rinks*, 112.

14. Calder to Adams, 26 Oct. 1926, quoted in Wong, *Lords of the Rinks*, 112; "Rangers and Boston Are Awarded Players," *Toronto Mail and Empire*, 18 Oct. 1926, 9.

15. Calder to Hammond, 28 Feb. 1927, and Hammond to Calder, 2 Mar. 1927, quoted in Wong, *Lords of the Rinks*, 113.

16. "Ten Teams Operate in National League," *TG*, 14 Sept. 1926, 9; "Hockey Body Admits Chicago and Detroit," *NYT*, 26 Sept. 1926, S4; Holzman and Nieforth, *Deceptions and Doublecross*, 287–88; "Boston Downs Detroit, 2–0, for Second Victory," *NYHT*, 19 Nov. 1926, 25; US Department of the Interior, National Park Service, "Olympia Arena," 4. Jack Adams recalled the Cougars lost eighty-four thousand dollars. Ed Fitkin, "Footloose and Fancy Free," [Maple Leaf Gardens program], n.d., 33, LAC, Mayer fonds, vol. 18, Jack Adams 1952 file.

17. "Hockey Body Admits Chicago and Detroit"; James Crusinberry, "Skaters Try Out Ice at Coliseum Hockey Arena," *CDT*, 4 Nov. 1926, 19; Email from William McLaughlin to author, 12 Mar. 2004; Minutes of 25 Sept. 1926 NHL Meeting, cited in Brian O'Neill to Trent Frayne, 1 May 1973, LAC, Frayne Fonds, vol. 2, file 3; "Ice Hockey to Make Comeback Here Wednesday," *CDT*, 14 Nov. 1926, A5; Johnny Gottselig Submission, HHFM, Major Frederic McLaughlin file; "Ice Hockey to Make Comeback Here Wednesday," *CDT*, 14 Nov. 1926, A5. See also Wong, "Rise of the Chicago Blackhawks," 259, 280n85. Since McLaughlin's unit was named after a chief whose name is usually rendered in two words (as is the Black Hawk War in which he fought), the two-part version of the name into "Black Hawks" became the norm for most newspapers, with the general exception of the *Chicago Daily Tribune*, whose orthographical independence was also seen in its consistent use of the spelling "hocky" until the late 1930s. It was not until the 1980s that the club consistently resumed the unitary name. In this text, "Black Hawks" is used throughout.

18. "Junior League Takes over Ticket Sale for Opening Hockey Game," *CDT*, 11 Oct. 1926, 33.

19. Wong, *Lords of the Rinks*, 129; "Chicago Hockey Team Defeats St. Pats, 4 to 1," *NYHT*, 18 Nov. 1926, 26; "Sports Gentry and Society Rub Elbows at Ice Hockey Match," *CDT*, 18 Nov. 1926, 29, 38; Holzman and Nieforth, *Deceptions and Doublecross*, 283.

20. Wong, *Lords of the Rinks*, 109; "Chicago's Two Hockey Clubs Use Same Rink," *CDT*, 15 Oct. 1926, 31.

21. Telegram from Livingstone to Calder, 7 Aug. 1926, cited in Wong, *Lords of the Rinks*, 114; "Cardinal Hockey Team Opens Here against Detroit," *CDT*, 25 Oct. 1926, 23; "Chicago Hockey Out at Arena," *Toronto Telegram*, 29 Oct. 1926, cited in Holzman and Nieforth, *Deceptions and Doublecross*, 378n481. On the Coliseum lease arrangements, see Wong, *Lords of the Rinks*, 114, 213–14n33; and "Canadian Sues for $700,000 in Hockey Case," *CDT*, 30 Sept. 1930, 19.

22. "Gambled Huge Sum on Hockey," *G&M*, 21 Jan. 1944, 15; Holzman and Nieforth, *Deceptions and Doublecross*, 288, 291; "Ed Livingstone Sells Cardinal Hockey Club," *CDT*, 9 Mar. 1927; "Hockey Bosses Refuse to O.K. Sale of Cards," *CDT*, 21 Mar. 1927, 21. On Black Hawks ticket giveaways, see also George Vass, *The Chicago Black Hawks Story*, 21.

23. Letters from Warren to Calder, 9 and 12 May 1927, and McLaughlin to Calder, 25 May 1927, quoted in Wong, *Lords of the Rinks*, 114; ibid., 115; "Hockey Overtime Cut to 10 Minutes," *NYT*, 25 Sept. 1927, S7; [Statement of Claim], *Edward J. Livingstone v. Frederic McLaughlin, William J. Foster,*

and John S. Keogh; Wong, *Lords of the Rinks*, 214n41. The suit finally went to trial in October 1930 and featured two mistrials. Livingstone refiled in January 1931, but the outcome is unknown.

24. On Livingstone's later involvement in Toronto amateur hockey, see Holzman and Nieforth, *Deceptions and Doublecross*, 335–36.

25. Wong, *Lords of the Rinks*, 116–17.

26. Ibid., 117–18.

27. The Minute Book of the NHL [1917–25] lists addresses for the NHL and Frank Calder at 335 Craig Street and then 2281 John Street, likely Calder's home addresses. In 1920–21, *Lovell's Montreal Street Guide* lists Calder as a newspaper reporter with an office at 40 Hospital Street, and in 1926–27 he is listed as president of the NHL with an office at 714–1410 Stanley Street, on the corner of Ste. Catherine. In 1934–35 the NHL office moved to the tower of the prestigious Sun Life building at 1155 Metcalfe St.

28. Wong, *Lords of the Rinks*, 102, 209n46; McLaughlin to Calder, 10 Jan. 1927, quoted in ibid., 103; "Toronto St. Pats of Hockey League Sold for $160,000," *NYHT*, 15 Feb. 1927, 23. McLaughlin later found the waiver agreement in the files of the club's former secretary. Wong, *Lords of the Rinks*, 210n57.

29. Wong, *Lords of the Rinks*, 102, 210n55.

30. Correspondence between Calder and McLaughlin, 26 and 29 Apr., 29 June, 5 July 1927, quoted in Wong, *Lords of the Rinks*, 105–6. Despite his homicidal musings, McLaughlin had little empathy for rough play, which he expected to have "a serious sporting and financial effect on the future of professional hockey." McLaughlin to Calder, 22 Apr. 1927, quoted in Wong, *Lords of the Rinks*, 105.

31. "Stanley Cup Clash on Again Tonight," *NYT*, 9 Apr. 1927, 24.

32. "Pro Hockey Drew Total of 1,221,305," *NYT*, 28 Apr. 1927, 19. The club average is derived from the *New York Times* figure for total league attendance. Individual club totals exist for nine clubs and imply more than 245,000 attendance for the tenth club, the Rangers, making it the best-attended club. See table 2 in the appendix.

33. US Department of the Interior, National Park Service, "Olympia Arena," 2, 3. The Olympia's ice-making process was modeled on the techniques perfected at Madison Square Garden. Terry Mitchell, "Largest Indoor Skating Rink in the United States Installed in Olympia Arena, Detroit," *American Architect*, 20 May 1928, 689, 691.

34. Kitchen, *Win, Tie, or Wrangle*, 254–55. For a comparison of ticket scales in 1930, see Wong, *Lords of the Rinks*, 123, 216–17n8.

35. "Senators Away to Play Pirates," *Ottawa Journal*, 12 Jan. 1927, 12.

36. "Toronto St. Pats of Hockey League Sold for $160,000"; "New Owners Take over the St. Patricks Club," *TDS*, 15 Feb. 1927, 10. Querrie had initially sold Bickell and Nathanson on the idea that they "would have a lot of fun" owning a hockey team, but that Nathanson eventually decided it was "not so funny." Querrie, "25 Years in Sports," *TDS*, 21 Nov. 1927, 12.

37. Querrie, "25 Years in Sports"; *TG*, 17 Feb. 1927, 8; Conn Smythe and Scott Young, *Conn Smythe: If You Can't Beat 'Em in the Alley*, 82–86. The other directors of the company were a sample

of Toronto's business elite: Bickell, Hugh Aird, E. W. Bickle, E. H. Blake, Major R. Cecil Cowan, Allan Case, Peter G. Campbell, Fred J. Crawford, Max S. Haas, T. A. McAuley, and Blake Jackson. "New Owners Take over the St. Patricks Club." The Leafs crest and colors were also reminiscent of City of Toronto emblems.

38. "Rickard Would Buy Control of Giants, Plans Arena Chain," *NYT*, 4 Mar. 1927, 1, 7. The Philadelphia interests looking at acquiring the St. Patrick's may have been affiliated with Tex Rickard. Given Bickell and Nathanson's apparent hostility to Rickard, it would have been extra incentive for them to help keep the club in Toronto.

39. The Americans traveled eighteen thousand miles compared to eleven thousand for the Canadiens. Al Wilson, "Calder of Montreal Asks Franchise Limit," *New York Evening World*, 15 Mar. 1927, LAC, HHOF fonds, vol. 2, New York Americans—Scrap-book, season 1926–27.

40. "Charlie Querrie Favors N.H.L.'s Play-Off System—Says It Keeps Up Interest," *HH*, 18 Mar. 1925, 14.

41. Wong, *Lords of the Rinks*, 98; Coleman, *Trail of the Stanley Cup*, 2:35.

42. Wilson, "Calder of Montreal Asks Franchise Limit"; "Bruin Six Ready for Cup Struggle," *NYT*, 6 Apr. 1927, 31; "Pro Hockey Drew Total of 1,221,305," *NYT*, 28 Apr. 1927, 19; Coleman, *Trail of the Stanley Cup*, 1:461.

43. "Adopt New System in Hockey Play-Offs," *NYT*, 23 Sept. 1928, S8; Coleman, *Trail of the Stanley Cup*, 2:73; "Sports of the Times," *NYT*, 20 Nov. 1928, 43. Joseph Gordon discussed the logic of regrouping in "Hockey Shifts May Hold Fate of Ice League," *New York Morning Telegraph*, 22 Nov. 1928, II2.

44. "Lady Byng Gives Hockey Cup for Canada's Fairest Player," *NYT*, 9 Mar. 1925, 13; Coleman, *Trail of the Stanley Cup*, 2:30; Frederick Edwards, "Twinkle, Winkle, Hockey Star," *Maclean's*, 1 Dec. 1929, 21; photo in LAC, HHOF fonds, vol. 5, New York Americans—Scrap-book, season 1929–30, 91. Many of the clubs had local trophies for most valuable players. Two examples are the Mappins & Webb Trophy and the George Marois Cup. *La Presse*, 14 Mar. 1924, 20; *La Presse*, 9 Mar. 1925, 16.

45. NHL Minutes, 24 Sept. 1927, cited in Wong, *Lords of the Rinks*, 123; Ahearn to Calder, 23 Jan. 1928, cited in Wong, *Lords of the Rinks*, 124; ibid., 123–24; Kitchen, *Win, Tie, or Wrangle*, 292. The league also created a referee-in-chief position to oversee officials, with Cooper Smeaton appointed to fill it.

46. Coleman, *Trail of the Stanley Cup*, 2:32–34; "Hockey Overtime Cut to 10 Minutes," *NYT*, 25 Sept. 1927, S7.

47. Coleman, *Trail of the Stanley Cup*, 2:33, 59–60; "Hockey Overtime Cut to 10 Minutes." In the fall of 1928, the overtime period was also changed from sudden death to a full ten minutes.

48. Grover Theis, "Pro Hockey Rules to Stay Unchanged," *NYT*, 5 Feb. 1929, 34; "Worters and Roach Lead the Goalies," *NYT*, 8 Mar. 1929, 27. *Le Petit Journal* had noted goals-against averages as early as 1935 (10 Feb. 1935, 31). Statistics tended to be erratically kept, a problem beginning with inconsistent standards at the rinkside scoring officials. Each game's statistics were to be forwarded to the league office, and Calder had the *Montreal Herald*'s Elmer Ferguson (who was also the Forum scorer) compile them. At some point, he began mimeographing them for the NHL clubs and wire

services. In the meantime, most reporters seemed to have kept their own compilations. As an example, see the files of Harold Kaese, BPL, Harold Kaese fonds, vol. 1.

49. "Rangers End Race by Beating Pirates," *NYT*, 18 Mar. 1929, 31; "Bruins Will Try New Hockey Rules," *NYT*, 16 Mar. 1929, 19; Alfred Dayton, "Hockey Rules to Be Enforced," *New York Sun*, n.d., LAC, HHOF fonds, vol. 5, New York Americans—Scrap-book, season 1929–30, 10.

50. William E. Brandt, "Americans on Ice at Garden Tonight," *NYT*, 19 Nov. 1929, 40; Coleman, *Trail of the Stanley Cup*, 2:85, 87.

51. Coleman, *Trail of the Stanley Cup*, 2:87; "Radical Rule Changes for Hockey Opposed," *NYT*, 8 Dec 1929, S6; George Trevor, "Blue Lines," *Outlook and Independent*, 4 Feb. 1931, 184. The modified new rule took effect 21 December. "Amend Hockey Rule to Modify Attack," 17 Dec. 1929, 38; Coleman, *Trail of the Stanley Cup*, 2:87.

52. Ed Fitkin, "Footloose and Fancy Free," [*Maple Leaf Gardens Program*], n.d., 36, LAC, Mayer fonds, vol. 18, Jack Adams 1952 file; Hardy "Long before Orr," 266; "New Boston Terminal to Have Sports Arena," *NYT*, 25 Mar. 1928, 146; "Boston Threatens Suspension," *NYT*, 6 Feb. 1929, 32; "1,350,000, a Record, Saw League Hockey," *NYT*, 31 Mar. 1928, 16.

53. "Harmon's Dream of Huge Sport Arena Nears Reality," *CDT*, 1 July 1928, A2; "Chicago's New Sport Palace to Rival Madison Square Garden," *Chicago Defender*, 7 July 1928, 9; Chicago Stadium Corporation bond prospectus, published in *CDT*, 2 July 1928, 28; "Norris Group Given Control of Stadium," *CDT*, 26 Feb. 1935, 17, 18; "Harmon's Dream of Huge Sport Arena Nears Reality."

54. Duggan to A. B. Smythe, 2 Mar. 1928, Duggan Collection, file 2; telegram from Funk to Duggan, 17 Jan. 1928, Duggan Collection, file 2; "Pirate Six Bought by Benny Leonard," *NYT*, 8 Oct. 1928, 17; "Leonard Acquires Title to Pirate Six," *NYT*, 9 Oct. 1928, 42; "Henry Townsend," *NYT*, 16 Jan. 1927, 30. On Leonard, see "Benny Leonard," in *Encyclopedia of Jews in Sports*, edited by Postal, Silver, and Silver, 162–64.

55. "Adopt New System in Hockey Play-Offs," *NYT*, 23 Sept. 1928, S8; "To Put the Brakes on Trading in Players," *TDS*, 4 Oct. 1927, 8; Duggan to A. B. Smythe, 2 Mar. 1928, Duggan Collection, file 2; Wong, *Lords of the Rinks*, 124; telegram from Joe Page to T. J. Duggan, 29 Jan. 1928, Duggan Collection, file 2; Duggan to Smythe, 2 Mar. 1928, Duggan Collection, file 2; "Plans Call for Arena Seating for 15,000 People," *Cleveland Plain Dealer*, 5 Feb. 1928.

56. Dwyer's reemergence seems to be the first time his involvement with the Americans was made public. "Pro Hockey Season Opens Here Nov. 18," *NYT*, 8 Sept. 1928, 21. On the Dwyer-Leonard connection, see "Benny Leonard Becomes a Business Man," n.p., n.d., LAC, HHOF fonds, vol. 4, New York Americans—Scrap-book, season 1928–29, 8. On Leonard's observations about boxing and hockey attendance, see Benny Leonard, "Hockey and Other Sports Hit Blow at Ring Receipts," *New York World*, 25 Nov. 1928, 5S. After the Pirates had moved to Philadelphia, Dwyer was the acknowledged owner. See Cooper Smeaton to Frank Calder, 13 Feb. 1931, 1930–31 Philadelphia Quaker Hockey Club file, NHL Archives. (My thanks to John Wong for this reference.)

57. "Leonard's Hockey Stars Balking at Contracts," *Washington Post*, 28 Oct. 1928, M21; "Hold-Out Hockey Stars Given League Ultimatum," *Washington Post*, 29 Oct. 1928, 12; "3 Hockey

Stars Banned," *NYT*, 3 Nov. 1928, 19; "American Six Fails in Bid for Worters," *NYT*, 29 Nov. 1928, 39; James S. Collins, "Almost the Naked Truth," *Washington Post*, 5 Dec. 1928, 15.

58. Grover Theis, "Will Decide Status of Worters Today," *NYT*, 5 Dec. 1928, 43; Grover Theis, "Calder Sustained in Worters Case," *NYT*, 6 Dec. 1928, 42; "Governors Uphold Refusal to Ratify Sale to Americans," *New York World*, 6 Dec. 1928, 12.

59. Pat Robinson, "Garden Control Fight On," n.p., n.d., LAC, HHOF fonds, vol. 4, New York Americans—Scrap-book, season 1928–29, 95. Calder's numbers put the Americans lease payment at 56 percent of the gate. Wong, *Lords of the Rinks*, 221n60.

60. Hardy, "Long before Orr," 267; W. E. Belcher, "Old North Station at Boston Replaced by a Modern Structure Including a Coliseum," *Engineering News-Record*, 28 Feb. 1929, 340. It is noteworthy that George Funk was responsible for the ice engineering plans for the Chicago, Detroit, Boston, and New York arenas. Joseph Gordon, "Sports' 'Growing Boy,'" *New York Morning Telegraph*, 30 Nov. 1928, 3.

61. The arena claimed $200,000 in damages. Foulds, *Boston's Ballparks and Arenas*, 81. The *New York Times* reported the Bruins 1929–30 gross gate much higher, at $575,000. Even with this figure, the profit margin was 35 percent. "Bruins' Six Drew $575,000, Made $200,600 Last Season," *NYT*, 4 July 1929, 13.

62. "Rickard's Body Lies in State in Garden as Thousands Mourn," *NYT*, 9 Jan. 1929, 1.

63. James S. Collins, "Almost the Naked Truth," *Washington Post*, 11 Jan. 1929, 15; "Sports in Chicago Failure Financially," *New York World*, 9 Dec. 1928, S1; Edward Burns, "Harmon, Ousted from Stadium, Tells Why," *CDT*, 20 Nov. 1929, 21; telegram from Norris to Calder, 5 Nov. 1928, cited in Wong, *Lords of the Rinks*, 134; "$750,000 Rink Seating 12,000 to Be Built for Black Hawks," *NYT*, 27 Dec. 1928, 24; "Loughran Bout Delayed," *NYT*, 24 Feb. 1929, 155; telegrams from Tobin to Calder, 22 Feb. 1929, cited in Wong, *Lords of the Rinks*, 134. On Bill Tobin, who was an Ottawa native and a former goalie for the Edmonton Eskimos of the WCHL, see Vass, *Chicago Black Hawks*, 21–23.

64. "Chicagoans May Acquire Hockey Team at Ottawa," *CDT*, 23 Jan. 1929, 15; Wong, *Lords of the Rinks*, 218n25; "Ottawa Club, Faced by Dwindling Receipts, Decides to Shift Hockey Franchise to U.S.," *NYT*, 25 Jan. 1929, 23; Ahearn to Calder, 13 Jan. 1929, cited in Wong, *Lords of the Rinks*, 126; Kitchen, *Win, Tie, or Wrangle*, 292–93; "Ottawa Club, Faced by Dwindling Receipts, Decides to Shift Hockey Franchise to U.S."

65. Calder to McLaughlin, 17 Jan. 1929; and McLaughlin to Calder, 21 Jan. 1929, quoted in Wong, *Lords of the Rinks*, 124–25.

66. "President Calder Is Anxious to See Capital Pro Team," *Ottawa Journal*, 18 Feb. 1929, 1, 14; "Ottawa Six Sold; To Stay in City," *NYT*, 19 Feb. 1929, 32. See also Kitchen, *Win, Tie, or Wrangle*, 298–301.

67. [Fred] Burpee [president of the Auditorium Company, Ltd.] to Calder, 23 Apr. 1929, cited in Wong, *Lords of the Rinks*, 126; Kitchen, *Win, Tie, or Wrangle*, 301; Wong, *Lords of the Rinks*, 127, 218n30, 219n35. Calder characterized the Foran plan as a request for "preferential treatment." Calder to McLaughlin, 12 Sept. 1929, quoted in Wong, *Lords of the Rinks*, 126.

68. NHL Minutes, 10 Feb. 1930, cited in Wong, *Lords of the Rinks*, 127; "Four Hockey Games for Atlantic City," *NYT*, 7 Nov. 1929, 27; Wong, *Lords of the Rinks*, 126. For example, Ottawa netted only $4,654 against the Rangers at home on 8 February but $9,626 against the Rangers in Atlantic City the previous December. (My thanks to John Wong for details of Ottawa's game receipts.)

69. On switching players, see [Niven Busch Jr.], "Hockey," *New Yorker*, 22 Nov. 1930, 65; M. J. Rodden's *Kingston (ON) Whig-Standard* column of 10 May 1966; Whitney Tower, "Conversation Piece: Subject: Dick Irvin," *Sports Illustrated*, n.d., 30, 40–43; and Leslie Roberts, "The Most Dangerous Game in the World," *New McClure's* 62, no. 2 (1929): 20. For some observations on the attraction of violence for the New York audience, see Field, "Night at the Garden(s)," 82–83. There were also efforts to open up the game to press coverage. In May 1928, the governors decided all clubs must provide ten seats for press representatives, centrally located with a view of the entire rink and next to telegraph wires and telephones. Coleman, *Trail of the Stanley Cup*, 2:57.

70. Field, "Night at the Garden(s)," 60–61, 76, 81; Roberts, "The Most Dangerous Game in the World," 20; "Arthur Siegel, "Women Hockey Fans Show Enthusiasm More than Men in Opinion of Bruins' Owner," n.d., n.p., LAC, Hitchman fonds, vol. 4, Boston Hockey Club (the Bruins) Season 1930–31 scrapbook.

71. Charlie Querrie, "What Price Pro Hockey?," *Toronto Star Weekly*, 26 Jan. 1929, 23.

72. Kidd, *Struggle for Canadian Sport*, 205; A. Linde Fowler, "Building Processes of a Championship Hockey Team," [*Boston Transcript*], n.d., LAC, Hitchman fonds, vol. 3, Boston Hockey Club (the Bruins) Season 1929–30 scrapbook. Kidd previously espoused a preference for a contemporary all-Canadian league in Bruce Kidd and John Macfarlane, *The Death of Hockey*.

73. *MDS*, 24 July 1930, 11; Baz O'Meara, "The Passing Sports Show," *MDS*, 25 July 1930, 25; Elmer Ferguson, "Arena Dramas," [pt. 2], *Maclean's*, 1 July 1938, 26. There was also a greyhound connection between Rickard and Duggan, who promoted the International Greyhound Racing Association, which was formed in 1926 and survives as the National Greyhound Association to the present day. (At one point, the association's president was Al Capone.) "Tom Duggan Warned Not to Race at Chicago," *TDS*, 7 May 1930, 10; Riess, *City Games*, 192.

5. Becoming "the Big Thing"

1. "Tonight's the Night . . . ," *TG*, 12 Nov. 1931, 6. CFCA was owned by the *Toronto Daily Star*. As director of radio, Foster Hewitt arranged all the on-air advertising on a commission basis. Hewitt's father was W. A. Hewitt, the sports editor of the *Star*, an OHA executive of long standing, and the registrar-treasurer of the CAHA, who himself became the manager of all nonhockey events at Maple Leaf Gardens.

2. Charles Pasmore to Hector Charlesworth [of the Canadian Radio Broadcasting Commission], 13 Dec. 1932, LAC, RG41 (Canadian Broadcasting Corporation fonds) (hereafter CBC fonds), vol. 219, file 11-22-2-2 (pt. 1); *Historical Statistics of Canada*, table A1, "Estimated population of Canada, 1867 to 1977"; "GM Hockey Broadcasts Hang Up New High Marks in Quality and Coverage," *General Motors Hockey Broadcast News*, May 1934, 1, IOA. Newfoundland was not then part of Canada.

3. "GM Hockey Broadcasts," *General Motors Hockey Broadcast News*, 1; "That All Night Game," *General Motors Hockey Broadcast News*, 2. National broadcasts of baseball and football games were limited to playoff and all-star games until after the Second World War. Tygiel, *Past Time*, 68–73, 89; Rader, *Baseball*, 137; White, *Creating the National Pastime*, 218; Richard C. Crepeau, *Baseball: America's Diamond Mind*, 184–86; Coenen, *From Sandlots to the Super Bowl*, 100–101.

4. Clare Brunton, Ottawa Hockey Association, to Canadian Radio Broadcasting Commission (CRBC), 26 Oct. 1933. On the Senators and radio, see Kitchen, *Win, Tie, or Wrangle*, 246–47, 313–14.

5. The *Tribune* is cited in "Chicago Stadium"; Westbrook Pegler, "Harmon Opener Big Bust," *Los Angeles Times*, 30 Mar. 1929, 11. Contrary to the *Tribune* quotation, the stadium did have some obstructed views. Peter Daniel Ellsworth, "'The House That Conn Built': Why and How Maple Leaf Gardens Was Built and the Impact Its Construction Had on Toronto and Professional Hockey," 121.

6. "Harmon Seeks National League Hockey Berth," *CDT*, 16 Apr. 1929, 28; Wong, *Lords of the Rinks*, 134; "Black Hawks Secure a Home; To Play at Chicago Coliseum," *NYT*, 17 July 1929, 28; Edward Burns, "Harmon, Ousted from Stadium, Tells Why," *CDT*, 20 Nov. 1929, 21; Edward Burns, "Urge Sheldon Clark to Take Harmon's Job," *CDT*, 21 Nov. 1929, 23; Don Maxwell, "Maj. Southwick Accepts Ring Board Post," *CDT*, 4 Aug. 1929, A1.

7. When Baz O'Meara, who later became a *Montreal Star* sports reporter, went to Chicago to work for Harmon, James Norris told him he (Norris) was going to take control of the rink as Harmon was in "financial difficulties." Hearing this news and after deciding Harmon was "a bit of a gangster," O'Meara returned to Ottawa. Baz O'Meara to M. J. Rodden, n.d., QUA, Rodden fonds, Series I, vol. 1, Correspondence, Misc., n.d., file. On Norris, see David Cruise and Alison Griffiths, *Net Worth: Exploding the Myths of Pro Hockey*, 27–28, 30ff; Annual General Meeting Minutes, 18 Nov. 1898, and Committee Meeting Minutes, 6 Dec. 1898, LAC, MG28 I351 (Montreal Amateur Athletic Association fonds), vol. 6, Montreal Hockey Club Minute Book, Nov. 1893–Nov. 1901 file; and the 1897–1902 editions of *Lovell's Montreal Street Guide*. For a genealogy of the Norris family, see Alex W. Ormston, "The Children and Descendants of Captain James Norris, M. P. (1820–1891): A Genealogical Note" (unpublished ms., St. Catharines, ON, 2000).

8. Burns, "Urge Sheldon Clark to Take Harmon's Job"; Burns, "Harmon, Ousted from Stadium, Tells Why"; Westbrook Pegler, "Rich Group Now Courting," *Washington Post*, 26 Nov. 1929, 17; "Stadium Will Pick New Manager This Week," *CDT*, 11 Dec 1929, 25; "Stadium to Sue If Blackhawks Change Rinks," *CDT*, 10 Sept. 1932, 17. See also "Paddy Harmon Fired," *Los Angeles Times*, 20 Nov. 1929, A14.

9. Irene Castle, *Castles in the Air*, 232; "Majors Draft Six Players," *CSM*, 12 May 1930, 6. The opening of the hockey season became an annual social event.

10. Gene Curtis, "Only in Oklahoma: Tulsa Landmark Destroyed by Fire in '52," *Tulsa World*, 5 Sept. 2007; Wong, *Lords of the Rinks*, 137.

11. McLaughlin to Calder, 23 May 1930, cited in Wong, *Lords of the Rinks*, 137; "Buys Minneapolis Sextet," *NYT*, 24 May 1930, 18; Arch Ward, "In the Wake of the News," *CDT*, 23 May 1940, 25; "Hockey Body Grants Franchise in Chicago," *Washington Post*, 3 July 1930, 21. See also "Denies

Hockey Grant Violates Leagues' Pact," *CDT*, 3 July 1930, 17. On Shaughnessy, see "Shaughnessy Quits as Pilot of Blackhawks," *CDT*, 14 Jan. 1930, 21.

12. "Hockey Moguls Decided A.A. Is Outlaw League," *CDT*, 19 Oct. 1930, A4; *Chicago Herald Examiner*, 19 Oct. 1930, 5, quoted in Wong, *Lords of the Rinks*, 138.

13. "Blackhawks Shift Training Site to Chicago," *CDT*, 21 Oct. 1930, 19. See also "American Hockey League Heads Meet Here Monday," *CDT*, 7 Feb. 1931, 20. NB: This AHL has no relation to the later successor to the Can-Am and IHL.

14. "Shamrock Head Answers Threat to Bar Brydson," *CDT*, 7 Nov. 1930, 35; McLaughlin to Calder, 12 Jan. 1931, quoted in Wong, *Lords of the Rinks*, 139. Shaughnessy picked up Brydson after his salary was not paid by the London IHL club, the same tactic McLaughlin had used on Livingstone, and Shaughnessy characterized it as "Calder's own rule." "Shamrock Head Answers Threat to Bar Brydson."

15. "Schedule Adopted by Hockey League," *NYT*, 19 Oct. 1930, 155.

16. "Leonard Forms Ice Loop," *NYT*, 30 Dec. 1929, 26; Frederick Edwards, "Magnates under the Microscope," *Maclean's*, 1 Jan. 1932, 32; All Officers Re-elected," *Saskatoon Star-Phoenix*, 5 May 1930, 14; "Quakers Expect Capacity Crowd," *NYT*, 11 Nov. 1930, 33.

17. Kitchen, *Win, Tie, or Wrangle*, 304, 306–7; Minutes of Meeting of Board of Directors, 7 May 1930, QUA, Ottawa Hockey Association Limited fonds; Ahearn to Calder, 19 Apr. 1930, cited in Wong, *Lords of the Rinks*, 128. Clancy cost $35,000 cash plus two players, Art Smith and Eric Pettinger, valued at $15,000. "Huge Sum Paves Way for Big Hockey Deal," *CSM*, 11 Oct. 1930, 4. Over the winter of 1931, further sales of players were discouraged by the other governors. Wong, *Lords of the Rinks*, 129.

18. Ahearn to Calder, 17 Mar. 1931, quoted in Wong, *Lords of the Rinks*, 219–20n47; "Ottawa Hockey Move to Chicago Rink Is Defeated," *CDT*, 5 Mar. 1931, 23; telegram from Calder to McLaughlin, 15 Sept. [1931], cited in Wong, *Lords of the Rinks*, 130. Wong suggests that Harmon was part of the Norris-Shaughnessy group as well, but Harmon had died the year before. Wong, *Lords of the Rinks*, 129; "Paddy Harmon Dies in Auto Accident," *MG*, 23 July 1930, 17.

19. Kitchen, *Win, Tie, or Wrangle,* 309; Wong, *Lords of the Rinks*, 219n46; Coleman, *Trail of the Stanley Cup*, 2:116; "Two Sextets Out of Hockey League," *NYT*, 27 Sept. 1931, S2; NHL Minutes, 26 Sept. 1931, cited in Wong, *Lords of the Rinks*, 130; "Get Hockey Stars of 2 League Clubs," *NYT*, 28 Sept. 1931, 25; "Hockey Loop Drops Ottawa and Quakers," *CDT*, 27 Sept. 1931, A2; Ottawa Hockey Association Minutes, 26 Oct. 1931, cited in Kitchen, *Win, Tie, or Wrangle*, 309.

20. "Hockey Loop Drops Ottawa and Quakers," *CDT*, 27 Sept. 1931, A2. It was also predicted that the resulting player surplus might produce a 10 percent cut in salaries.

21. Selke with Green, *Behind the Cheering*, 79. The Maple Leafs had the exclusive right to play professional hockey in the Arena Gardens, and all its games had to be played there. The Arena Gardens was to get 30 percent of the gross receipts (less amusement tax) up to eighty thousand dollars and 35 percent above and controlled all ticket sales and refreshment sales. Agreement between Arena Gardens, St. Patrick's Professional Hockey Club, and Toronto Maple Leafs Hockey Club, dated 23 July 1927, AO, F223-3-1-3.

22. Scott Young, *Hello Canada! The Life and Times of Foster Hewitt*, 47. See also Scott Young, *The Boys of Saturday Night: Inside Hockey Night in Canada*, chap. 4. When the new Gardens came into being, Smythe obtained sponsorship and started charging a modest fee.

23. Maple Leaf Gardens Prospectus, 15 May 1931, AO, F223-3-1-53.

24. Selke with Green, *Behind the Cheering*, 87; Smythe and Young, *Conn Smythe*, 105; Selke with Green, *Behind the Cheering*, 100. See also Smythe to Howie Meeker, 13 Sept. 1957, AO, F223-3-1-25. The workers received 10 percent of their pay in stock. In 1967 Smythe estimated there were between eighty and one hundred original shareholders left, implying several were workmen. Smythe to Dorothy Bedggood, 11 Sept. 1967, AO, F223-2-6-3.

25. Selke with Green, *Behind the Cheering*, 89; "At the Opening of the Gardens," *Toronto Telegram*, 13 Nov. 1931, 26; Russell David Field, "Passive Participation: The Selling of Spectacle and the Construction of Maple Leaf Gardens, 1931," 44. For a rundown of the other sites Smythe considered, see Ellsworth, "'House That Conn Built,'" 84. On the spectator experience at Maple Leaf Gardens, see Field, "Night at the Garden(s)."

26. "$3,000,000 Arena to Be Built in Montreal for Canadiens," *NYT*, 19 Dec. 1931, 25. The Leafs were able to widen the ticket price scale significantly from Mutual Street, but while season tickets sales were said to be brisk, shareholders were still being sought in October—"Add to your hockey enthusiasm the thrill of profitable investment" (Bert Perry, "Detours through the Sport Maze," *TG*, 15 Oct. 1931, 7; display ad in *TG*, 15 Oct. 1931, 6).

27. Automobile sales in 1931 were a quarter what they were two years earlier, which seriously hurt the Detroit economy. On Ottawa's Depression experience, see Kitchen, *Win, Tie or Wrangle*, 304. Gate receipt percentage losses in 1931–32 were: Chicago (55 percent), Boston (45 percent), Americans (39 percent), Detroit (28 percent), Rangers (27 percent), Maroons (26 percent), and Canadiens (11 percent). Over the same period, Toronto actually gained 30 percent, but this figure does not account for the capacity of the new Gardens and after the first two Gardens seasons, 1931–32 and 1932–33, the gates fell 27 percent. See the appendix.

28. "Hockey Loop Drops Ottawa and Quakers," *CDT*, 27 Sept. 1931, A2; "Campaign in National Hockey League Will Get Under Way on Nov. 12," *NYT*, 20 Oct. 1931, 37.

29. Wong, *Lords of the Rinks*, 140; "Shamrocks Beat Buffalo," *CDT* 27 Nov. 1931, 27; "Plan Charity Game," *CDT* 27 Nov. 1931, 27; Arch Ward, "Talking It Over," *CDT*, 6 Feb. 1932, 17. The Black Hawks attendance number is from Edward Burns, "Blackhawks Tie, 1 to 1, on Coliseum Rink," *CDT*, 14 Nov. 1932, 23.

30. "Trustees Accept American League Cup Challenge," *CDT*, 4 Feb. 1932, 21; Ward, "Talking It Over"; "Trustees Accept American League Cup Challenge"; "Hockey Rulers Erase Ban on a Few 'Outlaws,'" *CDT*, 2 Feb. 1932, 25; "Stop! Look! Listen!," *TDS*, 9 Feb. 1932, 8; Foran to Calder, 19 Mar. 1932, cited in Wong, *Lords of the Rinks*, 224n45; Kerr N. Petrie, "Stanley Cup Trustees Rule Out American League Bid This Year," *NYHT*, 26 Mar. 1932, 16. The AHA had tried to file a challenge at the end of the previous season, and also in 1927, but in both cases it was too late to arrange a series. "Hawks Lose in Cup Series but Have Best Year," *CDT*, 27 Dec. 1931, A4; "Duluth Challenge Not to Be Accepted," *CSM*, 8 Apr. 1927, 8.

31. Holzman and Nieforth, *Deceptions and Doublecross,* 316; McLaughlin to Calder, 22 Mar. 1932, quoted in Wong, *Lords of the Rinks,* 141. Soon after the opening of the St. Louis Arena in September 1929, Ben Brinkman of the National Exhibition Company, the arena operators, announced his intention to form an NHL club. Hammond reportedly assured him that one would be forthcoming for a $50,000 fee. "St. Louis Plans to Enter Hockey League in 1930," *CDT,* 23 Dec. 1929, 24. For details on the arena, which could seat twenty-one thousand, see Louis La Coss, "Fate of Mongoose Agitates St. Louis," *NYT,* 29 Sept. 1929, E2.

32. Ahearn to Calder, 2 Feb. 1932, quoted in Wong, *Lords of the Rinks,* 130.

33. Wong, *Lords of the Rinks,* 141–42; "Hockey Teams Face Drastic Economies," *NYT,* 11 May 1932, 24; "Salary Limit in Ice Hockey," *CSM,* 11 May 1932, 10. The Detroit Hockey Club and Angie Scovel had defaulted on the mortgage in April. US National Park Service, "Olympia Arena," 5. In his biography, Conn Smythe recalled that the Detroit club "went bust" right after he sold it to Jimmy Herberts for $12,500, which would have been in April 1928. If dated correctly, Detroit's financial problems began even before the Depression set in, only two short years after starting up. Smythe and Young, *Conn Smythe,* 94–95.

34. Ward, "Talking It Over"; "Hockey Teams Face Drastic Economies," *NYT,* 11 May 1924, 24; "Salary Limit in Ice Hockey." The penalty for violating the cap was five times the amount overpaid for the club and ten times the amount overpaid to a player. NHL Minutes, 10 May 1932, cited in Wong, *Lords of the Rinks,* 131. Dipping into the league equity account would have amounted to $4,500 per club. Wong, *Lords of the Rinks,* 131.

35. Ahearn to Calder, 29 May 1932, cited in Wong, *Lords of the Rinks,* 131; "You and Ahearn Better Have a Talk, Mr. Norris," *CDT,* 29 May 1932, A2.

36. Kitchen, *Win, Tie, or Wrangle,* 312–13; Ahearn to Calder, 3 Aug. 1932, quoted in Wong, *Lords of the Rinks,* 131; Minutes of Meetings of Board of Directors, 29 June and 27 Oct. 1932, QUA, Ottawa Hockey Association Limited fonds.

37. "Falcons Not Sold," *CSM,* 11 Aug. 1932, 9; Lee Macdonnell, "Detroit Buys Goalie Roach from N.Y.," *Detroit Times,* 6 Oct. 1932, quoted in Holzman and Nieforth, *Deceptions and Doublecross,* 327. On Norris's involvement, see "Shamrocks Join N.L.; Will Move to Detroit Rink," *CDT,* 26 Aug. 1932, 17; Hughes to Calder, 16 July 1932, cited in Wong, *Lords of the Rinks,* 142. Different retrospective sources name price tags from $250,000 to $2.6 million. Paul Chandler, "Fair Game," *Detroit News,* 5 Dec. 1952; Neil Milbert, "Arthur Wirtz—Gone but Not Forgotten," *Hockey News,* 1 Sept. 1983, 3; "Arthur Wirtz Dead at 82," *Chicago Sun-Times,* 22 July 1983, HHFM, Arthur M. Wirtz file. Wirtz later recalled the Olympia deal taking place in 1931 and that he received 40 percent of the shares, James Norris 45 percent, and the public 15 percent. David Condon, "An Insight into Hall of Famer Arthur Wirtz," *CDT,* [reprinted in *HN,* Aug. 1971, 6]. On the naming of the club, see Jack Adams with Trent Frayne, "The High Spots of a Lifetime with the Red Wings," 58.

38. "Pittsburgh and Senators Back," *CSM,* 23 Aug. 1932, 4; "Shamrocks Join N. L.; Will Move to Detroit Rink." For a review of some of the Detroit reports on the negotiations, see Holzman and Nieforth, *Deceptions and Doublecross,* 320–25.

39. Calder to Grant, 30 Aug. 1932, cited in Wong, *Lords of the Rinks*, 142; "Dispute Is Ended by Hockey Leagues," *NYT*, 3 Sept. 1932, 8. The AHA was reduced to a midwestern agglomeration of Kansas City, St. Louis, Minneapolis, St. Paul, and Duluth (Tulsa dropped out before the season started, citing financial difficulties).

40. Coleman, *Trail of the Stanley Cup*, 2:195; "Hockey Holdouts Face Suspension," *NYT*, 1 Nov. 1932, 28; John H. Lewy, "Holdouts See Square Deal in New Ice Ruling," *Brooklyn Times-Union*, [3 Nov. 1932], Madison Square Garden Scrapbook #48 (Season 1932–33), 14; "Seibert Faces Suspension," *NYT*, 12 Nov. 1932, 13; Joseph C. Nichols, "Rangers Conquer Toronto Sextet," *NYT*, 21 Nov. 1932, 25; Joseph C. Nichols, "10,000 See Rangers Play 1–1 Deadlock," *NYT*, 25 Nov. 1932, 25. In 1934 the salary cap was reduced to $62,500 and $7,000 per player. "Free Penalty Shot Voted in Hockey," *NYT*, 23 Sept. 1934, S10.

41. Memorandum of Agreement, Glenbow Museum and Archives, Calgary Exhibition and Stampede Fonds, series 10, file M–2160–197. The trend to centralization of control and convergence of procedures is evident in the correspondence of WCHL president E. L. Richardson, who asked Calder to act as go-between with the other leagues on issues of tampering, reserve lists, and the like.

42. Ward, "Talking It Over." McLaughlin claimed the lease was void since the stadium had not given the club the dates to which it was entitled. "Stadium to Sue If Blackhawks Change Rinks," *CDT*, 10 Sept. 1932, 17.

43. "Seven U.S. Born Stars on Team," *CSM*, 5 Nov. 1932, 6; "Stadium to File Suit for $150,000 against Hawks," *CDT*, 14 Nov. 1932, 23; "Delay Stadium Suit against Blackhawks," *CDT*, 15 Nov. 1932, 21; "Hawks Try Again Tonight for 1st Win; Play Leafs," *CDT*, 17 Nov. 1932, 21. To boost attendance, Tobin announced the club would be reducing ticket prices across the board from the bottom box seats (down to $2.50 from $3) to the top balcony seats (now 55¢, tax included). "Hockey Club to Quit Coliseum for West Side," *CDT*, 30 Nov. 1932, 17.

44. "M'Laughlin Off Hockey League Ruling Board," *CDT*, 6 Nov. 1932, A4; "Seven U.S. Born Stars on Team," *CSM*, 5 Nov. 1932, 6. Gorman had left the Americans in 1929 and returned to horse racing as the assistant general manager of the Agua Caliente horse-racing track in Mexico and as secretary of the Quebec Jockey Club. To acknowledge Gorman's status, he was made "managing director," with Tobin handling the business aspects. Edward Burns, "Gorman Replaces Iverson as Hawks' Manager," *CDT*, 14 Jan. 1933, 23.

45. "National Hockey League Rejects Proposal to Eliminate Stalling from Defensive Play," *NYT*, 2 Feb. 1932, 33; Frank (Buck) O'Neill, "Hockey Chief Asks Changes in Ice Rules," n.p., ca. Feb. 1932, LAC, and Jim Hurley, "Hockey Dispute Places Calder in the Middle," *NYDM*, n.d., both in HOF fonds, vol. 7, New York Americans—Scrap-book, season 1931–32, 56.

46. "Shore Fined $100 and Given Warning," *TG*, 28 Jan. 1933, 9; A. Linde Fowler, [*Boston Transcript*], n.d., in LAC, MG30 C89, Fred Lionel Hitchman fonds, vol. 7, Boston Hockey Club (the Bruins) Season 1933–34 scrapbook.

47. "Shore Fined $100 and Given Warning"; "Unfair, Says President Adams," *TG*, 28 Jan. 1933, 9; "Threatens to Withdraw Team," *NYT*, 5 Feb. 1933, S5; John Kieran, "Sports of the Times," *NYT*, 27

Feb. 1933, 20; "Adams Avoids 'Gag' Rule," *CSM*, 13 Feb. 1933, 8. See also Stanley Woodward, "Hockey Here and There," *NYHT*, 15 Feb. 1933, 20. Duncan had represented Adams in litigation with Duggan, the NHL, and the Boston Arena. Other than as protest, Adams's intent may have been to have the lawyer evaluate Calder's constitutional judgments. "Hockey Notes," *CSM*, 18 Feb. 1933, 4.

48. "Take Away Powers of Hockey Head," *CDT*, 14 May 1933, A1; Barrette, *Léo Dandurand, Sportsman*, 168–69; "New Hockey Post to Frank Patrick," *NYT*, 14 May 1933, S6. It was probably in reference to these events that Elmer Ferguson wrote that Dandurand "undertook a personal crusade" and flew to every city in the league to enlist support for Calder. Elmer Ferguson, "The Last of Sports' Three Musketeers," *MDS*, 27 June 1964, 2:16.

49. "Hockey Rules Revised," *NYT*, 5 Dec. 1933, 34; "Hockey League to Try New Referee System, Officials Dividing Jurisdiction in Rink," *NYT*, 31 Oct. 1933, 26. Patrick also proposed a preseason training school for referees and numbering of their sweaters. "Will Put Hockey Referees through Their Paces," *Montreal Standard*, n.d., in LAC, Hitchman fonds, vol. 7, Boston Hockey Club (the Bruins) Season 1933–34 scrapbook.

50. "$27,969 in Bailey Fund," *NYT*, 13 Mar. 1934, 29.

51. "Patrick to Quit as Hockey League Head; Canadiens Are Not Anxious to Sell Morenz," *NYT*, 4 Apr. 1934, 27; "Observations of the Night by the *News*' Sports Staff," [*Detroit News*], n.d., LAC, Gorman fonds, vol. 5, Scrapbook. On Patrick's time with the Bruins and a later brief wartime stint with the Canadiens, see Whitehead, *Patricks*, 204–5, 210–12, 226–27.

52. "Pittsburgh and Senators Back," *CSM* 23 Aug. 1932, 4; "Nine Hockey Teams in National League," *NYT*, 2 Oct. 1932, S6; James P. Dawson, "M'larnin Is Victor by Knockout in 6th," *NYT*, 8 Oct. 1932, 20; Meeting of Board of Directors, 23 Mar. 1933, QUA, Ottawa Hockey Association, Ltd., fonds. The Ottawa debt figure presumably excluded the much larger debt to Ahearn himself.

53. "Expect Court to O.K. Norris Stadium Plan," *CDT*, 3 Feb. 1935, B3; "Norris Group Given Control of Stadium," *CDT*, 26 Feb. 1935, 17. Norris officially took charge on 13 Mar. 1935. "Norris Gets Chicago Stadium," *CSM*, 14 Mar. 1935, 8.

54. "Rickard's Body Lies in State in Garden as Thousands Mourn," *NYT*, 9 Jan. 1929, 35; "Sports in Garden Topped by Hockey," *NYT*, 7 Apr. 1934, 10; Westbrook Pegler, "Assault Title Usurped by Hockey," *Washington Post*, 30 Mar. 1930, M17; John Kieran, "Sports of the Times," *NYT*, 5 Dec. 1932, 24. For more on MSG financials, see Annual Reports to Stockholders, Madison Square Garden Corporation, Harvard Business School, Baker Library (hereafter MSG Annual Reports); "Madison Square Garden," *Fortune*, Nov. 1935; Stanley Woodward, "Frozen Ears Convinced Hammond Answer to Tex Rickard's Dream Lay in Hockey for the New Garden," *NYHT*, ca. Feb. 1933, LAC, HOF fonds, vol. 7, New York Americans—Scrap-book, season 1931–32, 101.

55. James A. Burchard, "Hockey Tickets Slash Clicks—Garden Attendance Rises 28 Per Cent," *New York World-Telegram*, 12 Jan. 1933, 22. Hammond aspired to become president of the Garden after Rickard's death in 1929, but Richard Hoyt installed Carey instead. Pat Robinson, "Bush Admits Dwyer Contract One-Sided," n.p., ca. 1929, LAC, HOF fonds, vol. 4, New York Americans—Scrapbook, season 1928–29, 96. Hammond later denied hockey prices were the issue. "Hammond's Group Acquires Garden," *NYT*, 3 May 1934, 23. The Bruins also reduced their ticket prices at the same time.

"Reduction in Hockey Prices Proves to Be Step in the Right Direction," n.p., 25 Dec. 1932, Madison Square Garden Scrapbook #48 (Season 1932–33), 92. Kilpatrick had been a Garden director for several years. His appointment as vice president in April 1933 suggests he was being groomed for the top post. "Kilpatrick Named for Garden Post," *NYT*, 19 Apr. 1933, 21. Kilpatrick's father was a founder of the New York Athletic Club, and his mother was from Ontario. "For God, Country, Yale, and Garden," *New Yorker*, 28 Jan. 1956, 35.

56. "Expect Court to O.K. Norris Stadium Plan"; "Hammond's Group Acquires Garden"; "Col. Hammond Sues in Garden Dispute," *NYT*, 20 Sept. 1935, 22; "Hammond Regains Garden's Control," *NYT*, 9 May 1934, 29; "B&M May Take Possession of Boston Garden," *Hartford Courant*, 9 July 1934, 11; "Home Control Sought for the Boston Garden," *NYT*, 10 July 1934, 28. Hoyt and his associates held their stock through Hayden, Stone & Co., a New York brokerage firm. Hoyt's motivation for selling is unclear, although he cannot have been happy with the financial performance of the Garden, even after Carey was replaced.

57. MSG Annual Reports, 1935, 1936; "Garden Has Profit of $179,568 in Year," *NYT*, 7 Aug. 1935, 33; "Col. Hammond Sues in Garden Dispute"; "Dispute at Garden Is Put to a Vote," *NYT*, 25 Sept. 1935, 19; "Kilpatrick Wins Garden Control," *NYT*, 28 Sept. 1935, 13; "Madison Square Garden Fight for Control Ends as Brokers Acquire Hammond Stock," *NYT*, 5 Mar. 1936, 33. See also "Garden Management Charged with Waste," *NYT*, 19 Aug. 1935, 18; "Garden Factions Active," *NYT*, 21 Aug. 1935, 17; "Col. Hammond Sues in Garden Dispute"; "Hammond Drops Garden Vote Suit," *NYT*, 24 Sept. 1935, 7. A Wirtz obituary stated Norris and Wirtz started buying Garden stock "shortly after" the acquisition of Chicago Stadium, and by the end of the Second World War had a controlling 40 percent interest. "Arthur Wirtz Dead at 82."

58. "Free Penalty Shot Voted in Hockey," *NYT*, 23 Sept. 1934, S10; John Kieran, "Sports of the Times," *NYT*, 15 Nov. 1934, 28; Alfred Dayton, "Hockey League Averts Break," *New York Sun*, 24 Sept. 1934, 28; Al Copland, "Outlaw Ice League Looms in Rent War," n.p., n.d., LAC, HOF fonds, vol. 10, New York Americans—Scrap-book, season 1934–35, 2. The Boston Garden wanted a one-thousand-dollar profit for each of the twenty-four Bruins home games. "Sporting around the Hub," *CSM*, 21 Sept. 1934, 4.

59. Woodward implied that the club had never made money and had "failed by a whisker to break even" in 1929. Appropriately, his lede was: "What's keeping Bill Dwyer in hockey?" Stanley Woodward, "Hockey—Here and There," *NYHT*, n.d., LAC, HOF fonds, vol. 7, New York Americans—Scrap-book, season 1931–32, 93. The new forty-sixty split was reported as a change from the previous fifty-fifty split, although this figure does not correspond with the split sixty-five to thirty-five given to Woodward. "Americans Ask Aid of League in Garden Contract Quarrel," n.p., n.d., LAC, HOF fonds, vol. 10, New York Americans—Scrap-book, season 1934–35, 2.

60. "Americans Ask Aid of League in Garden Contract Quarrel," 2; "Maroons Defeat Eagles, 2 to 1, in Extra Period," *CDT*, 14 Nov. 1934, 23; Jim Hurley, "Hammond, Dwyer Meet Today on Amerks' Contract," *NYDM*, ca. Nov. 1934, LAC, HOF fonds, vol. 10, New York Americans—Scrap-book, season 1934–35, 23; George Kenney, "Ice War Menaces Garden Franchise," n.p., n.d., LAC, HOF fonds, vol. 10, New York Americans—Scrap-book, season 1934–35, 2.

61. Jimmy Powers, "Truce in Hockey War as A's, Leafs Line Up for Garden's Opener," *New York Daily News*, 15 Nov. 1935, LAC, HHOF fonds, vol. 10, New York Americans—Scrap-book, season 1934–35, 4.

62. Copland, "Outlaw Ice League Looms in Rent War," 2; Jimmy Powers, "League Will Probe 'Garden Ice Trust,'" *New York Daily News*, ca. 16 Nov. 1935, LAC, HHOF fonds, vol. 10, New York Americans—Scrap-book, season 1934–35, 4; "Blackhawks Meet Maroon Six Tonight," *CDT*, 10 Jan. 1935, 19. The actual numbers reported before the deal was confirmed were 67 percent [*sic*] for the Americans and 32.5 percent for the Garden. Bill Boni, "Fans Can Juggle Figures as Rangers, A's Flip Each Other," *New York Post*, 15 Jan. 1935, 18. The Garden annual report for 1935 notes that "final adjustment of New York Hockey Club claims was $31,588.76."

63. "Report New York Americans in a 'State of Revolt,'" *CDT*, 14 Mar. 1935, 21; "Team and Owner Deny Reports of Hocky [*sic*] Strike," *CDT*, 15 Mar. 1935, 32; Jack Miley, "Hammond, Norris May Head Amerks!," *New York Daily News*, 19 Nov. 1935, 50.

64. "Short Shots on Sport by Ed Baker," *OC*, n.d., LAC, Gorman, fonds, vol. 5, Scrapbook; "Pittsburgh Gets Hockey League Franchise; Arena Seating 16,000 Will Be Constructed," *NYT*, 15 June 1934, 30. On the St. Louis Eagles, see Kitchen, *Win, Tie, or Wrangle*, chap. 16.

65. "League Hockey Race Will Start Tonight," *NYT*, 8 Nov. 1934, 32; "Blackhawks Meet Maroon Six Tonight"; *NYT*, 11 Jan. 1935, 31; "Finnegan of Eagles Sold to Toronto for $10,000," *NYT*, 14 Feb. 1935, 29. The deficit number is from Elmer Ferguson, "Red-Ink Hockey," *Maclean's*, 15 Nov. 1938, 33.

66. "St. Louis Drops from National Hockey League," *NYT*, 16 Oct. 1935, 32. The *Times* noted the payment for player rights was the first time the league had ever taken such action (ibid.).

67. "Conacher, Patrick, Ross Mentioned for 'Chi' Job," *TDS*, 21 Apr. 1934, 16; "Gorman, Manager of Hawks, Resigns," *NYT*, 21 Apr. 1934, 21. The fact that Strachan left the club without any sale being announced seems to confirm that the CAC had owned the club from the beginning and that Strachan had no significant stake. According to Barrette, Strachan later tried to buy the Canadiens (*Léo Dandurand, Sportsman*, 177).

68. Barrette, *Léo Dandurand, Sportsman*, 178; "St. Louis Takes Ottawa's Place in Hocky [*sic*] League," *CDT*, 13 May 1934, A7; "Blackhawks Get Morenz in Deal with Canadians," *CDT*, 4 Oct. 1934, 19. Barrette wrote that Cattarinich and Dandurand could have sustained losses indefinitely given their other interests, but wanted a better deal from the Forum as well as more favorable market conditions (*Léo Dandurand, Sportsman*, 179).

69. "Canadiens' Sale Decision Today," *NYT*, 10 Jan. 1935, 25; "Blackhawks Meet Maroon Six Tonight"; "Call Off Deal for Canadien Hocky [*sic*] Sextet," *CDT*, 11 Jan. 1935, 26; "Canadiens May Be Shifted to Cleveland Rink," *CDT*, 29 Mar. 1935, 22. On O'Hara's racing interests, see Riess, *City Games*, 189–90. See also "Al Sutphin Seeks National League Franchise," *Cleveland Plain Dealer*, 11 Jan. 1935, 18; and "Report Franchise of Montreal Canadiens to be Transferred to Cleveland," *Cleveland Plain Dealer*, 5 Apr. 1935, 23.

70. "Hockey Leagues to Continue to Play without Combining," *CSM*, 11 May 1935, 12; "Canadiens to Renew Lease on Forum," *NYT*, 12 May 1935, S10; "Establishment of National League Team

in Cleveland Abandoned," *Cleveland Plain Dealer*, 12 May 1935, B1; *La Presse*, 18 Sept. 1935, 21; Charles Mayer, "Il y a 24 ans," unpublished ms., LAC, Mayer fonds, vol. 17, Les Canadiens de Montréal 1928–68 file; Charles Mayer, "La situation du hockey professionnel à Montréal," *PJ*, 8 Dec. 1935, 27. Savard had apparently tried to buy the Canadiens as early as 1931. Brown, *Baseball's Fabulous Montreal Royals*, 35; Barrette, *Léo Dandurand, Sportsman*, 177. In 1960 Dandurand admitted it was the CAC that had bought the company. Léo Dandurand, "Story behind Fabulous Canucks Recalls How NHL Got Its Start," *MDS*, 14 Jan. 1960, 61.

71. George M. R. Holmes, "By-Plays," *CSM*, 25 Sept. 1934, 9.

72. In 1935 James Norris revealed that he had never been an official or even stockholder of the Shamrock Club, but that the club had owed him money. Verbatim Minutes of NHL Annual Meeting [and Board of Governors Meeting], 11 May 1935, 39, HHFM.

73. "Canadiens to Renew Lease on Forum"; Verbatim Minutes, 11 May 1935, 33; National Hockey League Constitution [adopted 25 Sept. 1926], 4, AO, F223-7-0-16. Some authors have even maintained that Charles Adams of the Bruins was also in thrall to Norris, who ostensibly underwrote some mortgages that "Adams couldn't pay in the early years of the Depression" (Cruise and Griffiths, *Net Worth*, 40). Since the Boston Garden was owned by the Boston & Maine Railroad, it is highly unlikely there was any mortgage at all, and there is no evidence suggesting that Adams was suffering financially in the 1930s. Indeed, he was doing well: his Bruins made money consistently in the decade, he had been able to offer to buy the Garden, he had bailed out the NL Boston Braves, and he made a large investment in a new racetrack, Suffolk Downs. More than likely, Adams has been confused here with Dwyer, and the "mortgages" were the loans to the New York club. See also Kidd, *Struggle for Canadian Sport*, 187.

74. For the text of the league agreement, see Wong, *Lords of the Rinks*, 170.

75. Verbatim Minutes of NHL Annual Meeting, 11 May 1935, 19, HHFM.

76. Barry Broadfoot, *Ten Lost Years, 1929–1939: Memories of Canadians Who Survived the Depression*, 248.

6. Integrating the Amateurs

1. "Le développement du hockey dû au professionnalisme," *PJ*, 10 Feb. 1935, 32; Charles Mayer, "D'un but à l'autre . . . ," *PJ*, 7 Feb. 1943, 52. (All *Le Petit Journal* quotations have been translated from the French.) *Hockey*—later subtitled "News and Picture Service" for "The World's Fastest Game"— seems to have made its debut in the 1934–35 season.

2. "Le développement." Calder did not mention that during his time as a journalist, he had been one of those individuals sowing suspicion, raising "considerable hell" about paid amateurs. Verbatim Minutes of NHL Annual Meeting, 11 May 1935, HHFM, 19.

3. Ibid. Howie Morenz, Aurel Joliat, Russ Blinco, and Nels Stewart were star players.

4. Edwards answered his question with a yes and a no. Of the sixty-five players of the NHA and PCHA of the 1912–13 season, sixteen were still involved in the business end of the game, mostly as managers, including Art Ross, Lester Patrick, and Odie Cleghorn. Frederick Edwards, "Is Pro-Hockey a Career?," *Maclean's*, 1 Jan. 1928, 9.

380 NOTES TO PAGES 242–47

5. Verbatim Minutes of NHL Annual Meeting, 12 May 1944, 17; Don O'Hanley, "Lester Patrick's 3-R's: Rovers–Ramblers–Rangers," n.d., NYRC; John Kieran, "Sports of the Times," *NYT*, 20 Jan. 1933, 24. The Rangers system also included players in Cleveland, which functioned as a Rangers "school" and was coached by former Rangers star Bill Cook. George E. Timpson, "The Sports Horizon," *CSM*, 21 Jan. 1938, 13. It was a question of timing: Patrick noted that by age twenty-one or twenty-two, Canadian players "don't care anymore" whom they play for.

6. By 1934 the Cubs were known as the Boston Bruin Cubs. The Olympics were sold in 1936 and moved to Pittsburgh in the new IAHL. "Minor Hockey Loops in New Combination," *NYT*, 5 Oct. 1936, 30. Dwyer seems to have sold his interest in New Haven to Nathan Podoloff sometime in the early 1930s, although the Eagles remained an Americans farm club until at least 1936. "Hockey Governors Meet," *NYT*, 18 Apr. 1932, 21.

7. James A. Burchard, "Passing the Puck," [*New York World-Telegram*], n.d., LAC, HHOF Fonds, vol. 9, New York Americans Scrapbook, 1933–34, 9; H. H. Roxborough, "The Maple Leafs Forever," *Maclean's*, 15 Nov. 1932, 48. The Gardens' support of the amateur Marlies came under scrutiny in a 1933 wrongful-dismissal lawsuit filed by Andrew B. Taylor, the first manager of the Gardens. "'Shamateur,' Says Judge," *Border Cities Star* (Windsor, ON), 21 June 1933, 6.

8. Lloyd McGowan, "Brown Recalls 'Tourist' Era in Hockey," *Montreal Standard*, 19 Mar. 1966, 20; Charles Mayer, "La situation du hockey professionnel à Montréal," *PJ*, 8 Dec. 1935, 27.

9. "U.S. Association May Seek Peace," *TG*, 21 Oct. 1925, 18. Athletes who competed against professionals or under false names were also ineligible for amateur status. *CAHA Official Hockey Rules, 1927, Amended to November 1926*, LAC, CAHA fonds, vol. 80. See also *CAHA Official Hockey Rules, 1929, Amended to March 1928*, LAC, CAHA fonds, vol. 80.

10. Hewitt to Calder, 30 June 1930, quoted in Wong, *Lords of the Rinks*, 145. There had also been a meeting of CAHA with Smythe, Calder, and Dandurand "some months ago" ("Hockey Officials to Aid Amateurs," *NYT*, 29 Mar. 1929, 31).

11. Frederick Edwards, "Bootleg Amateurs," *Maclean's*, 1 Nov. 1930, 48–49; H. H. Roxborough, "That Bootleg Bogey," *Maclean's*, 1 Dec. 1930, 59. The next year the MAAA players went professional with the Maroons (Kidd, *Struggle for Canadian Sport*, 80).

12. *CAHA Hockey Rules Explained 1932, Revised to 17 October 1931* and *CAHA Official Hockey Rules, 1933, Amended to August 1932*, LAC, CAHA fonds, vol. 80.

13. D. Leo Dolan, "High Cost Hockey," *Maclean's*, 1 Mar. 1932, 21; Minutes of 45th Annual Meeting of AAUC, 1932, 95–100, and Minutes of 45th Annual Meeting [of AAUC], 1932, 95–100, LAC, MG28 I150 (Amateur Athletic Union of Canada fonds), vol. 20, AAUC Minutes, 1910–36; Kidd, *Struggle for Canadian Sport*, 80–81. The Saskatchewan motion was sent to a committee for discussion, and Wong notes this proposed amendment first appeared at the 1928 meeting (*Lords of the Rinks*, 144).

14. *CAHA Official Hockey Rules, 1934* [amended to Aug. 1933], and Minutes of the 18th Annual Meeting of the Canadian Amateur Hockey Association, 1935, 6, 7, LAC, CAHA fonds, vol. 80.

15. "A Busy Season in Store," *Times* (London), 25 Sept. 1935, 5; Minutes of 19th Annual Meeting of CAHA, 1936, LAC, CAHA fonds, vol. 80, 8, 11. See also "Ice Hockey," *Times* (London), 12 Oct. 1935, 5.

16. Minutes of 19th Annual Meeting of CAHA, 1936, 19, 22–24. A. H. Schlegel of Ontario estimated there were 80 percent amateurs and 20 percent "camouflaged amateurs" (ibid., 24). Broken-time payments became a national issue in 1935–36 when Canada's Olympic representatives from Halifax were deprived of several players who claimed them (Marc Savoie, "Broken Time and Broken Hearts: The Maritimes and the Selection of Canada's 1936 Olympic Hockey Team," 120–38). See also Thomas Rorke, "Memory on Ice: Making the 1936 Canadian Olympic Hockey Team."

17. Minutes of 19th Annual Meeting of CAHA, 1936, 24, 26–28, 78. Responding to Fry's comment about a possible international ban, Gilroy responded: "I would not cry over that." No doubt he was still bitter over the recent controversial British Olympic win in Germany (ibid., 28). Campbell began working as a referee in the NHL the next season.

18. O'Coughlin, *Squaw Valley Gold*, 29, 105, 109; Minutes of the 20th Annual Meeting of the [CAHA] 1937, LAC, CAHA fonds, vol. 80, 5.

19. Mike Rodden, "On the Highways of Sport," *TG*, 25 May 1936, 6; Wong, *Lords of the Rinks*, 148, 149; Patrick to Calder, 16 June 1936, quoted in ibid. The 23 May 1936 meeting was attended by Calder, Smythe, and Ross for the NHL and Hewitt, Cecil Duncan (the CAHA president), and George Dudley for the CAHA. For more background on Dudley and the 1936 agreement, see Young, *100 Hundred Years of Dropping the Puck*, chaps. 10–11.

20. Wong, *Lords of the Rinks*, 143, 150; Kidd, *Struggle for Canadian Sport*, 226; Minutes of the 20th Annual Meeting of the CAHA, 1937, LAC, CAHA fonds, vol. 80, 4, 5. Lester Patrick thought the playing rules clause was the only good one for the NHL and that all the rest damaged the league (Wong, *Lords of the Rinks*, 227n20). A typescript exists in the CAHA fonds that seems to set out the preliminary demands of the CAHA for the 23 May 1936 meeting. "Suggestions for N.H.L.-C.A.H.A. Agreement, 1936," LAC, CAHA fonds, vol. 1, files 1–2. For a brief analysis of its contents, see Ross, "Hockey Capital," 252n66.

21. Ralph Allen, "Enter the Paid Amateur," *Maclean's*, 1 Nov. 1940, 29. Dudley also discussed the advisability of dropping *Amateur* from the CAHA name, but explained that the word had "a very definite value in distinguishing the Association from the professional organizations."

22. Dan Diamond, ed., *The Official National Hockey League 75th Anniversary Commemorative Book*, 76; Minutes of the 20th Annual Meeting of the [CAHA] 1937, LAC, CAHA fonds, vol. 80, 76. Amateur reinstatements continued to be a source of conflict, and as early as 1937 the CAHA and NHL were again in disagreement over renewing their one-year 1936 agreement. In 1938 the two sides negotiated another peace pact. Tommy Munns, "Scanning the Sports Field," *G&M*, 23 June 1938, 16.

23. George Dixon, "Dwyer's $60,000 Cages New A's," n.p., [ca. preseason 1935–36], LAC, HHOF fonds, vol. 11, New York Americans Scrapbook, 1935–36, 4; "Coney Island Track Goes into Receivership; Coney Receiver Named," *CDT*, 25 Oct. 1935, 30. Dwyer estimated the track had lost seventy-five thousand dollars in the race season just ended.

24. "Dandurand Offers to Buy Americans," *NYT*, 15 Nov. 1935, 27; "Gorman Walks Back to Maroons," n.p., n.d., LAC, HHOF fonds, vol. 11, New York Americans Scrapbook, 1935–36, 106; James Burchard, "Passing the Puck," *New York World-Telegram*, n.d., LAC, HHOF fonds, vol. 11,

New York Americans Scrapbook, 1935–36, 97. Dan Parker wrote: "They tell me Jim [Norris] owns the Americans under cover or at least has the reputed owner so indebted to him that he is virtually the boss" ([column], *NYDM*, 7 Mar. 1936, 23).

25. "N.Y. Americans to Continue in Hocky [*sic*] League," *CDT*, 17 July 1936, 25; Joseph C. Nichols, "Hockey Circuit Takes over Americans . . . ," *NYT*, 20 Oct. 1936, 32; Dwyer Case Settled," *CDT*, 11 Nov. 1936, 27; Joseph C. Nichols, "Hockey Campaign to Open on Nov. 5," *NYT*, 27 Oct. 1936, 34; "Americans Placed under New Group," *NYT*, 4 Nov. 1936, 49. One limitation on interest may have been the stipulation that the sale of the club was to be to New York interests and that the team had to remain in New York ("League Takes over New York Hocky [*sic*] Club," *CDT*, 20 Oct. 1936, 25).

26. "Americans Placed under New Group"; "Americans in Draw with Black Hawks," *NYT*, 6 Nov. 1936, 31; "Americans Tie Hawks in Hocky [*sic*] Opener, 1–1," *CDT*, 6 Nov. 1936, 31; "Bill Dwyer Out of N. Y. Amerks; Prosperous Year," *CSM*, 10 May 1937, 10. On Dwyer's debts to Dutton, see "Difficulties of Americans Ended with New Corporation in Control," *NYT*, 11 Nov. 1936, 31; "Dwyer Case Settled," *CDT*, 11 Nov. 1936, 27; Harold C. Burr, "Dutton Will Quit Hockey," *New York Post*, 4 Apr. 1938, 18; "Business Records," *NYT*, 10 July 1941, 28; Arthur Daley, "The Flamboyant Redhead," *NYT*, 21 May 1961, S2.

27. Alfred Dayton, "Hockey Moguls Will Honor Calder," *New York Sun*, 9 Dec. 1937, 39. Charles Adams had seen a similar situation before, when he took over the NL Boston Braves in 1935 after the owner forfeited it. Charles Segar, "Tribe Head to Fight," *NYDM*, 16 Jan. 1935, 34; Harold Kaese, *The Boston Braves*, 227–33.

28. "Pooled Receipts in Hockey Urged," *NYT*, 17 Jan. 1937, 77; Gorman to Herbert Molson, 10 June 1936, LAC, Molson fonds, vol. 363, Herbert Molson (Col.) Canadian Arena Company—Correspondence, Financial Reports, Architect's Reports file. The perceived threat to the Canadian clubs is discussed in John H. Lewy, "Montreal Ice Clubs to Launch Battle for Gate Percentage to Visiting Team," *Brooklyn Times-Union*, 21 Dec. 1936, LAC, HHOF fonds, vol. 12, New York Americans—Scrap-book, season 1936–37, 108. Gorman was nominally acting for the Maroons, but with the CAC's interests in the Canadiens, he no doubt wished a blanket policy, hence his reference to all the Canadian clubs.

29. Hector Charlesworth passed the decision to the newly created Canadian Broadcasting Corporation (CBC), which was to take over from the CRBC three weeks later. Charlesworth to F. E. Scott, 13 Oct. 1936, LAC, CBC fonds, vol. 219, file 11–22–2–2 (pt. 4). Chicago, Detroit, New York, and the Maroons tended to play at home on Sundays, Toronto on Saturdays, the Canadiens on Thursdays, and Boston on Tuesdays. C. M. Pasmore outlined the history of hockey radio in Montreal in a letter to Ted Hough, 11 Feb. 1948, AO, F4467-3 (MacLaren Advertising fonds), Re: Hockey Night in Canada file.

30. "Maroon définitivement à Cleveland," *PJ*, 23 May 1937, 54.

31. "Montreal Likely to Lose One Six," *NYT*, 15 July 1937, 25. The St. Louis rumor is mentioned in Brown, *Montreal Maroons*, 195. According to Charles Mayer, spectators particularly despised the Americans, Detroit, and Chicago, and he understood that it was the Maple Leafs that had killed the idea of the all-Canadian league by refusing to join and refusing to allow another club in Toronto.

썽

"Une ligue Canadienne de hockey majeur," *PJ*, 16 May 1937, 55; "One Montreal Hocky [*sic*] Team May Be Transferred," *CDT*, 15 July 1937, 22.

32. "Canadiens Aided by League Action," *NYT*, 8 May 1936, 29. The catch-22 of needing a building before getting a franchise was mentioned by Smythe in the verbatim minutes of the NHL meeting of 7 September 1945 (10). The creation of the IAHL eliminated five IHL and Can-Pro clubs and reduced the combined to only eight. Despite its name, there were no Canadian clubs (London and Windsor were left out), and the league had also retreated from the NHL cities (Boston and Detroit).

33. James A. Burchard, "Morenz Hockey Benefit Nets $23,000 Despite Poor Attendance at Contest," *New York World-Telegram*, 3 Nov. 1937, LAC, HHOF fonds, vol. 13, New York Americans—Scrap-book, season 1937–38, 14; Brown, *Montreal Maroons*, 201; "Maroons' Troubles Will Be Main Topic at NHL Meet Today," *G&M*, 22 June 1938, 14; Tommy Munns, "Scanning the Sports Field," *G&M*, 23 June 1938, 16. Five Maroons players went to the Black Hawks and six to the Canadiens. "Maroon Players Sold," *NYT*, 16 Sept. 1938, 28. The Morenz charity game held at the Forum in November did not even sell out, drawing only 8,653, but a tribute game in Stratford (population 17,742 in 1931) pulled in 3,000. "All-Stars' Sextet Tops Montreal, 6–5," *NYT*, 3 Nov. 1937, 33; "Morenz Game at Stratford," *Leader-Post* (Regina, SK), 8 Nov. 1937, 17. See also "Financial Report—Howie Morenz Memorial Fund," LAC, Mayer fonds, vol. 18, Howie Morenz file.

34. In 1937–38, the combined Maroons and Canadiens gates were $221,827, and the Canadiens drew only $144,009 alone in the next season. In 1943–44 they reached $238,431. Mayer later wrote that English Montrealers maintained that the Maroons should be the ones to continue, but French Canadian Montrealers had threatened a boycott if the Canadiens disappeared. Mayer perceived that the CAC was under English influence, notwithstanding the controlling ownership of Donat Raymond. Charles Mayer, "Il y a 24 ans," unpublished ms., LAC, Mayer fonds, vol. 17, Les Canadiens de Montréal 1928–68 file. On Montreal's population, see Norbert Lacoste, *Les caractéristiques sociale de la population de Grand Montréal*, 77.

35. "Calder Is Honored by Hockey League," *NYT*, 23 Dec. 1937, 28; Charles Mayer, "Le hockey majeur restera au Canada," *PJ*, 26 Dec. 1937, 54. Mayer called the week's meetings a "congrès," claiming it was the first time all the leagues had gathered in one place (ibid.). It was reported that Art Ross was one of the men behind the dinner, despite the fact that "for years Ross fought Frank Calder on every conceivable point, but all the time he kept proclaiming that if the league did not have Calder, it would lose its balance wheel." John P. Carmichael, "The Barber Shop," n.p., n.d., BPL, HKP, Bruins (2) file.

36. Reported in Charles Mayer, "Le hockey majeur restera au Canada," *PJ*, 26 Dec. 1937, 54.

37. Elmer Ferguson, "Red-Ink Hockey," *Maclean's*, 15 Nov. 1938, 33. See also J. Lewis Brown, "Tragedy and Glamor in Hockey," *National Home Monthly*, Jan. 1939, 4. On league rationalization in football, see Coenen, *From Sandlots to the Super Bowl*. On basketball, see Nelson, *National Basketball League*.

38. Wong, *Lords of the Rinks*, 125. See also 124, 150.

39. Kidd, *Struggle for Canadian Sport*, 203.

40. Marshall McLuhan, *Understanding Media: The Extensions of Man*, 297–307; Cosentino, "Concept of Professionalism," 10, 346. See also 342–48.

41. "Chicago Six to Be Called Yanks, with All Players American-Born," *NYT*, 26 Jan. 1937, 26; "Sports," *Literary Digest*, 13 Mar. 1937, 38; John Kieran, "Sports of the Times," *NYT*, 28 Jan. 1937, 20, and 15 Feb. 1937, 23; "Chicago Releases Five American-Born Players," *CSM*, 26 Mar. 1937, 12.

42. Bob Considine wrote in 1938 that the salary cap was still in effect, but exceeded by every club. Bob Considine, "On the Line," *NYDM*, 30 Dec. 1938, 28. It is not clear when the negotiation list was created, but it was in place by 1930 and in 1937 provoked a set of critical columns by Mike Rodden. See M. J. Rodden, "On the Highways of Sport," *G&M*, 2 Apr. 1930, 10; and 10 June 1937, 21.

43. Roy Worters, as told to H. H. Roxborough, "Professionals Earn Their Dough," *Maclean's*, 15 Jan. 1939, 6, 24; "Trottier Proves Business Acumen," *CSM*, 15 Dec. 1938, 12.

44. Andy Lytle, "Speaking on Sports," *TDS*, 20 Mar. 1939, 13; Coleman, *Trail of the Stanley Cup*, 2:231; "To Insure Hockey Clubs," *NYT*, 30 Nov. 1938, 27. See also H. H. Roxborough, "Is Hockey Losing Color?," *Maclean's*, 1 Nov. 1939, 8.

45. "Andy Lytle, "League Funds Allocated Regularly to G. Parsons," *TDS*, 27 Dec. 1939, 12. The Injured Players' Fund was renamed the Players' Emergency Fund during the Second World War.

46. Alfred Dayton, "Seeks Uniform Ice Rulings," *New York Sun*, [ca. fall 1936], LAC, HHOF fonds, vol. 12, New York Americans Scrapbook, 1936–37, 56; "Connie Smythe to Beef No More—Not about Garden Hockey Timer," n.p., [12 Jan. 1935], LAC, HHOF fonds, vol. 10, New York Americans Scrapbook, 1934–35, 58; Brown, *Montreal Maroons*, 175–76.

7. Managing a Morale Business

1. Copy of Ross to Selke, 20 Jan. 1943, BPL, Harold Kaese fonds, vol. 1, Bruins 2 file.

2. Ibid.

3. Ibid.

4. Ibid.

5. Sections of this chapter appear in: J. Andrew Ross, "The Paradox of Conn Smythe: Hockey, Memory, and the Second World War" and "Arenas of Debate: The Continuance of Hockey in the Second World War" (reprinted with permission of the publisher). On the NHL player participation in the Second World War, see Bruce McIntyre, "Which Uniform to Serve?"; Bill Twatio, "Wartime Wonders"; and Gabriel Stephen Panunto, "For Club or Country? Hockey in Wartime Canada, 1939–1945." See also Douglas Hunter, *War Games: Conn Smythe and Hockey's Fighting Men*.

6. Jim Hurley, "Meeting to Decide Hockey Fate Today," *NYDM*, 7 Sept. 1939, 37; James Walvin, *The People's Game: A Social History of British Football*, 137–38.

7. George Strickler, "Hockey and Olympics Are Periled by War," *CDT*, 4 Sept. 1939, 29; Charles Mayer, "Si la ligue national n'opérait pas ce serait un coup pour le hockey amateur," *PJ*, 10 Sept. 1939, 55. In the first few weeks of September, there was no shortage of volunteers, to the point that all nonarmy recruiting was suspended on 24 September.

8. Bill Roche, "NHL Clears Decks to Carry on Next Winter," *G&M*, 8 Sept. 1939, 17; "Hockey League Plans to Carry on Despite War," *NYHT*, 8 Sept. 1939, 29; "An Excellent Decision," *NYHT*,

cited in "National Hockey League Praised for Its Decision to Carry On," *Hockey* [n.d.], LAC, Mayer fonds, vol. 55.

9. Hy Turkin, "Hockey Sked Okay; War's Fever Cools," *New York Daily News*, 14 Oct. 1939, 29; Charles Mayer, "Déclaration du président Calder à l'occasion de l'ouverture d'une autre saison de hockey majeur," *PJ*, 5 Nov. 1939, 55.

10. Coleman, *Trail of the Stanley Cup*, 2:372.

11. "On se viendra à diviser les recettes dans la N.H.L.," *PJ*, 24 Dec. 1939, 55; Lewis Burton, "The Lowdown," *New York Journal-American*, 18 Dec. 1939, Madison Square Garden Scrapbook #34 (Season 1939–40); "Norris' Ire Subsides at Hockey Meeting," *CDT*, 14 Dec. 1939, 35. See also Jimmy Powers, "The Powerhouse," *New York Daily News*, 23 Nov. 1939, 56; Andy Lytle, "Speaking on Sports," *TDS*, 27 Dec. 1939, 12; Coleman, *Trail of the Stanley Cup*, 2:377–78; and Verbatim Minutes of NHL Meeting of Governors, 16 Jan. 1942, 22, HHFM.

12. The ad was signed by Smythe and read in full: "'Attention, Hockey Fans!' If You're Tired of seeing the kind of hockey the Boston Bruins are playing COME TO THE GARDEN TONIGHT and see a real hockey club, The TORONTO MAPLE LEAFS." *Boston Globe*, 19 Dec. 1939, 19. In his later years, Smythe wrote that "every place Ross and I met, we fought" (Smythe and Young, *Conn Smythe*, 129).

13. Canadian industrial expansion was rapid, and its balance of payments deficit with its southern neighbor ballooned from CDN\$116 million in 1939 to CDN\$292 million in 1940.

14. Calder to E. M. Johnson, Enforcement Section, FECB, 6 June 1940; A. Duncan of the Dominion Bank, Montreal, to Commercial Section of FECB, 14 June 1940; Gibbons to Fricker, 27 June 1940; and R. F. B. Taylor to Montreal Office [FECB], 3 July 1940, all in Bank of Canada Archives (BCA), Foreign Exchange Control Board (FECB), vol. 143, Hockey Players file.

15. Calder to Muir, 24 Oct. 1939, BCA, FECB, vol. 143, Hockey Players file; copy of Smythe to G. R. Cottrelle, Canadian Bank of Commerce, 20 July 1940, BCA, FECB, vol. 143, Hockey Players file; Wong, "Rise of the Chicago Blackhawks," 267–68. Smythe copied the letter to Cottrelle to D. B. Mansur of the FECB, and possibly also to Calder.

16. "Franchise Given to Indianapolis in Int-Am Loop," *CSM*, 12 July 1939, 13; "Smythe-Buffalo Squabble Is Turned over to Calder," *TDS*, 14 Dec. 1939, 16; memorandum from D. B. Mansur to J. E. Coyne, 24 July 1940, BCA, FECB, vol. 143, Hockey Players file. The ten-club IAHL had not had any non-American clubs since 1936. (This AHL should not be confused with the earlier "outlaw" version of the AHA.)

17. Gibbons to Calder, 29 July 1940, Calder to Gibbons, 21 Aug. 1940, and Gibbons to W. G. Hardy, President of International Ice Hockey Association, 7 Sept. 1940, BCA, FECB, vol. 143, Hockey Players file. The IIHA was formed in 1941 by the CAHA, AHA of US, British Ice Hockey Association, and Scottish Ice Hockey Association, after a dispute over amateur definitions with the Ligue Internationale de Hockey sur Glace. After the war, the IIHA disbanded and reaffiliated with the LIHG, using the name International Ice Hockey Federation in North America. For more details, see Minutes of CAHA Semi-Annual Meeting, 8 and 9 Jan. 1955, 6–7, LAC, CAHA fonds, microfilm reel C-4852.

18. For more on the FECB program, see Ross, "Hockey Capital," 266–72. On FECB policy more generally, see Alan O. Gibbons, "Foreign Exchange Control in Canada, 1939–51," 43; and Robert B.

Bryce, *Canada and the Cost of World War II: The International Operations of Canada's Department of Finance, 1939–1947*, chap. 5.

19. See the appendix for gate receipts and attendance.

20. Michael D. Stevenson, *Canada's Greatest Wartime Muddle: National Selective Service and the Mobilization of Human Resources during World War II*, 18–19; J. L. Granatstein and J. M. Hitsman, *Broken Promises: A History of Conscription in Canada*, 138–40, 143. For a description of the call-up procedure, see Stevenson, *Canada's Greatest Wartime Muddle*, 18–21ff.

21. Smythe to Maple Leafs players, 17 July 1940, AO, F223-3-1-57; Herb Goren, "War Menace Affects Hockey," *New York Sun*, 10 Sept. 1940, Madison Square Garden Scrapbook #35 (Season 1940–41; Andy Lytle, "Governors Clearing Decks," *TDS*, 5 Sept. 1940, 14. The NPAM would be considered as "reserves" in current parlance, compared to the Permanent Active Militia who would be considered "regulars."

22. Andy Lytle, "Governors Clearing Decks," *TDS*, 5 Sept. 1940, 14; "Hockey Players Unaffected by War Situation," *NYHT*, 13 Sept. 1940, Madison Square Garden Scrapbook #35 (Season 1940–41); Jim Hurley, "Moguls Plan Ice Season in Spite of War Threat," *NYDM*, 11 Sept. 1940, 36; Minutes of the 25th Annual Meeting of the [CAHA] 1942, 74, 75, LAC, CAHA fonds, vol. 81 (microfilm reel C-4852). The amounts paid for amateurs were later halved.

23. The practice of recording verbatim minutes was apparently started at the behest of Tex Rickard after a dispute over what was actually said at a meeting. The set of minutes at the Hockey Hall of Fame and Museum is incomplete but has records of forty-seven board of governors, semiannual, annual, and general managers meetings from 1935 to 1957.

24. Gene Kiczek maintains that Indianapolis and Philadelphia, the only two AHL clubs owned by NHL clubs, supported Smythe's application, but the NHL minutes make it clear Norris supported another applicant. See Kiczek, *Forgotten Glory: The Story of Cleveland Barons Hockey*, 44; and Verbatim Minutes of Meeting of Governors, 17 Oct. 1940, 13–15ff.

25. Verbatim Minutes of Meeting of Governors, 17 Oct. 1940, 14.

26. Ibid., 15–16. For the text of the league agreement, see Wong, *Lords of the Rinks*, 170.

27. On *Federal Baseball*, see chap. 1, note 58.

28. Verbatim Minutes of Meeting of Governors, 17 Oct. 1940, 16.

29. Ibid., 18.

30. Ibid., 20–24.

31. Ibid., 23, 24.

32. Ibid., 24, 25, 26, 28.

33. Ibid., 25, 29.

34. Adam Smith, *An Inquiry into the Nature and Causes of the Wealth of Nations*, bk. 1, chap. 10, para. 82.

35. Verbatim Minutes of Meeting of Governors, 17 Oct. 1940, 31–32.

36. Ibid., 34.

37. Ibid.

38. Ibid., 34–35.

39. Ibid., 33.

40. Ross outlined the Bruins lease details: the club paid 35 percent up to $250,000 in gate receipts, 25 percent from $250,000 to $300,000, and 50 percent above $300,000. It had worked out to $99,000 in the previous year, and Kilpatrick called the lease "very advantageous." Verbatim Minutes of Meeting of Governors, 17 Oct. 1940, 36–37.

41. For a discussion of the prospects of expansion to Washington, Buffalo, St. Louis, and Cleveland, see Verbatim Minutes of Meeting of Governors, 15 Feb. 1941, 26–31.

42. See the appendix; and Coleman, *Trail of the Stanley Cup*, 2:422.

43. J. Lewis Brown, "Hockey Despite Hitler," *National Home Monthly*, Dec. 1940, 18.

44. Rodney Adamson, MP for West York, to Conn Smythe, 27 May 1941, AO, F223-1-2-45. Ironically, the theater lobby was led by the president of Famous Players, N. L. Nathanson, the former NHL governor and St. Patrick's part-owner.

45. Canadian Parliament, *House of Commons Debates*, 30 May 1941, 3325; 2 June 1941, 3382.

46. "US Puck Teams Lose Western Talent," *WFP*, 13 Sept. 1941, 22; "Army Comes First," *WFP*, 13 Sept. 1941, 22. Under Section 4 of the NWS Regulations, a man in an age class liable to be called had to obtain permission, and the twenty-one to twenty-four age classes were the first liable class. The boards were in major regional centers in Canada and generally corresponded to the thirteen military districts.

47. "Army Comes First"; "Recruiting Problems," *WFP*, 22 Sept. 1941, 13; "Why Pick on Hockey Players," *G&M*, 16 Sept. 1941, 22. See also Ralph Allen, "Mostly Incidental," *G&M*, 13 Sept. 1941, 14.

48. "Saskatchewan to Bar," *WFP*, 15 Sept. 1941, 10; "Saskatchewan Divisional Board Firm Stand on Hockey Question," *OC*, 16 Sept. 1941, 11; "Allen Kuntz and Gordie Bruce Seek Permission from Board," *OC*, 15 Sept. 1941, 15; "Famous Hockey Line of Boston May Be Ruined," *WFP*, 17 Sept. 1941, 1, 8; "Bulletin: Trainee Exemptions for Reserves Ended," *London Free Press*, 18 Sept. 1941, 1.

49. "No Further Applications," *WFP*, 16 Sept. 1941, 1, 7; Wayne S. Cole, *America First: The Battle against Intervention, 1940–1941*.

50. "21 to 25," *OC*, 17 Sept. 1941, 12.

51. "Crack Whip on Western Players," *G&M*, 15 Sept. 1941, 16. By 27 October, AHL President Maurice Podoloff was predicting that the board decisions would cost the AHL fifteen to eighteen players *Philadelphia Post*, 27 Oct. 1941.

52. Charles Mayer, "Frais sur la glace . . . ," *PJ*, 28 Sept. 1941, 48; "Hockey Moguls Ready for Worst," *OC*, 19 Sept. 1941, 14; "Seek Lifting Passport Ban on Hockeyists," *WFP*, 7 Oct. 1941, 1; "Alberta Will Let Hockey Players in Reserve Army Enter the States," *MG*, 7 Oct. 1941, 17; "No Comment from Calder," *MG*, 7 Oct. 1941, 17; "Hockey Players in Wartime," *WFP*, 16 Oct. 1941, 13.

53. "N.H.L. President Converses with Head of Manitoba Board," *WFP*, 16 Oct. 1941, 12; "Calder n'obtient rien au Manitoba," *LP*, 17 Oct. 1941, 31; "Passport Ban Stands for Hockey Players," *NYT*, 17 Oct. 1941, 30; H. H. Roxborough, "Is This a Time for Pro Sport?," *Maclean's*, 1 Jan. 1942, 8. Dutton also met with the Saskatchewan Board, to no avail. "Saskatchewan War Services Boards [*sic*] Maintains Stand," *WFP*, 18 Oct. 1941, 23. The different treatment of the players by regional authorities is briefly discussed in Ross, "Arenas of Debate," 121n65. Stevenson singles

out Justices Manson of Vancouver and Embury of Regina for specific criticism (*Canada's Greatest Wartime Muddle*, 25–26).

54. C. P. Stacey, *Arms, Men and Governments: The War Policies of Canada, 1939–1945*, 399–402, 404; Stevenson, *Canada's Greatest Wartime Muddle*, 20.

55. Franklin Roosevelt to Kenesaw Landis, 15 Jan. 1942, National Baseball Hall of Fame, http://education.baseballhalloffame.org/; "Adams, of Wings, Threatens to Buck Any Plan to Drop Hockey during War," *NYHT*, 15 May 1942, 23; Verbatim Minutes of Annual Meeting, 15 May 1942, 22–23.

56. "Wartime Fate of Pro Hockey Hangs on Case by President," *OC*, 8 Aug. 1942, 11; "NHL Has Good Chance to Survive Big Crisis," *G&M*, 10 Aug. 1942, 16; Granatstein and Hitsman, *Broken Promises*, 193.

57. Letters from Frank Calder to Elliott Little, 7 and 17 Aug. 1942, LAC, RG25 (External Affairs fonds), vol. 3041, file 4198-A-40. The AHL sent a high-powered American lobbyist, Charles Sawyer. Keenleyside to Moffat, 21 Aug. 1942, and Charles Sawyer to Elliott Little, 17 Aug. 1942, LAC, RG25, vol. 3041, file 4198-A-40.

58. L. E. Westman, for Director of NSS, to Keenleyside, 21 Aug. 1942, and Keenleyside to Moffat, 21 Aug. 1942, and press release from National Office, National Selective Service, Ottawa, 22 Oct. 1942, LAC, RG25, vol. 3041, file 4198-A-40; [press release] PM-3948, 15 Sept. 1942, National Archives and Records Administration, RG2111 (War Manpower Commission Records); "Ottawa and Washington Flash Green Light to Hockey," *TDS*, 15 Sept. 1942, 16. For background on McNutt and the formation of the WMC, see George Q. Flynn, *The Mess in Washington: Manpower Mobilization in World War II*, 9–20.

59. "Ottawa and Washington Flash Green Light to Hockey"; "League Members Cheered" and "Gorman, Selke Pleased," *NYT*, 16 Sept. 1942, 32; Coleman, *Trail of the Stanley Cup*, 2:451. The draft was a subject of some resentment for the AHL owners; they had been trying to avoid it when the war started.

60. Verbatim Minutes of the Meeting of the Board of Governors, 23 Nov. 1942, 1–2, 16–18. Maurice Richard missed the first six games played in the United States, Terry Reardon missed five, Emile Bouchard five, and Elmer Lach four. Jean-Patrice Martel, Society for International Hockey Research Listserv post, 20 Dec. 2011.

61. Verbatim Minutes of the Special Meeting of the Governors, 24 Oct. 1941, 13, 14, 17. The option was based on the one given to Dwyer in 1936, but Calder was trying to get it for Dutton at less than the strike price of two hundred thousand dollars that had been suggested.

62. Verbatim Minutes of the Special Meeting of the Governors, 24 Oct. 1941, 18–20. Calder said, "If we are going to flourish together let us flourish; if we are going to sink, let us sink together. You have nothing to sell, you have no future" (18).

63. Ibid., 21–22. When Lester Patrick suggested changing the Americans name to reflect its new borough, Kilpatrick resisted, thinking it was premature.

64. Verbatim Minutes of Annual Meeting, 15 May 1942, 4, 8–13, 14, 15, 16, 29–21. Norris's comments about the lease make one wonder about his ability to influence Garden policy—he was, after all, a major MSG shareholder.

65. "Rangers Dangle Scalps of Amerks at Wampum Belts," *TDS*, 25 Sept. 1942, 14; Andy Lytle, "Speaking on Sport," *TDS*, 29 Sept. 1942, 15.

66. "New York Americans Switch Hockey Allegiance to Brooklyn," *NYHT*, 13 Nov. 1941. The Americans' debt continued to be unpaid, however, and was discussed in Verbatim Minutes of Annual Meeting and Meeting of Governors, 8 May 1943. Dutton's option on a postwar franchise is referred to in Verbatim Minutes of Meeting of the Board of Governors, 21 Jan. 1944, 50.

67. Verbatim Minutes of Board of Governors Meeting, 24 Oct. 1942, 3. Duncan had also stepped in when Charles Adams had resigned in 1933.

68. Verbatim Minutes of Annual Meeting, 15 May 1942, 6, 7. A reference to a previous iteration of the management committee is in Andy Lytle, "Speaking on Sports, *TDS*, 2 Nov. 1940. The reference to "disputes" is interesting, as Calder's right to judge had been reaffirmed in a previous case.

69. "Calder Taken Ill at Hockey Meeting," *NYT*, 26 Jan. 1943, 23; Andy Lytle, "Hockey's Fearless Leader Reports to Great Referee," *TDS*, 4 Feb. 1943, 16.

70. Charles Mayer, "D'un but à l'autre . . . ," *PJ*, 7 Feb. 1943, 52; Verbatim Minutes of Meeting of Governors, 5 Mar. 1943, 22. See also "Frank Calder: A Canadian," *MG*, 5 Feb. 1943, 8.

71. For a similar assessment of Calder's influence, see Wong, *Lords of the Rinks*, 154–55. For a more tendentious one, see Holzman and Nieforth, *Deceptions and Doublecross*, 332–33.

72. Verbatim Minutes of Meeting of Governors, 5 Mar. 1943, 30; 21 Jan. 1944, 46. Dutton asked for bonuses for both staff members, including two hundred dollars for Pinard, who "works late every night." She was later promoted to assistant office manager.

73. Verbatim Minutes of Meeting of Governors, 5 Mar. 1943, 23. (The NHL also paid to insure the trophies.) Holzman and Nieforth believe that Calder appointed himself president of the league and imply that the use of Calder's name in the conduct of league business suggests fraud, but it is preposterous to believe that oversight was so weak or governors so ignorant that Calder could line his pockets for a quarter century without detection (*Deceptions and Doublecross*, 150, 198, 213).

74. Verbatim Minutes of Meeting of Governors, 23 Nov. 1942, 12.

75. Verbatim Minutes of Annual Meeting and Meeting of Governors, 8 May 1943, 3; Charles Mayer, "Frais sur la glace . . . ," *PJ*, 19 Dec. 1943, 53. See the appendix for attendance and gate receipts. As war measures, the governors decided to eliminate overtime games so as not to interfere with train schedules and also experimented with weekday afternoon games. "No Overtime New Chapter," *Hockey*, no. 4, 26 Nov. 1942, LAC, Mayer fonds, vol. 18, Hockey Maurice Richard file; "Afternoon Game Is New History," *Hockey*, no. 5 (7 Dec. 1942), LAC, Mayer fonds, vol. 57.

76. Stevenson, *Canada's Greatest Wartime Muddle*, 6–10.

77. Andy Lytle, "Speaking on Sports," *TDS*, 18 Aug. 1943, 12; "Hockey Seeks Standing for War Manpower," *CSM*, 17 Aug. 1943, 23; "Hockey Group Told of Player Status," *NYT*, 17 Aug. 1943, 23; Andy Lytle, "Speaking on Sports," *TDS*, 20 Aug. 1943, 10; Andy Lytle, "Speaking on Sports," *TDS*, 29 Sept. 1942, 15. John Ebbs was a partner in the firm Haydon & Ebbs and was likely recommended by Donat Raymond, who was a Liberal senator with close ties to the firm.

78. Memorandum from MacNamara to C. F. Needham, Associate Director [Civilian], 13 Mar. 1943, LAC, RG27, vol. 153, file 611.19–4; Needham to Keenleyside, 8 Apr. 1943, LAC, RG25, vol.

3041, file 4198-A-40; Lester B. Pearson to N. A. Robertson, 14 Apr. 1943, LAC, RG25, vol. 3041, file 4198-A-40; McNutt to MacNamara, 25 Aug. [1943], cited in Teletype EX-4108 sent by B. M. Bridge of External [Affairs] Ottawa to Canadian Minister in Washington, 20 Oct. 1943, authored by "NR" [presumably Norman Robertson], LAC, RG25, vol. 3041, file 4198-A-40; National Selective Service Circular Memorandum No. 283, 16 Sept. 1943, LAC, RG25, vol. 3041, file 4198-A-40. Pearson based his view on a jaundiced rant by Dave Egan, "Hard to Jubilate over Bruin Victory," *Boston Daily Record*, 1 Apr. 1943, 29. For a summary of essential and nonessential occupations, see Stevenson, *Canada's Greatest Wartime Muddle*, table 1, 32.

79. Teletype message WA-5236 from Canadian Minister [in Washington] to Secretary of State (External Affairs), 21 Oct. 1943, LAC, RG25, vol. 3041, file 4198-A-40. See also Norman Robertson, the undersecretary of state for external affairs, to Director of NSS [MacNamara], 25 Oct. 1943, LAC, RG27, vol. 134, file 601.3–7.

80. MacNamara to McNutt, 30 Oct. 1943; telegram from MacNamara to McNutt, 11 Nov. 1943; telegram from McNutt to MacNamara, 12 Nov. 1943; and telegram from McNutt to MacNamara, 19 Nov. 1943, all in LAC, RG27, vol. 134, file 601.3-7; MacNamara to Robertson, 8 Dec. 1943, LAC, RG25, vol. 3041, file 4198-A-40; Robertson to MacNamara, 10 Dec. 1943, LAC, RG27, vol. 134, file 601.3–7. See also Ross, "Arenas of Debate," 104.

81. "WMC Ruling Helps Hockey Personnel," *NYT*, 23 Oct. 1943, 30; "Heller, Hextall Called in Draft," *New York Daily News*, 1 Feb. 1944, 37; "Mobilization Board May Bar Hextall from Ranger Team," *New York Sun*, 18 Oct. 1944, 37.

82. A. C. Stewart to NSS Associate Director Allan Mitchell, 30 Nov. 1943; Memo of Reply to Letter of Resignation of Mr. A. C. Stewart, K. C., [from Anderson] to Hon. Humphrey Mitchell, Minister of Labour, 30 Nov. 1943; Mobilization Board—Regina, Dec. 23rd, 1943 [Riley's Report]; H. J. Riley to MacNamara, 21 Apr. 1944, all in LAC, RG27, vol. 128, file 601.3-1-12. C. W. McCool was the founder of the Saskatoon Wesleys hockey organization, for which Bentley had played in 1933–34. Anderson was fully aware of this fact and explained that McCool recused himself in cases of hockey players seeking permits. "Chairman Explains Why One 'A' Player Got Permit," *Leader-Post* (Regina, SK), 4 Dec. 1943, 1, 19.

83. "Jury Convicts Orlando," *NYT*, 31 July 1943, 15; "Orlando in Canadian Army," *NYT*, 3 Mar. 1944, 20; "By Jim Coleman," *G&M*, 3 Nov. 1944, 16.

84. "By Jim Coleman." Coleman's father, D. C. Coleman, was the vice president of the Canadian Arena Company, which owned the Canadiens. D. C. had accompanied Calder on at least one lobbying trip. Ross, "Arenas of Debate," 94.

85. Verbatim Minutes of Meeting of Governors, 16 Jan. 1942, 22, 25, 27, 28; A. H. Weiler, "Fury on Ice," *NYT*, 14 Jan. 1940, SM6. See also "Hockey Governors Move to Curb Fights," *NYT*, 16 Jan. 1941, 28.

86. Frank Boucher with Trent Frayne, *When the Rangers Were Young*, 183; Lester Rice, "Attack Emphasis Hits Goalies," *New York Journal-American*, 13 Jan. 1940, 19; Marshall Smith, "Puck's Bad Boy," *Life*, ca. 5 Mar. 1951, 82, 84.

87. Boucher wrote the new book with Vern Thomas of Baltimore, an AHL representative. Boucher with Frayne, *When the Rangers Were Young*, 184.

88. Ibid., 179; T. P. Gorman to Joe Gorman, 3 Sept. 1943, LAC, Gorman fonds, vol. 1, file 6. The *1942–43 Official Rule Book* listed 83 players in the services and the next year's edition listed 128. Charles Mayer listed all the daytime employments of the Canadiens in "Les Canadiens jouent en hockey, c'est vrai, mais ils contribuent aussi à l'effort de guerre," *PJ*, 12 Dec. 1943, 55.

89. Coleman, *Trail of the Stanley Cup*, 2:481. Conn Smythe had left strict instructions that there was to be "no reduction in price" and "no passes—very important." Smythe to Cottrelle, 9 Jan. 1941, AO, F223-1-2-9. Selke defended the policy in Andy Lytle, "Speaking on Sports," *TDS*, 1 Feb. 1944, 10. On Boston and Chicago charity efforts, see "Bruins Champion Bond Sellers, Too," *Hockey*, no. 10, 17 Jan. 1942, LAC, Mayer fonds, vol. 57; "All Hawks' Profits Will Go to Charity," *NYT*, 22 Mar. 1942, S1; Judith Cass, "Hockey Season Start Is Signal for Party Plans," *CDT*, 26 Oct. 1944, 25. Ross was always skeptical of McLaughlin's promise to donate Black Hawks profits.

90. Verbatim Minutes of Annual Meeting, 12 May 1944, 11–15. The full resolution had exemptions for students and farmers.

91. Verbatim Minutes of Meeting of the Board of Governors, 12 May 1944, 4–5, 6; *NYT*, 10 Sept. 1944, S1; "On semble à tout prix vouloir démolir les CANADIENS," *PJ*, 10 Sept. 1944, 47; "'War Comes First,' Sports Officials Agree," *CDT*, 24 Dec. 1944, A1–A2; "Watson Joins Rangers after Army Rejection," *NYHT*, 7 Nov. 1944. The Canadiens actually complained directly to the minister of labor, Humphrey Mitchell, without success. Though still a longtime senator and fund-raiser, Donat Raymond's influence with the government had waned. Memorandum from George G. Greene, Private Secretary to Minister of Labour Humphrey Mitchell, to MacNamara, 31 May 1944, LAC, RG27, vol. 134, file 601.3-7. See also Whitaker, *Government Party*, 285.

92. Richard Goldstein, *Spartan Seasons: How Baseball Survived the Second World War*, 199–202.

93. NSS Circular No. 283-3, 18 Jan. 1945, LAC, RG27, vol. 134, file 601.3-7; Joe Perlove, "Border Crossing Bar Up for Hockey Players Only," *TDS*, 22 Jan. 1945, 10. Billy Reay of the Detroit Red Wings and Neil Colville of the Rangers were two players affected. "Rangers Get Colville for Canadian Games," *NYDM*, 27 Jan. 1945, 17.

94. "Untrained Troops Hazard at Front, Smythe Complains," *G&M*, 19 Sept. 1944, 1. See also Ross, "Paradox of Conn Smythe," 26–27. Bruce Hutchison later wrote that Smythe's comments "angered Canada, disturbed King, and staggered Ralston" (*The Incredible Canadian*, 341).

95. Verbatim Minutes of Meeting of the Board of Governors, 2 Feb. 1945, 29.

96. The interview with O'Meara is cited in "Smythe Demands Fair Hockey Deal," *NYT*, 6 Feb. 1945, 14.

97. It is clear that baseball and football had some of the same morale industry characteristics, although there has been no detailed study of this issue. There are parallels in other consumer products industries making the case for being "essential." See, for example, Lisa Jacobson, "Beer Goes to War: The Politics of Beer Promotion and Production in the Second World War." On baseball's

war experience, see Steven P. Gietschier, "'Uncle Sam Needs Only to Call': Baseball and the United States' Peacetime Military Draft, 1940–1941"; Goldstein, *Spartan Seasons*; and Steven R. Bullock, *Playing for Their Nation: Baseball and the American Military during World War II*. On football's, see Coenen, *From Sandlots to the Super Bowl*.

98. "Maj. M'Laughlin Dies; Wife and Son at Bedside," *CDT*, 18 Dec. 1944, 3.

99. Personal patriotism is even harder to measure, but it may be worth noting that Art Ross, James Norris, and Jack Adams had become naturalized Americans and may have been more acutely attuned to national differences in club behavior.

100. Jerry Geran to Frank Calder, 3 May 1941. My thanks to the late John Halligan of the NHL for supplying a copy of this letter. See also "Sports of the Times," *NYT*, 18 Apr. 1941, 28; and Charles Mayer, "Ici et là dans la L.N.H.," *PJ*, 9 Jan. 1944, 45.

Conclusion

1. On the importance of culture in firm formation, see Lamoreaux, Raff, and Temin, "Beyond Markets and Hierarchies," 405, 407–8; Mark C. Casson, *Economics of Business Culture: Game Theory, Transaction Costs and Economic Performance*; and W. W. Powell, "Neither Market nor Hierarchy: Network Forms of Organization."

2. W. O. McGeehan, "Down the Line," *NYHT*, 6 Mar. 1927, 2:2.

3. The major league need to balance the national with the local is emphasized by Leifer in *Making the Majors*, and Colin Howell sees a similar process in Canadian baseball in *Northern Sandlots: A Social History of Maritime Baseball*. Wiebe makes the classic argument of the general American shift from local-regional to national society in *Search for Order*.

4. J. C. H. Jones, "The Economics of the National Hockey League," 2.

5. Hardy notes that profit seeking and risk taking, the "normally central dimensions of entrepreneurship," have not always been central to sports and finds it telling that the industry was often subsidized by the state or philanthropic organizations ("Entrepreneurs, Organizations, and the Sports Marketplace," 347).

6. Smythe and Young, *Conn Smythe*, 113.

7. Micheline Keating, "The Boss' Son," *Collier's*, 16 Jan. 1937, 10; Lester Patrick is quoted in Dan Parker, "Ladies Love Mayhem," *New York Journal-American*, 4 Feb. 1939, Madison Square Garden Scrapbook #58 (Seasons 1936–39).

8. The importance of shifting to larger national markets to the definition and survival of a sport has parallels in other leisure industries. Bill Osgerby writes that "mediation by commercial industries . . . gave surf culture both national exposure and stylistic coherence. Without this commercial intervention it is unlikely that the burgeoning surf scene would have existed as a recognizable cultural formation—instead remaining a vaguely defined, locally based leisure culture" (*Playboys in Paradise: Masculinity, Youth and Leisure in Modern America*, 106).

9. Charles Mayer of *Le Petit Journal* noted that speed was supplanting stickhandling "now that American clubs are in the majority and the speed game is what the spectators from over the border want." Given that the move to speed had occurred with the move to Hamilton as well, it is hard to

qualify it as entirely a national preference, but certainly the postexpansion years had seen further refinement of the playing rules, often as a result of American criticism. "Plus de vitesse avec cinq joueurs d'avant," *PJ*, 23 Oct. 1938, 48.

10. Another innovative Canadian export to the United States, box lacrosse (boxla), was criticized by American field lacrosse adherents for having a negative influence on their own field game— a nice counterexample to Canadian worries about the negative American influence on hockey. See Fisher, *Lacrosse*, 157–67.

Bibliography

Archival Sources

Archives de Montréal
 Various subject files
Archives of Ontario, Toronto
 F223 Conn Smythe fonds
 F4669 MacLaren Advertising Co., Ltd., fonds
 Various civil litigation files
Baker Library, Harvard Business School, Boston
 Madison Square Garden Corporation Annual Reports
Bank of Canada Archives, Ottawa
 Foreign Exchange Control Board fonds
Bibliothèque et Archives nationales du Québec
 Dwyer v. Fraid et al.
Boston Public Library
 Boston Garden Collection
 Harold Kaese fonds
 Tex Rickard fonds
Detroit News Library
Duggan, Thomas, Collection (private)
Glenbow Museum and Archives, Calgary
 M-2160 (Series 10) Calgary Exhibition and Stampede fonds
Hamilton Public Library, Hamilton, ON
 Hamilton Herald Scrapbooks
Hockey Hall of Fame and Museum, Toronto
 Various subject files
 NHL Minute Book, 1917–25
 Verbatim minutes of NHL meetings, 1935, 1940–45

Library and Archives Canada, Ottawa

Manuscripts

MG27 III B11	James Layton Ralston fonds
MG28 I99	Hockey Hall of Fame fonds
MG28 I150	Amateur Athletic Union of Canada fonds
MG28 I151	Canadian Amateur Hockey Association fonds
MG28 I167	Ontario Hockey Association fonds
MG28 I263	Hockey Canada fonds
MG28 I351	Montreal Amateur Athletic Association fonds
MG28 III 57	Molson fonds
MG30 C76	Charles Mayer fonds
MG30 C84	Harry Connor fonds
MG30 C89	Fred Lionel Hitchman fonds
MG30 C129	Thomas Patrick Gorman fonds
MG30 D67	E. Austin Weir fonds
MG30 D98	Philip Dansken Ross fonds
MG30 E419	W. Lea Gault fonds
MG31 B23	Howard Irwin Ross fonds
MG31 D171	Trent Frayne fonds

Government Records

R1135	Rutherford Report fonds
RG9	Militia and Defence fonds
RG14 D2	House of Commons fonds (Sessional Papers)
RG24	National Defence fonds
RG25	External Affairs fonds
RG27	Department of Labour–National Selective Service fonds
RG33-55	Commission to Investigate into and Report upon the Conditions Pertaining to the Running of Race Meets and Betting in Connection Therewith in Canada fonds
RG41	Canadian Broadcasting Corporation fonds
RG95	Canadian Department of Consumer and Corporate Affairs, Corporations Branch fonds

Madison Square Garden Scrapbooks, New York

McGill University Archives, Montreal
    MG4151/08 Austin (Dink) Carroll fonds
National Archives and Records Administration, Washington, DC
    RG2111   War Manpower Commission Records
New York Rangers Collection, New York
    Rangers programs and clipping files
Queen's University Archives, Kingston, ON
    Michael James Rodden fonds
    Ottawa Hockey Association, Ltd., fonds
University of Western Ontario Business Library, London, ON
    Maple Leaf Gardens, Ltd., Annual Reports

Newspapers and Periodicals

American Architect
Border Cities Star (Windsor, ON)
Boston Daily Record
Boston Evening Globe
Boston Globe
Boston Herald
Boston Traveler
Brooklyn Eagle
Brooklyn Times-Union
Calgary Daily Herald
Chicago Daily Tribune
Christian Science Monitor
Civil Service Review
Cleveland Plain Dealer
Collier's
Detroit Free Press
Detroit News
Engineering News-Record
Financial Post (Toronto)
Fortune
Gazette (Montreal)
Globe (Toronto)
Globe and Mail (Toronto)
Halifax (NS) Reporter

Hamilton (ON) Herald
Hartford (CT) Courant
Harvard Crimson
Hockey News
Kingston (ON) Whig-Standard
Leader-Post (Regina, SK)
Liberty
Life
Literary Digest
London (ON) Free Press
Los Angeles Times
Maclean's
McGill News
Montreal Daily Herald (and Daily Telegraph)
Montreal Daily Witness
Montrealer
Montreal Evening Star
Montreal Standard
Montreal Weekend Magazine
National Home Monthly
New McClure's
New York Daily Mirror
New York Daily News

New Yorker
New York Herald Tribune
New York Journal-American
New York Sun
New York Times
New York World-Telegram
Ottawa Citizen
Ottawa Evening Citizen
Ottawa Journal
Outlook and Independent
Patrie, La (Montreal)
Petit Journal, Le (Montreal)
Philadelphia Post
Presse, La (Montreal)

Saskatoon Star-Phoenix
Saturday Night
Sports Illustrated
Time
Times (London)
Toronto Daily News
Toronto Daily Star
Toronto Mail and Empire
Toronto Star
Toronto Star Weekly
Toronto (Evening) Telegram
Washington Post
Winnipeg (MB) Free Press
World (Toronto)

Printed Government Documents

Canadian Department of Labour. *Investigation into an Alleged Combine in the Motion Picture Industry in Canada.* Report of Commissioner, 30 Apr. 1931. Ottawa: F. A. Acland, 1931.

Canadian Parliament. *House of Commons Debates,* 1917–45.

———. *Royal Commission on Racing Inquiry.* [Sessional Paper no. 67.] Ottawa: J. De Labroquerie Taché, 1920.

US Department of the Interior. National Park Service. "Olympia Arena." Historic American Buildings Survey no. MI-252.

Printed Primary Documents

Articles of Organization, Boston Professional Hockey Association, Inc., 24 Oct. 1924. Available at Commonwealth of Massachusetts Corporations Division. http://corp.sec.state.ma.us/.

Campbell, Clarence. "Hockey as a Business and as a Career" [delivered 21 Mar. 1963]. In *The Empire Club of Canada: Speeches, 1962–1963,* edited by Douglas Best et al. Toronto: Empire Club Foundation, 1963. http://www.empireclub foundation.com/.

City of Hamilton Directory. [Hamilton, ON: Vernon's, 1920.]

Constitution of the American League of Professional Baseball Clubs (1926). http://www.businessofbaseball.com/1926alconstitution.htm.

Lovell's Street Directory of Montreal, 1898–1940.

National Agreement for the Government of Professional Base Ball Clubs, [1903],
[between the National League and American Association of Professional
Base Ball Clubs and the American League of Professional Base Ball Clubs].
http://www.businessofbaseball.com/1903nlagreement.htm.

*Official Souvenir Programme of the Toronto Musical Festival, October 7th, 8th,
9th, 10th, 11th, and 12th, 1912, to Commemorate the Opening of the Arena,
Toronto, Canada.* CIHM No. 87057. N.p., [1912].

Ontario Law Reports. Vols. 55 (1924) and 57 (1925). Toronto: Canada Law Book,
1924, 1925.

*The Ontario Weekly Notes: Notes of Judgments of the Supreme Court of Ontario
and Other Ontario Courts.* Vol. 15. Toronto: Canada Law Book, 1919.

Online Databases

Ballparks of Baseball. http://www.ballparksofbaseball.com/.
BaseballReference.com. http://www.baseball-reference.com/.
HockeyDB.com. The Internet Hockey Database. http://www.hockeydb.com/.
Hockey Summary Project. http://hsp.flyershistory.com/.
Rodney Fort's Sports Business Data Pages. https://sites.google.com/site/rodsweb
pages/codes.
Society for International Hockey Research. http://www.sihrhockey.org/main.cfm.

Other Sources

Adams, Jack, with Trent Frayne. "The High Spots of a Lifetime with the Red
Wings." In *Canada on Ice: 50 Years of Great Hockey,* edited by Michael Bene-
dict and D'Arcy Jenish, 58–64. Toronto: Viking, 1998.

Adelman, Melvin L. *A Sporting Time: New York City and the Rise of Modern Athletics, 1820–70.* Urbana: Univ. of Illinois Press, 1986.

Alito, Samuel A., Jr. "The Origin of the Baseball Antitrust Exemption: *Federal
Baseball Club of Baltimore, Inc. v. National League of Professional Baseball
Clubs.*" *Journal of Supreme Court History* 34, no. 2 (2009): 183–95.

Amatori, Franco, and Geoffrey Jones, eds. *Business History around the World
at the Turn of the Twenty-First Century.* New York: Cambridge Univ. Press,
2003.

Aycock, Colleen, and Mark Scott. *Tex Rickard: Boxing's Greatest Promoter.* Jefferson, NC: McFarland, 2012.

Banner, Stuart. *The Baseball Trust: A History of Baseball's Antitrust Exemption.*
New York: Oxford Univ. Press, 2013.

Barlow, John Matthew. "'Scientific Aggression': Irishness, Manliness, Class, and Commercialization in the Shamrock Hockey Club of Montreal, 1894–1901." In *Coast to Coast: Hockey in Canada to the Second World War*, edited by John Chi-Kit Wong, 35–85. Toronto: Univ. of Toronto Press, 2009.

Barnouw, Erik. *The Golden Web: A History of Broadcasting in the United States.* Vol. 2, *1933–1953*. New York: Oxford Univ. Press, 1968.

Barrette, Rosaire. *Léo Dandurand, Sportsman.* Ottawa: Le Droit, 1952.

Beckert, Sven. *The Monied Metropolis: New York City and the Consolidation of the American Bourgeoisie, 1850–1896*. New York: Cambridge Univ. Press, 2001.

Beckert, Sven, and Julia B. Rosenbaum, eds. *The American Bourgeoisie: Distinction and Identity in the Nineteenth Century*. New York: Palgrave Macmillan, 2010.

Beers, W. G. *Lacrosse: The National Game of Canada*. Montreal: Dawson, 1879.

Betts, John R., "The Technological Revolution and the Rise of Sport, 1850–1900." *Mississippi Valley Historical Review* 40 (1953): 231–56.

Boucher, Frank, with Trent Frayne. *When the Rangers Were Young*. New York: Dodd, Mead, 1973.

Bouchier, Nancy. *For the Love of the Game: Amateur Sport in Small-Town Ontario, 1838–1895*. Montreal and Kingston: McGill-Queen's Univ. Press, 2003.

Broadfoot, Barry. *Ten Lost Years, 1929–1939: Memories of Canadians Who Survived the Depression*. Toronto: Doubleday Canada, 1973.

Brown, William. *Baseball's Fabulous Montreal Royals*. Montreal: Robert Davies, 1996.

———. *The Montreal Maroons: The Forgotten Stanley Cup Champions*. Montreal: Véhicule Press, 1999.

Bruneau, Pierre, and Léandre Normand. *La glorieuse histoire des Canadiens*. Montréal: Les Éditions de l'Homme, 2003.

Bryce, Robert B. *Canada and the Cost of World War II: The International Operations of Canada's Department of Finance, 1939–1947*. Edited by Matthew J. Bellamy. Montreal and Kingston: McGill-Queen's Univ. Press, 2005.

Bullock, Steven R. *Playing for Their Nation: Baseball and the American Military during World War II*. Lincoln: Univ. of Nebraska Press, 2004.

Burton, C. M., William Stocking, and Gordon K. Miller. *The City of Detroit, Michigan, 1701–1922*. Vol. 4. Detroit and Chicago: S. J. Clarke, 1922.

Butsch, Richard. *For Fun and Profit: The Transformation of Leisure into Consumption*. Philadelphia: Temple Univ. Press, 1990.

Cain, Louis P., and David D. Haddock. "Similar Economic Histories, Different Industrial Structures: Transatlantic Contrasts in the Evolution of

Professional Sports Leagues." *Journal of Economic History* 65, no. 4 (2005): 1116–47.

Casson, Mark C. *Economics of Business Culture: Game Theory, Transaction Costs and Economic Performance.* Oxford: Clarendon Press, 1991.

Castle, Irene. *Castles in the Air.* New York: Da Capo Press, 1980.

Chandler, Alfred D., Jr. "The Opportunities for Business History at the Beginning of the Twenty-First Century." In *Business History around the World at the Turn of the Twenty-First Century,* edited by Franco Amatori and Geoffrey Jones, 394–405. New York: Cambridge Univ. Press, 2003.

———. *Strategy and Structure: Chapters in the History of the Industrial Enterprise.* Cambridge: MIT Press, 1962.

———. *The Visible Hand: The Managerial Revolution in American Business.* Cambridge: Belknap Press, 1977.

"Chicago Stadium." *Jazz Age Chicago: Urban Leisure from 1893 to 1945.* Archived at http://web.archive.org/web/20110917053831/http://chicago.urban-history .org/ven/sas/chi_stad.shtml.

Clancy, K., and B. McFarlane. *Clancy: The King's Story.* Toronto: ECW Press, 1997.

Clark, Donald M. "Early Artificial Ice: The Development of Refrigeration Allowed the Game to Spread." In *Total Hockey: The Official Encyclopedia of the National Hockey League,* edited by Dan Diamond, 564–65. Toronto: Total Sports, 1998.

Clawson, Mary-Anne. *Constructing Brotherhood: Class, Gender, and Fraternalism.* Princeton, NJ: Princeton Univ. Press, 1989.

Coenen, Craig. *From Sandlots to the Super Bowl: The National Football League, 1920–67.* Knoxville: Univ. of Tennessee Press, 2005.

Cole, Wayne S. *America First: The Battle against Intervention, 1940–1941.* Madison: Univ. of Wisconsin Press, 1953.

Coleman, Charles L. *The Trail of the Stanley Cup.* 3 vols. [Montreal]: National Hockey League, 1964–69.

Condon, George. *The Man in the Arena: The Life & Times of A. C. Sutphin.* Cleveland, OH: A. C. Sutphin Foundation, 1995.

Cosentino, Frank. "A History of the Concept of Professionalism in Canadian Sport." PhD diss., York Univ., 1973.

Cox, Allan Elton. "A History of Sports in Canada, 1868–1900." PhD diss., Univ. of Alberta, 1969.

———. *The Renfrew Millionaires: The Valley Boys of Winter 1910.* Burnstown, ON: General Store, 1990.

Crepeau, Richard C. *Baseball: America's Diamond Mind.* Lincoln: Univ. of Nebraska Press, 2000.

———. "The Sports Song of Patriotism." http://www.poppolitics.com/articles /2003-02-28-flagprotest.shtml.

Cruise, David, and Allison Griffiths. *Net Worth: Exploding the Myths of Pro Hockey.* Toronto: Viking, 1991.

De Wilde, Ari C. "'The Dizzy Race to Nowhere': The Business of Professional Cycling in North America, 1891–1940." PhD diss., Ohio State Univ., 2010.

Diamond, Dan, ed. *The Official National Hockey League 75th Anniversary Commemorative Book.* Toronto: McClelland & Stewart, 1991.

———, ed. *Total Hockey: The Official Encyclopedia of the National Hockey League.* Toronto: Total Sports, 1998.

———, ed. *Total Hockey: The Official Encyclopedia of the National Hockey League.* 2nd ed. Toronto: SportClassic Books, 2003.

Dufresne, Sylvie. "Le Carnaval d'hiver de Montréal." *Urban History Review* 11, no. 3 (1983): 25–47.

Durand, Marc. *La coupe à Québec: Les Bulldogs et la naissance du hockey.* Quebec: Éditions Sylvain Harvey et Commission de la Capitale Nationale du Québec, 2012.

Durso, Joe. "The Four Gardens and How They Grew." In *Madison Square Garden: A Century of Sport and Spectacle on the World's Most Versatile Stage,* edited by Zander Hollander, 1–66. New York: Hawthorn Books, 1973.

———. *Madison Square Garden: 100 Years of History.* New York: Simon and Schuster, 1979.

Dutton, Mervyn. *Hockey: The Fastest Sport on Earth.* New York: Funk & Wagnalls, 1938.

Dyreson, Mark. "The Emergence of Consumer Culture and the Transformation of Physical Culture: American Sport in the 1920s." *Journal of Sport History* 16, no. 3 (1989): 261–81.

Egnal, Marc. *Divergent Paths: How Culture and Institutions Have Shaped North American Growth.* New York: Oxford Univ. Press, 1996.

Ellsworth, Peter Daniel. "'The House That Conn Built': Why and How Maple Leaf Gardens Was Built and the Impact Its Construction Had on Toronto and Professional Hockey." Master's thesis, Univ. of Guelph, 2005.

Farrell, Arthur. *Hockey: Canada's Royal Winter Game.* Montreal: C. R. Corneil, 1899. http://epe.lac-bac.gc.ca/100/200/300/corneil_cr/hockey/hockey_canadas _royal_winter_game.pdf.

Field, Russell David. "A Night at the Garden(s): A History of Professional Hockey Spectatorship in the 1920s and 1930s." PhD diss., Univ. of Toronto, 2008.

———. "Passive Participation: The Selling of Spectacle and the Construction of Maple Leaf Gardens, 1931." *Sport History Review* 33, no. 1 (2002): 35–50.

———. "Profits, Playoffs and the Building of Maple Leaf Gardens, 1931." In *Putting It on Ice*, edited by Colin D. Howell, 47–58. Halifax, NS: Gorsebrook Research Institute, St. Mary's Univ., 2002.

Fischler, Stan, with Tom Sarro. *Metro Ice*. Flushing, NY: H&M Productions II, 1999.

Fisher, Donald M. *Lacrosse: A History of the Game*. Baltimore: Johns Hopkins Univ. Press, 2002.

Fitsell, J. W. *Hockey's Captains, Colonels and Kings*. Erin, ON: Boston Mills Press, 1987.

———. "The Rise and Fall of Ice Polo and Its Influence of Maritime Hockey." *SIHR Journal* (1999): 11–17.

Flaherty, David, and William McKercher, eds. *Southern Exposure: Canadian Perspectives on the United States*. Toronto: McGraw-Hill Ryerson, 1986.

Fleming, George Thornton. *History of Pittsburgh and Environs, from Prehistoric Days to the Beginning of the American Revolution*. 5 vols. New York and Chicago: American Historical Society, 1922.

Flynn, George Q. *The Mess in Washington: Manpower Mobilization in World War II*. Westport, CT: Greenwood Press, 1979.

Fort, Rodney. "Market Power in Pro Sports: Problems and Solutions." In *The Economics of Sports*, edited by William S. Kern, 7–19. Kalamazoo, MI: W. E. Upjohn Institute for Employment Research, 2000.

Foster, Charles J. "Other Winter Games." In *Our Young Folks: An Illustrated Magazine for Boys and Girls* [Apr. 1867]. Boston: Ticknor and Fields, 1867.

———. "The Winter Sports: Skating." In *Our Young Folks: An Illustrated Magazine for Boys and Girls* [Mar. 1867]. Boston: Ticknor and Fields, 1867.

Foulds, Alan E. *Boston's Ballparks and Arenas*. Hanover, NH: Univ. Press of New England, 2005.

Frayne, Trent. *The Mad Men of Hockey*. Toronto: McClelland & Stewart, 1974.

Galambos, Louis. "The Emerging Organizational Synthesis in Modern American History." *Business History Review* 44, no. 3 (1970): 279–90.

———. "Identity and the Boundaries of Business History." In *Business History around the World at the Turn of the Twenty-First Century*, edited by Franco Amatori and Geoffrey Jones, 11–30. New York: Cambridge Univ. Press, 2003.

————. "Recasting the Organizational Synthesis: Structure and Process in the Twentieth and Twenty-First Centuries." *Business History Review* 79 (2005): 1–38.

Gallico, Paul. *Farewell to Sport*. New York: Alfred A. Knopf, 1944.

Gibbons, Alan O. "Foreign Exchange Control in Canada, 1939–51." *Canadian Journal of Economics and Political Science* 19, no. 1 (1953): 35–54.

Gietschier, Steven P. "'Uncle Sam Needs Only to Call': Baseball and the United States' Peacetime Military Draft, 1940–1941." Paper presented to the North American Society for Sport History, Halifax, NS, 25 May 2013.

Goldstein, Richard. *Spartan Seasons: How Baseball Survived the Second World War*. New York: Macmillan, 1980.

Gomery, Douglas. *Shared Pleasures: A History of Movie Presentation in the United States*. Madison: Univ. of Wisconsin Press, 1992.

Goyens, Chrystian, and Allan Turowetz. *Lions in Winter*. Toronto: Prentice Hall Canada, 1986.

Goyens, Chrystian, with Allan Turowetz and Jean-Luc Duguay. *Montreal Forum: Forever Proud*. Westmount, QC: Les Éditions Effix, 1996.

Granatstein, J. L., and J. M. Hitsman. *Broken Promises: A History of Conscription in Canada*. Toronto: Oxford Univ. Press, 1977.

Greif, Avner. *Institutions and the Path to the Modern Economy: Lessons from Medieval Trade*. Cambridge: Cambridge Univ. Press, 2006.

Gruneau, Richard S., and David Whitson, eds. *Hockey Night in Canada: Sport, Identities and Cultural Politics*. Toronto: Garamond Press, 1993.

Guay, Donald. *L'histoire du hockey au Québec: Origine et développement d'un phénomène culturel*. Chicoutimi, QC: Les Éditions JCL, 1990.

Guttmann, Allen. *Games and Empires: Modern Sports and Cultural Imperialism*. New York: Columbia Univ. Press, 1994.

Halligan, John. "Confessions of Some More New York Rink Rats." Unpublished ms.

————. "February 25, 1940: Hockey's First Telecast." http://www.newyorkrangers .com/tradition/alumnispotlight.asp?Alumni=TVhistory.

Handley, Peter. *Anent Michael J.: The Life & Times of Michael J. Rodden in Northern Ontario in His Own Words*. Cobalt, ON: Highway Book Shop, 1999.

Hardy, Stephen H. "Entrepreneurs, Organizations, and the Sports Marketplace." In *The New American Sport History: Recent Approaches and Perspectives*, edited by S. W. Pope, 342–65. Urbana: Univ. of Illinois Press, 1997. Reprinted from *Journal of Sport History* 13, no. 1 (1986): 14–33.

———. "Entrepreneurs, Structures, and the Sportgeist: Old Tensions in a Modern Industry." In *Essays on Sport History and Sport Mythology*, edited by Allen Guttmann et al., 45–82. College Station: Texas A&M Univ. Press, 1990.

———. *How Boston Played: Sport, Recreation, and Community, 1865–1915*. Boston: Northeastern Univ. Press, 1982.

———. "Long before Orr: Placing Hockey in Boston, 1897–1929." In *The Rock, the Curse, and the Hub: A Random History of Boston Sports*, edited by Randy Roberts, 245–72. Cambridge: Harvard Univ. Press, 2005.

———. "Memory, Performance, and History: The Making of American Ice Hockey at St. Paul's School, 1860–1915." *International Journal of the History of Sport* 14, no. 1 (1997): 97–115.

———. "Polo at the Rinks: Shaping Markets for Ice Hockey in America, 1880–1900." *Journal of Sport History* 33, no. 2 (2006): 156–74.

———. "Two-Way Hockey: Selling Canada's Game in America, 1885–1935." Unpublished ms.

Hardy, Stephen, and Andrew Holman. "Periodizing Hockey History: One Approach." In *Now Is the Winter: Thinking about Hockey*, edited by Jamie Dopp and Richard Harrison, 19–35. Hamilton, ON: Wolsak and Wynn, 2009.

Hardy, Stephen, Brian Norman, and Sarah Sceery. "Toward a History of Sport Branding." *Journal of Historical Research in Marketing* 4 no. 4 (2012): 482–509.

Harper, Frank C. *Pittsburgh of Today, Its Resources and People*. Vols. 3–4. New York: American Historical Society, 1931–32.

Harper, Stephen J. *A Great Game: The Forgotten Leafs and the Rise of Professional Hockey*. Toronto: Simon and Schuster Canada, 2013.

Harvey, Adrian. *The Beginnings of a Commercial Sporting Culture in Britain, 1793–1850*. Aldershot: Ashgate, 2004.

———. *Football: The First Hundred Years, the Untold Story*. London and New York: Routledge, 2005.

Helyar, John. *Lords of the Realm: The Real History of Baseball*. New York: Villard Books, 1994.

Hewitt, William Abraham. *Down the Stretch: Recollections of a Pioneer Sportsman and Journalist*. Toronto: Ryerson Press, 1958.

Hinnegan, K. A. "The 'Services Exemption' under the Combines Investigation Act." *University of Toronto Law Journal* 19, no. 2 (1969): 234–35.

Holman, Andrew C. "Playing in the Neutral Zone: Meanings and Uses of Ice Hockey in the Canada-US Borderlands, 1895–1915." *American Review of Canadian Studies* 34, no. 1 (2004): 33–57.

———. *A Sense of Their Duty: Middle-Class Formation in Victorian Ontario Towns*. Montreal and Kingston: McGill-Queen's Univ. Press, 2000.

Holzman, Morey, and Joseph Nieforth. *Deceptions and Doublecross: How the NHL Conquered Hockey*. Toronto: Dundurn Press, 2002.

Houda, Patrick, and Carl Giden. "Stick and Ball Game Timeline." http//www .sihr.org.

Howell, Colin D. *Blood, Sweat and Cheers: Sport and the Making of Modern Canada*. Toronto: Univ. of Toronto Press, 2001.

———. *Northern Sandlots: A Social History of Maritime Baseball*. Toronto: Univ. of Toronto Press, 1995.

Howland, William. *Chicago Jazz: A Cultural History, 1904–1930*. New York: Oxford Univ. Press, 1993.

Hunter, Douglas. *War Games: Conn Smythe and Hockey's Fighting Men*. Toronto: Viking, 1996.

Hutchison, Bruce. *The Incredible Canadian*. Toronto: Longmans, Green, 1952.

Isaacs, Neil D. *Checking Back: A History of the National Hockey League*. New York: W. W. Norton, 1977.

Jacobson, Lisa. "Beer Goes to War: The Politics of Beer Promotion and Production in the Second World War." *Food, Culture, and Society* 12 (Sept. 2009): 275–312.

Janson, Gilles. "George Washington Kendall, dit George Kennedy." *Dictionnaire biographique du Canada*. http://www.biographi.ca/.

Jenish, D'Arcy. *The NHL: 100 Years of On-Ice Action and Boardroom Battles*. Toronto: Doubleday Canada, 2013.

Jones, J. C. H. "The Economics of the National Hockey League." *Canadian Journal of Economics* 2, no. 1 (1969): 1–20.

———. "The Economics of the National Hockey League Revisited: A PostScript on Cultural Change, Behaviour and Government Policy." In *Canadian Sport: Sociological Perspectives*, edited by Richard S. Gruneau and John G. Albinson, 249–25. Don Mills, Toronto: Addison-Wesley (Canada), 1976.

Jones, Kevin. "Sport and Games from 1900–1920." PhD diss., Univ. of Alberta, 1970.

Jose, Colin. *American Soccer League, 1921–1931: The Golden Years of American Soccer*. Lanham, MD: Scarecrow Press, 1998.

Joyce, Charles Anthony. "'From Left Field': Sport and Class in Toronto, 1845–1886." PhD diss., Queen's Univ., 1997

Kaese, Harold. *The Boston Braves*. New York: G. P. Putnam's Sons, 1948.

Kahn, Roger. *A Flame of Pure Fire: Jack Dempsey and the Roaring 20s.* New York: Harcourt Brace, 1999.

Kiczek, Gene. *Forgotten Glory: The Story of Cleveland Barons Hockey.* Euclid, OH: Blue Line, 1994.

Kidd, Bruce. "Improvers, Feminists, Capitalists and Socialists: Shaping Canadian Sport in the 1920s and 1930s." PhD diss., York Univ., 1990.

———. *The Struggle for Canadian Sport.* Toronto: Univ. of Toronto Press, 1996.

Kidd, Bruce, and John Macfarlane. *The Death of Hockey.* Toronto: New Press, 1972.

Kitchen, Paul. "Before *The Trail of the Stanley Cup*." In *Total Hockey: The Official Encyclopedia of the National Hockey League,* edited by Dan Diamond, 8–15. 2nd ed. Toronto: SportClassic Books, 2003.

———. "P. D. Ross: How He Came to Be a Stanley Cup Trustee." *Hockey Research Journal* 10 (2006): 4–6.

———. *Win, Tie, or Wrangle: The Inside Story of the Old Ottawa Senators, 1883–1935.* Manotick, ON: Penumbra Press, 2008.

Kroeber, A. L., and Charles Kluckhohn. *Culture: A Critical Review of Concepts and Definitions.* New York: Vintage Books, 1963.

Lacoste, Norbert. *Les caractéristisques sociale de la population de Grand Montréal.* Montreal: Les Presses de l'Université de Montréal, 1958.

Lamoreaux, Naomi R., Daniel M. G. Raff, and Peter Temin. "Beyond Markets and Hierarchies: Toward a New Synthesis of American Business History." *American Historical Review* 108, no. 2 (2003): 404–33.

Lears, T. J. Jackson. *No Place of Grace: Antimodernism and the Transformation of American Culture, 1880–1920.* New York: Pantheon, 1981.

Leifer, Eric. *Making the Majors: The Transformation of Team Sports in America.* Cambridge, MA: Harvard Univ. Press, 1996.

Lipartito, Kenneth. "Culture and the Practice of Business History." *Business and Economic History* 24 (Winter 1995): 1–41.

Lorenz, Stacey. "'In the Field of Sport at Home and Abroad': Sports Coverage in Canadian Newspapers, 1850–1914." *Sport History Review* 34 (2003): 133–67.

MacDonald, D. A. L. "A Winter Stadium." *McGill News* (Winter 1956).

Manning, Frank. "Reversible Resistance." In *The Beaver Bites Back? American Popular Culture in Canada,* edited by David Flaherty and Frank E. Manning, 1–27. Montreal: McGill-Queen's Univ. Press, 1993.

Marks, Lynne. *Revivals and Roller Rinks: Religion, Leisure and Identity in Late-Nineteenth-Century Small-Town Ontario.* Toronto: Univ. of Toronto Press, 1996.

Mason, Daniel S. "The International Hockey League and the Professionalization of Ice Hockey, 1904–1907." *Journal of Sport History* 25, no. 1 (1998): 1–17.

———. "The Origins and Development of the International Hockey League and Its Effects on the Sport of Professional Ice Hockey in North America." Master's thesis, Univ. of British Columbia, 1994.

Mason, Daniel S., and Barbara Schrodt. "Hockey's First Professional Team: The Portage Lakes Hockey Club of Houghton, Michigan." *Sport History Review* 27, no. 1 (1996): 49–71.

Mayer, Charles. *L'épopée des Canadiens de Georges Vézina à Maurice Richard: 46 ans d'histoire, 1909–1955*. Montreal: Dow Breweries, 1956.

McDonald, Kevin. "Antitrust and Baseball: Stealing Holmes." *Journal of Supreme Court History* 2 (1998): 89–128.

McFarlane, Brian. *One Hundred Years of Hockey*. Toronto: Summerhill Press, 1990.

McIntyre, Bruce. "Which Uniform to Serve?" *Canadian Journal of History of Sport* 24 (Dec. 1993): 68–89.

McKinley, Michael. *Hockey: A People's History*. Toronto: McClelland & Stewart, 2006.

———. *Putting a Roof on Winter: Hockey's Rise from Sport to Spectacle*. Vancouver, BC: Greystone Books, 2000.

McLuhan, Marshall. *Understanding Media: The Extensions of Man*. Toronto: McGraw-Hill, 1965.

McParland, Kelly. *The Lives of Conn Smythe: From the Battlefield to Maple Leaf Gardens: A Hockey Icon's Story*. Toronto: FENN/McClelland & Stewart, 2011.

Metcalfe, Alan. *Canada Learns to Play: The Emergence of Organized Sport, 1807–1914*. Toronto: McClelland & Stewart, 1987.

———. "The Evolution of Organized Physical Recreation in Montreal, 1840–1895." In *Histoire sociale/Social History* 11, no. 21 (1978): 144–66.

———. "Organized Sport and Social Stratification in Montreal, 1840–1901." In *Canadian Sport: Sociological Perspectives*, edited by Richard S. Gruneau and John G. Albinson, 77–101. Don Mills, Toronto: Addison-Wesley (Canada), 1976.

———. "Power: A Case Study of the Ontario Hockey Association, 1890–1936." *Journal of Sport History* 19, no. 1 (1992): 5–25.

Mills, David. "The Blue Line and the Bottom Line: Entrepreneurs and the Business of Hockey in Canada, 1927–1989." In *The Business of Professional Sports*, edited by J. A. Mangan and P. Staudohar, 175–201. Urbana: Univ. of Illinois Press, 1991.

———. "The Visible Hand and the Management of Hockey." In *Method and Methodology in Sport and Cultural History*, edited by K. Wamsley, 244–80. Dubuque, IA: Times Mirror Higher Education Group, 1995.

Monk, Craig. "When Eustace Tilley Came to Madison Square Garden: Professional Hockey and the Editorial Policy of the *New Yorker* in the 1920s and 1930s." *American Periodicals* 15, no. 2 (2005): 178–95.

Morrow, Don. "A Case Study in Amateur Conflict: The Athletic War in Canada, 1906–08." *British Journal of Sports History* 3, no. 2 (1986): 173–90.

———. "The Institutionalization of Sport: A Case Study of Canadian Lacrosse, 1844–1914." *International Journal of the History of Sport* 9, no. 2 (1992): 236–51.

———. "The Little Men of Iron: The 1902 Montreal Hockey Club." *Canadian Journal of History of Sport* 12 (1981): 51–65.

———. *A Sporting Evolution: Montreal Amateur Athletic Association, 1881–1981.* Montreal: Montreal Amateur Athletic Association and Don Morrow, 1981.

Morrow, Don, and Kevin B. Wamsley. *Sport in Canada: A History.* Toronto: Oxford Univ. Press, 2005.

Mott, Morris. "Flawed Games, Splendid Ceremonies: The Hockey Matches of the Winnipeg Vics, 1890–1903." *Prairie Forum* 10, no. 1 (1985): 169–87.

Nelson, Murry R. *The National Basketball League: A History, 1935–1949.* Jefferson, NC: McFarland, 2009.

———. *The Originals: The New York Celtics Invent Modern Basketball.* Bowling Green, OH: Bowling Green State Univ. Popular Press, 1999.

Norrie, Kenneth, Douglas Owram, and J. C. Herbert Emery. *A History of the Canadian Economy.* 4th ed. Toronto: Nelson Education, 2008.

"Oakland: Duquesne Garden." Carnegie Library of Pittsburgh. http://www.clpgh .org/exhibit/neighborhoods/oakland/oak_n268.html.

"Oakland: The World's Most Perfect Ice Palace." *Bulletin,* 9 Oct. 1920, reprinted at Carnegie Library of Pittsburgh. http://www.clpgh.org/exhibit/neighbor hoods/oakland/oak_n26a.html.

O'Coughlin, Seamus. *Squaw Valley Gold: American Hockey's Olympic Odyssey.* New York: Writer's Showcase, 2001.

Oriard, Michael. *King Football: Sport and Spectacle in the Golden Age of Radio and Newsreels, Movies and Magazines, the Weekly and the Daily Press.* Chapel Hill: Univ. of North Carolina Press, 2001.

———. *Reading Football: How the Popular Press Created an American Spectacle.* Chapel Hill: Univ. of North Carolina Press, 1993.

Orlick, E. M. "McGill's Contribution to the Origins of Ice Hockey." *McGill News* (Winter 1943): 13–17.

Osgerby, Bill. *Playboys in Paradise: Masculinity, Youth and Leisure in Modern America*. Oxford: Berg, 2001.

Panunto, Gabriel Stephen. "For Club or Country? Hockey in Wartime Canada, 1939–1945." Master's thesis, Carleton Univ., 2000.

Postal, Bernard, Jesse Silver, and Roy Silver, eds. *Encyclopedia of Jews in Sports*. New York: Bloch, 1965.

Poulter, Gillian. *Becoming Native in a Foreign Land: Sport, Visual Culture, and Identity in Montreal, 1840–1885*. Vancouver, BC: UBC Press, 2009.

Powell, W. W. "Neither Market nor Hierarchy: Network Forms of Organization." *Research in Organizational Behavior* 12 (1990): 295–336.

Quirk, James P., and Rodney D. Fort. *Pay Dirt: The Business of Professional Team Sports*. Princeton, NJ: Princeton Univ. Press, 1992.

Rader, Benjamin G. *American Sports: From the Age of Folk Games to the Age of Televised Sports*. Englewood Cliffs, NJ: Prentice Hall, 1996.

———. *Baseball: A History of America's Game*. Urbana: Univ. of Illinois Press, 1994.

———. "The Quest for Subcommunities and the Rise of American Sport." *American Quarterly* 29 (1977): 255–69.

Regehr, T. D. *The Beauharnois Scandal: A Story of Canadian Entrepreneurship and Politics*. Toronto: Univ. of Toronto Press, 1990.

"Rene Boileau." Hockey Hall of Fame and Museum. http://www.legendsof hockey.net.

"The Retirement of William Foran." *Civil Service Review* (Mar. 1939).

Riess, Stephen A. *City Games: The Evolution of American Urban Society and the Rise of Sports*. Urbana: Univ. of Illinois Press, 1991.

———, ed. *Sports in North America: A Documentary History*. Vol. 6, *Sports in the Progressive Era, 1900–1920*. Gulf Breeze, FL: Academic International Press, 1998.

Robinson, Dean. *Howie Morenz: Hockey's First Superstar*. Erin, ON: Boston Mills Press, 1982.

Roche, Wilfrid Victor (Bill), ed. *The Hockey Book*. Toronto: McClelland and Stewart, 1953.

Rook, Charles Alexander, et al., eds. *Western Pennsylvanians: A Work for Newspaper and Library References*. Pittsburgh: Western Pennsylvania Biographical Association, 1923.

Rorke, Thomas. "Memory on Ice: Making the 1936 Canadian Olympic Hockey Team." Master's thesis, Carleton Univ., 2010.

Ross, J. Andrew. "Arenas of Debate: The Continuance of Hockey in the Second World War." In *Coast to Coast: Hockey in Canada*, edited by John Chi-Kit Wong, 223–57. Toronto: Univ. of Toronto Press, 2009. Reprinted with permission of the publisher.

———. "Explaining Exceptionalism: Approaches to the Study of American Sport Business History." In *A Companion to American Sport History*, edited by Steven A. Riess. Malden, MA: Wiley Blackwell, 2014.

———. "Hockey Capital: Approaches to the Study of Sports Industry." *Business and Economic History On-Line* 3 (2005). http://www.thebhc.org/publications /BEHonline/2005/ross.pdf.

———. "Hockey Capital: Commerce, Culture and the National Hockey League, 1917–1967." PhD diss., Univ. of Western Ontario, 2008.

———. "The Paradox of Conn Smythe: Hockey, Memory and the Second World War." *Sport History Review* 37 (May 2006): 19–35.

Roxborough, H. H. *One Hundred—Not Out: The Story of Nineteenth-Century Canadian Sport*. Toronto: Ryerson Press, 1966.

———. *The Stanley Cup Story*. Toronto: Ryerson Press, 1964.

Rutherford, Paul. *A Victorian Authority: The Daily Press in Late Nineteenth-Century Canada*. Toronto: Univ. of Toronto Press, 1982.

Samuels, Charles. *The Magnificent Rube: The Life and Gaudy Times of Tex Rickard*. New York: McGraw-Hill, 1957.

Scranton, Philip. *Endless Novelty: Specialty Production and American Industrialization, 1865–1925*. Princeton, NJ: Princeton Univ. Press, 1997.

Selke, F. J., with H. G. Green. *Behind the Cheering*. Toronto: McClelland & Stewart, 1962.

Seymour, Harold. *Baseball: The Early Years*. New York: Oxford Univ. Press, 1960.

Shea, Kevin, and John Jason Wilson. *Lord Stanley: The Man behind the Cup*. Bolton, ON: Fenn, 2006.

Shubert, Howard. "The Changing Experience of Hockey Spectatorship: Architecture, Design, Technology and Economics." In *Putting It on Ice*. Vol. 1, *Hockey and Cultural Identities,* edited by Colin D. Howell, 59–54. Halifax, ON: Gorsebrook Research Institute, St. Mary's Univ., 2002.

———. "The Evolution of the Hockey Arena: Building Better Hockey Barns, 1860 to 2000." In *Total Hockey: The Official Encyclopedia of the National*

Hockey League, edited by Dan Diamond, 553–59. 2nd ed. New York: Total Sports, 2000.

Slater, Kevin. *Trolley League: The Complete History of the Ontario Professional Hockey League, 1908–1911*. E-book.

Smith, Adam. *An Inquiry into the Nature and Causes of the Wealth of Nations*. 2nd ed. London: W. Strahan and T. Cadell, 1778.

Smythe, Conn, and Scott Young. *Conn Smythe: If You Can't Beat 'Em in the Alley*. Toronto: McClelland & Stewart, 1981.

Society for International Hockey Research. *Report of the Sub-Committee Looking into Claim That Windsor, Nova Scotia, Is the Birthplace of Hockey*. http://www.sihrhockey.org/.

Sotiron, Minko. *From Politics to Profit: The Commercialization of Canadian Daily Newspapers, 1890–1920*. Montreal: McGill-Queen's Univ. Press, 1997.

Stacey, C. P. *Arms, Men and Governments: The War Policies of Canada, 1939–1945*. Ottawa: Queen's Printer, 1970.

Staudohar, Paul D. *Playing for Dollars: Labor Relations and the Sports Business*. Ithaca, NY: ILR Press, 1996.

Staudohar, Paul D., and James A. Mangan, eds. *The Business of Professional Sports*. Urbana: Univ. of Illinois Press, 1991.

Stevenson, Michael D. *Canada's Greatest Wartime Muddle: National Selective Service and the Mobilization of Human Resources during World War II*. Montreal and Kingston: McGill-Queen's Univ. Press, 2001.

Surdam, David G. *The Rise of the National Basketball Association*. Urbana: Univ. of Illinois Press, 2012.

Susman, Warren I. *Culture as History: The Transformation of American Society in the Twentieth Century*. New York: Pantheon Books, 1984.

Taylor, Matthew. *The Leaguers: The Making of Professional Football in England, 1900–1939*. Liverpool: Liverpool Univ. Press, 2005.

Tuthill, J. A. *Ice Hockey and Ice Polo Guide*. New York: American Sports, 1898. http://www.library.unh.edu/digital/object/digital:00190.

Twatio, Bill. "Wartime Wonders." *Queen's Quarterly* 100 (Winter 1993): 833–40.

Tygiel, Jules. *Past Time: Baseball as History*. New York: Oxford Univ. Press, 2000.

Vamplew, Wray. "The Economics of a Sports Industry: Scottish Money-Gate Football, 1890–1914." *Economic History Review* 35 (Nov. 1982): 549–67.

———. *Pay Up and Play the Game: Professional Sports in Britain, 1875–1914*. Cambridge: Cambridge Univ. Press, 1988.

Van Bottenburg, Maarten. "Beyond Diffusion: Sport and Its Remaking in Cross-cultural Contexts." *Journal of Sport History* 37, no. 1 (2010): 41–53.

Vass, George. *The Chicago Black Hawks Story.* Chicago: Follett, 1970.

Vigneault, Michel. "La naissance d'un sport organisé au Canada: Le hockey à Montréal, 1875–1917." PhD diss., Univ. Laval, 2001.

————. "Out of the Mists of Memory: Montreal's Hockey History, 1875–1910." In *Total Hockey: The Official Encyclopedia of the National Hockey League,* edited by Dan Diamond, 10–18. New York: Total Sports, 1998.

Voigt, David Quentin. *American Baseball.* 2 vols. Norman: Univ. of Oklahoma Press, 1966–70.

Walkinshaw, Lewis Clark. *Annals of Southwestern Pennsylvania.* New York: Lewis Historical, 1939.

Walvin, James. *The People's Game: A Social History of British Football.* London: Allen Lane, 1975.

Whitaker, Reginald. *The Government Party: Organizing and Financing the Liberal Party of Canada, 1930–58.* Toronto: Univ. of Toronto Press, 1977.

White, G. E. *Creating the National Pastime: Baseball Transforms Itself, 1903–1953.* Princeton, NJ: Princeton Univ. Press, 1996.

Whitehead, Eric. *Cyclone Taylor: A Hockey Legend.* Toronto: Doubleday, 1977.

————. *The Patricks, Hockey's Royal Family.* Toronto: Doubleday Canada, 1980.

Wiebe, Robert. *The Search for Order, 1877–1920.* New York: Hill and Wang, 1967.

Wilson, J. J. "Skating to Armageddon: Canada, Hockey and the First World War." *International Journal for the History of Sport* 22, no. 3 (2005), 315–43.

Wong, John Chi-Kit. "Boomtown Hockey: The Vancouver Millionaires." In *Coast to Coast: Hockey in Canada,* edited by John Chi-Kit Wong, 223–57. Toronto: Univ. of Toronto Press, 2009.

————. "The Development of Professional Hockey and the Making of the National Hockey League." PhD diss., Univ. of Maryland–College Park, 2001.

————. "Entrepreneurship and the Rise of the Chicago Blackhawks." In *The Chicago Sports Reader: 100 Years of Sports in the Windy City,* edited by Gerald Gems and Steven Riess, 254–80. Urbana: Univ. of Illinois Press, 2009.

————. *Lords of the Rinks: The Emergence of the National Hockey League, 1875–1936.* Toronto: Univ. of Toronto Press, 2005.

Wong, John Chi-Kit, and Michel Vigneault. "An English Team in a French Environment: The Rise and Fall of Professional Hockey in Quebec City, 1911–1920." In *Putting It on Ice.* Vol. 1, *Hockey and Cultural Identities,* edited by

Colin D. Howell, 17–23. Halifax, ON: Gorsebrook Research Institute, St. Mary's Univ., 2002.

Wood, William. *The Storied Province of Quebec, Past and Present.* 4 vols. Toronto: Dominion, 1931–32.

Young, Scott. *The Boys of Saturday Night: Inside Hockey Night in Canada.* Toronto: Macmillan of Canada, 1990.

———. *Hello Canada! The Life and Times of Foster Hewitt.* Toronto: Seal Books, 1985.

———. *100 Years of Dropping the Puck: A History of the OHA.* Toronto: McClelland & Stewart, 1989.

Young, Scott, and Astrid Young. *O'Brien.* Toronto: Ryerson Press, 1967.

Index

Italic page number denotes illustration.

Miami (FL), 177

military participation. *See under* hockey players; *individual clubs and leagues*

Milks, Hib, 96

Miller, Jim, 175

Milne, Alex, 46

Milot, Hubert, 148

Minneapolis (MN), 276

Minneapolis Millers hockey club (CHA/ AHA), 129, 206, 215

minor leagues: formation of, 144–51. *See also* individual leagues

Mitchell (ON), 84

Mitchell, John J., Jr., 152, 173

modernity: antimodernism, 54; imposition of rules, 12; paradox of, 136–37; of sport, 10, 12. *See also under* hockey (ice)

Molson, Herbert, 109

monopoly, 2, 28, 124, 278. *See also* Madison Square Garden; National Hockey League: business and economic aspects

monopsony, 2. *See also* National Hockey Association; National Hockey League: business and economic aspects

Montreal, 12, 142, *191*; club culture of, 11–16, 314; English (Anglophone) community in, 11–14, 53–54, *191*, 320; as environment for hockey, 12–13, 53–54; French (Francophone) community in, *191*, 320; population of, 40; as viable two-club market, 254. *See also* Montreal Amateur Athletic Association

Montreal Amateur Athletic Association (MAAA), 15–16, 55, *188*, 204, 217; Allan Cup-winning team, 243, 245; business aspect of, 22; and lobbying for amateur rules reform, 34–35; objects of, 15; social class composition, 15

Montreal Arena. *See* Westmount Arena (Montreal Arena)

Montreal Arena Company, 24, 32. *See also* Westmount Arena (Montreal Arena)

Montreal Canadiens (hockey club), 39–40, 67, 71, 85, 89, 92, 101, 126, 132, 142, 150, 163–65, 171–72, 176, 217, 256, 269, 317, 326; gate receipts, 232, 254, 256–57, 268–69, 284; join NHL, 58; lease with Forum, 232–33; 1921 sale of, 80, 183; 1935 sale of, 233; and player recruitment, 243; and radio, 202, 237, 254–55; relationship with Forum, 130; relationship with Mount Royal Arena, 110, 116–17; right to French Canadian players, 40, 82, 120, 214, 243; and rumored move to Chicago, 129, 131; sale/move threats, 232–33; wartime border-crossing problems, 292–93; wartime exhibition game in California, 300; wartime goalscoring, 305; and wartime improvement, 293; and wartime players lost due to Ross resolution, 307; and wartime players working in essential industries, 306–7; and Westmount fire, 64. *See also* Canadian Arena Company (CAC)

Montreal Carnival, 14–15; hockey tournaments, 14; influence of, 18, 19

Montreal Exhibition Company, 233

Montreal Football Club, 9, 11

Montreal game. *See under* hockey (ice)

Montreal Hockey Club (HC), 14, 15, 16, 29, 30, 35, 109, *198*; commercial aspects of, 22–23

Montreal Lacrosse Club, 11, 15, 24

Montreal Maroons hockey club (NHL), 90, 110, 114–15, 130–31, 138, 150, 164, 169, 171–72, 227, 317, 326; dormant franchise, 269; gate receipts, 232, 254; and player recruitment, 243, 245; and radio, 202, 237, 254–55; and rumours of move, 255; suspends, 256–57. *See also* Canadian Arena Company

National War Services Board (Canada) (*cont.*)
287, 288; in Saskatchewan, 287, 288; in
Toronto, 287, 289. *See also* Adamson, J. E.;
Department of National War Services;
National Selective Service (NSS); passport
(permissions)

negotiation list. *See under* National Hockey
League

networks, 12, 122, 136, 185

Neurological Institute of New York, 90

Newark (NJ), 148

New Haven (CT), 104, 148

New Haven Eagles (Can-Am), 242

New Liskeard (ON), 36

New Madison Square Garden Corporation,
106. *See also* Madison Square Garden

New Westminster hockey club (PCHA Royals), 48

New York (NY), 56, 73, 88, 105, 124, 127, 129,
163; early hockey in, 21, 94

New York American Hockey Club, Inc. *See*
New York Americans

New York Americans (NHL), 89, 92, 106, 108,
116, 120, 122, 124–25, 130, 137, 163, 174,
183, *195*, 221, 235, 269, 285, 317, 320, 326;
attendance, 171–72; balance sheet, 228;
deal with MSG, 111–12, 229; and dispute
with MSG, 228–29; and dispute over temperature with MSG, 128; franchise suspension, 295, 311; lease, 228–29, 251, 294;
move to Brooklyn, 294; and New Haven
Eagles, 242; player unrest, 230; potential
sale, 251; purported Garden subsidy of,
294; takeover by league, 252–53, 293. *See
also* Dwyer, William V. (Bill)

New York Giants (NL), 162

New York Giants Professional Hockey Club,
130–31, *192*. *See also* New York Rangers

New York Life Assurance Company, 95, 106

New York Metropolitan League, 241–42

New York Rangers, 142, 163, 165, 171–72, 177,
182, *192*, *197*, 227, 235, 326; and Geran
benevolent society proposal, 313; name,
132; player recruitment system, 241–2;
wartime player permissions to play, 301–
2; and wartime swoon, 293; and Watson
situation, 307–8. *See also* Madison Square
Garden; New York Giants Professional
Hockey Club

New York Rangers Hockey Club, Inc. *See*
New York Rangers

New York Rovers (EAHL), 241, 249, 283

New York Yankees (AL), 123

Niagara Falls (ON), 125, 150

Noble, Reg, 68, 115, 218

Non-Permanent Active Militia (NPAM), 274,
275

Normandy campaign, *198*, 307, 309

Norris, James E. (Sr.), 203, 321; on Americans lease, 294; as amateur player, *188*,
234; arena ownership, 259, 276; background, 204–5; berates Bill Stewart, 269;
creation of arena chain, 276; as Detroit
NHL owner, *194*; and Dutton contract,
309; IAHL franchise, 277; and Indianapolis Arena interest, 276; involvement
with AHA and Shamrocks, 206, 208,
215–16, 234; involvement with multiple
NHL clubs, *194*, 235; and loan to Dwyer,
230, 251; as NHL governor, 266; on NHL
territorial rights, 278, 283; opinion on
Calder bond, 298; and Ottawa Senators,
208, 217; ownership position in MSG,
226–27; and quest for NHL franchise,
205, 215, 216, 217–18; and relationship
with McLaughlin, 219; role in Chicago
Stadium, 173, 177–78, 204–5; and takeover of Olympia and Detroit Falcons,
217; understanding of antitrust of, 278,
280–82